Teaching Them to Read

TEACHING THEM TO READ

Fourth Edition

Dolores Durkin
University of Illinois

Allyn and Bacon, Inc.
Boston · London · Sydney · Toronto

Library of Congress Cataloging in Publication Data

Durkin, Dolores.
  Teaching them to read.

  Bibliography: p.
  Includes index.
  1. Reading. I. Title.
LB1050.D84 1983   372.4'1   82-16458
ISBN 0-205-07933-4

Printed in the United States of America
10 9 8 7 6 5 4 3 2 1   88 87 86 85 84 83

To Gene

CONTENTS

PREFACE

Whenever how to teach reading is considered, the urge to say everything at once is inevitable because all of its facets seem so important. However, since neither written nor oral language allows for a simultaneous treatment of different topics even when they are closely related, a sequence for dealing separately with the many pieces that make up an instructional program had to be selected for this textbook.

Part I, which consists of two chapters, is meant to serve as an introduction. The first of the two chapters can be described with its title, "Teaching Reading: An Overview." A general survey of effective reading instruction was chosen as the subject for the initial chapter on the assumption that seeing the whole picture before its parts are examined is helpful. Chapter 2 goes on to discuss in a thorough way the roles that oral and silent reading ought to play in an instructional program. This topic merits both thorough and early treatment because of the large amount of classroom time that is spent on having students take turns reading aloud. While this questionable practice, commonly referred to as "round robin reading," is usually associated with the primary grades, classroom observations indicate it is often used in the middle and upper grades when social studies is taught. That the goal of all instructional activities is comprehension via silent reading is underscored in Chapter 2, which, while making that point, does not overlook the unique contributions that oral reading can make when it is used in certain ways at certain times.

The next two chapters constitute Part II and look at reading ability and reading instruction in their earliest stages. Chapter 3 deals with "Readiness for Reading;" Chapter 4, with "Reading in the Kindergarten." Although these chapters should be of particular interest to kindergarten and first-grade teachers, the topics they cover have relevance for all teachers because, over the years, each has prompted controversy. In addition, even though readiness has been traditionally associated with the start of reading, it is, in fact, a concept that has significance for any teaching at any level. How it applies to reading instruction beyond the beginning is explained with a number of examples.

Chapter 5, "Whole Word Methodology," starts Part III, "Instruction: Words." Chapter 5 also marks the beginning of a detailed, multiple-chapter treatment of the specifics of instruction. Starting the treatment with a look at whole word methodology is recognition of the fact that, at all grade levels and for various reasons, some words will have to be directly identified for students. Chapter 5 concentrates on how words are taught as wholes; when they should be taught as wholes; what facilitates or impedes word learning; what effect nonstandard dialects and bilingualism have on the meaning of "correct" response; and what can be done to provide what is always necessary: interesting, productive practice.

Like good parents, good teachers foster independence in their students; consequently, to ensure that they are able to figure out new or forgotten words on their own, instruction in using three types of cues (contextual, graphophonic, and structural) is essential. How to teach students to use the context in which an unknown word appears in order to get it identified is the subject of Chapter 6, which is followed by two others that deal with graphophonic cues. The first of the two tells what is taught in phonics; the second, Chapter 8, specifies how it can be taught. Chapter 9 then deals with structural cues, thus with ways for figuring out the pronunciation *and* meaning of derived and inflected words. All these chapters attend both to the details of instruction and to suggestions for practice and assignments. Like all of the other chapters concerned with the specifics of instruction, recommendations are based on elementary school teaching experience, countless numbers of observations in classrooms, frequent discussions with teachers, close analyses of instructional materials, and findings from research. Like all the other chapters, too, the fact that the essence of reading is comprehension is never forgotten.

As the next chapter, Chapter 10, concentrates on "Vocabulary Knowledge," it deals with a topic that should be uppermost in the minds of all teachers, since word meanings are an essential ingredient of successful reading. The chapter that comes next, entitled "Comprehension," recognizes that understanding connected text is the usual concern of readers. It thus shows what can be done to help elementary school students grow in their ability to understand authors' messages found in sentences, paragraphs, pages, and more. To supplement this direct and detailed treatment of comprehension, Chapter 12 follows and deals with "Content Subjects and Study Skills."

Even though instructional materials are referred to in all the prior chapters, Chapter 13, entitled "Basal Reader Programs," is one of two chapters that deals with them more directly. Basal series are considered first because they commonly structure a program. Chapter 14, "Language Experience and Other Materials," focuses on what loosens it up and makes it more personal for students.

Knowing what to teach, how to teach it, and how to select and use materials are all important prerequisites for superior instruction. Of no less importance, however, is getting a classroom organized to facilitate such instruction. Ways for doing that are discussed in Chapter 15, "Organizing for Instruction." Means for finding out who needs what kind of instruction are described in the final chapter, "Diagnosis for Instruction." Treatment of that topic was left until the end because knowing *what* to diagnose requires knowing the components of reading ability. Chapters 5 through 12 are, therefore, preparation for Chapter 16.

As the various chapters in *Teaching Them to Read* are studied, the use of "she" when teachers are being referred to will be apparent. This practice is followed (except when an actual case is cited in which the teacher was male) not because elementary school teaching is thought to be a feminine profession but to avoid the cumbersome "she or he." In contrast, reference to a pupil will use "he" unless a specific girl is the referent. This is done to avoid ambiguity when a pronoun for a teacher and another for a pupil are necessary in the same sentence.

Dolores Durkin

Teaching Them to Read

PART I

INTRODUCTION

CHAPTER 1

TEACHING READING: AN OVERVIEW

What Contributes to Reading Ability
    Extensive Sight Vocabularies
    Ability to Figure Out Words Independently
    Word Meanings
    Ability to Comprehend Connected Text
Diagnostic Teaching
Instructional Materials
    Role of Materials
    Relevant Materials
The Total School
    A Philosophy about Reading
    The Reading Program
    The Principal
Review

At the risk of starting with the obvious, let me acknowledge right away that achieving excellence in the teaching of reading is no small, ordinary accomplishment. As the best teachers demonstrate, however, it is not an impossible one.

Although it is true that highly successful instructional programs are not identical in every detail, teachers who have them do share certain characteristics. As a start, for example, effective teachers like and respect their students. This shows up not only in the way they talk and listen to them but also in the amount of effort they are willing to expend in order to ensure that each student's potential for reading is realized. "Contrary to popular myths," writes one observer of classrooms, "teachers in 'schools that work' are not charismatic figures generating unforgettable experiences. They are simply hard-working organized teachers moving crisply through a well-planned day" (2, p. 3).

Not to be forgotten is that successful teachers work hard *on the right things*. In short, they know what contributes to reading ability and concentrate on that.

WHAT CONTRIBUTES TO READING ABILITY

Describing *reading ability* is not an easy task. Why it is difficult is explained well in an observation made many years ago by a reading specialist named Edmund Huey, who in 1908 wrote, "To completely analyze what we do when we read would almost be the acme of a psychologist's achievements, for it would be to describe very many of the most intricate workings of the human mind" (1, p. 6).

While Huey's contention would be hard to dispute, a textbook that proposes to help teachers and those preparing to teach do an effective job with reading has an obligation at least to describe what contributes to reading ability.

Extensive Sight Vocabularies

Although the ability to read requires much more than expertise in identifying individual words, such identifications—especially when they are automatic—make a considerable contribution to proficient reading. This is verified by the fact that even a single sentence may be difficult (or impossible) to comprehend if an important word is unknown or if several words are identified with great hesitation or much uncertainty.

The importance of individual words is the reason effective teachers see to it that their students are able to identify on sight a sizable number of words, especially those that appear frequently in print. This is accomplished with the help of practice, which wise teachers try to make as interesting as possible since involvement and achievement go hand in hand.

Ability to Figure Out Words Independently

Knowing that new or forgotten words will inevitably show up in the materials that students need or want to read, successful teachers provide instruction for developing the understandings and skills that allow students to figure out themselves the pronunciation of words. Concern for this kind of independence accounts for the carefully planned attention given to letter-sound relationships and to parts of words called *roots, prefixes,* and *suffixes.* Thoroughly knowledgeable about phonics and word structure, these teachers are able to pick and choose from materials like workbooks only those pages that stand a chance of contributing to their students' ability to cope with the identity of words without outside help. The same knowledge also allows them to fill in gaps and to offer extra instruction and practice for any student who needs them. Essentially, then, superior teachers are *independent* professionals who *know* what needs to be taught.

Word Meanings

Because they are aware of what is vital for success with reading, the best of teachers—whether working with kindergartners or older students—do whatever they can to add to the number of words whose meanings will be familiar when they show up in print. Recognizing that experiences, direct and vicarious, are the primary source of vocabulary development, these teachers view schooling as one important means for enlarging and deepening students' knowledge of the world. In addition, they plan special lessons for vocabulary development and also take advantage of unexpected opportunities to teach the meanings of one or more words.

Ability to Comprehend Connected Text

Underlying everything that is done in an effective instructional program is the realization that reading is comprehending. Aware that authors' messages come in many sizes and forms, successful teachers provide instruction that will help their students comprehend as little as a phrase or as much as a book. Recognizing that different types of text make different demands of readers, the instruction of competent teachers is also marked by balance as it focuses on narrative discourse (such as a fable), expository discourse (such as an explanation of how dew forms), and procedural discourse (such as directions for making a pinwheel). And poets who have something to say to children are not overlooked either.

DIAGNOSTIC TEACHING

While knowing what contributes to mature reading ability is essential for effective teaching, knowing exactly what to teach to whom is equally mandatory if an instructional program is ever to succeed in getting each student to realize his or her potential. That is why identifying what children do and do not know, and can or cannot do, is viewed as a daily task by superior teachers. It also accounts for calling the work of such individuals *diagnostic teaching*. What such teaching accomplishes is *individualized instruction,* the major concern of this textbook. As used in *Teaching Them to Read,* individualized instruction is any instruction that (a) deals with what contributes to reading ability; (b) concentrates on something that has not been learned or is not understood by those being instructed; and (c) proceeds at a suitable pace. Conceivably, individualized instruction can be carried on with a group as large as one hundred—or one thousand, for that matter. And it can also take place with a single child. In the latter case, the description "individualized" is appropriate not because someone is being taught individually but because what is getting attention is what he or she needs and is ready to learn. Obviously, individualized instruction in the setting of a classroom is a tall order. It also is central to the concerns of conscientious teachers.

The components of one kind of direct, individualized instruction start with a goal and proceed as follows:

1. *Instruction:* Explanations, information, illustrations, modeling, questions, and so on.
2. *Application:* Attempts by students, supervised by a teacher, to use what was taught.
3. *Practice:* Independent attempts by students to use what was taught, often carried out in written assignments.
4. *Evaluation:* Examination of students' independent responses in order to see whether further attention to the same goal is necessary.

While preplanned instruction like that just described is at the core of successful programs, the use of unexpected opportunities to teach something significant is also characteristic. An example of the unexpected is described in the following section since it pertains to instructional materials.

INSTRUCTIONAL MATERIALS

Instructional material, as used in *Teaching Them to Read,* encompasses anything that displays print. It thus encompasses textbooks, library books, magazines, comic books, signs, labels, menus, calendars, newspapers, billboards, stamps, greeting cards, license plates, telephone directories, candy wrappers, and so on. Why this broad concept of instructional materials is highlighted as early as Chapter 1 can be explained with a reference to what was seen in a third grade.

At the start of the observation, the teacher had just started working with five boys who were much more interested in a pencil than they were in the basal reader they were being told to open. The pencil's attraction was both the die that had been attached to one end and the advertisement for a new furniture store that was printed on its side. The latter said, "Don't gamble on quality. See us first." At the time the pencil was taken from its owner, he and the other boys were doing their best to read the two sentences. Since they did anything but try hard to read the basal story—they kept insisting they had read it in second grade—a question had to be raised about why the basal reader was not temporarily laid aside in order to allow for attention to the slogan on the pencil because it had so much potential for reading comprehension. For example, the meaning of "Don't gamble on quality" could have been contrasted with the meaning of something like "Don't gamble on a horse," immediately setting up a chance to talk about literal and figurative language. Or, the words *die* and *dice* could have been written and discussed in the context of unusual ways to form plural nouns. Words like *quantity* and *quality* might also have been considered along with such directions as, When is quality more important than quantity? Is quantity ever more important than quality? Instead of doing anything like this, however, the teacher spent the time on some very poor oral reading, all the while the boys insisting that they had read the story when they were in second grade.

The reference to this classroom incident is not meant to convey the notion that instructional programs should proceed according to students' whims. Rather, it was made in order to allow for some comments about two related matters: effective teaching and the judicious (thus flexible) use of materials.

Role of Materials

The most important point to make about instructional materials is that they are meant to assist teachers, not to direct them. From a teacher's perspective, the difference between the two roles can be portrayed as follows:

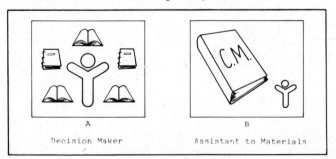

A
Decision Maker

B
Assistant to Materials

Superior teachers, symbolized above by Teacher A, are thoroughly acquainted with available materials; however, *they* decide what will be taught. Once decisions are made about instructional needs, they use whatever materials are likely to forward their efforts to deal with them. In contrast, Teacher B is subordinate to materials and thus allows them to dictate both what will be taught and how it will be presented. The concern now is to carry out whatever suggestions materials make, thus demoting the role of the teacher to little more than "assistant to materials." Among the by-products of such a role is less flexibility than effective instruction requires.

Perhaps it is needless to say that the aim of *Teaching Them to Read* is to encourage the development of a sizable number of Teacher A's.

Relevant Materials

Recognizing the importance of motivation and interest for successful learning, Teacher A does whatever is possible to demonstrate to students why it makes sense to be a reader. With something like the slogan on the pencil, for example, Teacher A not only would recognize its potential for helping with comprehension but also would value it as a means for showing the children that reading ability is highly relevant for everyday living. Concern for relevance explains why a teacher who was seen in a second-grade classroom took the time to assemble a bulletin board display that effectively demonstrated the omnipresence of print. Featured on the board were such items as an addressed envelope, a page from a cookbook, a gum wrapper, headlines from a newspaper, a TV guide, and a T-shirt. Concern about showing the importance of reading ability with the help of materials also explains why a fifth-grade teacher prepared a news corner for displaying newspaper articles brought in by students.

All this is to say that Teacher A, with the help of a wide variety of both commercially prepared and homemade materials, succeeds in demonstrating that print is a valuable source for information, practical help, relaxation, and even inspiration. It is not accidental, then, that a child who is fortunate enough to have had a succession of Teacher A's not only *can* read but *does* read.

THE TOTAL SCHOOL

A discussion of reading that portrays teachers and classrooms as though they existed in isolation is unrealistic because the two are integral parts of a total school. This means that what any one teacher is able to do, or even wants to do, is very much affected by all that makes up the school. The principal, the other teachers, the neighborhood, the students, their parents—all have important effects on what happens in a classroom.

Because of the significance of the total school, it might be helpful to describe the kind that offers maximum opportunity to develop a superior instructional program. The ideal school portrayed here has been assembled by selecting from a variety of actual schools those factors that seem crucial in fostering success in teaching reading. Like all other ideals, it can serve as a standard against which schools might be evaluated. It also suggests some goals toward which faculties and administrators can work.

A Philosophy about Reading

It is accurate to say that the obvious success that some schools experience in teaching reading is not an accident. They work for their success, and they work not haphazardly but guided by a philosophy that views the development of all of the verbal skills—listening, speaking, reading, and writing—as the *major* responsibility of the elementary school.

At first glance, this focus might seem narrow. It should be remembered, however, that a child learns to listen by listening to *something;* learns to speak and to write by speaking and writing about *something;* and learns to read by reading about *something.* When that *something* is the content of science, social studies, literature, or mathematics, the apparent narrowness of the philosophy fans out considerably—but without losing the special language focus. And, at the elementary school level, *that* is important.

The Reading Program

A faculty's acceptance of the fundamental importance of language skills certainly is a first step in developing an effective program for teaching them. But it is not enough. Without a specific enumeration of the abilities and understandings that comprise the verbal skills—and at least an approximate sequence for teaching them—acceptance of their importance is ineffectual. I say this because in those schools in which every student is given maximum opportunity to achieve in reading, it is very apparent that the faculty not only appreciates its special importance but also has a clear, detailed picture of the goals of the total reading program. In that picture there is enough content to challenge the brightest of the children, but there also is a flexibility in expectations based on the fact that differences among students mean there will be differences in what they can achieve. Within this setting, decisions about the content of reading instruction are not restricted either by a grade-level outlook of the teacher or by the grade-level placement of a child. Instead, the reading program throughout the school moves along as a knowledgeable, flexible response to instructional needs.

Such flexibility contrasts with what is sometimes seen:

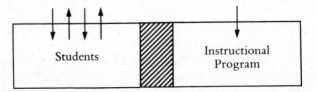

Portrayed above is a rigid type of school organization in which the instructional program at each grade level is set (usually by commercial materials) in spite of the fact that, each year, the students at any given level are different. It is as if a wall kept children from affecting the program.

The Principal

As more and more elementary schools are visited (and as more and more research on successful schools is done), it becomes increasingly evident that school-wide excellence in reading instruction occurs only when a principal has a very special concern for reading (2, 3, 4, 5). Without such a concern, time and energy are too easily diverted to other matters, many of which have little to do with education. But even with the special concern, a successful reading program is not guaranteed. Other factors are important too.

While elementary school teaching experience is not an absolute prerequisite for the successful administration of a reading program, it would be difficult to name another experience that gives an administrator the same realistic understanding of the many factors that either impede or promote effective classroom instruction. It would be difficult, too, to think of another experience that makes the principal more keenly aware of all that he or she still needs to learn about teaching children to read.

Still another characteristic that stands out among principals who administer superior reading programs is an astuteness about decision making. This allows them to distinguish between occasions that call for independent administrative decisions and, on the other hand, occasions when faculty help should be sought and when faculty decisions will prevail. Under the leadership of such principals, a reading program is the end result of just the right combination of administrative directives, principal-faculty discussion, and faculty decisions.

Related to ability in decision making is the principal's knowledge of the teaching competency of each staff member. With a detailed awareness of what every teacher is able to do, a principal is in a position to give maximum freedom to those who merit it through their demonstrated competence; to the teachers who are less able, he or she is in a position to give much specific help and a little less freedom.

Finally—and this characteristic is especially necessary today—successful reading programs are found in schools in which principals are sufficiently secure in what they know and want to accomplish that they are able to resist the rather constant temptation to win temporary acclaim by jumping on some current bandwagon in reading. This does not mean that they find nothing worthwhile in what is new, and certainly it does not mean that they are persons who see the past as "the best of times." Rather, they are administrators who view progress as the maintenance of what is good in the old and the selection of what is valuable from the new. While this mosaic of the old and the new is not likely to result either in fame or fortune, it does create a school in which a faculty member is given every chance to become as good a reading teacher as she or he truly wants to be.

REVIEW

1. The meaning of *diagnostic teaching* was implied, not stated directly, in Chapter 1. What did you infer the meaning to be?
2. Explain the connection between *diagnostic teaching* and *individualized instruction*.
3. Give an example of (a) individualized instruction offered to 100 students (at any grade level) and (b) instruction offered to one child that is not individualized.
4. Briefly characterize what is referred to as Teacher A in the chapter. Next, explain why the third-grade teacher who overlooked the potential of the slogan on the pencil was, at least on that occasion, Teacher B.

REFERENCES

1. Huey, Edmund B. *The Psychology and Pedagogy of Reading.* New York: Macmillan, 1908.
2. Salganik, M. William. "Researchers Team with Reporter to Identify Schools That Work." *Educational R and D Report* 3, no. 1 (Winter 1980): 2–7.
3. State of New York. Office of Education Performance Review. *School Factors Influencing Reading Achievement: A Case Study of Two Inner City Schools.* Albany, N.Y., 1974.
4. Venezky, Richard L., and Winfield, Linda. "Schools That Succeed Beyond Expectations in Teaching Reading." Studies on Education, Technical Report No. 1. Newark, Dela.: University of Delaware, August 1979.
5. Weber, George. "Inner-city Children Can Be Taught to Read: Four Successful Schools." Occasional Paper No. 18. Washington, D.C.: Council for Basic Education, 1971.

CHAPTER 2

TEACHING READING: ORAL VERSUS SILENT

PREVIEW

Anyone who reads this chapter probably attended one or more elementary schools in which around-the-group oral reading was a common, taken-for-granted practice. Little risk is involved in making an even more specific prediction: taking turns at oral reading was especially noticeable in the primary grades during the reading period and was equally conspicuous in the middle and upper grades when subjects like social studies received attention.

Since these portrayals of past decades also describe the present, one goal of Chapter 2 is to show that what perseveres is not necessarily what is desirable. Another goal is to establish a correct perspective for oral and silent reading, which, in turn, should provide guidelines for making decisions about the use of instructional time.

The suggested procedures for comprehending Chapter 2 are applicable to all subsequent chapters:

1. *Skim the chapter in order to get a general impression of the content. Headings and subheadings will help with the overview, as will the summary that concludes the chapter.*
2. *Examine the questions listed at the end; then keep them in mind to guide a second, more careful reading. This time, give studied attention to important terms, which will be in italics, and to the teaching procedures being recommended. Why they are recommended (and why something else is not) should be noted, too.*

Like many of the other chapters, Chapter 2 includes reproductions of instructional materials. Please take the time to examine their details when the chapter presents them. Each was selected to make this textbook specifically helpful and, in addition, to acquaint its readers with both good and questionable materials in order to facilitate decisions about what to use and what to bypass.

Because schools have relatively little time to accomplish a great many objectives concerned with reading, usefulness must be considered when decisions are made about priorities. Whenever usefulness affects judgments about the relative importance of silent and oral reading, the latter clearly ends up in second place.

To demonstrate the relatively slight value of oral reading in your own life, try to recall the last time it was a necessity. Perhaps not too long ago somebody in another room in your home asked you to read a telephone number aloud. Or maybe someone was curious about the next day's weather; not near a newspaper, she or he asked you to read the forecast. While isolated instances like these do exist, it is still safe to predict that your recollections of a need for oral reading will show that the examples are sparse and brief. In contrast, recalling when it was necessary (or desirable) to read silently would result in a very long list of examples, including the reading of this textbook right now.

To underscore with these recollections and comparisons the special and very practical value of silent reading is not to suggest that oral reading is useless and thus ought to be bypassed when teachers plan each day's work. Instead, the comparisons are designed to put oral and silent reading into a realistic perspective and, in the process, to point out that *the primary but not exclusive focus of a reading program ought to be on comprehension via silent reading.*

If it were, certain procedures would not be used as routinely as they are. In order to show why one very common procedure—taking turns at oral reading while others follow silently—is highly questionable, certain differences between oral and silent reading need to be highlighted first.

DIFFERENCES BETWEEN ORAL AND SILENT READING

Three differences will be discussed. They were selected because each has important implications for instruction at all grade levels.

Vocalization

The most apparent difference between oral and silent reading is that the former is heard whereas the latter is not. The observable pronunciation of words that is the very essence of oral reading is referred to as *vocalization*.

Vocalization contrasts with *subvocalization,* which is sometimes present in silent reading. As the name suggests, subvocalization (also called *inner speech*) is a mental pronunciation of words that is neither heard nor seen.

Whether some subvocalizing assists with comprehension is one of the many questions about reading that lacks a carefully documented answer. When Gibson and Levin (13) reviewed existing research on this topic, they described the difficulties in studying subvocalization and the conflicting findings when it has been examined but suggested nonetheless that subvocalization may serve to facilitate the comprehension of difficult material by focusing a reader's attention on meaning.

A different hypothesis about why difficult material and an increase in subvocalization often go together has been proposed by Frank Smith (20). He believes that "the explanation is more likely to be that reading a difficult passage automatically reduces speed, and we have a habit of articulating individual words when we read at a speed slow enough for individual words to be enunciated" (p. 200).

Until facts about the relationship between subvocalization, difficult material, and comprehension become available, the position taken here is as follows:

1. Probably everyone subvocalizes far too much even with easy material.
2. Such subvocalization not only reduces speed but also is "annoying and difficult to turn off" (13).
3. Since ability to read (comprehend) silently at a reasonably fast rate is desirable, nothing should be done in an instructional program that might foster needless subvocalization.
4. It is possible that the habitual practice of taking turns at oral reading (while others are expected to follow the same material silently) may do just that.

More will be said about the final point later. Now, let us continue with the discussion of differences between oral and silent reading.

Eye Movements

Before explaining how eye movements account for a second difference, let me discuss these movements more generally. To do that, some research will be reviewed.

Studies of eye movements.   When researchers first began to study reading, many ideas about its nature were generated from the method of introspection (17). That is, research subjects were directed to think about what was happening within themselves as they read. From such a method, hypotheses were formulated, some of which included hunches about eye movements. Among the latter was the notion that people's eyes sweep steadily across each line of print as they read.

Later, this conclusion was replaced by another, thanks to newly invented cameras that allowed for eye movement monitoring that was not only more objective but also more precise.⋆ Although cameras did not figure extensively in research until the 1920s and 1930s, initial studies using them showed that a reader's eyes stop intermittently as they move rapidly across a line (2, 8). Eye behavior is thus characterized not by a steady sweep but by stop-and-go movements. The active part is called *saccades* (sŭ căd¢). The periods of inactivity are referred to as *fixations*. (To understand eye movements correctly, it is essential to keep in mind that each eye fixation is so brief that its duration has to be measured in milliseconds; 1 msec = one-thousandth of a second.) Research also showed that "the leaping eye is practically blind" (20). Consequently, "the reading of text occurs only during fixations" (18). What seems like visual continuity, then, is provided by the brain, not by the eyes.

Another characteristic identified with the more sophisticated research is that the eyes move backward on occasion. The right-to-left movement, referred to as a *regression,* has a variety of causes. In some instances, for example, readers might miss a word or two and have to return to pick them up. At other times, they might be reading something like the following paragraph. To read it is to identify still another reason for regressions.

> The boys' arrows were nearly gone so they sat down on the grass and stopped hunting. Over at the edge of the woods they saw Henry making a bow to a little girl who was coming down the road. She had tears in her dress and also tears in her eyes. She gave Henry a note which he brought over to the group of young hunters. Read to the boys it caused great excitement. After a minute but rapid examination of their weapons they ran down the valley. Does were standing at the end of the lake making an excellent target. [7, p. 87]

Written by a researcher named Buswell, the previous paragraph figured in an eye movement study. Reading it now demonstrates that multiple pronunciations of identically spelled words are another reason for regressions. A different but related reason has to do with the fact that reading involves certain expectations. When a text does not conform to them, regressive eye movements occur in order to correct what was erroneously anticipated.

Still another reason for eye regressions is linked to a reader's need to move from the end of one line to the start of the following one. (This essential right-to-left movement is called a *return sweep.*) In returning to the next line, the eyes do not always pick up what is at the beginning. Should this happen, a return sweep might be followed by one or more regressions.

One further reason for regressions relates only to oral reading—specifically, to the eye-voice span of an oral reader. Before discussing that, let me synthesize this more general discussion with some definitions.

Eye fixation. Pause in eye movements at which time print is seen. Duration of fixations is so brief it is measured in milliseconds.

⋆ The ensuing description of eye movements continues to be verified in current research in which computers are used (18).

Saccade. Movement of eye from one fixation to the next. "The average length of saccades during reading is about 8–10 letter positions. . . . This is about the size of the region seen during a fixation" (18, p. 163).

Eye regression. Backward (right-to-left) movements caused by such factors as missed words, multiple pronunciations of identically spelled words, concern or confusion about meaning, and incorrect predictions.

Return sweep. The necessary right-to-left eye movement required by the start of each new line of text.

How these terms figure in studies of eye movements can be demonstrated with data collected by Buswell while children at different grade levels read silently (8). They are listed in Table 2.1, which shows that progress in reading is accompanied by a reduced number of fixations, by shorter fixations, and by fewer regressions.

How eye movements differ in oral and silent reading.   The reference to Buswell's data noted that they were collected while subjects read silently. That was essential to mention because eye movement records for the same children reading the same material aloud (with the possible exception of the first graders) would yield noticeably different data. You should be able to predict the details of the differences once some comments are made about the *eye-voice span.*

With oral reading, it is necessary to pronounce and carefully enunciate every word. Such care and attention take time, far more than the eye requires to span the same material. The difference in rate causes a conflict; of necessity, the voice wins out as the eye yields (unconsciously) to the slower pace. The accommodation accounts for what is called the *eye-voice span,* which is "the number of words or letter spaces that visual processing is ahead of oral reading" (15, p. 640).

The eye, while accommodating the voice, is still active; for as it waits, it wanders and regresses. Now, regressions "operate to reduce the separation between the eyes and the voice" (2, p. 125). The eye also fixates longer than would be the case were the reading silent.

All of these consequences of the eye's accommodation to the voice can be verified when eye movement records of the same person reading orally and then silently are compared. Predictably—at least when the reader is past the initial stage of learning to read—eye movements for oral reading show more and longer

Table 2.1   Children's Eye Movements at Different Grade Levels

Grade	Average number of fixations per line	Average duration of fixation pauses	Average number of regressive movements per line
1	18.6	660 msec	5.1
5	6.9	252 msec	1.3
11	5.5	224 msec	0.7

fixations and more regressions. That is why it can be said that the eye movements associated with oral reading are inefficient for the silent reader.

It is relevant to note in this context a conclusion reached by Golinkoff (15) after she reviewed research on comprehension: "Poor comprehenders' eye movements showed greater correspondence in oral and silent reading than did the good comprehenders' eye movements. Poor comprehenders seemed to continue laborious word-by-word reading even when reading silently" (p. 637).

Functions

The third difference between oral and silent reading that has implications for instructional programs pertains to their respective functions. With silent reading, the primary purpose is to get the author's message. Other purposes may also exist—for instance, to critique the message. Nonetheless, the first concern is to receive and understand it. This makes silent reading similar to listening but different from speaking and writing, since the latter two express messages:

Verbal Communication

Listening ⟵———— receive
Reading   message

Speaking ————⟶ express
Writing   message

Except in school, the usual function of oral reading is to communicate an author's message to one or more listeners. While an effective delivery often indicates that the oral reader understands what the author says, comprehension is not an essential requirement. What *is* required is the correct pronunciation of words, correct phrasing, a suitable volume, and appropriate expression. And all this can be present even when the oral reader fails to understand everything the author says.

While there is a merited place in classroom activities for oral reading, it is essential that students know right from the beginning that "reading is not saying something *to* another but is, instead, getting something *from* another" (1, p. 23). When the correct objective is kept in mind, correct decisions will be made about how to use the time allotted to reading instruction. Whether correct decisions *are* made will be considered next.

IMPLICATIONS OF DIFFERENCES FOR INSTRUCTIONAL PROGRAMS

The foregoing sections highlighted differences between oral and silent reading having to do with vocalization, eye movements, and functions. What their implications are for instructional programs will now be considered.

To do that, let me first provide a context for the discussion by referring again to what childhood experiences and visits to classrooms point up as being a daily practice not only when reading is taught but also when the day's schedule calls for something like social studies (9). The practice, called *round robin reading,* has students take turns reading aloud while others in the group are directed to follow the same material silently. To encourage the silent following, a teacher might call on children unexpectedly and may reprimand them if they do not have the place.

Usually, some preparations are made for round robin reading. For example, attention might go to new or troublesome words, and even to a silent reading of the entire selection. Less often, nothing is done. When that is the case, the oral reading is noticeably poor even when the best students have their turn. Specifically, it is difficult to hear, is done in a monotone, and is interrupted by the reader's inability to identify words or by mispronunciations that the teacher corrects.

Whether preparations are made or not, the oral readers are usually encouraged to read with expression, with a big voice, and so on. Only on rare occasions, however, does the advice result in oral reading that is a joy to hear.

Having considered what often occurs when round robin reading takes place, let us move on now to implications for instruction of the differences between oral and silent reading that have been discussed.

Around-the-Group Oral Reading and Subvocalization

Regardless of the position taken on the function of subvocalization, I believe everyone would agree (based on introspection) that much of the subvocalizing that goes on in silent reading results in little more than needlessly slow rates—and annoyance. If that is so, what must be taken seriously is the strong likelihood that asking students to follow silently what another is reading aloud is encouraging the silent followers to pronounce mentally the words they are hearing. Or, said differently, the common use of round robin reading is likely to foster what everyone should object to: purposeless subvocalization.

Around-the-Group Oral Reading and Eye Movements

While no researcher has examined the hypothesis that the routine use of round robin reading leads to excessive and useless amounts of subvocalization in children's silent reading, one did look into its effects on eye movements. Gilbert (14) reported a study in 1940 whose findings have been neither supported nor questioned because subsequent research was never done.

Gilbert studied his subjects (children in grades 2 through 6) by photographing their eye movements while they read silently and, in addition, while they followed silently what another subject was reading aloud. (Deliberately, Gilbert chose oral readers with varying abilities.) When the two sets of eye movement records were analyzed and compared, predictable differences were found. To begin, the eye movements for the silent reading that was accompanied by oral reading showed more fixations and regressions than did the silent reading done independently. Expectedly, the fixations were longer. Also shown was that the poorer the oral reading, the poorer (that is, the less efficient) were the eye movements of the subjects who were following the same material silently. The latter finding prompted Gilbert to write, "The data are unmistakable in condemning the routine practice of requiring silent readers to follow the oral reading of poor and mediocre readers" (p. 621). Since observations in classrooms uncover a paucity of excellent oral reading when around-the-group oral reading takes place, Gilbert's data offer a second reason to abandon, or at least seriously question, round robin reading.

To all this, a teacher working in a middle- or upper-grade classroom might say, "I rarely have students read aloud during the reading period." While that may be so, observations indicate that when round robin reading *is* used at those levels, participants are likely to be the poorest readers in the class. That practice makes Gilbert's conclusion relevant for all elementary teachers. It also is relevant for middle- and upper-grade teachers who have round robin reading during social studies, health, or science periods (9).

Around-the-Group Oral Reading in Relation to Function

The primary purpose of reading is to comprehend, and that is usually accomplished best with silent reading. With oral reading, on the other hand, the usual goal is to communicate what an author says to one or more listeners. Keeping the two functions in mind, let us take yet another look at round robin reading both when it is preceded by a silent reading of the selection and when it is not.

When it is not, the logical reason for round robin reading is comprehension. However, why a silent-oral combination is more likely than silent reading to achieve that goal is unclear, especially when it is remembered that the oral reading is likely to be a halting, listlike rendition of a text that obscures rather than elucidates meaning.

Although the oral reading is usually better when the selection was read silently beforehand, the reason to have oral reading under these circumstances is not obvious, except when certain parts of the selection are read aloud for such specific purposes as clarifying or verifying a point, recalling a vivid mental image, finding examples of what was taught earlier (for example, appositives), pointing out the clue that suggested a particular outcome, and so on.

A Summary

To sum up, then, the routine use of round robin reading is questionable for the following reasons:

1.   It is likely to foster useless subvocalizing.
2.   It probably encourages inefficient eye movements in children's silent reading.
3.   It may make comprehension more difficult.
4.   It fails to distinguish between the different functions of oral and silent reading.

TEACHERS' EXPLANATIONS FOR AROUND-THE-GROUP ORAL READING

Since round robin reading remains common, a consideration of what teachers say when asked why they continue to have it seems necessary.

Provides Evidence of Comprehension

Some claim that if the oral part of round robin reading is done with appropriate expression, it indicates that the reader is comprehending. The problem with this explanation is that an effective oral delivery may be little more than expressive word naming (12). A related problem is that early, persistent attention to expression can lead students to conclude erroneously that reading is a performing art, not a thought-getting process. When such a conclusion *is* reached, children might not comprehend when they read silently because they do not know that that is what they are supposed to do.

Kenneth Goodman (16) offers still another thought about expression and comprehension. He observes:

> There are periods in the development of reading competence when oral reading becomes very awkward. Readers who have recently become rapid, relatively effective silent readers seem to be distracted and disrupted by the necessity of encoding oral output while they are decoding meaning. Ironically, then, "poor" oral reading performance *may* reflect a high degree of reading competence rather than a lack of such competence. [p. 489]

Ensures That Children Read

Some teachers defend round robin reading on the grounds that it is one way to make sure that students *will* read, since they are either following a passage silently or reading it aloud themselves. In this case, it is necessary to keep in mind that what any child reads aloud is likely to be brief. This makes it necessary to ask, "Do children follow when others are reading orally?"

Classroom observations indicate that, most of the time, children try to follow until they get a turn to read aloud. Afterward, effort is less obvious. Based on what has been seen, it is possible that the thoughts of some of the children who are supposed to be following a text may be something like:

> Well, I've had my turn. Nobody ever gets a second turn, so I think I'll take another look at my new pocketknife.

> I think I'd better see what's on the next page. By that time, it'll be my turn.

> Suzie really is a terrible reader. I wonder what the next story is about. I'll take a peek.

> Gee, I wish we didn't have to read the same story so many times. I wonder how many more stories are in this book. I think I'll count them.

Teachers who are concerned about making sure that students do read might be well advised to exchange round robin reading for supervised silent reading of an entire selection or subsections of it. Now the reading would be preceded by questions and followed by discussion. (This way of working will be considered later.)

Allows for Monitoring Word Identification Ability

Still another reason given for round robin reading is found in the comment of a teacher who, after listening to an account of the problems associated with around-the-group oral reading, asked, "But if I omitted it, how would I know if the children remember the new words in a selection?"

What needs to be recalled in this case is that what any child remembers is uncovered in round robin reading only when he has a turn to read aloud. Since that usually is done with a brief passage that may include neither new nor troublesome words, reliable conclusions are ruled out. Because teachers do need to know which words are being remembered and which are not, alternative ways for learning about word identification abilities need to be considered.

To begin, it should be emphasized that when teachers give ample time to new words before a selection is read, most students will remember them. ("Ample time" often requires doing much more with new words than is suggested in teaching manuals, especially those prepared for middle- and upper-grade levels.) Once students read the selection silently, a number of procedures are possible for checking up on vocabulary.

To illustrate, let us say the new words are *selfish, guilty, confused,* and *privacy.* Let us further assume that they are in a story about a grandmother who comes to live with her daughter, son-in-law, and two granddaughters. With her arrival, the two girls are required to share a bedroom so that the grandmother can have one, which is acceptable to Jean but not to her sister, Marie. How Marie behaves, how she feels about her behavior, and why and how she eventually changes constitute the plot.

Once the story is read silently, a teacher might choose to display cards on which the new words are written. Holding up *selfish,* she says to the children, "Think of this word. Think what it says and means. Does it describe anyone in the story you just read?"

After all the words have been reidentified and discussed in relation to plot and characters, a teacher-compiled worksheet that displays rows of words across the top is distributed. Underneath the words, names of the five story characters appear in a way that will allow for a column of words under each. Now the children are asked to read silently the words at the top (which include the new vocabulary) and to write under each character's name all the words that pertain to him or her. Responses will provide the teacher with further information about both word learning and comprehension.

To collect even more information, the teacher might decide to use one other procedure. (Remember: time not used for round robin reading is available for other things.) For this, she distributes to each student two small cards on which *yes* and *no* have been printed. She then holds up sentence cards that correctly or incorrectly report what occurred in the story. If a sentence is correct, the children hold up *yes* cards; if incorrect, the ones that display *no.* As the activity progresses, individual children are asked to read the sentences aloud, all of which include new vocabulary.

To sum up, then, multiple ways exist (other than the use of round robin reading) for checking both word learning and comprehension.

BASAL READERS AND AROUND-THE-GROUP ORAL READING

A complete explanation of why round robin reading persists cannot omit the fact that manuals for basal readers foster it, especially in the primary grades (see Figure 2.1).★ This is reflected in the type of lesson they promote:

Traditional Basal Reader Lesson

Preparation period, in which new vocabulary is introduced, interest in reading the selection is created, and background for understanding it is developed.

Silent reading, which is generally preceded by stipulated questions and followed by responses and discussion.

Oral reading, which proceeds by having students take turns in round robin fashion.

Skill development, which might include further attention to new vocabulary, word analysis skills, or comprehension.

Assignments, which are pages in the basal reader workbook and ditto-sheet exercises.

★ Although basal reader materials are not discussed in detail until Chapter 13, you are probably familiar with them since they have been used in classrooms for many decades. If you are not, examining a basal series now (readers, manuals, workbooks) would be helpful.

Figure 2.1

—Describe some of the experiences and adventures we read about Jim Beckwourth, the Mountain Man.

Directing Oral Reading

Reading with meaningful phrasing   Have pupils read the selection orally. Remind them to use the punctuation clues such as commas, quotation marks, and question marks as guides for proper phrasing and expression.

★ **Skimming for details**   Have pupils skim the following pages to locate and read aloud the paragraph that answers each question.

Page 163: Who wanted to stop walking?
Page 164: Why did the men have to keep on walking?

Page 165: Who was the better walker, Jim or Harris?
Page 166: What did Jim do when the first bear got his friend?
Page 167: What did the Indians do to make Jim feel like their brother?
Page 169: What is Beckwourth Pass?

Rereading the selection   Have pupils select their favorite parts of the story. Then tape record each pupil reading his or her favorite part. Let pupils listen to the tapes to evaluate their own performance.

Interpreting the Selection/Critical Reading

● **Recognizing different forms of writing: biography**   Review that a biography tells about a real person's life. Compare ''Jim Beckwourth, Mountain

From *World of Surprises and Reading Skills 6,* Teacher's Edition by Margaret Early et al., copyright © 1979 by Harcourt Brace Jovanovich, Inc. Reprinted and reproduced by permission of the publisher.

●   *This is part of a manual page in which recommendations are made for oral reading. What is recommended comes after a silent reading of the selection, which is done page by page with questions asked about each one.*

   The recommendations show why round robin reading is common in the primary grades. (This manual is for a second-grade reader.) The recommendations also point up why children might erroneously conclude that reading is a performance, not a thought-getting endeavor.

How manual suggestions can be altered to substitute more helpful procedures for round robin reading will be discussed when Chapter 13 looks at basal
reader materials in detail.

ACCEPTABLE COMBINATIONS OF ORAL AND SILENT READING

With all the criticism that has been directed to round robin reading, you may have
inferred that the recommendation is to eliminate *all* combinations of oral and
silent reading. To correct that erroneous conclusion, let me describe a few examples of acceptable combinations.

Dramatizations will serve as the first illustration. Let us assume that certain
children need to improve their oral reading, so the teacher decides to use a play to
help.★ Because it is oral reading and not a perfect play that is of concern, this
teacher does not have the children memorize the lines; instead, she has them read
from a script, which requires one child to read lines while the others follow them
silently in order to be ready with their parts. For special occasions, the teacher
might combine play reading with puppet making. Now, speaking parts for the
play are taped by the children, thus freeing them to give full attention to manipu-
lating the puppets while the pretaped dialogue runs smoothly in the background.
(Reference 21 at the end of the chapter provides guidelines for using puppets and
directions for making various kinds: paper bag, stick, sock, finger, fist, and
hand.) What is pertinent to emphasize for this discussion is that dramatizations—
whether simply or elaborately presented—occur infrequently and thus are different from the habitual, day-by-day use of round robin reading that has
been criticized.

But, you might be wondering, what about day-by-day practices? Should
they ever combine oral and silent reading? Surely, but only in certain ways. To
illustrate, let us say a teacher is working with a group of nine students, all of
whom are about the same in their general achievement in reading. The group has
just finished reading (silently) some particular selection, which might be material
the teacher wrote, a story in a basal reader, or perhaps a newspaper article. What
was read does not matter; what does is how the teacher combines silent and oral
reading. (It is possible, of course, that oral reading will not be used at all.) In this
case, the teacher might decide to discuss questions that were raised before the
silent reading began. If some call for a subjective answer (Which paragraphs
include descriptions that make you feel as if you were right at the scene?), the
teacher might have individual students read aloud the passages that succeeded in
transplanting them right into the scene of the story or article. But, please note, the

★ Sources for plays are many. *Thirty Plays for Classroom Reading* (10) includes scripts plus
commentary about the use of play reading in the classroom. The children's magazine *Plays* also
provides material, as does the teacher magazine, *Instructor*.

others just listen while the paragraphs are read because the reason for the oral reading is to communicate to others.

It could turn out that even factual questions elicit different responses. Should this happen, oral reading again might be required, this time to allow for comparisons and verification. As individual children read aloud, the others listen—critically, it is hoped.

To sum up, then, certain circumstances do call for a combination of silent and oral reading. Such circumstances are not a daily occurrence, nor are they usually a time to require students to follow silently what another is reading aloud. To hold to such a requirement is to encourage subvocalization and inefficient eye movements among the silent followers. Why round robin reading is also questionable for the student doing the oral reading will be clarified in the following discussion.

ORAL READING

Even though oral reading is much less important than silent reading, the former should not be automatically bypassed when plans are made for a day's activities since it has unique contributions to make. With beginners, for example, oral reading (followed by adequate praise) is a pleasant confirmation of the fact that they *can* read. At the very beginning, oral reading also demonstrates the connection between what is familiar (spoken language) and what is not (written language).

With all children, oral reading of sentences is required to show the significance for comprehension of such graphic signals as exclamation and question marks, and italics, all caps, and underlining. Obviously, oral reading is also necessary for sharing with others what has been learned, discovered, or enjoyed very much. Some oral reading is also necessary because certain kinds of materials—many poems, for instance—were written as much for their sound as for their sense and are fully appreciated and understood (much as if they were music) only when read aloud (19).

Since oral reading does merit classroom time, additional comments about it follow.

Requirements for Oral Reading Done to Share

When the purpose of oral reading is to share, teachers should make certain that two requirements are met. First, the oral reader ought to have an audience (big or small) that has a desire, or at least a willingness, to listen. Whether a genuine audience is likely to exist depends upon a combination of factors, one of which is the material being read. If it is dull or is already familiar (which is often the case in round robin reading), children will listen only out of courtesy—or maybe out of fear of being chastised. Since courtesy is not usually full blown in children and since fear hardly is a worthy goal, it is a wise teacher who sees to it that the selection of material for oral reading is made with care.

One other factor affects whether an oral reader is likely to have a genuine audience. It relates to the reader himself, for it is the quality of the reading. This factor, then, suggests a second requirement for oral reading done to share: preparation. If what is to be read is short and simple, a quick skimming usually is sufficient. On the other hand, when it is difficult or lengthy, adequate preparation might be a complete, careful (and silent) prereading. Special attention is given to this requirement because teachers sometimes ask students to read aloud for others without giving them a chance to look over the material. Yet recall, if you will, the times you yourself have been asked to read something suddenly. Even as a mature reader you felt just a little tense, didn't you? When you teach, remember that sudden, unexpected requests have the same effect on children.

Requirements for Oral Reading Used for Diagnosis

Although the usual reason for reading aloud is to communicate to others, oral reading in school may also be used as a medium for identifying a student's abilities and shortcomings. Serving that purpose, oral reading has different—in fact, opposite—requirements. Now a child should not have a chance to prepare since the reason for the oral reading is to learn what he does in the very act of reading. Since such reading is likely to be flawed, it should be done as privately as possible, preferably with only the teacher listening.

To sum up, then, oral reading done for different purposes has different requirements:

Requirements for Oral Reading

To share: audience
            familiar material

To diagnose: privacy
            unfamiliar material

Teachers who have developed the habit of asking themselves, *Why* am I doing this? first decide whether they are interested in sharing or diagnosis and then see to it that the appropriate requirements are met. They may also decide that it is silent reading that is called for because of what they are trying to accomplish.

TEACHING FOR EFFECTIVE ORAL READING

The primary goal of this book is to show what helps to develop reading comprehension. Because all of the remaining chapters have that as their underlying concern, the rest of this chapter considers what helps with oral reading viewed as a means for sharing. (Oral reading for placement and diagnosis is dealt with in Chapters 15 and 16.)

In any consideration of what can be done to help students become adept communicators when they read aloud, it is important to remember at the outset that some will never succeed, and they may include highly skilled silent readers. This note of pessimism is sounded because how effectively anyone reads aloud is partially dependent on factors outside the domain of a teacher—for instance, on personality and the quality of speech. Therefore, children who are shy or quiet or somewhat stumbling in their speech will not usually excel in oral reading. Better performances come from those who are more aggressive or self-confident or who have a little of the "ham" in them. In this group there might even be a child who is able to read a telephone directory and make it sound interesting.

Fortunately, reading programs have no obligation to produce students who read directories with gusto. Instead, the more modest and realistic aim is to help them read orally with a moderate amount of skill. In some instances, individual children will go far beyond this. In other cases, however, they will not reach the goal; and that is acceptable too, because it is comprehension through silent reading that really counts.

That comprehension *is* what matters is not always reflected in classroom practices. Here I cannot help but recall a conversation with a fourth-grade teacher who works with low achievers. Surprisingly, her overwhelming concern was for an effective oral delivery expressed with the complaint, "I just can't get these children to read fluently even when I have them practice over and over again." Such a worry suggests that this teacher may hold to an elocution concept of reading in which success is equated with fluent, oral reading. Yet with her students, who are still struggling with basic skills, fluency in oral reading is like frosting on a cake—nice but not necessary.

To work on the frosting, when this seems appropriate, teachers can do a number of things, which will now be discussed.

Read to Children

An assumption of this text is that good oral reading is as much caught as it is taught; consequently, the occasions when a teacher reads to students assume importance because they provide a model. Ideally, it will demonstrate the importance of careful pronunciation and enunciation of words, appropriate volume, and an expression that succeeds in communicating feelings as well as facts.

Since children always enjoy being read to—assuming appropriate material has been selected and is presented effectively—teachers *at all grade levels* should always allow time for reading to their students. While this might occur less frequently with the older ones, it should never be omitted in any classroom. Reading aloud once a week, in fact, should be viewed as the minimum in middle- and upper-grade classes.

To be a worthy model for oral reading, beginning teachers often find it helpful to rehearse. This builds up confidence and allows for sufficient acquaintance with the material that they can establish eye contact from time to time with their audience. A rehearsal also frees teachers to show illustrations at appropriate times.

An interesting article by Artley (5) reminds all teachers of how children both enjoy *and* remember being read to. The article is based on responses from junior and senior education majors when they were asked to recall elementary school experiences in order to identify "what turned them on or off reading." After describing the bleak picture drawn by the college students' responses, Artley shifts to the positive and notes:

> The greatest number said that teachers reading to the class on any level was the thing they remembered and enjoyed most. In some cases the teacher read the opening chapter of a book or an interesting episode from it as a starter, the pupils then finishing it themselves, in some instances having to wait in turn because of the book's sudden popularity. Other teachers read a book to completion, chapter by chapter. . . . Some students reported that their teachers frequently talked about books they thought some of them might enjoy, and in other cases a teacher told about a book that she was reading for her own information or enjoyment. In this way the pupils saw that reading was important to the teacher. [5, p. 27]

Another article (6) by a fourth-grade teacher should help any who feel unsure of their ability to make selections that will win the attention of older children. The article includes brief descriptions of books that were especially captivating.

Make Commercial Recordings Available

The many commercial recordings that are available also provide models for oral reading and have the advantage of allowing students to analyze what it is that makes them excellent, poor, or just average. Children may also enjoy comparing a professional recording with what they themselves read into a tape recorder. Such comparisons ought to be done privately unless a child happens to have unusual skill. They might also be done with a checklist or a written set of guidelines so that students have something definite to listen for as they make comparisons. A sheet like Figure 2.2 is helpful.

Use Choral Reading

Another way to foster effective oral reading is to have group choral reading (also called *choral speaking* or *verse choirs*). For students whose potential for oral reading is diminished by shyness, choral reading can be especially effective because it allows them both to participate and to hide within the group. (The dramatizations

Figure 2.2

Oral Reading:
Self-Evaluation Checklist

When I read aloud, do I

		Yes	No
1.	Pronounce all the words correctly?	___	___
2.	Enunciate each word so that all my words can be understood?	___	___
3.	Read smoothly, not stopping when there is no reason to stop?	___	___
4.	Read loud enough to be easily heard?	___	___
5.	Read with an expression that helps my audience understand and enjoy what I read?	___	___

I need to work on:

referred to earlier also help because they encourage shy children to forget themselves as they assume the role of another person.)

For teachers, the most important point to remember about choral reading is that it should not be treated as an end in itself. Perfectly polished performances are fine for the theater but unnecessary in the classroom. In fact, demands for perfection may become petty, ignoring the very reason for having choral reading, which is to promote both ability in oral reading *and* enjoyment. With the twin goals in the foreground, choral reading will be handled with an appropriate amount of seriousness.

Books are available to help teachers (a) choose material, (b) organize students, and (c) plan the details of a reading. One helpful source is *Time for Poetry,* for which the authors, Arbuthnot and Root, assembled 735 poems plus specifically helpful suggestions for using them in choral reading (4). Another text by Arbuthnot, *Children and Books,* deals with literature more broadly, but it too provides specific help with choral reading (3).

For any teacher who lacks experience with this type of reading, the Benefic Press Oral Readers provide a suitable starting point (see Figures 2.3 and 2.4). They offer explicit directions and include material that ranges from a first- to about a third-grade level of difficulty. The range makes the material useful not only in primary grades but also in the middle and upper grades where students with reading deficiencies and those who are more able can work together. The same books include other types of material that are suitable for oral reading— riddles and tongue twisters, for instance.

PRACTICING ORAL READING

If skill in oral reading is to be maintained, it must be used. To conclude the discussion, therefore, examples of oral reading practice will be described, each of which can be adapted for different grade levels.

> Prepare written descriptions of objects and scenes.
> Direct students in an instructional group to draw a picture that corresponds to a description. Later, each will display his drawing and read the description. Others will be asked to listen in order to see whether all the details appear in the picture.

Comment. This activity illustrates how a single assignment can achieve more than one goal. First, students were given practice in reading aloud to communicate to an audience, and they also had practice in reading silently in order to get a mental picture, which is important for comprehension. Notice, too, that the oral reader had a chance to preread the material while the audience was given a definite purpose for listening.

> Assign children to pairs. Each member of a pair will be responsible, first, for finding material likely to be of interest to a partner (for example, a short magazine article or part of a book) and, second, for preparing to read it to the partner on some designated day. Following each reading, the material can be discussed by the pair.

Comment. Whenever students are unaccustomed to doing something, preparation or even a rehearsal is often required. With the activity described above, a teacher might have to present a model before the paired reading can be successful. To do this, she could select two students (to whom she has given help in making a selection and in discussing it) to illustrate what is to be done. The same teacher might learn through experience that having students select and read what is of

Figure 2.3

Music with ng Endings

Listen to the word sounds as your teacher reads this poem. Listen for the music of the ng words.

Next read the poem with your teacher. The boys may read the boy's part, the girls may read the girl's part.

The City Things

Boys: Hear them trotting, jumping, running.
Hear them whizzing down the street!

Girls: Hear them yowling, tooting, humming!
Hear their wheels or hear their feet!

Boys: Working, playing, racing, chasing,
Up above or down below;

Girls: Flying, wiggling, rumbling, grumbling,
City things are on the go!

Lucy Sprague Mitchell

Dawson, Mildred A., and Newman, Georgina. *Say and Hear*. Westchester, Ill.: Benefic Press, 1969, p. 27.

Figure 2.4

Speaking in Refrain

Listen as your teacher reads this poem. As she reads it a second time, say the refrain softly.

Now, as the teacher reads the poem again, whisper the part you will read along with her.

Speak clearly now as you say your part of the poem. Make sure you keep together as a group. After you have practiced saying this poem, try speaking the poem to other classes.

Boys: 'Tis a lesson you should heed,

All: Try again;

Boys: If at first you don't succeed,

All: Try again;

Girls: Then your courage should appear,
For if you will persevere,
You will conquer, never fear,

All: Try again.

Boys: If you find your task is hard,

All: Try again;

Boys: Time will bring you your reward,

All: Try again;

Girls: All that other folk can do,
Why, with patience, may not you?
Only keep this rule in view,

All: Try again.

T. H. Palmer

32

Dawson, Mildred A., and Newman, Georgina. *Loud and Clear.* Westchester, Ill.: Benefic Press, 1969, p. 32.

interest to themselves works better. In either case, the activity gives students a chance to read aloud in order to share.

> Periodically, have able readers write questions (on a chalkboard or for a ditto sheet) about interesting material covering topics related to social studies, current events, or science. Their second job is to prepare to read the material to less able readers whose responsibilities are threefold: (1) read the questions silently, (2) listen to the reading, and (3) answer the questions.

Comment.   This activity provides one possible solution (not to be overdone) for a problem that middle- and upper-grade teachers mention frequently: the need to cover certain content in textbooks even though some students are unable to read it. As time passes and the previous activity is used more than once, able readers can usually carry on postreading discussions without supervision, thus freeing a teacher to give time to others.

> To promote interest in word meanings and word histories, distribute to members of an instructional group copies of books that tell about words. (Titles of such books are in Chapter 10.) Have each child skim through a book to find a word with an especially interesting history and to prepare to read it to the others. Prior to each reading, write the word (or have a student do this) so that all can see what it looks like. Following a reading, encourage the group to respond with comments and questions.

Comment.   Once more, an assignment aims toward multiple goals: development of an interest in words and practice in skimming, oral reading, and group discussion. What might be achieved, too, is a budding interest in mythology because many words in our language are tied to myths.

> Collect wordless picture books covering a wide variety of topics. Let individual children who are interested compose anything from brief captions to a well-developed text to go with the pictures. Later, a composer can read what he wrote while the teacher or another student displays the illustrations to the audience.

Comment.   Reading one's own material is another type of oral reading practice. As was just described, the material can be written in connection with commercial picture books, or a student's own artwork might be the stimulus. In either case, an audience should be available.

> To provide a reason for improving oral reading skills, let students who are interested take turns reading to younger children—kindergartners and first graders, for instance.

Comment.   If the older students select an appropriate story (with the help of a teacher or librarian) and if they prepare well, they will be rewarded with a most appreciative and attentive audience. On the other hand, if the reading is done poorly or if the wrong material was selected, they will learn very quickly the error of their ways.

A FINAL COMMENT ABOUT ORAL READING

To conclude the discussion of oral reading done to share, one more comment needs to be made because of a question that teachers frequently raise: "When a child is reading to others and is unable to identify a word, should I tell him what it says?"

As with many other questions about teaching, the answer to this one is found in a consideration of purpose and goals. (That is why it is correct to say that the most important question for teachers to ask is, *Why* am I doing this?) Since the reason for the oral reading is communication, the only teacher response that makes sense is to supply the word so that the reader can move on.

Consideration of purpose also provides an answer for any who wonder what to do when an oral reader misidentifies a word. If the misidentification distorts or confuses meaning, it should be quickly corrected in a way that is not embarrassing to the reader. If it does not cause confusion, correction is unnecessary.

Should it happen that one or more students frequently require help when they read aloud to an audience, it might indicate insufficient preparation. This should be discussed and remedied. It might also be that they are reading material that is too difficult, in which case a change to easier material will resolve the problem.

SUMMARY

That classroom time is often spent on a procedure that may impede students' progress in becoming successful comprehenders of print is the central theme of Chapter 2. The procedure, referred to as round robin reading, has students take turns reading aloud what others are expected to follow silently. Classroom observations uncover frequent use of such a practice not only when reading is taught but also when time goes to content subjects. Why the habitual use of around-the-group oral reading is questionable was explained as follows.

Having students both follow, and listen to, what another is reading aloud may foster both excessive subvocalizing and inefficient eye movements when they read silently. The two consequences, which are especially likely to occur when the oral reading is poor, slow down silent reading, making it more difficult to comprehend because of the increased burden placed on the reader's memory. Since excessive subvocalization and inefficient eye movements are symptoms of problems, they can be corrected by eliminating their causes, which suggests that teachers who routinely use round robin reading would do well to consider abandoning it. The same teachers also need to keep in mind that giving frequent praise to oral readers who perform with a big voice and with expression may unintentionally foster the erroneous conclusion that an effective oral delivery is what is important when, in fact, comprehension is what counts.

That comprehension through silent reading *is* the primary concern is not a reason to eliminate oral reading, but it does point up the need to help students make a distinction between the purpose of silent reading and the concern of oral reading done to share. As the chapter stressed, round robin reading is effective only in muddying the distinction.

REVIEW

1. To discuss eye movements and to understand research about them, it is necessary to be familiar with certain terminology. Therefore, see whether you can define the following terms:

saccadic movement	return sweep	eye-voice span
fixation	regression	

    Which have to do with silent reading, which pertain to oral reading, and which enter into both?

2. Explain why the two statements below are false.

    (a) Ideally, eye fixations would be nonexistent, especially in silent reading.
    (b) Even though return sweeps cannot be reduced to zero, they should still be kept to a small number.

3. Explain why some eye regressions may be evidence of a reader's efforts to comprehend.

4. A parent who was preparing to be a teacher was heard to say, "I used to see round robin reading so often when I visited my children's classrooms that I assumed it was the way reading was supposed to be taught." In contrast, the theme of Chapter 2 is that it ought to be eliminated.

    (a) Cite all the reasons mentioned in the chapter why the habitual use of round robin reading may be detrimental for the silent followers.

(b)   Keeping in mind the two functions of oral reading (communication and diagnosis), comment on the oral part of round robin reading when it is preceded by a silent reading of the selection and, second, when it is not.

5.   Acceptable combinations of oral and silent reading are described in Chapter 2. In what important ways do these combinations differ from round robin reading?

6.   Let us say you taught in a school in which the principal made the following announcement: "This year, money will be available to purchase taped recordings of books, the books themselves, and earphones so that students can listen to the recordings without disturbing others. Any teacher who is interested in having these materials should let me know within a week or two." Would *you* be interested? If so, why? If not, why not? If yes, how would you have students use the materials? What would be your purposes for using them?

REFERENCES

1.   Adams, Marilyn J.; Anderson, Richard C.; and Durkin, Dolores. "Beginning Reading: Theory and Practice." *Language Arts* 55 (January 1978): 19–25.
2.   Anderson, Irving H., and Dearborn, Walter F. *The Psychology of Teaching Reading.* New York: Ronald Press, 1952.
3.   Arbuthnot, May Hill, and Sutherland, Zena. *Children and Books.* Chicago: Scott, Foresman, 1972.
4.   Arbuthnot, May Hill, and Root, S. L. *Time for Poetry.* Glenview, Ill.: Scott, Foresman, 1968.
5.   Artley, A. Sterl. "Good Teachers of Reading—Who Are They?" *Reading Teacher* 29 (October 1975): 26–31.
6.   Brown, Jennifer. "Reading Aloud." *Elementary English* 50 (April 1973): 635–636.
7.   Buswell, Guy T. *An Experimental Study of the Eye-Voice Span in Reading.* Supplementary Educational Monographs, No. 17. Chicago: University of Chicago Press, 1920.
8.   Buswell, Guy T. *Fundamental Reading Habits: A Study of Their Development.* Supplementary Educational Monographs, No. 21. Chicago: University of Chicago Press, 1922.
9.   Durkin, Dolores. "What Classroom Observations Reveal about Reading Comprehension Instruction." *Reading Research Quarterly* 14, no. 4 (1978–1979): 481–533.
10.   Durrell, Donald D., and Crossley, B. Alice. *Thirty Plays for Classroom Reading.* Boston: Plays, 1957.
11.   Edfeldt, A. W. *Silent Speech and Silent Reading.* Stockholm: Almquist and Wiksell, 1959.
12.   Erickson, Sheryl E. *Conference on Studies in Reading.* Washington, D.C.: U.S. Department of Health, Education and Welfare, 1978.
13.   Gibson, Eleanor J., and Levin, Harry. *The Psychology of Reading.* Cambridge, Mass.: MIT Press, 1975.

14. Gilbert, Luther C. "Effect on Silent Reading of Attempting to Follow Oral Reading." *Elementary School Journal* 40 (April 1940): 614–621.

15. Golinkoff, Roberta M. "A Comparison of Reading Comprehension Processes in Good and Poor Comprehenders." *Reading Research Quarterly* 11, no. 4 (1975–1976): 623–659.

16. Goodman, Kenneth S. "Behind the Eye: What Happens in Reading." *Theoretical Models and Processes of Reading.* Edited by Harry Singer and Robert B. Ruddell. Newark, Dela.: International Reading Association, 1976.

17. Huey, Edmund B. *The Psychology and Pedagogy of Reading.* New York: Macmillan, 1908.

18. McConkie, George W.; Hogaboam, Thomas W.; Lucas, Peter A.; Wolverton, Gary S.; and Zola, David. "Toward the Use of Eye Movements in the Study of Language Processing." *Discourse Processes* 2, no. 3 (1979): 157–177.

19. Sloan, Glenna. "Profile: Eve Merriam." *Language Arts* 58 (November–December 1981): 957–964.

20. Smith, Frank. *Understanding Reading.* New York: Holt, Rinehart and Winston, 1971.

21. Weiger, Myra. "Puppetry." *Elementary English* 51 (January 1974): 55–64.

PART II

AT THE BEGINNING

CHAPTER 3

READINESS FOR READING

PREVIEW

One's initial experience with anything—a person, an event, a task, an object—has unique influence on subsequent contacts because it establishes a mental set for the next encounter. The maxim "Success breeds success" reflects that link, as does the educator's interest in the question that is of primary concern in Chapter 3: When are children ready to learn to read? Realizing that readiness allows for success, educators naturally want to be sure that students are ready when reading instruction is initiated with the hope that, if ready, they will get off to a good, positive start. Although a successful beginning does not guarantee future success, it certainly leads a child in the right direction.

You who are about to embark on Chapter 3 probably received initial instruction in reading in first grade. For some, it may have begun immediately whereas with others, not until a reading readiness program was completed. Were you much younger and starting school now, making the same predictions would be risky because, currently, reading in kindergarten—even in nursery school—is common. Why the change? Are children different, or is our conception of what constitutes readiness for reading different?

Chapter 3 answers questions like these. Although answering them is its first concern, the chapter does not neglect the significance of the readiness concept for later levels. This means that its content should be relevant for any reading teacher who is doing her best to make sure that her students, young or old, have the chance to enjoy success.

After reading Chapter 3, you should be able to respond to such questions as:

When should reading instruction begin?
Is chronological age the most important factor to consider when decisions are made about when to start teaching reading?
Are all kindergartners ready for reading? For some, might a later start be better? What about first graders? Are they ready?
How does the readiness concept enter into decisions about instruction beyond the beginning level?

Before starting the chapter, you might want to read the summary at the end in order to get an overview of the content.

Based on what is seen in kindergartens, many must believe that five year olds are ready to profit from reading instruction because most kindergartens are offering some. Yet, not too many years ago it was taken for granted that children are not ready for reading until they have a mental age of about 6.5 years. Which position is correct? Why the great change? To answer, it is necessary to understand developments that go as far back as the beginning of the century.

HISTORICAL PERSPECTIVE

In American schools, a close association has traditionally existed between being in first grade and starting to read. Because the age of six has been the common criterion for admission into first grade, a parallel development was the expectation that "being six" and "starting to read" occur simultaneously.

Not to be overlooked, nonetheless, is that reports and articles published many years ago identify well-known scholars who objected to the idea that entrance into school should automatically mean the start of reading. Edmund Huey, best known for his 1908 text *The Psychology and Pedagogy of Reading* (35), quoted John Dewey as recommending the age of eight as an appropriate time for beginning instruction. But he emphasized that Dewey was objecting as much to the mechanical and passive way in which the schools taught reading as he was to the time when they initiated instruction.

Huey's own objections were also directed as much to the nature of existing instruction as to when it began. His complaints focused on the "unnatural" ways in which the schools introduced reading, which he contrasted with the "natural, every-day activities" of preschool children that sometimes teach them to read. Huey's language is a little old-fashioned but the theme in his 1908 description of preschoolers is strictly up to date:

> The child makes endless questionings about the names of things, as every mother knows. He is concerned also about the printed notices, signs, titles, visiting cards, etc., that come in his way, and should be told what these "say" when he makes inquiry. It is surprising how large a stock of printed or written words a child will gradually come to recognize in this way. [35, p. 313]

Even though well-known, highly regarded educators did speak out against the routine practice of initiating school instruction in reading at the start of first grade, it still must be concluded that the years from 1900 to 1920 were relatively quiet about when to begin. Subsequently, however, books and journals became heavy with questions and answers about the best time to start teaching reading. Why the change?

One of the most important indirect causes was the new interest during the 1920s and 1930s in the "scientific" measurement of children's behavior, including their achievement in school (53). Among the results of what became almost a craze to measure everything was the appearance of school surveys. Of special relevance for this discussion is a finding that was common to many of the survey reports: large numbers of children were failing first grade, most often because of insufficient achievement in reading (13, 34, 46).

Within a short time, interest in this finding was widespread, and for at least two reasons. The successful teaching of reading, then as now, was considered uniquely important among elementary school responsibilities. In addition, the failures that were occurring resulted in a number of "overage" children in first-grade classrooms. Behavior problems blossomed; so did concern about why first graders were having problems with reading.

Logically, a study of inadequate achievement—at any grade level and in any period of time—would look to such multiple and commonsense causes as insufficient teacher preparation, poor instruction, inappropriate instructional materials, large classes, low IQs among the children, or, perhaps, a lack of motivation. In the study of beginning reading problems that went on in the 1920s and 1930s, however, the factor given *singular* attention can be identified in a pronouncement that appeared frequently in the professional literature of that period: first graders are having difficulty with reading because they were not ready when instruction began (13, 34). Why reading problems were attributed so exclusively to a lack of readiness and why delaying instruction was subsequently proposed as the way to alleviate the problems can be understood only when the broader psychological and educational setting of the 1920s and 1930s is brought into focus (47).

Prevailing Psychological Beliefs

To show why the concept of readiness received such singular attention in the 1920s and 1930s, it is necessary to go back to prior decades in order to bring the name G. Stanley Hall into the discussion. Hall was a psychologist who, because of his numerous publications, had a striking influence on psychological interpretations of human behavior at the start of the century. Prominent in Hall's writings was his belief in the unique importance of heredity in a child's development. Equally prominent was his acceptance of the theory of recapitulation (45). To remind you of the tenets of this theory, a quotation from one of Hall's own texts follows:

> The most general formulation of all the facts of development that we yet possess is contained in the law of recapitulation. This law declares that the individual, in his development, passes through stages similar to those through which the race has passed, and in the same order. [28, p. 8].

Hall's combined emphases on heredity and recapitulation theory resulted in a view of humans that stressed *a predetermined nature that unfolds in stages*. This interpretation of growth and development had a pronounced effect on the thinking of Hall's students, who included prominent individuals like Frederick Kuhlmann, Lewis Terman, Patty Smith Hill, and Arnold Gesell. Because Gesell's work is so directly related to the concept of readiness and because his writings were uniquely influential during the 1920s and 1930s, he also must get special attention in this attempt to explain why (a) lack of readiness and (b) postponed instruction were once viewed as the cause and the solution for beginning reading problems.

Arnold Gesell was a physician; thus his special interest in the maturation process is not surprising. Nor is his description of maturation as something that occurs in distinct stages (23–26). Such a description clearly shows the influence of G. Stanley Hall. Hall's influence seems even greater, however, in Gesell's proposed explanation of how development moves from one stage to the next. Bypassing such possible causes as practice and learning, he singled out instead what he called at various times "intrinsic growth," "neural ripening," and "automatic and unfolding behavior."

Early Interpretation of Beginning Reading Problems

With the foregoing sketch of the psychological climate of the 1920s, you should now be able to understand why the first-grade reading problems that were uncovered in the surveys referred to earlier were "explained" with a reference to a lack of readiness rather than to such possible causes as poor instruction, large classes, or inappropriate materials. The reasoning behind such an explanation can be outlined as follows.

1. Development takes place in stages that follow one another in an inevitable order.
2. Growth from one stage to another is the result of a maturation (internal neural ripening) that occurs automatically with the passing of time.
3. The ability required to learn to read occurs at one of these stages.
4. Reading problems disclosed by the surveys suggest that most beginning first graders have not yet reached that stage of development and thus are not yet ready to read.
5. The solution is to postpone reading instruction so that, with the passing of time, the children will become ready.

Mental-Age Concept of Readiness

Given the circumstances of the 1920s, it would have been unusual to find contentment with a concept of readiness that related it to some vague stage in a child's development. After all, that hardly reflected the interest in exact measurement that characterized the times. With that in mind, it should come as no surprise that efforts were made to define with more precision that stage of development thought to ensure a child's success with reading.

The form these efforts eventually took was influenced by the appearance of group intelligence tests, because with their availability came many reports about the relationship between a child's intelligence and achievement in reading. Often, too, the focus was on reading achievement in first grade. In fact, as early as 1920 one author of a report claimed that the children who were having difficulty with reading and thus failing first grade had mental ages of less than six years (14). Subsequently, other authors in the 1920s moved toward proposals that would establish a certain mental-age level as a requirement for starting instruction (2, 34, 57). Arthur, for example, writing in 1925, maintained that a mental age of 6.0 to 6.5 years was "necessary for standard first-grade achievement" (2).

The type of thinking about readiness that is reflected in these reports was crystallized in an article that was published in 1931 and that became widely known and uncommonly influential for a long period of time (42). Written by Mabel Morphett and Carleton Washburne, the report described the reading achievement of first-grade children when one particular method was used in one school system (Winnetka, Illinois). Based on the children's achievement as it related to mental age, the authors concluded:

> It seems safe to state that, by postponing the teaching of reading until children reach a mental age level of six and a half years, teachers can greatly decrease the chances of failure and discouragement and can correspondingly increase their efficiency. [42, p. 503]

How seriously Washburne took his own proposal is reflected in an article that he wrote in 1936 entitled—quite in keeping with the prevailing psychological views—"Ripeness." He observed:

> Nowadays each first grade teacher in Winnetka has a chart showing when each of her children will be mentally six-and-a-half, and is careful to avoid any effort to get a child to read before he has reached this stage of mental growth. [54, p. 127]

Evidence of how seriously other educators took the Morphett-Washburne proposal is in reading methodology textbooks that appeared not long after their report, but also in some published as many as ten and twenty years later (8, 11, 15, 30, 32, 39, 41). In fact, textbooks published in the 1960s still took it seriously (29, 43, 50).

Reasons for Acceptance of Mental-Age Concept

Knowing how influential the mental-age concept of readiness has been, you might wonder why findings from a study of one teaching method in one school system were accepted as being applicable to all children. Too, you might wonder why the acceptance persisted so long. A subsequent section in the chapter helps with the latter question; here, the one that asks why the Morphett-Washburne proposal was quickly accepted will be considered.

To begin, their proposal matched perfectly the temper of the times in which it was offered. It gave support to the "doctrine of postponement," since most children entering first grade do not have a mental age of 6.5 years. It also supported the notion that development proceeds in stages, and it honored the measurement and testing movement by being precise and "objective."

Any attempt to explain the unique influence of the mental-age concept of readiness must also take into account the prominence of Carleton Washburne. He was not only superintendent of the Winnetka schools—widely admired and copied in the 1930s—but also one of the most prestigious leaders of the progressive education movement. That meant that what Washburne said was listened to, and not only in the field of reading. Even earlier than 1931, he had made specific proposals about what was to be taught in arithmetic and at which mental-age level (55). With all these facts in mind, neither his mental-age description of readiness nor the influence it wielded is surprising.

Early Objections to Mental-Age Concept

Even though the mental-age concept of readiness was widely accepted, objections were still raised, the most important coming from Arthur Gates. Conclusions reached in two of his studies merit attention not only because they raised questions about the concept but also because they were in reports that appeared soon after the Morphett-Washburne article.

In 1936, in a report entitled, "Reading Readiness: A Study of Factors Determining Success and Failure in Beginning Reading," Gates described reading achievement in four first-grade classes (21). Of relevance to the present discussion is that in March, he identified the ten lowest achievers and assigned them tutors. By June, all ten were enjoying success. Referring to that success, Gates wrote:

> The study emphasizes the importance of recognizing and adjusting to individual limitations and needs . . . rather than merely changing the time of beginning. It appears that readiness for reading is something to develop rather than merely to wait for. [21, p. 684]

In the same report Gates also pointed out:

> Correlations of mental age with reading achievement at the end of the year were about 0.25. When one studies the range of mental ages from the lowest to the highest in relation to reading achievement, there appears no suggestion of a crucial or critical point above which very few fail and below which a relatively large proportion fail. [21, p. 680]

In concluding the report, Gates stated:

> The optimum time of beginning reading is not entirely dependent upon the nature of the child himself, but it is in a large measure determined by the nature of the reading program. [21, p. 684]

Another study reported by Gates in 1937 reached the same conclusion (20). This one had examined different methods of teaching reading and the achievement that resulted. Commenting on the findings, Gates observed:

> Reading is begun by very different materials, methods, and general procedures, some of which a pupil can master at the mental age of five with reasonable ease, others of which would give him difficulty at the mental age of seven. [20, p. 508]

As the two research reports clearly indicate, a concept of reading readiness emerged from Gates's research that was at odds with the Morphett–Washburne description. Within the Gates frame of reference, the burden of responsibility was moved to the instruction and away from the child. In addition, questions were raised about the wisdom of postponement and of equating readiness with a particular mental age.

Essentially, Gates's message was simple: Improve your instruction and watch the children read! Apparently the simplicity of the Morphett–Washburne proposal was more appealing because just as the publications of the 1930s and subsequent decades provide ample evidence of the wide and prolonged acceptance of the mental-age concept of readiness, so too do they reveal how little attention went to Gates's findings. His simply did not move with the stream of popular thought. What did, though, were further descriptions of the child thought to be ready for reading. Here I refer to what became the common practice of listing all kinds of attributes—almost in litany fashion—that were also supposed to be requirements for success. For instance, in the Thirty-eighth Yearbook of the National Society for the Study of Education, published in 1939, the following were cited as being some of the "requisites of readiness for reading" (27, p. 195):

Keen interest in reading
Reasonably wide experiences
Facility in the use of ideas
Ability to solve simple problems
Ability to do abstract thinking of a very elementary type
Ability to remember ideas, word forms, and the sounds of words
A reasonable range of vocabulary
Command of simple English sentences
Good health, vision, and hearing
Ability to see likenesses and differences in word forms and to discriminate sounds
    of words
Normal speech organs
Emotional stability
Some degree of social adjustment

With such a list, it is easy to forget that the concern was only for beginning reading. Probably the saving feature of the proposed requirements is that they generally were described in vague terms. With the vagueness they could be interpreted according to each person's particular biases.

Reading Readiness Tests

One more effort to describe the child who is ready to read led to the birth of readiness tests, references to which appear in the literature as early as 1927 (6, 51). The initial and naive hope held out for the tests is effectively portrayed in an editorial in a 1927 issue of *Childhood Education:*

> In the field of reading it is essential that a joyous attitude of success shall be cultivated from the first. This necessitates a stage of development in which the learner is capable of getting meaning from the crooked marks which symbolize ideas. When does this period come? . . . In which direction shall we look to discover the truth regarding this confused situation? Fortunately the scientific method points the way toward the solution of this and of other baffling problems. The first steps have been taken. First, the problem has been recognized. Second, a name has been coined for the characteristic which is sought, Reading Readiness, a term not only alliterative but meaningful. Third, tests are in process of developing which shall be applicable to any young child. . . . So we may look forward to the day when the measure of readiness will rest in objective tests and parent and teacher will both be governed thereby. [37, p. 209]

What did the tests, which were "in the process of developing," turn out to be? They were group pencil-and-paper tests made up of subtests that typically dealt with vocabulary and visual and auditory discrimination.

When a subtest focused on vocabulary, children were usually asked to circle or underline a picture that went with a word named by the one administering the test, generally a teacher. Or the administrator might be directed by the test manual to read aloud a particular sentence; again, children would be told to select from a row of pictures the one that pertained to its content.

Subtests for visual discrimination also relied on pictures. In this case, the unverified assumption was that if a child sees similarities and differences in pictures, he has the ability to distinguish among similar and dissimilar letters and words. That the same assumption held for geometrical figures also seems to have been accepted because many of the early visual subtests focused on circles, squares, triangles, and so on. Now a child would be asked to look at the first figure in a row and to underline all the others that were the same (or different).

Evidently those who constructed readiness tests figured that sooner or later phonics would be taught. This is suggested by the frequent inclusion of subtests dealing with auditory discrimination, typically involving rhyme. Now the administrator might be directed to name each picture in a given row and to have the children underline or circle all of the pictures whose names rhymed with the name of the first one. Sometimes, but less often, an auditory subtest dealt with initial sounds in words. When this was the case, the one administering the test might say: "Put your finger under the picture of the door. I am going to name the other pictures in this row. Listen, because I want you to draw a line around the one whose name begins with the sound you hear at the beginning of *door*."

In addition to explaining how tests were to be administered, manuals usually suggested that results ought to be used diagnostically. That is, subtest scores should be studied in order to identify each child's particular strengths and weaknesses. What happened in practice, though, was quite different: schools used total scores to make global judgments. The end result was groups of first graders who were labeled "ready" or "unready."

What then? What came next depended on when the readiness test was administered. And dealing with that requires attention to reading readiness programs.

Reading Readiness Programs

When it was agreed in the 1930s that most beginning first graders were unready to read, a decision had to be made about what was to be done while they were "growing into readiness." The term used to describe the product of the decision was *reading readiness program*.

Content of readiness programs.   Although called by the same name, what went on at the beginning of the first-grade year varied from school to school. Some of the variation, no doubt, reflected variation among teachers, but some also reflected differences in viewpoints about the nature of readiness. Thus, educators who held staunchly to the notion that the passing of time *automatically* results in readiness concluded that the content of a readiness program does not have to show any obvious, direct relationship to the reading process. On the other hand, those who believed that what occurred as time passed was significant for readiness had quite different conceptions of a readiness program. Under their direction, the content was more likely to focus on goals like those commonly assessed in the readiness tests.

What also promoted attention to what was being assessed in those tests—and this turned out to be uniquely influential over several decades—was the appearance of the reading readiness workbook. Often, the publisher of a readiness test was the publisher of one or more workbooks. Whether or not this was so, however, the content of the tests and the content of the workbooks were very similar. In time, the content of the workbooks and the content of the readiness programs were remarkably similar, too.

Duration of readiness programs.   In theory, a readiness program was for "unready" children and should last until they became "ready." In practice, however, that is not the way it worked. Instead, the typical procedure was to administer a readiness test (sometimes a group intelligence test was given too) close to the start of the first-grade year. Evidently, the purpose was *not* to learn whether some might be ready for reading but, rather, to see how much time the children were to spend in a readiness program. The assumption seemed to be that it would be good for everybody—ready or not.

If a school had decided that the shortest amount of time to be spent on readiness was, let us say, two months, then the first graders with the highest readiness and IQ scores would be in a readiness program for two months. The remaining children participated for some longer amount of time, often determined somewhat arbitrarily and without consideration of particular children.

Other schools were more flexible. For instance, they might administer readiness tests more than once in order to make more frequent decisions about whether the readiness program needed to be continued for individual children. In such schools, nonetheless, it was still the total scores that were the concern. Probably very few schools ever used subtest scores diagnostically, matching carefully what was taught with what individual children needed to learn.

Reasons for Questionable Practices

In retrospect, it is easy to be critical of practices like those just described; however, one must keep in mind some of the reasons for them. While such reasons do not endow the flaws with quality, they at least make them comprehensible.

Certainly one reason for many of the questionable practices was the large number of children typically found in first-grade classrooms when the readiness concept was in the spotlight. Ideally, readiness programs should have been highly individualized and should have included only children who seemed unready. Being responsible for large numbers of children—sometimes forty or even fifty—teachers were hardly able to achieve the ideal.

Further, the whole idea of readiness and of readiness programs was new. In addition, the programs were viewed not humbly but as a means of solving all the reading problems. No wonder they were greeted with what now seems like naive enthusiasm, which, among other things, appears to have resulted in the notion that readiness programs are good for everybody, ready or not.

Why the content of the programs was often sterile and routine also has a very human explanation. When first-grade teachers were suddenly called upon to do something other than teach reading at the start of the year, many, if not most, must have felt insecure to say the least. After all, a good program—whether for readiness or something else—is not created overnight. It is no wonder, then, that readiness workbooks were greeted with enthusiasm and just about took over when decisions were made about what to do in the readiness program.

Reasons for Maintenance of Questionable Practices

Whereas it is easy to see how questionable practices developed when readiness programs were a novelty, it is difficult to understand why they continued for so long—more specifically, from the 1930s into the 1960s. Among the collection of reasons is the tendency of schools to be conservative (56). That is, they often want to keep what they are doing and sometimes actively resist change. With readiness programs, unchanging and sometimes questionable routines were also linked with instructional materials, specifically with readiness workbooks. As was mentioned, not long after the programs came into existence, the workbooks appeared. And they came, sometimes two and three to a set, as part of the various basal reader programs. Because the vast majority of elementary teachers used these materials, readiness workbooks were used too, and not always because their content allowed for individualized instruction. As one first-grade teacher explained not too many years ago, "Our principal buys the workbooks, so we use them."

One more reason why certain practices connected with readiness continued for so long relates to another tendency among educators: to place too much faith in test scores. This has been true of readiness scores even though researchers examining their predictive value have been raising questions almost from the time the tests came into existence (18, 22). While the critics had some effect on the content of the revised editions of tests, they have had little effect on their use. Even now, readiness tests continue to be published, apparently because schools continue to buy them.

Still one more factor needs to be mentioned in this attempt to explain why certain practices connected with readiness assessment and readiness programs continued for so long. It moves the focus away from the schools and toward psychology, because psychologists were yet another reason for too little change over too many years (47). Here I refer to the fact that psychological conceptions of human growth and development changed very little from the early 1920s until the late 1950s. Supported by Gesell and his students and his disciples, the popular view during the 1940s and 1950s was like the popular view of the 1920s and 1930s: Readiness for various tasks, including reading, results from maturation; therefore, the passing of time is the solution for problems connected with a lack of it.

In the 1940s and 1950s, support for these contentions came from psychologists other than Gesell. Willard Olson, for instance, was especially popular among educators of young children, and his ideas about child development, expressed in terms of "organismic age," did anything but go contrary to Gesell's (44). Robert Havighurst, also well known to educators, offered no reason to question traditional practices as he wrote about "developmental tasks" and even referred to the notion of a "teachable moment" (31).

And so, having little reason to do otherwise, schools continued with what became the routine practice of administering readiness tests in first grade and of having all the children—ready or not—participate in readiness programs. But then came Sputnik and what is accurately called a revolution in education.

A NEW ERA

Although educational changes hardly occur on one specific day, it is customary to designate the start of major, midcentury changes by citing the date when the

Soviet Union launched Sputnik I: October 4, 1957. Expectedly, the launching of a satellite by a foreign power produced a variety of repercussions in the United States. Easily heard among the clamor was criticism that pounced on public school education, increasing the tempo of the already existing debate about the quality of instruction in American schools (7). Now the debate stressed the inferiority of our educational endeavors compared to those of the Soviet Union (5, 12).

One result of the furor was an atmosphere characterized by the plea, "Let's teach more in our schools, and let's teach it earlier!" Such an atmosphere, as time has demonstrated, fostered rapt attention to new proposals from psychologists. Relevant to this chapter's consideration of readiness are those that highlighted both the learning potential of young children and the unique importance of the early years for intellectual development.

Different Emphases in Psychology

One of the first books to receive the friendly blessing of the post-Sputnik era was *The Process of Education* (10) by Jerome Bruner. This was a psychologist's account of a ten-day meeting convened "to discuss how education in science might be improved in our primary and secondary schools" (10, p. vii). Bruner gave special attention to the importance of the "structure of a discipline" in teaching that discipline to others. More specifically emphasized was the claim that the "fundamental character" of a discipline enables one "to narrow the gap between 'advanced' knowledge and 'elementary' knowledge" (10, p. 26). A chapter entitled "Readiness for Learning" followed the claim and was introduced by a statement that was quoted with great frequency: "We begin with the hypothesis that any subject can be taught effectively in some intellectually honest form to any child at any stage of development" (10, p. 33).

Those who took the time to read all of Bruner's book would find little that was startling in this statement. It simply urged in a somewhat different way that the schools take another look at how they organized and presented instruction in fields like science and mathematics. However, when the statement was quoted out of context—and it often was—it fostered what could only be called wishful thinking about the learning potential of young children.

That was the beginning. Later, in 1961, a book by another psychologist became unusually popular. This one, *Intelligence and Experience* (36), by J. McV. Hunt, was a review and reinterpretation of earlier research that had examined the effects of training and practice on certain aspects of development. According to the original interpretation, readiness to learn—whether a motor skill or an intellectual skill—was the product of maturation, not of environmental factors like training or practice. In the interpretation Hunt proposed, a great variety of practices and experiences were said to affect the emergence of a skill; especially highlighted in his hypothetical explanation was the critical importance of *early* experiences.★

★ To understand and appreciate the new interpretation, one must read the whole of Hunt's book *Intelligence and Experience* (36).

With the broader concept of what constitutes practice and with the new emphasis on the importance of early stimulation, it was natural that the young child's environment emerged as a popular topic for discussion. Predictably, it became the theme of still another book from which it became fashionable to quote. This one, *Stability and Change in Human Characteristics,* appeared in 1964 and was written by Benjamin Bloom (9). Like Hunt's work, Bloom's was a detailed reexamination of earlier research—in this instance, of long-term studies concerned with the development of certain measurable characteristics. Concluding that the most rapid period for the development of many characteristics—including intelligence—is in the first five years of life, Bloom again stressed the crucial importance of the child's early environment.

New Social Concerns

At the start of the 1960s, in the midst of the new excitement about the importance of early environmental factors, another development occurred. In this case, it was a new interest in an old problem: children from the lowest socioeconomic levels start school with disadvantages that preclude adequate achievement. Why such a concern was unusually vocal and widespread at this particular period of time is to be found in factors that were political, social, and economic (49). Why the concern led to plans for prekindergarten schooling for "culturally disadvantaged" children—plans later formalized in Head Start programs—was clearly related to the psychological climate of the times.

Still later, in 1966, the Educational Policies Commission of the National Education Association published a statement supporting earlier schooling not just for the "culturally disadvantaged" but for all children (19). A portion of the introduction to the commission's statement serves well in characterizing this new era in both psychology and education:

> A growing body of research and experience demonstrates that by the age of six most children have already developed a considerable part of the intellectual ability they will possess as adults. Six is now generally accepted as the normal age of entrance to school. We believe that this practice is obsolete. All children should have the opportunity to go to school at public expense beginning at the age of four. [19, p. 1]

Changes in Timing of Reading Instruction

Given this collection of new emphases, it was only natural that the post-Sputnik years heard numerous complaints about the traditional interpretation of reading readiness. After all, an era that assigned critical importance to learning opportunities during the pre-first-grade period was not likely to be patient with practices that postponed reading instruction beyond the start of first grade on the assumption that the passing of time automatically ensures readiness for it later.

The typical response to the impatience was neither complicated nor imaginative. For the most part, schools simply altered the timing of traditional practices. Readiness tests were administered earlier, often in kindergarten where readiness workbooks could now be found. In first grade, reading instruction usually was started sooner, although readiness programs still went on in some first-grade classrooms, especially in school districts that had no kindergartens. In a few places, the difference in timing was more radical: reading was introduced in kindergarten. In other areas, opposition to this was as great and as vocal as it had been in decades gone by.

Results of the Changes

What was learned from the changes? Not much. The greatest difference, reading in the kindergarten, was not usually accompanied by changes in materials or methodology. Instead, it tended to be like what existed in a typical first grade (1, 4, 38, 48, 52). One consequence is that restrictions were placed on what could be learned both about earlier reading and about the basic nature of readiness. The end result is that the 1960s, with all the excitement about young children and earlier learning, contributed little to what could have been an enlightened discussion of the optimal time for beginning reading.

During the 1970s and continuing in the 1980s, the one apparent development is a growing number of kindergartens attempting to teach reading, not in ways that match children's abilities and interests but following a form that comes directly from phonics workbooks. Because such uniform instruction (commonly given to an entire class) hardly reflects what the readiness concept implies for teaching beginning reading, the following sections deal with both the concept and the implications.

PROPOSED DEFINITION OF READINESS

The concept of readiness offered here is not an original one. It was articulated by Gates in the 1930s and at least inferred by others since then. In 1959 it was stated effectively by David Ausubel in an article in *Teachers College Record* (3). Although the focus of the article was not reading, Ausubel's description of readiness for any learning is useful for the present discussion. Readiness, Ausubel proposed, is *"the adequacy of existing capacity in relation to the demands of a given learning task"* (3, p. 246). Let us examine the details of this definition to see what they suggest (a) for the best time to initiate school instruction in reading and (b) for how it ought to be taught.

Existing capacity.   Nothing that is known about humans indicates that heredity alone accounts for an individual's capacity to learn, nor does anyone insist that only environmental factors determine it. At various times, it is true, both nature and nurture are placed on special pedestals of honor; yet even amid the adulation, the one not being raised on high is never completely cast aside. The assumption of this discussion, therefore, is that each child's capabilities at any given time are the product of both nature and nurture. That is, they are the result of an interplay among genetic endowment, maturation, experiences, and learnings. Just how such an interplay takes place awaits a definitive explanation, but for now it seems correct to say that a child's attained capabilities at any given time are something he has inherited, grown into, and learned.

Demands of the learning task.   What learning to read requires *depends on the method that is used* to teach it *and,* second, *on how the method is executed.* More specifically, a methodology that requires children to memorize every word they are to read has requirements that are not identical to what is demanded by another that stresses letter-sound relationships to identify words. But even with the same methodology, demands may differ. Here, teachers enter the picture, making it necessary to consider not only methodological differences but also variation in what teachers do with a method. What they do and how well they do it always affect what success in learning to read requires. Even the pacing of what is done makes a difference.

Adequacy of capacity in relation to demands.   Probably the most important feature of Ausubel's definition is the explicit attention it gives to the *relational* aspect of readiness, which is commonly overlooked. The aspect points up that the question of a child's readiness for reading has a *two*fold focus: (a) his capacity *in relation to* (b) the instruction that will be available. Since different kinds of instruction make different demands of learners, what is adequate for dealing with them also differs. This means that we must learn to think in terms of readiness for reading rather than to assume that one certain combination of abilities (that can be measured in a readiness test) makes children ready for every conceivable kind of

Figure 3.1

Readiness is a relationship
between

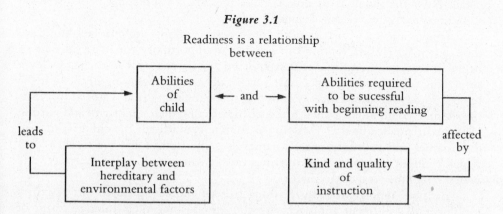

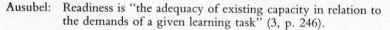

Ausubel: Readiness is "the adequacy of existing capacity in relation to the demands of a given learning task" (3, p. 246).

instruction. Equally important to remember is that certain deficiencies do not make children *un*ready for every type of teaching.

What has now been said about Ausubel's conception of readiness is summarized in Figure 3.1.

PRACTICAL IMPLICATIONS OF THE DEFINITION

With the attention it gives to the relational nature of readiness, Ausubel's definition suggests how questions about readiness ought to be worded. To ask—as is the common practice—Is this child ready? is to ask the wrong question, because it is an unfinished one. Instead, the concern must be, "Is the child ready for this particular kind and quality of instruction?" (More ideally, the educator's question would be, "Given this child's particular abilities, what type of instruction will make use of them and thus allow the child to experience success?")

A second implication of the Ausubel definition has to do with readiness assessment. If, as Ausubel suggests, readiness is the adequacy of existing capacity in relation to the demands of the learning task, it follows that the only meaningful way to test for adequacy is to give children opportunities to learn to read in order to see what their capacity actually is. The definition further indicates that the opportunities should vary in the methodology they represent, since it is possible that a child will be successful with one method but unsuccessful with another. By observing what a child does or does not learn from each, much can be gleaned not only about readiness but also about the kind of instruction that makes the best use of that child's interests and abilities.

You might now be wondering what this recommendation would lead to, say, in a kindergarten. Let me show you with illustrations featuring typical kindergarten activities. (Chapter 4 discusses reading in the kindergarten in greater detail. Now the intent is to give specific meaning to the concept of readiness subscribed to in the present chapter.)

Some time in every kindergarten goes to taking attendance. Mundane though it is, attendance taking can provide an opportunity for five year olds to begin to read and—and this is the point being stressed—for a teacher to learn something about existing capacities. Specifically, at the beginning of the year the teacher could take attendance by showing first names on cards. Later in the year, the children could indicate their presence by selecting their name card and putting it on an attendance board. This simple routine could teach the children to read their names and probably others' names as well. And, it helps a teacher learn which children remember (read) names easily, which have more difficulty, and which remember few if any names.

Because opportunities for learning to read should be varied, art activities can illustrate a different approach. Without diminishing their value as forms of free expression, finished products in art provide a reason for kindergartners to learn to print their names and, later, to write captions and to read those composed by others. Pertinent to the theme of this discussion is that such activities give an observant teacher a chance to identify children for whom writing and spelling might be an easy way into reading, to identify those who remember whole words with a minimum of exposure to them, and to become aware of children for whom the motor skill of writing is a formidable task or for whom it is difficult to compose even the briefest of captions.

Still another activity found in kindergartens is that of reading to the children. While this should always be for enjoyment, a story can be used occasionally to learn still more about the children's readiness for reading. Let us say, for example, that a couple of stories have been about Ping, a duck. Let us also say that two children in the class are named Paul and Penny. In such a case, a kindergarten teacher might decide to print *Ping* on the chalkboard, allowing for the question, "Does anybody [pointing to the *P*] have a name that starts the way *Ping* starts? If you do, I'll write your name with Ping's." Soon the board shows:

Ping
Paul
Penny

Other questions (their number and kind will depend upon the children's abilities and interest) follow: "Does anybody know the name of the letter [pointing to *P*] at the beginning of these three names? . . . Have you ever seen any other word that begins with this letter *P*? . . . Now we have five words that begin with *P*. I'll read them all. As I do, listen to see if you can hear how they all start with the same sound. . . . Can someone make the sound that these names start with? . . . I'll say the words again. Watch how I put my lips together when I start to say each of them. Listen to the way each word starts. . . . Can someone think of other words that start the way *Ping* and *Paul* and *Penny* and *Punch* and *Pat* begin? If you can, I'll write them, too."

On another day, another word and letter might be given attention; or the teacher might decide to repeat the attention given *P* using different words to illustrate the sound it commonly records. Whatever the decision, an opportunity exists for children to respond and for a teacher to identify who among them might know letter names and even have skill in auditory discrimination of speech sounds. At the same time, the teacher may also become aware of other kindergartners who appear to have no knowledge of letter names or, more likely, no understanding of what is meant by "begin with the same sound."

Perhaps these few illustrations of ordinary activities are enough to give specific meaning to what has been proposed as a way to assess children's readiness for reading: Give them varied opportunities to begin, and note what they are able to learn. Implied even in the few illustrations are other ideas that are important for teachers.

ASSESSMENT, READINESS INSTRUCTION,
AND READING INSTRUCTION

One way to deal with these ideas is through descriptions of two children in the kindergarten class just referred to who were present on the day the teacher wrote *Ping, Paul,* and *Penny* and asked questions about them. We will call the children Paul and Mary Anne.

PAUL.   Paul shows signs of being mentally slow. Even his physical move-ments are sluggish and awkward. When the teacher wrote *Ping* on the board and asked whether anyone had a name that began with the same letter, he remained silent. A concentrated look from the teacher plus a nudge from the child next to him (Mary Anne) eventually led to Paul's volunteering his name. It is doubtful that he would have mentioned it had there not been these hints from others. Once his name appeared on the board, he seemed interested in the discussion, although he remained silent during all of it. The question now is, What meaning did the discussion and questioning have for both Paul and the teacher?

For his teacher, the situation was assessment and allowed for further evi-dence of Paul's slowness. Even though the letter being highlighted was in his name and even though he had seen it written many times before, he did not seem to be aware that his name and Ping's begin the same way. It is also unlikely that Paul had any understanding—at least his behavior showed none—of the concept "sound alike" when applied to parts of words.

For Paul himself the situation was very special because everybody was talking about his name. He did not remember anyone telling him before—they had, actually—that the first letter in his name is *P.* And he did not know until the day of the *Ping* lesson that other words start with it too.

Now, what about Mary Anne? What did the very same discussion and questioning mean for her?

MARY ANNE.   Mary Anne is an alert child who doesn't believe in hiding her candle under a bushel basket. In the discussion of words be-ginning with *P,* she was quick to say that she knew its name because it was in her big sister's name (Pat). She said she could write her sister's name, and her mother's and daddy's names, too. As the discussion proceeded, she enjoyed making the sound of *P*—this seemed new for her—and quickly recalled words beginning with it. *Punch, princess,* and *Pat* were her contributions when the teacher inquired. "Can anyone think of some words that begin the way *Ping* begins?" (Mary Anne was eager to explain that *Punch* was the name of the detergent that her parents used to wash clothes.)

Obviously, what the discussion and the questioning meant for Mary Anne was totally different from what they had meant for Paul. With both, however, the teacher had an opportunity to assess their readiness. In the case of Mary Anne, much was learned—including the fact that she had already begun to read. She knew the name of *P*, enjoyed making the sound it represented in *Ping*, and was able to name words beginning with it. That she did some writing at home and was attentive to words in her environment also became clear.

While the teacher was seeking out behavioral signs of readiness, what was Mary Anne getting out of the discussion and questions? Primarily, they helped her recall and use what she already knew. Two new learnings were the understanding that words have a beginning sound and, second, that the sound that *p* represents is /p/.* With Mary Anne, then, the teacher's assessment efforts provided an opportunity for her to have reading instruction, specifically, instruction in phonics.

What the discussion and questioning turned out to be for both children is summarized below:

	Assessment	Readiness instruction	Reading instruction
Paul	X	X	
Mary Anne	X		X

One other point needs to be made about readiness. This can be done by describing still another child in the kindergarten just discussed.

JOEY. Joey is an enthusiastic participant in all activities. At the start of the year he generally went to the blocks at free-choice time, but quiet table games and puzzles soon became attractive. He also is an inevitable joiner whenever the teacher makes available other choices: "Today I'm going to be reading a story over in that part of the room" or "Today I'm going to be playing a game" (such as, bingo played with numerals, letters, or words). When words enter into a game, Joey is both involved and successful because of his wonderful ability to remember words with minimal help. He learned to read all the days of the week as a result of the quick, early morning discussions related to "What day is today?" In addition, with the attention given to *September, October,* and *November* in connection with the calendar displayed in the room, he can read those words, too.

With word games, Joey's teacher has heard him make interesting comments. When *Sunday* was used he observed, "Sandy's name looks like a short Sunday." On another day when the teacher wrote *silk* on the

* A detailed discussion of phonics, including the isolation of sounds, comprises Chapters 7 and 8.

board in connection with a discussion of fabrics and textures, Joey quickly observed, "That almost looks like salt." Asked, "Where did you see *salt?*" he explained, "It's on our salt shaker at home."

Interestingly, Joey's excellent visual memory is not matched by excellence in auditory discrimination. In fact, he rarely responds when the teacher makes requests like: "I'm going to say two words. Can you tell me whether they start with the same sound or a different sound: *ball, fence.* . . . I'm going to say some words. Tell me which of these words begins with the same sound: *mouse, table, mother.* . . . Can anyone think of another word that starts with the sound you hear at the beginning of *Ping* and *Paul* and *Penny?*"

What all these observations correctly indicate about Joey is that in some ways he is more than ready for reading—he has already begun. In other ways, however, he is still learning to be ready. What the same observations mean more generally is that efforts to assess readiness should not have an either-or focus. That is, a teacher's thoughts ought *not* to be, "Is he or is he not ready?" but, rather, "In what ways is he ready, and in what ways is he not?" This more correct concern has implications for the way we think about instruction. It reminds us— or should—that readiness instruction and reading instruction go on simultaneously. With Joey, for instance, reading ability is developing as a result of help with whole word identification. *At the same time,* the attention going to sounds is readiness instruction for him. Graphically, this point can be made as follows:

September ────────────────────────────────▶ June

readiness instruction

reading instruction

Notice how essentially different the conception above is from the traditional practice of separating the readiness program from the reading program:

September ────────────────────────────────▶ June

readiness instruction	reading instruction

Still another important point is to be found in the observations made about Joey. This one relates to readiness assessment—specifically to the idea that it is a daily occurrence, not a special event carried out once each year. All the reasons why this is so have been summed up perfectly by Walter MacGinitie: "When a child is taught a little, he is then ready for a little more" (40, p. 399).

The disarming simplicity of MacGinitie's statement should not overshadow another of its implications. It is the fact that beginners in reading are just that—*beginners*. As such, they do not have to master *immediately* all that constitutes "reading ability." Instead, they achieve that ability piece by piece over a long period of time. This means that if reading instruction begins with the identification of a few carefully chosen words, the only requirement is the ability to distinguish among the words and, second, to remember what each says. If it happened—but this is unlikely—that each word began with the same letter and sound and, as a result, a teacher later decided to introduce a little phonics, new requirements come into existence: the ability to see that each word begins with the same letter and, second, the ability to hear that each begins with the same sound. With such abilities, a child is ready to associate a certain letter with a certain sound.

Even these few comments should identify a major flaw in traditional questions and tests dealing with readiness: they are concerned with the whole of reading ability rather than with those beginning steps that, when joined with many subsequent steps, *eventually* culminate in reading.

READINESS AT LATER LEVELS

Admittedly, readiness is most often referred to when the timing of beginning reading is discussed; however, its significance for success at subsequent levels should not be forgotten by those who teach older children. After all, every step of the way to becoming a proficient reader has certain requirements, which is what the readiness concept is all about.

Whether viewed in the context of the Ausubel definition or in the category of requirements or prerequisites, readiness beyond the beginning may be one thing or a combination of things that could include—depending on what is to be learned—an attitude, an experience, a skill, or an understanding. Let me illustrate prerequisites with a variety of examples.

If students find it difficult to follow a sequence in written discourse, their teacher might decide to help by instructing about words that signal sequence (for example, *first, later, next*). Before that can be done, however, she needs to make sure that the children are ready. In this case, being ready means (a) having an understanding of what is meant by sequence, (b) being able to identify the selected signal words, and (c) knowing what they mean. Any of these prerequisites that is missing needs to be taught first.

To cite another example, if a story in a reader takes place in years gone by, preparing students to comprehend it might well include more than teaching new vocabulary. To be more specific, if a central character runs from house to house to warn neighbors of an approaching fire, the children need to know that at the time the story took place, telephones were nonexistent. Otherwise they will find it hard to understand why such an inefficient and possibly dangerous means was chosen for dealing with the emergency. Providing the necessary background information, therefore, constitutes readiness instruction.

If a selection that students will be reading includes underlined words to indicate special stress, explaining the function of the underscoring also exemplifies readiness instruction. Now, using orally read sentences like the following in order (a) to show underscoring, (b) to explain how it may signal special stress, and (c) to demonstrate the effect of stress on meaning may be all that is required:

I won't go with you.

I won't go with you.

I won't go with you.

The need for teachers of older students to take readiness into account almost invariably shows up when something like a chapter in a social studies textbook is about to be read. In this case, readying students to comprehend the content may require attention to how the author organized the content, what the author does to explain technical terms, how the end-of-the-chapter questions can be used to guide the reading, and how certain graphic aids (such as maps and graphs) are to be interpreted.

Teachers who want to learn whether certain students can distinguish among five short vowel sounds must also consider readiness requirements, one of which is an understanding of "short vowel sounds." A second-grade teacher who overlooked prerequisites was recently observed working with seven children who had been given a list of short, one-syllable words that they could read. The teacher began by asking, "What's the first word in the list that has a short vowel sound?" Silence resulted. The teacher continued, "The first word says 'slow.' Do you hear any short vowel sound in 'slow'?" Now some said "yes" while others were saying "no." Clearly there was confusion, in this case originating from the children's inability to remember the meaning of "short vowel sounds." Eventually, the teacher did what should have been done in the first place: reviewed the meaning, as well as the individual sounds themselves.

It is possible that teachers sometimes bypass attention to prerequisites in order to save time. Yet what the second-grade teacher just referred to demonstrated is that attending to review is a way to save, not waste, time. It also is a way to maximize success for students.

The implication of all this is clear. Whenever teachers plan a lesson to achieve a selected goal, they should think through its prerequisites. Asking a question like, What do these children need to know, or understand, or be able to do in order to reach the goal? is one way to do this. It also is a way of recognizing that readiness should be a concern of all teachers, whether they work with beginners or advanced readers.

SUMMARY

The timing of beginning reading instruction was the central theme of the chapter. It merits detailed attention because a child's initial experience with learning to read is of unique importance, since success at the beginning fosters more success later.

In considering the best time to start reading, educators and psychologists who dominated the scene from the 1920s to the 1950s correctly gave attention to readiness when they asked, "When are children ready to be successful with reading?" Many answered, "When they have a mental age of about 6.5 years." Others turned to special testing as a way of finding an answer, and so was born the reading readiness test. Routinely, the concern of those administering it was not about the possibility that some beginning first graders might be ready for reading but, rather, about the question of how long each should spend in a readiness program, conceived of as being separate and distinct from the reading program.

The chapter identified flaws in the early interpretations and use of the readiness concept. One was an exaggeration—specifically, an exaggerated appreciation of the contributions that heredity and maturation make. In contrast, the position taken in the chapter is that whatever constitutes readiness for reading is the product not only of genetic endowment and maturation but also of prior experiences and learnings. Within this framework, much about readiness is teachable.

Another point emphasized in the chapter is the need to look at instruction as well as the students' abilities when readiness is considered. With the twofold focus, the question that the earlier psychologists and educators asked—Is the child ready?—can be seen as being incomplete and thus incorrect. It assumed that success with different kinds of reading instruction demands the same abilities and that readiness, therefore, has a single meaning and can be assessed in a test. Or maybe the assumption was that there is one way to teach reading and so the question to ask is: "When are children ready to be successful with it?"

Whatever the explanation, Chapter 3 tried to show that the correct and complete question is more specific, for it asks, "Is the child ready to succeed with this particular kind and quality of instruction?" Such a question recognizes the *equal* significance of the child's abilities and of the instruction that will be available. Or, to put it differently, it reflects the relational aspect of readiness—an aspect effectively underscored in Ausubel's conception of readiness as being "the adequacy of existing capacity in relation to the demands of a given learning task" (3, p. 246). This concept has implications for how readiness can be assessed: Give children varied opportunities to learn to read, and what they do or do not learn tells something not only about their readiness but also about the way of teaching reading that takes advantage of their particular abilities and interests.

Such assessment, the chapter showed, has the advantage of being two other things as well. It will be readiness instruction for some children and reading instruction for others. Since this way of assessing readiness uses different methodologies, teachers will usually learn that most children are neither totally ready nor totally unready for reading. Such awareness ought to encourage schools to give up the idea that "getting ready to read" and "beginning to read" occur at separate points on some time line, as well as the related practice of having a readiness program followed by a reading program. Instead, *readiness instruction* will be viewed as *reading instruction in its earliest stages*. The early stages will be illustrated in the next chapter, which deals with reading in the kindergarten.

The chapter ended by stressing that the readiness concept has as much significance for middle- and upper-grade teachers as it does for those at the kindergarten and first-grade levels. With examples, it underscored the need for all teachers to think through prerequisites whenever they make plans to attain a preselected goal. The same examples also served to show that progress in learning to read is a matter of moving from what is known to what is new but related.

REVIEW

1. Using the time line shown below, explain how the interpretation of readiness for beginning reading changed between the 1920s and the 1960s.

G. Stanley Hall	Arnold Gesell	Testing movement	C. Washburne A. Gates			Sputnik	J. Bruner J. M. Hunt B. Bloom
1900	1910	1920	1930	1940	1950	1960	1970

2. Because of the changes referred to in the first question, some now seem to think that the readiness concept no longer has any meaning for those who make decisions about the timing of beginning instruction.

    (a) How would you correct this erroneous conclusion?
    (b) With an example, explain why readiness must also be considered by teachers of older children.

3. In your own words, describe Ausubel's conception of readiness. Does his interpretation put the blame on the teacher if beginners in reading do not succeed?

4. Let us assume that you accept the interpretation of readiness that Ausubel proposed. Within that framework, how would you respond to a teacher who, in October, made the following request: "I teach first grade in a school where we're required to use the _____ basal readers.* All the children are doing well with the exception of two boys who seem to be

* The series referred to starts by teaching phonics. The pace of instruction is fairly quick.

learning little or nothing. Evidently, they're not ready for reading. What readiness materials would you recommend?"

5. Explain (a) why unready children will be unsuccessful with beginning reading and (b) why unsuccessful children are not necessarily individuals who were unready when instruction got under way.

6. Let us assume you are a fifth-grade teacher and it is time for parent conferences. During one conference, a mother of four children expresses curiosity about the fact that her oldest child, who is the brightest of the children, was not taught to read until some time after she started first grade, yet her youngest, now in kindergarten, is already learning. She wonders about the difference. How would you answer?

7. When the readiness concept was considered in past decades, the notion of a "teachable moment" was often introduced into the discussions. Do *you* think there is a particular moment when it is best for a child to begin to get help with reading?

8. Apparently, some professional educators still hold to the idea of there being a teachable moment. For example, a recent letter from a curriculum director contained the following sentence: "My concern involves the most effective way to determine when children are ready to read." A subsequent sentence asks, "Would you send information about the best way to determine readiness for reading?" How would you respond to the writer of this letter?

REFERENCES

1. Appleton, Edith. "Beginning with Enthusiasm." *Education* 86 (February 1966): 347–349.

2. Arthur, Grace. "A Quantitative Study of the Results of Grouping First Grade Children According to Mental Age." *Journal of Educational Research* 12 (October 1925): 173–185.

3. Ausubel, David P. "Viewpoints from Related Disciplines: Human Growth and Development." *Teachers College Record* 60 (February 1959): 245–254.

4. Bacci, W. "Children Can Read in Kindergarten." *School Management* 5 (May 1961): 120–122.

5. Benton, William. *This Is the Challenge*. New York: Associated College Presses, 1958.

6. Berry, Frances M. "The Baltimore Reading Readiness Test." *Childhood Education* 3 (January 1927): 222–223.

7. Bestor, Arthur E. *Educational Wastelands: The Retreat from Learning in Our Public Schools*. Urbana: University of Illinois Press, 1953.

8. Betts, Emmett A. *The Prevention and Correction of Reading Difficulties*. Evanston, Ill.: Row Peterson, 1936.

9. Bloom, Benjamin S. *Stability and Change in Human Characteristics*. New York: Wiley, 1964.

10. Bruner, Jerome. *The Process of Education.* Cambridge: Harvard University Press, 1960.

11. Cole, Luella. *The Improvement of Reading: With Special Reference to Remedial Instruction.* New York: Farrar and Rinehart, 1938.

12. "Crisis in Education." *Life,* 49 (March 24, 1958): 26–35.

13. Dickson, Virgil E. *Mental Tests and the Classroom Teacher.* New York: World Book Co., 1923.

14. Dickson, Virgil E. "What First Grade Children Can Do in School as Related to What Is Shown by Mental Tests." *Journal of Educational Research* 2 (June 1920): 475–480.

15. Dolch, Edward W. *Teaching Primary Reading.* Champaign, Ill.: Garrard Press, 1950.

16. Durkin, Dolores. *Getting Reading Started.* Boston: Allyn and Bacon, 1982.

17. Durkin, Dolores. "When Should Children Begin to Read?" *Innovation and Change in Reading Instruction,* chap. 2. Sixty-seventh Yearbook of the National Society for the Study of Education, Part II. Chicago: University of Chicago Press, 1968.

18. Dykstra, Robert. "The Use of Reading Readiness Tests for Prediction and Diagnosis: A Critique." In *The Evaluation of Children's Reading Achievement.* Edited by T. C. Barrett. Newark, Dela.: International Reading Association, 1967.

19. Educational Policies Commission. *Universal Opportunity for Early Childhood Education.* Washington, D.C.: National Education Association, 1966.

20. Gates, Arthur I. "The Necessary Mental Age for Beginning Reading." *Elementary School Journal* 37 (March 1937): 497–508.

21. Gates, Arthur I., and Bond, Guy L. "Reading Readiness: A Study of Factors Determining Success and Failure in Beginning Reading." *Teachers College Record* 37 (May 1936): 679–685.

22. Gates, A. I.; Bond, G. L.; and Russell, D. H. *Methods of Determining Reading Readiness.* New York: Bureau of Publications, Teachers College, Columbia University, 1939.

23. Gesell, Arnold L. *The First Five Years of Life.* New York: Harper and Bros., 1940.

24. Gesell, Arnold L. *Infancy and Human Growth.* New York: Macmillan, 1928.

25. Gesell, Arnold L. *The Mental Growth of the Preschool Child.* New York: Macmillan, 1925.

26. Gesell, A., and Ilg, F. *The Child From Five to Ten.* New York: Harper and Bros., 1946.

27. Gray, William S. "Reading." *Child Development and the Curriculum,* Chap. 9. Thirty-eighth Yearbook of the National Society for the Study of Education, Part I. Bloomington, Ill.: Public School Publishing Co., 1939.

28. Hall, G. Stanley. *The Psychology of Adolescence.* New York: D. Appleton, 1904.

29. Harris, Albert J. *Effective Teaching of Reading.* New York: David McKay, 1962.

30. Harrison, M. Lucille. *Reading Readiness.* Boston: Houghton Mifflin, 1936.

31. Havighurst, Robert. *Human Development and Education.* New York: Longmans, Green, 1953.

32. Hester, K. B. *Teaching Every Child to Read.* New York: Harper, 1955.

33. Holdaway, D. *The Foundation of Literacy.* Sydney, Australia: Ashton Scholastic, 1979.

34. Holmes, Margaret C. "Investigation of Reading Readiness of First Grade Entrants." *Childhood Education* 3 (January 1927): 215–221.

35. Huey, Edmund B. *The Psychology and Pedagogy of Reading.* New York: Macmillan, 1908.

36. Hunt, J. McVicker. *Intelligence and Experience*. New York: Ronald Press, 1961.

37. Jenkins, Frances. "Editorial." *Childhood Education* 3 (January 1927): 209.

38. Kelley, Marjorie L., and Chen, M. K. "An Experimental Study of Formal Reading Instruction at the Kindergarten Level." *Journal of Educational Research* 60 (January 1967): 224–229.

39. Lamoreaux, Lillian A., and Lee, Dorris M. *Learning to Read Through Experience*. New York: Appleton-Century-Crofts, 1943.

40. MacGinitie, Walter H. "Evaluating Readiness for Learning to Read: A Critical Review and Evaluation of Research." *Reading Research Quarterly* 4 (Spring 1969): 396–410.

41. Monroe, Marion. *Children Who Cannot Read*. Chicago: University of Chicago Press, 1932.

42. Morphett, M. V., and Washburne, C. "When Should Children Begin to Read?" *Elementary School Journal* 31 (March 1931): 496–503.

43. Newton, J. Roy. *Reading in Your School*. New York: McGraw-Hill, 1960.

44. Olson, Willard. *Child Development*. Boston: D. C. Heath, 1949.

45. Partridge, G. E. *Genetic Philosophy of Education*. New York: Sturgis and Walton, 1912.

46. Reed, Mary M. *An Investigation of Practices in First Grade Admission and Promotion*. New York: Bureau of Publications, Teachers College, Columbia University, 1927.

47. Resnick, Lauren B. "Social Assumptions as a Context for Science: Some Reflections on Psychology and Education." *Educational Psychologist* 16 (Spring 1981): 1–10.

48. Shapiro, B. J., and Willfred, R. E. "i.t.a.—Kindergarten or First Grade?" *Reading Teacher* 22 (January 1969): 307–311.

49. Shaw, Frederick. "The Changing Curriculum." *Review of Educational Research* 36 (June 1966): 343–352.

50. Smith, Henry P., and Dechant, Emerald V. *Psychology in Teaching Reading*. Englewood Cliffs, N.J.: Prentice-Hall, 1961.

51. Smith, Nila B. "Matching Ability as a Factor in First Grade Reading." *Journal of Educational Psychology* 19 (November 1928): 560–571.

52. Sutton, Marjorie H. "Readiness for Reading at the Kindergarten Level." *Reading Teacher* 17 (January 1964): 234–240.

53. Thorndike, Robert L., and Hagen, Elizabeth. *Measurement and Evaluation in Psychology and Education*. New York: Wiley, 1969.

54. Washburne, Carleton. "Ripeness." *Progressive Education* (February 1936): 125–130.

55. Washburne, Carleton. "The Work of the Committee of Seven on Grade-Placement in Arithmetic." *Child Development and the Curriculum*, Chap. 16. Thirty-eighth Yearbook of the National Society for the Study of Education, Part I. Bloomington, Ill.: Public School Publishing Co., 1939.

56. Wayson, W. W. "A New Kind of Principal." *National Elementary Principal* 50 (February 1971): 8–19.

57. Zornow, T. A., and Pachstein, L. A. "An Experiment in the Classification of First-Grade Children Through Use of Mental Tests." *Elementary School Journal* 23 (October 1922): 136–146.

CHAPTER 4

READING IN THE KINDERGARTEN

PREVIEW

Although most schools continue to administer reading readiness tests, the position taken here is that the tests' flaws are sufficiently major as to warrant discontinuing their use as instruments for deciding whether a child is ready to read. Flaws having to do with assumptions of readiness tests are reviewed below.

Questionable Assumptions

That one certain collection of abilities (which are measured in the tests) constitutes readiness for every kind of reading instruction.

That a deficiency in one or more of these abilities makes a child unready for every kind of reading instruction.

That all of the abilities that are measured are necessary at the start and that if any are lacking, the child should be placed in a readiness program thought to be separate and different from a reading program.

Some of the contrasting assumptions underlying recommendations made in Chapter 4 can be summarized as follows:

Whether children will be successful with reading depends on the match that exists between their abilities and what the instruction requires for success.

Most children entering kindergarten are neither totally ready nor totally unready to begin reading.

It is the school's responsibility to offer types of reading instruction that use what children can do; meanwhile, attention can go to whatever ability is lacking.

Kindergartens that offer only one kind of instruction (for example, phonics) are unfair to those children who would be more successful with a different approach.

How a kindergarten program can provide for both readiness and reading instruction is described in Chapter 4.★ The essential theme is that five year olds can be eased into reading in ways that are enjoyable and that add to their self-esteem and self-confidence.

★ References 13 and 15 at the end of the chapter provide much more detailed descriptions.

For many children, the first step into school is through a kindergarten doorway. Like most other first steps, this one is often accompanied by fears and insecurities. New expectations, new routines, new adults, and many new children combine to create a world away from home that can be threatening. With that possibility in mind, there can be nothing but agreement about the need for kindergarten teachers to give special attention to making the initial weeks of school psychologically comfortable for every child. All this is to say that whether kindergartners are or are not ready to read should hardly be a teacher's initial concern.

STARTING THE YEAR

As soon as comfort, routines, and expectations are at least somewhat established, kindergarten teachers will naturally want to learn what the children know and are ready to do for, like all other teachers, their objective should be individualized instruction. Since the ability to name colors, numbers, and letters allows children to carry on a variety of independent assignments, it helps to know fairly soon what each has already learned about all three. Identifying what is known can be accomplished easily and quickly in individual testing with the help of an aide or older, elementary school students. The diagnostic information that results will indicate some of what needs to be taught and to whom. It also tells a teacher the kinds of assignments that can be made and to which children.

A SAMPLE SCHEDULE

In addition to learning which colors, numbers, and letters are known, a kindergarten teacher also has to make decisions about a schedule. To illustrate one (and to provide a setting for the instruction that will be described later), a schedule that one kindergarten teacher followed is shown below. She had twenty-three children and an aide.

8:30–8:45	Conversation groups
8:45–9:00	Attendance taking; attention to date, weather, and current interests
9:00–9:20	Academic period for one group, free choice for other group
9:20–9:40	Groups reversed for above activities
9:40–10:00	Music
10:00–10:30	Playtime, bathroom, milk

10:30–11:00	Art
11:00–11:15	Storytime
11:15–11:20	Preparation for home

At conversation time, the children spontaneously divided into two groups of approximately equal size, although on some days the boys made up a group while the girls composed a second one. The teacher sat at a table with one group, while the aide conversed informally with the other.

The next period of approximately fifteen minutes began with attendance taking and ended with current interests. All of the children were together for this, sitting on the floor in front of the teacher. Meanwhile, the aide prepared materials for use later in the morning.

At about nine o'clock, the academic goals of the program received explicit attention; consequently, this was a time for working with less than an entire class. (As will be shown later, more casual attention went to academic goals at other times.) At the start of the year, the academic period on Monday provided help with color identification; soon afterward, teaching color words was the goal for some children. Still later, Monday was the day when either extra help (with anything) or extra challenge was provided. On Tuesday, letter names and printing received special consideration, although attention went to both at other times too. For the more advanced children, Tuesday soon became the day for teaching simple phonics.

On Wednesday, ready children were given carefully planned opportunities to learn to read words, generally selected in relation to current interests and activities. As words were learned, sentences were constructed, and homemade books began to accumulate. Thursday was a time for the teacher to get her bearings and to do whatever needed to be done. The usual activity was work with small numbers of children who needed extra help or challenge. On Friday, the academic period singled out numeral identification with the help of materials like birthday cards, calendars, measuring tapes, license plates, television dials, clocks, store catalogs, and telephones. As the year passed, simple mathematical concepts were introduced to some children. Although not officially in the schedule, the teacher's special interest in word meanings pervaded almost everything that was done. In addition, she commonly used an academic period to do something special with meanings.

While the teacher worked on the above activities with various groups— members were selected on the basis of ability—the aide was with the others. Her responsibility was to supervise activities selected by the children from prescribed possibilities that included, at the beginning of the year, blocks, trucks, dolls, dishes, telephones, and so on. Possibilities were gradually altered to include activities such as writing on small chalkboards or slates, working puzzles, and playing with sequence cards, concept cards, or bingo cards that, at different times, displayed colors, numerals, letters, and words. Eventually three learning centers were established (listening, reading, writing), and the aide divided her time among them. Now children could be found involved with activities such as listening to stories on earphones, making signs for block constructions, dictating descriptions of their pictures to the aide, and playing with a variety of number and word games.

At approximately 9:20, the children who were with the teacher changed to free-choice activities; those who had been with the aide worked with the teacher.

Music followed the academic periods and was a time for fun and relaxation. In ways that would not take away from either, songs were used occasionally to help with academic goals. Next came playtime. For that, the children went outdoors whenever weather permitted. Bathroom and refreshment needs were taken care of afterwards.

During art, which lasted approximately thirty minutes, both the teacher and the aide worked with the children. Usually the teacher gave directions, and then both she and her assistant distributed materials and, later, helped or talked with individuals. During art, the atmosphere was relaxed but never rowdy. Conversations among the children and between teacher and child were taken for granted. At times, art projects were also used to attain academic goals. Next came a story, and then it was time to prepare for home.

While the assistance of the aide contributed substantially to the program just described, it could still function successfully without the extra help. Certain things would have to be done differently, however. For instance, at the start of the year, the children would have to be given time to learn to work independently. For a while, therefore, the teacher would supervise while the entire class was engaged in free-choice activities. Once the children seemed to know what was expected, the academic periods could begin. Whenever new free-choice possibilities were made available, more temporary supervision would be required, this time to make certain that everyone knew how the new choices were to be used. Essentially, then, the program would be the same whether or not the teacher had an aide; but with an unassisted teacher, it would progress more slowly and probably less smoothly.

READING GOALS AT THE VERY BEGINNING

You will recall from the previous chapter that readiness instruction is viewed as being *reading instruction in its earliest stages*. Since it is, let me list and then discuss instructional goals for the very start of reading. (The goals are stated from a teacher's perspective.) Even though some kindergartners will be beyond such goals, teachers need to be aware of what they are so that they will know where to start with beginners. What is listed is relevant for any kind of reading methodology.

Goals at the Beginning

1. Motivate the children to want to learn to read.
2. Help them acquire some understanding of what reading and learning to read are all about.

3. Teach about the left-to-right, top-to-bottom orientation of our written language.
4. Teach the meaning of *word* and the function of space in establishing word boundaries.
5. Teach the meaning of terms that figure in reading instruction.
6. Teach the children to discriminate visually among letters and words.
7. Teach the names of letters.

Some might view the above as reading; others might call them prereading goals. Actually the label does not matter. What does is that teachers do not overlook those attitudes, learnings, and understandings that promote a child's success with beginning reading no matter what methodology is used to teach it.

SOME COMMENTS ABOUT THE BEGINNING GOALS

Before discussing how to achieve some of the initial goals, let me comment more generally about the entire list. To begin, the list is not meant to suggest a mandatory sequence for instruction, nor should it be interpreted to signify that one goal must be realized before plans are made to work on another. Correctly interpreted, therefore, the list points to what gets attention concurrently, not sequentially. This means that on any given day, a teacher may be working on several of the listed goals.

What was *not* listed also merits a comment. Among the omissions is, "Give children opportunities to learn to read words." That was omitted because it is taken for granted that kindergarten teachers are always looking for opportunities to teach words that are of special interest; meanwhile, for the less advanced children, one or more of the listed goals receive attention.

Other goals were omitted because they do not contribute to success with reading (1, 2, 5, 21, 24, 25, 27). I refer to visual discrimination that concentrates on pictures and geometrical shapes and to other activities that are supposed to prepare children for phonics—distinguishing among musical and environmental sounds, for instance. And speaking of phonics, some may have wondered why teaching letter-sound relationships was not in the list, especially those who are aware of the countless number of phonics workbooks now found in kindergarten. It was omitted because teaching phonics at the very start presents children with some facts about language that are foreign and difficult for them to understand—for instance, that a word is composed of more than one sound, that a word has such characteristics as a beginning sound, that words are recorded with letters that represent sounds. None of this is to say that pre-first-grade programs ought to omit phonics instruction. It *is* to say, however, that teaching phonics is neither the easiest nor the most interesting way to introduce children to reading.

To summarize, if the list of beginning goals steers teachers toward important concerns and away from the irrelevant and the difficult, it will have accomplished its purpose.

ACHIEVING BEGINNING GOALS

Almost all of the listed goals can be reached in the most meaningful and personal way with language experience materials. How they enter into early instruction is dealt with in Chapter 14, one of the two chapters that concentrate on instructional materials. Now, therefore, just a few of the beginning goals will be considered.

Meanings of Instructional Terms

Failure to keep in mind the limitations of children's experiences and vocabularies may result in the use of terms in instruction that have little or no meaning for them. (This may also be true of older students.) That this is so will be pinpointed with some illustrations.

In one kindergarten, the teacher wrote *you* and *me* on the board and then asked, "How many words did I just write?" With much enthusiasm the group responded, "Five!" (I was impressed with both the quick counting and the confusion about the meaning of *word* and *letter*.)

At another time, I had been invited to observe in a classroom occupied by four- and five-year-olds who were being prepared for reading. It was early in the year, and the teacher was working on visual discrimination. On the day of the visit, she had placed word cards in the slots of a chart and was asking individuals in a small group to find any two words that were the same. (Earlier work had concentrated on smaller combinations of letters, beginning with comparisons of just two.) All went well until the teacher pointed to a card displaying *Monday* and asked if anyone could find the same word on the chalkboard. (At the start of the morning, *Monday* and *October* had been written and discussed.) Now, in contrast with the earlier work, nobody could. Upon reflection, the children's failure to respond was no longer unexpected, although at the time it was because of the earlier success. *Monday* had been printed on the board in large, white letters, whereas much smaller letters in black appeared on the card. Clearly, what these children needed to learn was the meaning of *same* and *different* applied to words. Eventually, they needed to learn that to all of the following, the same response must be given: Monday, MONDAY, *Monday* , and   Monday

Instructional terms also caused problems in a first grade. In this instance, a student teacher had been asked to work with a boy who, unlike his classmates, could not remember the names of letters. Following a procedure she had seen the teacher use, the student teacher had arranged a series of carefully printed letters and was asking the boy such questions as, "This letter is *t*. What letter comes before *t*? This letter is *c*. What's the name of the letter that's after *c*?" One would conclude that the child really did need special help, for the number of incorrect answers equaled the number of questions about the array of letters. As it happened, however, the student teacher finally asked a different kind of question: "Do you know what I mean when I say *before* and *after*?" The boy did not, so the teacher wisely changed to a different procedure that involved pointing to a letter and asking, "What's the name of this letter?" Now, although not all answers were correct, many were.

In another first grade, some of the children were busy with a workbook page, the directions for which had been, "Draw a line over all the pictures that . . ." In response, some were drawing lines above certain pictures, and others were drawing lines through them.

Misunderstandings similar to those identified during visits to classrooms have also received attention in articles and research reports (4, 11, 22, 32). In one, entitled "Component Skills in Beginning Reading," Robert Calfee and Richard Venezky (4) describe an experience that is as pertinent for teachers as it is for researchers:

> Although many children use the words *same* and *different* . . . , their interpretation of these terms . . . may be different from the experimenter's. The writers ran headlong into this problem early in their testing program when one of the children replied "different" when shown two cards containing identical geometrical forms. When asked to justify his answer, the child pointed out that one of the cards had a smudge on it. With older or more test-sophisticated children, it is easier to communicate the dimensions with regard to which identity is to be judged. With younger children . . . the relevant dimension may be extremely difficult for the child to interpret. [p. 107]

Just how complex the language of instruction can be is further underscored in some observations made by Thomas Sticht.

> It seems likely that many children who are being taught to read may not know what they are to look for and focus upon, and may therefore have difficulty in learning to read. . . . For instance, suppose the teacher says, "Look at the word 'cat' on the blackboard." The child must aud the message, comprehend what a word is, understand that the utterance "cat" is a word in the spoken language, direct the gaze to the blackboard, visually examine the printed configuration and somehow understand that all three letters—not just "c" and "t" and "c" and "a"—are important elements of the graphic display of the spoken word "cat."
>
> The foregoing is quite different from the child's ordinary looking which is subservient to the child's self-imposed cognitive task. The teacher-imposed task may completely bewilder the child, making looking an almost pointless activity. This may be especially important if the teacher at one time expects the child to focus on whole words and at other times on elements of words. . . . A type of looking confusion could result, in that the child would not precisely know where to direct his focal attention. [32, p. 62]

Although of immediate importance, the meaning of instructional terms is not something that is best taught in a given lesson on a given day. Instead, they come to be understood most precisely in a gradual way that is enhanced with many, many examples. While understandings are growing, teachers of beginners (and of older students as well) need to bear in mind that when wrong answers occur, they may be rooted in confusion about the meaning of instructional language.

Visual Discrimination Ability

Although reading is essentially a cognitive skill, it also is visual. Visual discrimination ability, therefore, is one prerequisite for success since readers do have to be able to see when letters and words are the same or are different.

Children who arrive in kindergarten able to name letters have no need for visual discrimination exercises that focus on comparisons of individual letters; after all, the ability to name them is unquestionable evidence of the ability to see which are identical and which are different. The same children, however, *may* need to work with series of letters. ("Are these two letters like those two, or are they different?") If series do figure in work with visual discrimination, some should spell words so that they can be named. For instance:

bu	ite	room	wall	effi
bu	ice	raam	mell	eff

When children know whether pairs of letters have or do not have identical sequences, any (for example, *ice*) that spell a word should be identified as such. ("These three letters spell the word *ice*.") This is recommended not on the assumption that one telling is always sufficient for remembering a word but with the hope that *some* children might remember some words with a single identification. (This illustrates the meaning of "Give children varied opportunities to begin reading.") Identifying a string of letters as being a word that is known in its spoken form will also help children understand the difference between a letter and a word.

With individuals who come to kindergarten unable to name letters, questions about single-letter comparisons like those shown here will soon develop letter discrimination ability:

n	o	e	y	v
n	e	e	y	m
		e	u	n
				v

Listing letters in columns rather than rows facilitates making comparisons, which are prompted by questions like "Does this letter look just like that letter?" (pointing to the one at the top), and "Are these two letters the same or are they different?"

Children who have difficulty responding to such questions should work with comparisons of two letters that are either maximally different or are the same. In time, they will come to understand that it is shape, not color or size, that is the key element in making comparisons. Gradually, when letter pairs are compared (*oc* with *co, ti* with *it*), they will learn that sequence must be considered too. Meanwhile, the meaning of *same* and *different* applied to letters and words is being clarified.

One important point to keep in mind is that visual discrimination (like auditory discrimination) is not a global ability but, instead, is composed of specific abilities. For those preparing children for reading, the specificity means that the only way to help them learn to discriminate among letters and words is by using letters and words—*not* pictures, shapes, numerals, or anything else. Admittedly, commercially prepared materials continue to claim to help children by having them complete workbook pages filled with nonverbal stimuli; however, over several decades research consistently shows that such exercises contribute little or nothing to what is required for success with reading (1). As Marie Clay puts it so well, they are "a devious route to reading" (8, p. 1).

Letter-Naming Ability

Although many children arrive in kindergarten knowing the names of letters, a question that continues to be posed is, "Should letter names be taught before reading instruction begins?" In some cases, the wondering is prompted by studies reporting a fairly high correlation between letter-name knowledge at the start of first grade and reading achievement at a later date (5, 16, 30, 31). Implied in some interpretations of the reports is the notion that the two are causally related, this in spite of the fact that correlation data say nothing about what is causing what. An interpretation more likely to be valid is one that Samuels offers:

> Speed of learning to name letters of the alphabet is a paired-associate task and may be taken as an index of intelligence. Since we already know that in the elementary school I.Q. is highly correlated with reading achievement, it is not surprising that letter-name knowledge is also correlated with reading achievement.
>
> Another explanation of the correlation between letter-name knowledge and reading achievement is that the kind of home background which enables a child to enter first grade knowing many of the letters of the alphabet would be the kind of home in which academic achievement is stressed. Again, it is well known that socioeconomic status and home environment are highly correlated with school achievement. [30, p. 72]

Even though knowing the names of letters is not likely to play a causative role in successful reading, knowing some is sufficiently helpful that time should be given to letter naming, sometimes in connection with visual discrimination practice. ("Yes, these two letters are the same. The name of both is *t*.") The result will be kindergarten children who know at least the names of the most frequently used letters by the time increased attention goes to reading instruction. This makes it easier for a teacher to call attention to the distinctive features of words ("This word is *doll*. It does look like *dog*, but it ends with *ll*, not *g*."). Letter naming also enters into phonics instruction ("All of these words begin with the same letter, with *b*. If you listen as I read them, you'll hear that they also begin with the same sound".) And it goes without saying that knowing letter names is required for spelling.

MORE ADVANCED READING INSTRUCTION

The goals listed earlier in the chapter pointed out what merits attention in kindergartens in which readying children for reading is thought to be one major responsibility. Whether the instructional program does or does not go beyond readiness, providing what the previous chapter called varied opportunities for children to begin to read should never be omitted. The more ready the children are, of course, the more time should go to such opportunities.

In the following sections, illustrations of opportunities are offered. Initially, they are divided according to three methods for teaching beginning reading; subsequently, illustrations relate to traditional kindergarten subjects like music and art.

Whole Word Emphasis*

For some children, remembering what written words say is easy, especially when the words are meaningful and, most of all, personal. An obvious example of an easy word is the child's own name, which explains why the initial words in a kindergarten reading vocabulary might be *Art, Nora, Donald,* and so on. Personal words can be taught—that is, displayed, identified, discussed, and reidentified— in connection with routines like attendance taking. It also is natural for a teacher to write and thus display children's names on drawings, crayon boxes, and lockers or storage shelves. The probable results of such exposure, especially when it is frequent in an activity like attendance taking, is that every kindergarten child will read his own name, and some will read almost everybody's name. And so, reading begins.

Other kinds of words also enter quite naturally into the kindergarten curriculum. For example, when a color is identified and discussed, the teacher can write its name on a chalkboard or large sheet of paper so that the children can see what it looks like. Eventually, many color words might be summarized on a chart showing differently colored pieces of paper with labels identifying each one. By then, all the colors will be familiar, and some children will be able to read their names as well.

Later, perhaps in connection with painting, mixing colors to make another one might be demonstrated. A meaningful summary for such an experience—and more reading practice as well—could be one or more bulletin-board displays. For example:

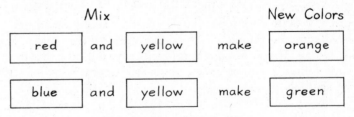

* Chapter 5 discusses in considerable detail how to build reading vocabularies with whole word identifications. The intent now is simply to show how kindergartners can be taught to read some words in easygoing, natural ways in which mastery by all is *not* the goal.

Another display of written language might result from a conversation about the children's birthdays, always a popular topic. In this case, after the children have had many opportunities to see the names of their classmates and the names of the months, a teacher might deliberately plan for a discussion of birthdays. A visual supplement to the discussion could be a cutout train with a car for every month. Printed on each car are the names of the children for whom that is a birthday month. By the time such a train is displayed, some might be able to read all the words shown; others will know considerably fewer, but they might also

learn more before the train is taken down. (Notice how the engine is placed to the left in order to foster a left-to-right direction when attending to words.)

Another natural way to bring written words into the kindergarten is with labels and signs. School buildings offer the chance to look at *Office, Girls, Boys,* and *Grade.* Outside, traffic signs provide other possibilities for a reading vocabulary, as do labels on packages, cans, and bottles if a visit to a grocery store is included in kindergarten plans or if food products are brought into the classroom. With such variety, of course, too much too soon can create problems, or at least inhibit permanent retention. That is why a teacher needs to make selections for special emphasis.

To illustrate, after the children have taken a walk outdoors, she might highlight a small traffic-sign vocabulary by displaying labeled signs or enlarged photographs showing actual signs. At another time, she might choose to dwell on food names in connection with playing house or going to an imaginary grocery store. From such an emphasis, a scrapbook collection of labeled pictures might develop so that words like *milk, egg, bread,* and *meat* can be looked at as often as a child or group is interested.

Snack time is another occasion for using written words. In the beginning, place cards can both display names and simplify the matter of who sits where. Later, simple menu cards might be left at each child's place until the majority of children recognize most of the few words that cover menu possibilities in a kindergarten.

At still another time, repeated attention to high-frequency words (for example, *is* and *a*) can be achieved with sentences that are completed with pictures:

It is a

In sentences like the one above, small picture cards replace unknown words. If the words are printed on the backs of the picture cards, they can be used to show the children what the unknown words look like.

Other types of sentences allow for attention to one of the ways for forming plurals. For instance:

I like a

I like

Again, words are printed on the back of the cards; they should also be printed on a chalkboard in order to highlight how they are the same and how they are different:

flower

flowers

Pictures standing for words is known as *rebus* reading. Although it should not be used too often or for too long, rebus reading can be helpful at the beginning when reading vocabularies are limited.

Reading via Writing

Identifying words is not the only procedure for getting reading started. Studies of children who first learned to read at home reveal that its roots can lie in scribbling (12). With "scribblers," progress typically advances from aimless scribbling to copying objects to copying letters to copying words. The end result for the children is the ability to read the words they write. Such findings suggest that the easiest way into reading for some kindergartners might be through writing. For that reason, kindergarten programs should offer interested children opportunities to learn to write.★

In school, watching a teacher write on a chalkboard can be a sufficient reason for a child to want to learn. Or a kindergarten visit to a first-grade classroom might be just enough to get a five-year-old to the point of, "I want to write, too." As with reading, the easiest word for children to learn to write is their own name, regardless of length or intricate letters. This suggests that teachers should prepare models of first names printed on lined cards. At first, the

---

★ Writing (printing) in the kindergarten ought to follow the manuscript system used in first grade. In spite of the tradition of using extra thick pencils with primary-grade children, ordinary pencils should be available because they are what preschoolers use at home (12).

children will copy all or part of their names carefully and slowly. Later, as they get more and more practice signing their names to pictures and possessions, name cards can be put away.

With individuals who show both dexterity and interest in printing, additional words can be supplied for copying—perhaps names of family members or streets or colors or whatever else is of interest. For some of the necessary practice, small lined chalkboards are useful, preferably those displaying letters and numerals at the top. Periodically, working at a chalkboard can be one of the possibilities at free-choice time when self-selected activities are scheduled.

Attention to printing provides numerous opportunities for identifying letter names, and the printing of letters, combined with a knowledge of their names, almost inevitably results in a child's asking, "How do you spell . . . ?" At the beginning, most answers about spelling come from the teacher. Later, collections of labeled pictures can provide more of the assistance. If children who are playing house, for example, decide they want to make a grocery list, a scrapbook collection of pictured foods, labeled, will allow them to proceed independently. If some are drawing pictures of animals they saw at the zoo and they want to write the names of the animals on their drawings, a collection of animal pictures with labels will help with that.

Whenever there are kindergartners whose interest in making words exceeds their ability to form letters, supplies of cutout letters ought to be available for pasting on pictures. Sometimes, too, a child might enjoy making words by laying paper or plastic letters on a table or the floor. In any case, whether children are doing their own printing or using already formed letters, the end result of word-making activities may be ability in both spelling and reading.

Letters and Sounds

The fact that a word is composed of distinct but blended sounds is unknown by most kindergartners, but it is a basic understanding for phonics. To foster it, teachers can use many different procedures during the kindergarten year.

An understanding of the concept "sound alike at the beginning" can begin to develop without written language. (Avoiding written words is important; otherwise, a teacher cannot be certain whether children are responding to a letter or to a sound.) Following a discussion of a story about a boy named Mike, a teacher might ask, "Do any of you have a name that starts with the same sound as 'Mike'?" If silence results, she might continue with, "Watch my lips when I say 'Mike,' and see whether you can think of anybody right here in this room who has a name that starts with the sound you hear at the beginning of 'Mike.' " If a correct answer still is not heard, the teacher can supply it herself, thus demonstrating with the example the meaning of her request.

With questioning like this, done often enough and over a long enough period of time, it is likely that *some* individuals will show a surprisingly keen perception of initial sounds in words. (Generally, the beginning sound in a short word is the easiest to hear as a distinct sound; therefore it makes sense at the start to concentrate on differences and likenesses in beginning sounds. Because consonants are more consistent than vowels in the sounds they record, it is also better to begin with them.) To provide ready kindergartners with further practice, a teacher might have them sort unlabeled pictures into categories of names that start with the same sound. (Using *un*labeled pictures puts the focus on beginning sounds rather than beginning letters.) Or collections of trinkets and miniature toys and animals might be organized into groups, again on the basis of the initial sounds in their names. Then, of course, there is the familiar practice of asking questions like, "Does anybody see something in this room that starts with the sound that's at the beginning of 'boy'?"

Once some children display auditory discrimination ability, further work with them combines attention to auditory and visual discrimination in order to teach the concept "sound alike, look alike." To illustrate, a teacher might write a list of children's names in a way that makes the visual similarity maximally apparent:

> Jeanne
> Jack
> Jessica
> John

After each name is read and the similarity of initial sounds is discussed, it would be appropriate to comment, "When I said these names, you heard that they began with the same sound. If you look at the four names, you'll see something at the beginning of each that's the same, too. What do you see that's the same at the beginning of all these names?"

After the *J*'s are pointed out, the teacher sums up: "Yes, all these words begin with the same letter and sound. Words that begin with *J* start with a sound that is like the one you hear at the beginning of *Jeanne,* and *Jack,* and *Jessica,* and *John.* Let me write other words that begin with *J.* When I say them, you'll hear the same sound at the beginning." The teacher then writes and reads aloud.★

> jello
> jam
> jet

As a result of these lessons, some children will know the sound recorded by *j.* Later, with the help of words like *Michelle, Mark,* and *Matthew* or, perhaps,

---

★ In this instance, the teacher deliberately selected her own examples because words like *gym* and *ginger* also begin with the sound being discussed. Since this hardly is the time to introduce spelling complexities, responses from the children were not requested. On the other hand, had the listing been highlighting *Michelle, Mark,* and *Matthew,* the teacher would have encouraged the children to suggest additional examples.

monkey, milk, meat, and *mumps,* what *m* records can be taught. And still later, to show the usefulness of knowing about letter sounds, the teacher might write *mumps* on the board and have it reidentified. Under it she could write the unfamiliar word *jumps* and, following that, a sentence; so that the chalkboard shows:

                    mumps
                              Jeanne jumps.
                    jumps

If nobody is able to read the two-word sentence (*Jeanne jumps*) because of the new word (*jumps*), the teacher should refer the children back to the column showing *mumps* and *jumps,* thus reemphasizing the similarity between the known word (*mumps*) and the new one (*jumps*). If *jumps* still cannot be identified, the teacher should read it, thus demonstrating the connection between the two words. To reinforce the phonic connection she should write more word pairs, naming the first herself and asking the children to identify the second. For example:

mean	merry	May	mail	met
Jean	Jerry	jay	jail	jet

Again—and this is common at the beginning—the teacher may have to identify all the new words herself; however, with each identification, she is demonstrating the usefulness of letter-sound connections for reading unfamiliar words. And that is the very essence of phonics.

For any instruction in phonics, whether in this somewhat easygoing fashion in kindergarten or in a more structured and concentrated way later on, no one best sequence exists for introducing sounds. Thus the attention given *j* and *m* in the illustrative material is just that—an illustration of one possible procedure and one possible sequence. Actually, the only "rule" for beginning phonics that gets support in this textbook is the general principle of starting with initial consonant sounds. Another "rule" is common sense: practice makes perfect. And children will need practice in identifying, remembering, and using sounds whether the level is kindergarten or a later grade. (Suggestions for practice are in Chapter 8, the whole of which deals with phonics instruction.)

STILL MORE OPPORTUNITIES FOR TEACHING READING

Thus far, illustrations of opportunities to teach reading have been presented in relation to (a) a whole word emphasis, (b) a writing and spelling emphasis, and (c) a phonics emphasis. Now, additional illustrations will be given, this time using activities that are customary in kindergarten.

Reading to Children

No matter what changes are made in kindergarten programs, time for reading daily to the children *should never be omitted*. For some children, kindergarten marks the first occasion for this contact with books; with others, it is the continuation of a pleasant experience begun at home. For all, being read to will contribute not only to their interest in reading and learning to read but also to a growing awareness of book language and of diversity in stories (3). As was mentioned in Chapter 2, reading to children also provides a model for good oral reading and, in addition, yields information that will facilitate reading comprehension later. In spite of all these important contributions, however, enjoyment remains *the* reason for reading to young children.

Even when enjoyment *is* the key concern, reading allows for calling attention to a basically important fact that not all kindergartners understand: reading is not a matter of holding a book and speaking. Rather, it is saying what is printed.

Not to be overlooked, either, is that reading to children may help them learn to read. Titles of books, for example, provide repeated contact with hard-to-remember words like *the, was,* and *have.* (Such words are difficult because they have no specific or interesting referent.) Showing children the pages being read may prompt one or more to ask, "Where does it say that?" Still other books will suggest ideas for a bulletin-board display of labeled pictures arranged to show the sequence of a story. A large sheet of heavy paper, folded in accordion fashion, also allows for drawing sequential pictures.

While reading to children does provide many productive opportunities to help them with their own ability to read, a word of caution is in order: it should not always turn into an occasion for teaching reading, just as every instance of attention to colors, to cite another illustration, should not automatically become "a reading lesson." Reading to children is primarily for enjoyment, and anything that detracts from that should be bypassed.

To ensure enjoyment, what is read needs to be chosen with care. It is important, therefore, to know that young children have little patience with excessive detail and slowly moving plots. Like us all, they enjoy suspense—but not too much—and happy endings. Stories of other children or of animals are usually attractive, as is a book whose theme or content relates to their own experiences. Unlike an adult audience, young children soon let the oral reader know when a poor choice was made.

Art

Earlier illustrations showed how art activities provide opportunities for attending to written language. Signing names to artwork, writing simple captions about a picture, labeling objects in a display of clay figures—all of these are perfect activities for helping children become both artist and author. But other "perfect occasions" connected with art occur, too. For instance, a teacher might encourage kindergartners to look for various shapes in the world surrounding them, both indoors and outdoors. When circles are discussed, the children might find them in buttons, bracelets, flowers and flower pots, doorknobs, pillows, lampshades, ice cream cones, wheels, fans, jar covers, coins, coasters, and traffic lights.

Then rectangles are identified and talked about so that children begin to see that shape in the outlines of cookie sheets, books and magazines, desk blotters, pictures, chalkboards, drawers, tablets, crayon boxes, envelopes, air conditioners, highway signs, license plates, window frames, and doors. Later, attention can go to other shapes in the child's everyday world, now turned into something far more interesting.

To add written language to the effort to make "looking" a little more exciting, labeled magazine pictures showing various shapes might be collected, sorted, and put into appropriate books. Hooked to a string or wire, strung low enough for the children to reach, picture books might look something like this:

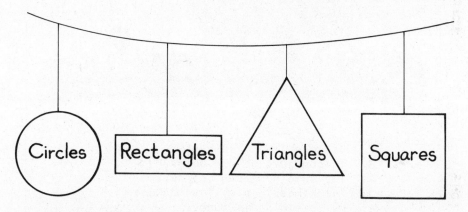

Although elaborate covers are unnecessary, any booklike collection of pictures (including homemade picture dictionaries) creates a need not only to illustrate a cover but also to spell and write words for titles. At another time, bookmarks might be made and decorated.

A bulletin-board display of artwork can provide still more contacts with print. After the children have drawn self-portraits, for example, they can be displayed under the title, "Who Are You?" When the children have finished drawing pictures of their homes, the art could be displayed under the question, "Where Do You Live?" The positive feature of such titles is that they not only point out the function of a question mark but also provide practice in reading hard-to-remember words like *what, who, where,* and *why* in meaningful contexts.

Figures 4.1 and 4.2 show other uses of children's artwork. In both instances, a teacher composed the text, using it to review words that had received attention earlier. Use of the names of children in her class (for example, *Tom* and *Kane*) personalized the accounts. Obviously, so did the children's art.

Figure 4.1

I See Something

1. I see something.
2. "It can jump," said Tom.
3. It can jump up and down.
4. The something can go fast.
5. "It likes to play," said Kane.
6. My something is funny.
7. It is my dog.

Figure 4.2

Come With Me

1. I see something.
2. Look boys and girls.
3. I want to ride.
4. See me ride up and down.
5. See me jump.
6. See me jump fast.
7. "Come ride with me," said Diane.
8. See me ride the funny merry-go-round.
9. It is yelllow, green, red and blue.

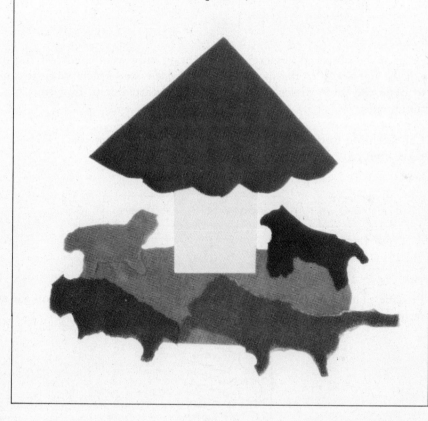

One further example of an art activity will be described because it illustrates what was said earlier: How much should be done with an activity depends on the children's abilities and interest. In this instance, the activity was seen during a visit to a kindergarten.

After discussions about safety (coupled with a walk to examine traffic lights), the children made their own lights out of construction paper:

In the case of the observed kindergarten, attention only went to identifying the colors of the lights and to the meaning of *top, middle,* and *bottom* when it came time to paste the three circles. With more advanced children, however, other possibilities exist:

1.   Call attention to the written words *red, orange,* and *green.*
2.   Have children match word cards:

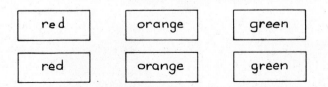

3.   Provide practice in identifying *red, orange,* and *green* in preparation for attaching small word cards to the traffic lights:

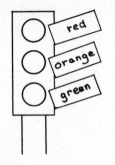

Music

As with art, the fun and freedom of music should never be stifled with nagging efforts to get reading into a kindergarten program. Nonetheless, occasions do occur when attention to written language can add to the music as well as to the children's ability to read. For instance, a much enlarged copy of a page from a song book, displayed for all to see, will show how notes tell singers when to go up and down with their voice and how the written words tell them what to say as they sing.

If attention is going to musical instruments, perhaps with the help of recordings, a bulletin-board display of labeled pictures showing horns, violins, and drums can add specificity to the lesson. If the instruments are only those of the kindergarten rhythm band, pictures with identifying labels will still be of interest—perhaps of even greater interest.

As children learn songs, additional ways to feature written words are possible. In a song about four farm animals, with a verse for each, the teacher can show a picture of the appropriate animal each time a new verse is begun. Later, when the song is repeated, she could show the same pictures, this time with identifying labels. After this procedure has been followed on a number of occasions, the teacher might next show cards on which only an animal's name is written, asking, "Who can tell me what this animal is?" And then, "Let's sing that verse."

With other songs, only one word might be highlighted. A song about children's games, for instance, can be an opportunity to call attention to *games*. (It might also be a time to compare *games* and *game*.) A song called "Getting to Know You" could naturally lead to attention to *you*.

COMMENTS ABOUT THE ILLUSTRATIONS

Unfortunately, it is possible that the illustrative material presented in the chapter fostered an erroneous conception of what teaching is all about. That is, as you read about the many examples of kindergarten instruction, you may have concluded that a teacher's job is to come up with a variety of procedures and activities with the hope that at least some will interest the children, keep them occupied, and teach them something as well. Such a picture, however, omits attention to an important responsibility—in fact, the *first* responsibility of the professional teacher: to identify goals (skills, abilities, understandings) that have educational significance and that have not yet been attained by the children for whom the instruction is being planned. It is only *after* one or more goals are identified that a teacher is ready to begin thinking about the means (materials, activities, assignments) that will be instrumental in achieving them. An example of this necessary sequence will be the best description of it.

When reading opportunities connected with art were discussed earlier, the possibility of teaching the concepts "circle," "rectangle," "square," and "triangle" was proposed. One goal, it was stated, was to make looking a little more interesting; however, the development of these concepts was chosen for the illustrative material because it can also be a means for achieving goals related to reading. More specifically, attention to the various concepts could not only extend the children's oral vocabulary but also provide words that some might learn to read as a result of repeated identifications connected with discussions, bulletin-board displays, and scrapbook collections of labeled pictures.

With the concept of "circle" as an example, a teacher's plans for reading, written in a way that highlights what she will do, might look something like this:

Goals	Procedures
1. To introduce the concept "circle."	1. Begin a discussion with the question, "Does anybody know what a circle is?" (Write word on chalkboard.)
	2. Show circular objects. (Later, display them on a table with the sign circles.)
	3. Show and discuss pictures of circular objects. (Save for bulletin board and, later, for scrapbook.)
	4. Encourage children to look for circular objects at home and on their way to and from school. Talk about their discoveries the next day.
	5. Assemble and discuss bulletin board entitled "Circles," showing pictures of circular objects labeled circle.
2. To reinforce children's understanding of "circle."	1. Show red cutout circles of identical size. Discuss the similarity in color and size. Then show other circles that vary in both size and color. With questions, help children conclude that the concept "circle" encompasses variation in size and color but not shape.
	2. Let children paste cutout circles on paper, making a design if they wish. While the pasting is being done, write Circles on each paper. Display papers in the classroom.

Goals	Procedures
3. To introduce <u>s</u> to denote plural.	1. Prepare a bulletin-board display entitled "Circles," showing cutout circles of various sizes and colors. Below each one write <u>Circle</u>.
	2. Diseuss the display with the children. Have them read all the labels. Ask whether the labels and the title are exactly the same. To emphasize the difference, write on a chalkboard:

Circle
Circles

Read the two words. Discuss the one difference. Explain that <u>s</u> at the end of a word sometimes shows it means more than one. Write, read, and discuss other pairs of words, for instance:

girl	boy	color	day
girls	boys	colors	days

Goals	Procedures
4. To summarize attention to circles.	1. Prepare a circle-shaped scrapbook for pictures of circular objects. Write <u>Circles</u> on the cover, and label each picture <u>Circle</u>. Show and discuss the scrapbook. Put it with other books that can be used at free-choice time.
5. To help children begin to print letters composed of circles.	1. Have children make circles in the air.
	2. Have children trace circles drawn on dittoed sheets. (Make certain correct direction is used.)
	3. Have them make their own circles on paper.
6. To practice printing <u>o</u>.	1. Using the chalkboard, print known words that include <u>o</u>. Name and discuss the words. Call attention to the <u>o</u>'s.

<u>Goals</u>   <u>Procedures</u>

2. Show children sample of lined writing paper with <u>o</u>'s printed on it.
   On another sheet, demonstrate with
   care how they are to make the letter <u>o</u> so that it sits on a line.
   Distribute writing paper and have
   them try to print <u>o</u>'s.

7. To practice printing   1. Follow the same procedures, empha-
   <u>c</u>.   sizing that <u>c</u> is an unfinished
                                circle.

   While reviewing the teaching plans for circles, which would require different amounts of time with different groups, you probably noticed that they incor-
porated some ideas emphasized in earlier sections of the chapter. The plans show,
for example, how instruction can bring together such related learnings as word
meanings, the identification of written words, and, in this instance, the beginning
of skill in printing. The same plans exemplify how practice in word identification
can come from such sources as bulletin-board displays and scrapbook collections
of labeled pictures. The plans should also have made the point that productive
teaching does not just happen but is, instead, the fruit of thoughtful, knowledgeable decisions based, first of all, on an awareness of what children need to learn
and, second, on the selection of materials, procedures, and assignments that will
foster those learnings.

SUMMARY

The underlying assumption of Chapter 4 is that most kindergartners are neither
totally ready nor totally unready to learn to read. That is why a kindergarten
curriculum (insofar as reading is concerned) should be composed of various
combinations of readiness and reading instruction.

   Goals for readiness instruction were listed and discussed at the start of the
chapter. What will not contribute to readiness was considered, too, in order to
encourage kindergarten teachers to move away from nonproductive goals and
toward those that *will* foster success with reading.

   Because the success of each child is affected by methodology, reading instruction was described in a way that highlighted different methodologies: whole
word identifications, phonics instruction, and printing instruction. To show how
attention to reading can be linked to activities that have been in kindergartens for
a long time, further descriptions of instruction and practice were presented in the
context of reading to children, art activities, and music.

   In order to emphasize that kindergarten instruction should be carefully
planned in relation to preestablished goals, the chapter ended with a sample
teaching plan that dealt with a number of goals, all of which are relevant for
reading.

REVIEW

1. Alert kindergarten teachers learn a great deal about a child's readiness for reading by observing day-by-day behavior. Even in grocery stores, behavioral signs of readiness are noticeable. Just recently, for example, I had the opportunity in a store to observe a little girl of about three or four who, penny in hand, walked to a gumball machine. Taped to it was a sheet of paper displaying three handprinted words: *out of order.* Upon seeing the sheet, the child turned and asked a woman who was passing by, "What does that say?" "It says 'out of order,' " the woman answered. "What does that mean?" the little girl inquired. "It means the machine doesn't work. I hope you didn't put your money in." "No," responded the child and walked away. Specify the behavioral signs of readiness that became apparent during the brief conversation just described.

2. To help specify the meaning of "word," one kindergarten teacher uses dashes between words when she prints sentences. For instance:

   I—am—five.

   For the same purpose, another teacher lists brief sentences on a ditto sheet and has the children place a small paper square under each word. Which procedure is better? Why?

3. In a book called *Reading Readiness,* a suggestion for developing readiness is similar to what appears below.

   > Have the children close their eyes. Ask them to be as quiet as possible. Play a record of sounds (e.g., slamming door, bird noises, barking dog, drum). Have the children identify as many of the sounds as they can.

   What do you think about the suggestion? If followed, will it promote readiness for reading?

4. On one occasion, I observed a kindergarten teacher during the period she called "Reading Readiness." The children were seated on the floor around the piano listening to the teacher play pairs of notes. With some pairs the teacher's question was, "Which note was louder: the first or the second?" With others the question was, "Which note was softer: the first or the second?" At still other times, questions had to do with which note was lower or higher. Afterward, I asked the teacher why she thought what was done with the notes was a reading readiness activity. She explained it as teaching auditory discrimination, which she said would help later with phonics. Do *you* think that the piano activity is preparation for phonics?

5. Describe how a kindergarten teacher can learn (through individual testing) which numerals (1–20) each child is able to name at the start of the year. Specify what the test would look like, how the testing itself would proceed, and how what each child could and could not do should be recorded.

6. How would you respond to each of the following teachers?

Kindergarten teacher: "Personally, I think five-year-olds are too young to learn to read. What's the big hurry?"

First-grade teacher: "If they start teaching reading in kindergarten, what are first-grade teachers supposed to do?"

REFERENCES

1. Arter, Judith A., and Jenkins, Joseph R. "Differential Diagnosis—Prescriptive Teaching: A Critical Appraisal." *Review of Educational Research* 49 (Fall 1979): 517–555.

2. Barrett, Thomas C. "The Relationship between Measures of Prereading Visual Discrimination and First Grade Achievement: A Review of the Literature." *Reading Research Quarterly* 1 (Fall 1965): 51–76.

3. Bruce, Bertram. "Stories within Stories." *Language Arts* 58 (November–December 1981): 931–936.

4. Calfee, R. C., and Venezky, R. L. "Component Skills in Beginning Reading." In *Psycholinguistics and the Teaching of Reading*. Edited by K. S. Goodman and J. T. Fleming. Newark, Dela.: International Reading Association, 1969.

5. Chall, Jeanne S. "A Decade of Research on Reading and Learning Disabilities." In *What Research Has to Say about Reading Instruction*. Edited by S. Jay Samuels. Newark, Dela.: International Reading Association, 1978.

6. Chomsky, Carol. "Write First, Read Later." *Childhood Education* 47 (March 1971): 296–299.

7. Clark, Margaret. *Young Fluent Readers*. London: Heinemann Educational Books, 1976.

8. Clay, Marie M. *Reading: The Patterning of Complex Behavior*. London: Heinemann Educational Books, 1972.

9. Cohn, Margot. "Observations of Learning to Read and Write Naturally." *Language Arts* 58 (May 1981): 549–555.

10. Cutts, Warren G. "Does the Teacher Really Matter?" *Reading Teacher* 28 (February 1975): 449–452.

11. Downing, John. "The Child's Conception of 'A Word.'" *Reading Research Quarterly* 9, no. 4 (1973–1974): 568–582.

12. Durkin, Dolores. *Children Who Read Early*. New York: Teachers College Press, Columbia University, 1966.

13. Durkin, Dolores. *Getting Reading Started*. Boston: Allyn and Bacon, 1982.

14. Durkin, Dolores. "A Language Arts Program for Pre-First Grade Children: Two-Year Achievement Report." *Reading Research Quarterly* 5 (Summer 1970): 534–565.

15. Durkin, Dolores. *Teaching Young Children to Read*. 3d ed. Boston: Allyn and Bacon, 1980.

16. Durrell, Donald. "Success in First Grade Reading." *Boston University Journal of Education* 140 (February 1958): 2–47.

17. Gibson, Eleanor J., and Levin, Harry. *The Psychology of Reading*. Cambridge, Mass.: MIT Press, 1975.

18. Hall, Mary Ann; Moretz, Sara A.; and Statom, Jodellano. "Writing before Grade One—A Study of Early Writers." *Language Arts* 53 (May 1976): 582–585.

19. Halpin, G., and Halpin, G. "Special Paper for Beginning Handwriting: An Unquestioned Practice." *Journal of Educational Research* 69 (March 1976): 267–269.

20. Harris, Albert J. "A Reaction to Valtin's 'Dyslexia: Deficit in Reading or Deficit in Research?' " *Reading Research Quarterly* 14, no. 2 (1978–1979): 222–225.

21. Harris, Albert J. "Practical Applications of Reading Research." *Reading Teacher* 29 (March 1976): 559–565.

22. Holden, M. H., and MacGinitie, W. H. "Children's Conceptions of Word Boundaries in Speech and Print." *Journal of Educational Psychology* 63 (December 1972): 551–557.

23. Klink, Howard. "Words and Music." *Language Arts* 53 (April 1976): 401–403.

24. Leibert, R. E., and Sherk, J. K. "Three Frostig Visual Perception Sub-Tests and Specific Reading Tasks for Kindergarten, First, and Second Grade Children." *Reading Teacher* 24 (November 1970): 130–137.

25. Olson, A. V., and Johnson, C. I. "Structure and Predictive Validity of the Frostig Developmental Test of Visual Perception in Grades One and Three." *Journal of Special Education* 4 (Winter–Spring 1970): 49–52.

26. Paradis, Edward. "The Appropriateness of Visual Discrimination Exercises in Reading Readiness Materials." *Journal of Educational Research* 67 (February 1974): 276–278.

27. Paradis, Edward, and Peterson, Joseph. "Readiness Training Implications from Research." *Reading Teacher* 28 (February 1975): 445–448.

28. Past, K. C.; Past, A.; and Guzman, S. B. "A Bilingual Kindergarten Immersed in Print." *Reading Teacher* 33 (May 1980): 907–913.

29. Read, Charles. "Pre-School Children's Knowledge of English Phonology." *Harvard Educational Review* 41 (February 1971): 1–34.

30. Samuels, S. Jay. "The Effect of Letter-Name Knowledge on Learning to Read." *American Educational Research Journal* 9 (Winter 1972): 65–74.

31. Silvaroli, N. J. "Factors in Predicting Children's Success in First Grade Reading." *Reading and Inquiry*. Proceedings of the International Reading Association, 1965, pp. 296–298.

32. Sticht, T. G.; Beck, L. J.; Hauke, R. N.; Kleiman, G. M.; and James, J. H. *Auding and Reading*. Alexandria, Va.: Human Resources Research Organization, 1974.

33. Weeks, Thelma E. "Early Reading Acquisition as Language Development." *Language Arts* 56 (May 1979): 515–521.

PART III

INSTRUCTION: WORDS

CHAPTER 5

WHOLE WORD METHODOLOGY

PREVIEW

The ability to identify written words both correctly and quickly is only one of the many requirements of reading comprehension. It is, nonetheless, an essential ingredient. That is why Chapters 5 through 9 cover what can be done to ensure that students know (or will be able to figure out) whatever words are necessary for comprehending connected text.

Recognizing that individual children respond differently to the various means for developing reading vocabularies, the earlier chapters on readiness and kindergarten urged the use of all approaches as the best way to accommodate the most children. Anyone who accepts the proposal, however, must still decide which methodology to use first since everything cannot be done simultaneously. The recommendation here is to use whole word instruction initially, for reasons explained in the forthcoming chapter.

What is said there about whole word methodology applies not just to the beginning but to whenever it is used—for instance, when it is used with words like aisle, colonel, indict, *and so on. This means that the content of Chapter 5 is as relevant for upper-grade teachers as it is for those working with beginners. Not to be forgotten either is that the content applies as much to the vocabulary of science and social studies as it does to new words in a basal reader. What it says about whole word methodology also applies when language experience materials are used.*

As you read Chapter 5, you may encounter some new vocabulary yourself. Terms that teachers should know are in italics. As you read the chapter, you will also find answers to questions like:

Exactly what is whole word methodology?
How does a teacher decide which words to teach with this method?
What helps students remember words once they have been identified? On the other hand, is there anything that impedes word learning?
What is the best kind of practice for learning words? How can at least some of it be made interesting?

In recent years, the effect of nonstandard dialects on reading ability has been a concern. Among other things, the interest has fostered a closer, more thoughtful look at such basic questions as, What is a "correct" identification? That question is considered in Chapter 5 and in a way that also shows the relevance of the answer for bilingual students.

As students move from one grade to the next, various procedures are used to help them know what written words say. Even at the kindergarten level, as the previous chapter showed, they learn what they say through direct identifications and from help with letter-sound relationships, spelling, and writing. The present chapter singles out direct identifications as it concentrates on whole word methodology.

This methodology is sometimes called a *sight method* for teaching vocabulary because the expectation for it is that children will be able to identify words on sight without first having to go through conscious, letter-by-letter analyses. For the same reason, it is referred to as the *look-say method* since, as a result of its use, children are expected to say (identify) a word as soon as they look at it.

Regardless of the description, whole word methodology is simply a matter of naming words and is used frequently by teachers and nonteachers alike. In fact, whoever responds to the query, "What does that word say?" is employing whole word methodology. Since anyone who can read is able to use the method, some explanation does seem necessary as to why an entire chapter is devoted to it.

One reason is that a single identification rarely leads to permanent retention. Because nothing less than that can be the goal of school instruction, it is imperative that professional teachers know how to foster permanent recall. That explains why the chapter considers topics like *cues* and *practice*.

Because students must be able to read many more words than those they happen to inquire about, the professional teacher also needs to know which words to select for attention and, further, what to do to interest students in learning them. These requirements are additional reasons for the present chapter.

When to use whole word methodology is still another question for which a teacher must have an answer. Since part of the answer is related to how our language is recorded, it is appropriate to begin the discussion with a few comments about the nature of written English.

WRITTEN ENGLISH

Broadly speaking, writing systems are of three kinds. In the order of their historical development, they are (a) pictographic, (b) ideographic, and (c) alphabetic.

With pictographic, or hieroglyphic writing, symbols show a direct relationship to the visual appearance of their referents. A word thus looks like what it says. According to the linguist Leonard Bloomfield, "The important feature of picture writing is that it is not based on language at all. A reader who knows the conventions by which the pictures are drawn, can read the message even if he does not understand the language which the writer speaks" (4, p. 126). The obvious limitation of pictographic writing is that messages are not always picturable.

That drawback fostered the development of ideographic writing in which a word is assigned a symbol that shows no relationship to its pronunciation and, generally, none to its meaning either. Written Chinese is the best example of an ideographic system, although the Japanese (according to one author at least) still use about 1,850 ideographs along with "phonetic letters" (21). The same author points out that the difficulty of learning to read Japanese ideographs depends upon the extent to which a symbol has changed from the original pictogram—if one existed—to a simplified, conventionalized symbol.

Although written English is not ideographic, it does have some ideographs. Examples are mathematical signs (+, −) numerals (4), and abbreviations (Ms., Co.). As the illustrations point up, a reader either knows or does not know what an ideograph says. He either knows or does not know, for instance, that *10* is read as "ten"; and if he does not know it, there is no way he can reach that conclusion from the ideograph itself. With an alphabetic writing system, on the other hand, words are recorded with letters that stand for speech sounds; a knowledge of the sounds that letters represent, therefore, can function in figuring out what a series of letters "says."

One example of alphabetic writing is English.★ However, anyone who has learned to read English is aware that it does not have a perfectly consistent alphabetic system. If it did, it would have as many letters as it has speech sounds, and each letter would always stand for the same sound. As it is, English has about forty-two sounds—the number varies depending upon whose analysis is used— and twenty-six letters to represent them. The mismatch, coupled with some inconsistency in the way speech sounds are represented, results in irregular spellings that make it difficult to predict a pronunciation from a spelling. The difficulty is mentioned because it has to be taken into account when questions about the appropriate time for using whole word methodology are raised.

WHEN TO USE WHOLE WORD METHODOLOGY

Irregularly spelled words are the reason some use will always have to be made of whole word methodology. That is, there will be times at all grade levels when the correspondence between the spelling and pronunciation of an unknown word is sufficiently slight that the word should be directly identified for students. Words like *depot, clothes, vein, choir,* and *suite* are possible examples at middle- and upper-grade levels; earlier, irregularly spelled words include such frequently occurring ones as *of, was, should,* and *to,* and others like *one, busy,* and *eye.*

★ This is an appropriate time to point out that all languages are phonetic since all are composed of speech sounds. When the sounds are the basis of a writing system, that system is alphabetic. "Alphabetic" thus refers to a particular kind of written language, whereas "phonetic" characterizes the spoken form of all languages.

With beginners, a second factor accounts for the need to rely on whole word methodology: insufficient skill to figure out words. (Figuring out the identity of an unknown word on the basis of its spelling is called *decoding*.) This might prompt a question about the advisability of initiating a reading program by concentrating on letters and sounds so that students will be able to work out their own identifications. Starting that way is *not* recommended for several reasons. To begin, young children are much more interested in learning words since they are familiar in their spoken form. That letters stand for sounds, or that a single word is composed of multiple sounds, is foreign. Learning words also bears closer resemblance to their conception of what "learning to read" is all about, and, further, it allows them to do some reading immediately.

With these advantages, the recommendation is that instruction begin with whole word methodology but that *as soon as possible* attention should go to letters and the sounds they record. (The parallel development was illustrated when kindergarten reading was discussed.) Soon, word structure will require instructional time, too.

SELECTING WORDS FOR WHOLE WORD METHODOLOGY

At the very beginning, when whole word methodology is used routinely, teachers of beginners naturally wonder which words to choose for direct identifications.

Early Selections

The significance of motivation for success suggests that early selections should be words that are of interest. Practical considerations indicate, however, that they must also include words that appear in whatever materials are used to teach reading. If *pool* appears in a reader, for example, *pool* has to be taught. Words that occur frequently in any kind of text (for example, *the, and, have,* and *they*) also require early attention.

One of the first efforts to identify words that show up in any kind of text was made by Edward Dolch (11). Figure 5.1 shows his well-known list of 220 *service words,* so-called because their frequent appearance in print makes knowing them highly serviceable. Later on, other reading specialists also pursued the task of identifying high-frequency words (22). While factors like cultural change and the availability of computers produced slightly different lists, the one Dolch compiled is shown here because it is the best known and it is the standard against which the more recent lists are often compared. With or without all such lists, anyone acquainted with English is aware of the value of being able to identify automatically such frequently occurring words as *was, the, to,* and *it.* Also valuable for carrying out written assignments are words like *underline, circle, draw, color,* and *describe.*

Figure 5.1 The Dolch Basic Sight Vocabulary of 220 Service Words

a	could	had	may	said	under
about	cut	has	me	saw	up
after		have	much	say	upon
again	did	he	must	see	us
all	do	help	my	seven	use
always	does	her	myself	shall	
am	done	here		she	very
an	don't	him	never	show	
and	down	his	new	sing	walk
any	draw	hold	no	sit	want
are	drink	hot	not	six	warm
around		how	now	sleep	was
as	eat	hurt		small	wash
ask	eight		of	so	we
at	every	I	off	some	well
ate		if	old	soon	went
away	fall	in	on	start	were
	far	into	once	stop	what
be	fast	is	one		when
because	find	it	only	take	where
been	first	its	open	tell	which
before	five		or	ten	white
best	fly	jump	our	thank	who
better	for	just	out	that	why
big	found		over	the	will
black	four	keep	own	their	wish
blue	from	kind		them	with
both	full	know	pick	then	work
bring	funny		play	there	would
brown		laugh	please	these	write
but	gave	let	pretty	they	
buy	get	light	pull	think	yellow
by	give	like	put	this	yes
	go	little		those	you
call	goes	live	ran	three	your
came	going	long	read	to	
can	good	look	red	today	
carry	got		ride	together	
clean	green	made	right	too	
cold	grow	make	round	try	
come		many	run	two	

Contractions

Contractions are another type of word that should figure in whole word instruction. Even though many manuals delay teaching them, the earlier attention being recommended here is based on two facts. First, young children understand contractions because they enter into their own speech very early; and, second, ability to read contractions allows for the use of natural language (*I'm here* versus *I am here*). The second point is important because natural language constructions give students the opportunity to use what is familiar (oral language) to comprehend what is less familiar (print).

Although teaching manuals and workbooks convey the notion that once contractions *are* introduced, much attention must go to their special structure, the position taken here is that such attention is unnecessary. Again, it is based on a fact, namely, that the ability to read contractions has only two requirements: an understanding of their meaning and the ability to identify them in their written form. What is *not* required is illustrated in Figure 5.2 and can be further illustrated with a reference to one third grade.

During the observation, the teacher was directing a lesson whose goal was the ability to identify, and know the meanings of, eight contractions listed on the board. Apparently, they had been identified and practiced earlier because all three boys—the poorest readers in the class—were able to read most of them without help. Following the identifications, sentence cards were displayed. Now the teacher's request was to read a sentence silently and then explain its meaning. For the first one (*Don't cross in the middle of the street*), a boy explained, "It means you're not supposed to cross in the middle of the street. You're supposed to go to the corner." Even though the meaning of all the other sentences was explained equally well, the teacher still asked the boys to name the two words for which each contraction substituted and to name the letters that each apostrophe replaced. Now, fidgeting, guessing, and errors were characteristic. Clearly the lesson had become not only too demanding but—and this is the point to be underscored—it also exceeded what reading requires.

For teachers, this incident has a twofold message: first, keep in mind the basic requirements of reading and, second, do not go beyond them (even though workbook exercises commonly do), especially with slower children who, for the sake of their self-esteem, need all the success and encouragement they can get.

A description of what has been seen being done with contractions may prompt the question, "Is detailed attention to the unique structure of contractions ever warranted?" The answer is, "It depends." If students are curious about the appearance of a contraction the first time they see one, all that needs to be said is something like, "You'll see that mark—it's called an 'apostrophe'—in a few other words, too." Once additional contractions have been introduced with whole word methodology and it thus becomes time to teach the meaning of *contraction*, something specific needs to be said about the fact that the apostrophe serves to contract two words into one. Now it is appropriate to contrast and discuss the details of pairs like:

Figure 5.2

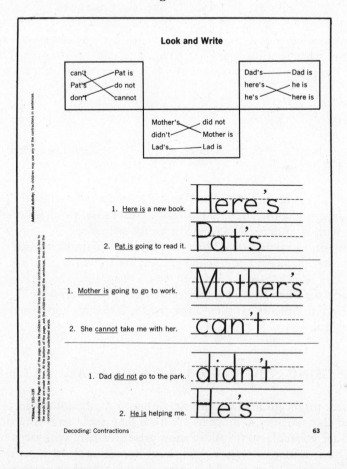

From Studybook for *May I Come In?* of READING 720, RAINBOW EDITION by Theodore Clymer and others, © copyright, 1979, 1976, by Ginn and Company (Xerox Corporation). Used with permission.

● *This teacher's edition of a workbook page (for which answers are supplied) is useful in making two points that apply to a number of pages in all workbooks. First, the exercise is mislabeled, since what children are asked to do is not required for decoding (reading) contractions. The second point is implied in the first: the content of workbooks does not always deal with what advances reading ability. The second characteristic means that teachers who ask children to do every page in workbooks sometimes assign what can only be called busy work. For those who want to concentrate on practice that is pertinent for reading, the suggestions for practice included in this textbook in Chapters 5 through 11 should be helpful.*

can't	I'll	she's	they're
cannot	I will	she is	they are

Once the term *contraction* is understood, no further need exists to spend time talking about what is substituted for what. The main concern is, Do students understand the meaning of contractions when they are part of a sentence?

A Summary

What has now been said about selecting words for whole word instruction can be summarized as follows:

1. Words should be directly identified for students only when they are unable to make the identifications themselves. Otherwise, proficiency in decoding (and, with it, independence) will never be achieved.
2. Insufficient or no decoding ability means that unfamiliar words will have to be directly identified for beginners. At first, words that are of interest should be selected; soon, however, words that appear in whatever materials children are asked to read must get attention. If children are expected to do written assignments on their own, words like *draw* and *underline* must be taught, too.

TEACHING NEW WORDS: A BASAL READER LESSON

How teachers might go about using whole word methodology in kindergarten was illustrated in Chapter 4. Since its use from first grade on is commonly linked to basal reader vocabulary, the illustration presented here will focus on preparations for a basal reader story, which is about hummingbirds. Nine third graders who have some ability in decoding comprise the subgroup participating in the lesson.

Teacher: It takes a lot of letters to name the most important character in the story you'll be reading today. I'll write three of them. [Prints *hum*.] What do these three letters say?
Group: Hum.
Teacher: I'll add more letters. [Adds *ming*.] Now what do all these letters say?
Group: Humming.
Teacher: Right. What does "humming" mean? Billy?
Billy: Humming is like singing, but there aren't any words. You don't have to open your mouth either.
Teacher: I have to add one more part to this word so that you'll know whom you'll be reading about. [Adds *bird*.] Today the story is about what?
Group: A hummingbird.

Teacher:	Right you are. I've never seen a hummingbird around here. They're very tiny birds, and they make a humming noise. That's how they got their name. Let me show you some pictures of hummingbirds. The ones in your reader are too small.

The teacher proceeds to show colorful pictures, which elicit comments from the children. She then continues:

Teacher:	The story is about a hummingbird, but it's also about [teacher finishes by printing *honey* on the board]. Who knows what this says? Nobody? I bet you'll know if I write something else. [Adds to board so that it shows *bee and honey*.]
Michael:	I know. Honey!
Teacher:	Right. I thought you'd think of honey if I wrote *bee*. Have any of you ever eaten honey?
Mary Ann:	My mother puts it on toast, but it makes me sick.
Trish:	Sometimes my mother puts it in carrots when she's cooking.
Teacher:	Yes, honey is sweet, so it's good on toast and in carrots.
Mary Ann:	It's too sweet and sticky. It makes me sick.
Teacher:	Mary Ann, when you read the story you'll have to see whether the hummingbird agrees with you. When all of you read the story you'll find a fairly long word, and I'm not sure you'll know what it means so we better look at that, too. [Writes *experiment*.] What does this say?
Bobby:	It says "ex" at the beginning and "ment" at the end, but I don't know the rest of it. I don't think I've ever seen that word before.
Teacher:	Maybe not. Scientists use it a lot. Does anyone know what it says? No? It says "experiment." What does it say?
Group:	Experiment.
Teacher:	Do you know what "experiment" means? Does anyone know what an experiment is?
Billy:	It's when you try something, and you have to be careful because it might blow up. The other night on television, two guys did an experiment and it almost killed them.
Teacher:	That was one kind of experiment, Billy. Not all experiments are dangerous. In fact, I'm carrying on an experiment right now at home. I have two plants that are the same. I'm watering one every week and the other about every ten days. I'm trying to learn which amount of water is better. It's not dangerous, but it's an experiment because I'm trying to learn something by doing different things. That's what your story for today is about. Someone is trying to find out something about hummingbirds. And it has to do with honey.
Trish:	I bet I know what happens. Some bees sting the hummingbird because they both want the honey.

Teacher:	I can't tell you because then there wouldn't be any mystery. Before you find out what happens, there's one more word I want you to look at because you might have trouble figuring it out. Let me write it. [Prints *touch*.] Can anyone read this? Jim?
Jim:	Touch? [Pronounces it to rhyme with *couch*.]
Teacher:	Jim, have you ever heard a word that sounds like "touch"? [Repeats Jim's pronunciation.]
Jim:	I don't think so. I guess I don't know what it says.
Teacher:	Let's see if you do now. Read everything I write, then see if you can read this new word. [Writes *touch football*.] Jim, with your eyes, read what I just wrote. What does this word [points to *touch*] say?
Jim:	Touch. Touch football.
Teacher:	Yes, in this case *touch* means a kind of football game in which you touch rather than tackle the players. But in the story about a hummingbird, it will just mean to touch something—the way I'm touching the top of Mary Ann's head. Jim, I think I know why you first thought this word said "touch" [pronounces it to rhyme with *couch*]. With this word [writes *couch* directly under *touch*], we do say "couch." We give that /ou/ sound to the digraph *ou*. But in "touch," the vowel sound is /ŭ/. What this shows is the importance of asking—what question should you always ask after you think you've figured out a word?
Group:	Does it make sense?
Teacher:	Correct. The reason I wrote *touch football* is to show you how words you can read help with words that you're not sure of. There are some other words in the story about the hummingbird that are new, but the way they're spelled should tell you what they say. If you have any problems, be sure to read all the other words in the sentence. They'll help, too. To make sure that you don't have problems with the words we've been talking about, let's read them a few more times.

In the story about the hummingbird, seven other regularly spelled words are cited in the basal manual as being new. After the story is read silently, the teacher will show the group a number of phrase and sentence cards, each containing at least one of the seven words. Sentences using the words that were formally presented before the reading was begun will also be used. By having individuals read the cards aloud, the teacher can learn which, if any, of the new words are causing problems. Further attention will then go to them.

WORD IDENTIFICATION AND SUCCESS WITH READING

As our own experiences confirm, the ability to identify most of the words that appear in a text is essential for comprehension. (It also is essential for developing self-confidence as a reader.) The same experiences tell us, too, that the faster such identifications are made, the easier it is to comprehend.

The importance of instantaneous identifications for comprehension is reflected in what is called *automaticity,* a term used in connection with automatic identifications (28). While such identifications do not guarantee success in comprehending, they do free a reader to give conscious attention to the meaning of connected text, much as the experienced automobile driver is free to attend to a radio program or to participate in a conversation with a passenger. Since reading *is* comprehending, the need at all grade levels for automatic identifications should be clear. Yet in spite of that, visits to middle- and upper-grade classrooms sometimes reveal little or no time being spent on word practice (12), a prerequisite for automaticity. Because of the importance of automaticity for comprehension, it is important for teachers to know the difference between recognizing words and identifying them.

"Recognizing" and "identifying," of course, are responses that apply to more than just words. Our encounters with people, for example, may be occasions when we can identify them ("Hello, Mr. White") or, on the other hand, times when we are aware that we met them before but cannot now recall their names without help. So it is with reading. Encountering a word that we can name independently is word *identification;* realizing that it is familiar, even though we cannot name it directly, describes word *recognition.* Obviously, it is identifications that provide optimal conditions for comprehending. More specifically:

LEVELS OF KNOWING A WORD

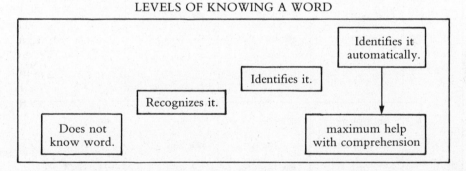

Even though it *is* identifications that are desirable, commercially prepared tests and workbooks commonly test word recognition (see Figure 5.3). In this case, the teacher names a word, and the children mark it. One possible explanation for the concentration on word recognition is the ease with which it can be assessed with a group. However, Figure 5.4 shows that testing word identification ability can also be achieved with a group and, in fact, can be done when they are working on their own. Figure 5.4 is also useful in making the point that the content of some workbook pages is helpful in providing ideas for teacher-made practice material. And practice is always essential for developing sight vocabularies. (A person's *sight vocabulary* is composed of all the words that he or she is able to name automatically, that is, "on sight.")

Figure 5.3

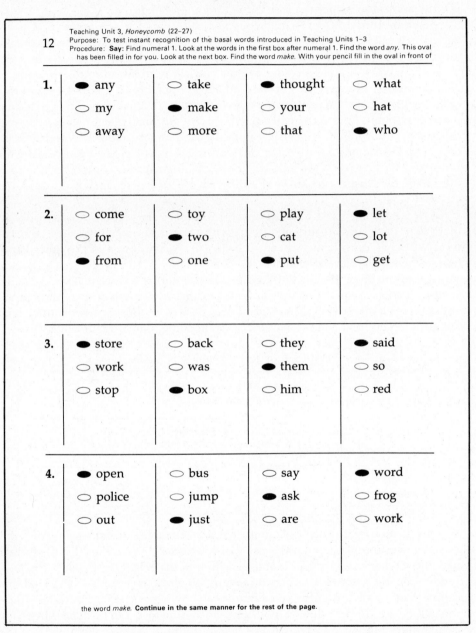

Teaching Unit 3, *Honeycomb* (22–27)
12   Purpose: To test instant recognition of the basal words introduced in Teaching Units 1–3
Procedure: **Say:** Find numeral 1. Look at the words in the first box after numeral 1. Find the word *any*. This oval has been filled in for you. Look at the next box. Find the word *make*. With your pencil fill in the oval in front of

1. ● any   ○ take   ● thought   ○ what
    ○ my   ● make   ○ your   ○ hat
    ○ away   ○ more   ○ that   ● who

2. ○ come   ○ toy   ○ play   ● let
    ○ for   ● two   ○ cat   ○ lot
    ● from   ○ one   ● put   ○ get

3. ● store   ○ back   ○ they   ● said
    ○ work   ○ was   ● them   ○ so
    ○ stop   ● box   ○ him   ○ red

4. ● open   ○ bus   ○ say   ● word
    ○ police   ○ jump   ● ask   ○ frog
    ○ out   ● just   ○ are   ○ work

the word *make.* **Continue in the same manner for the rest of the page.**

Durr, William K., LePere, Jean M., Alsin, Mary Lou, Bunyan, Ruth Patterson, and Shaw, Susan. Practice Book for *Honeycomb* (Teacher's Ed.). Boston: Houghton Mifflin Company, 1979, p. 12.

●   *This page is correctly called "word recognition"; however, it is not recognition that contributes maximally to reading. More specifically, the task of the reader is not to find a word named by another. Rather, the need is to name written words without help. Ability to produce a word independently is word identification.*

*   One way to deal with ability in word identification is illustrated on the following page in Figure 5.4. Why the exercise is called "Study Skills" (see the bottom of Figure 5.4) is not apparent.*

Figure 5.4

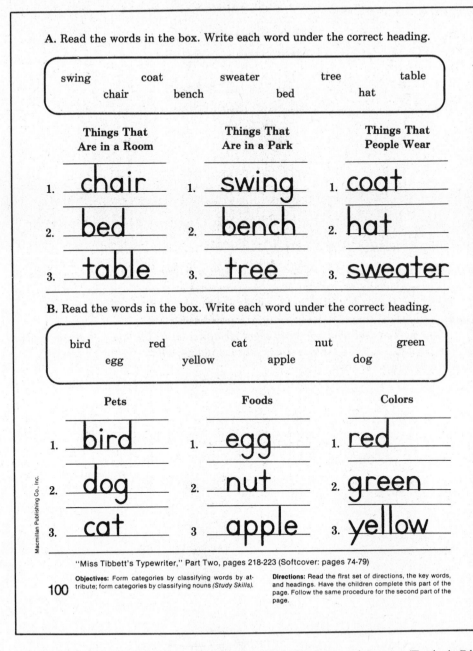

A. Read the words in the box. Write each word under the correct heading.

| swing | coat | sweater | tree | table |
| chair | bench | bed | hat | |

Things That Are in a Room
1. chair
2. bed
3. table

Things That Are in a Park
1. swing
2. bench
3. tree

Things That People Wear
1. coat
2. hat
3. sweater

B. Read the words in the box. Write each word under the correct heading.

| bird | red | cat | nut | green |
| egg | yellow | apple | dog | |

Pets
1. bird
2. dog
3. cat

Foods
1. egg
2. nut
3 apple

Colors
1. red
2. green
3. yellow

"Miss Tibbett's Typewriter," Part Two, pages 218-223 (Softcover: pages 74-79)

Objectives: Form categories by classifying words by attribute; form categories by classifying nouns *(Study Skills).*

100

Directions: Read the first set of directions, the key words, and headings. Have the children complete this part of the page. Follow the same procedure for the second part of the page.

Macmillan Publishing Co., Inc.

Smith, Carl, and Wardhaugh, Ronald. Workbook for *Secrets and Surprises* (Teacher's Ed.). New York: Macmillan Publishing Co., Inc., 1980, p. 100.

WORD LEARNABILITY

Anyone who has taught knows that some words are easier for students to remember than others. Why is there a difference?

For one thing, a word whose meaning is familiar is learned more quickly than one that is little more than a sound. Still easier are words whose referents are not only familiar but also of interest. Research further suggests that the learnability of a word is positively affected by the ease with which it evokes an image (23), which helps explain why nouns as a group are learned more readily than other classes of words. What all this suggests is the wisdom of dwelling on words (whenever it is possible) that are at least in the students' listening vocabularies, if not their speaking vocabularies, too. This guideline points to the need for definitions:

Listening Vocabulary. All the words that a person understands when another speaks them.
Speaking Vocabulary. All the words that a person can understand, pronounce, and use to communicate orally to others.
Reading Vocabulary. All the words that a person understands and can identify in their written form.
Writing Vocabulary. All the words that a person is able to spell, write, and understand well enough to use them for communicating to others.

Anyone working with students whose native language is not English needs to be especially sensitive to the guideline just referred to: select words that are at least in the students' listening vocabulary. The same teachers also need to keep in mind the basic importance of oral language for reading and, in addition, the constant need to expand vocabulary knowledge, a topic discussed in Chapter 10.

One further way to catalog words for the purpose of shedding light on their learnability divides them into *content* and *function* words. Content words contain meaning in and of themselves; thus they include nouns, verbs (with the exception of the verb *to be*), adjectives, and adverbs. The meaning of function words, on the other hand, is activated as they specify relationships among words that make up a phrase, clause, or sentence. Function words, as you can probably guess from the definition, are prepositions, conjunctions, auxiliary verbs, pronouns, articles, and the various forms of the verb *to be*. Because function words serve to hold the structure of connected text together, they are also called *structure* words. Examples of both content and function words follow:

Content words	*Function (structure) words*
people, chair, azure, silo,	at, but, an, not, or, the,
funnel, thumb, slow, exit,	been, off, were, the, be,
risky, herd, closet, candid	it, to, and, was, had, nor

Because of the significance of meaning for word learning, students have much more difficulty remembering function words than content words.

A section on word learnability cannot disregard the fact that some hold to the notion that words can be grouped according to grade levels. (I was reminded of this during a visit to a first grade on an excessively foggy morning. Although fog is a nuisance and even a hazard for motorists, it is a source of considerable excitement for six-year-olds, which is why I commented to the teacher, "I'm sure you'll be teaching the word *fog* today." Her response? "Oh, is that a first-grade word?") The fact that words get attached to grade levels is tied in with the notion that certain basal readers are to be used in certain grades; a word in a fourth-grade reader thus becomes a "fourth-grade word." While it is true that the meanings of words in more difficult readers are less likely to be known by six-year-olds than are the words in a beginning text, neat grade-level categories ignore the fact that children are ready to learn to read any word whose meaning is familiar regardless of when it appears in textbooks.

WHAT ELSE TEACHERS NEED TO KNOW ABOUT WHOLE WORD METHODOLOGY

Whether students succeed in remembering words presented as wholes depends on a number of factors, some of which have to do with how the words are taught. What contributes to effective teaching, therefore, will be considered now.

Words in Isolation versus Words in Context

A question that teachers commonly raise goes something like, "When I'm identifying a new word, should I put it in a sentence or should I write the word alone?" Like so many other questions about teaching, the answer to this one is, "It depends." Let me explain the hedging with illustrations.

For reading, individual words get attention as objects to study. This is different from oral language in which one word blends into the next, making for a continuous flow of speech rather than a series of clearly distinct words. Spoken words also receive unequal amounts of stress, making something like *blue and red* sound like "blue 'n red." One consequence of these characteristics of speech is that children are not always consciously aware of separate words. Therefore, in order to highlight them with word boundaries (to distinguish between *alone* and *a loan,* for example) and, further, to highlight the existence of such important but unstressed words as *and,* some new words should be introduced in context—in a phrase or sentence, for example. This is especially important at the start.

What *always* requires a context are function words, since they derive their meaning from other words. In this case, contexts may be as brief as *the girl* or *to the door,* as unusual as *red and blue and brown and yellow,* or as conventional as *The children ran to their bikes.*

In addition to function words, three other types require a context: homonyms, homographs, and homophones. A *homonym* is "a word of the same sound and spelling as another, but of different origin and meaning" (35, p. 87). Why contexts are essential when a homonym is introduced is illustrated below:

> I *can* do that.
> I need the *can* of fruit.
>
> A *host* of people were there.
> Mr. Lyle is a thoughtful *host.*

In contrast, a *homograph* is "a word with the same spelling as another but of different origin, sound, and meaning" (35, p. 87). Why homographs should also be introduced in the company of other words is demonstrated below:

> I *wind* the clock every night.
> Listen to that *wind* howl.
>
> The boy *dove* into the water.
> This *dove* is so white and soft.

Why *homophones* (words that are pronounced the same but spelled differently) require a context can be explained with a reference to what was heard in a classroom. The teacher wrote *I'll* on the board, pronounced it, then asked what it meant. Quickly one boy said, "It's where you walk in a store."

Visits to other classrooms have uncovered additional reasons for using contexts with new words. In one, the teacher wrote *am* on the chalkboard and told the children what it said. It happened that her pronunciation of *am* was sufficiently like the name of the letter *m* that it quickly generated a puzzled expression on one girl's face as well as the comment, "Mrs. _____, that's not an *m.* That's an *a* and an *m.*" Use of a context like *I am a teacher* would have eliminated the confusion and, simultaneously, assigned meaning to the function word *am.*

The importance of contexts—and of careful pronunciations—was underscored in another classroom in which *find* was a new word. After the teacher had written and identified *find,* she asked for examples of sentences that included it. The one offered first was revealing. With considerable pride a girl suggested, "It is a fine day."

While occurrences like these clarify the significance of contexts when new words are taught, others serve to explain when a context is unnecessary. In this case, a perfect example comes from a classroom observation that took place one Thursday morning. On Wednesday, a tornado had passed through the community, leaving behind ample evidence of its visit. To get Thursday started, the teacher wisely wrote *tornado* on the board, commenting, "I don't know if anyone can read this word, but I'm sure that everyone knows what it means." Although no child was able to identify *tornado,* once the teacher read it everyone could discuss it—and nobody needed a context. Clearly, experiencing the tornado had supplied a vivid one.

To sum up, then, content words whose meanings are familiar do not usually require a context when they are being taught; on the other hand, function words, homographs, homonyms, and homophones always require one. Whether a context is or is not needed, eventually new words should be presented alone so that students have the opportunity to examine their details in ways that the next section describes.

Attending to New Words

In its skeleton form, whole word methodology requires that a word be written and identified. ("The word that I just wrote says 'fence.' ") Learning theory suggests a further requirement: Be sure children look at the word *when* it is identified. At first, the reminder to get students to look at a word when it is named might seem unnecessary because it appears to be little more than common sense. Be that as it may, visits to classrooms reveal instances in which the importance of such a directive is overlooked. Let me cite just one example.

Using round robin reading, a second-grade teacher was with a group of ten. Pertinent to the present discussion is what happened while one child was reading aloud. When he was first asked to read, he immediately had difficulty with *toward,* so he looked up to the teacher for help. She told him what it said, and he continued. A few lines later he encountered *toward* once more, again did not know it, and again looked up to the teacher. Soon it was another child's turn; however, had the first one continued and come across *toward* once more, it is safe to predict that he still would not know what it said. Why not? Each time the teacher identified it, he was looking at her, not at *toward.*

Again, an important lesson can be learned from the observation: *Encourage students to look at a word at the time it is being identified.* Implied in this highly important guideline are two others:

New words should not be presented to as many as an entire class.
Whole word instruction should not begin until everyone seems ready to pay attention to the words.

In addition to looking at a new word at the right time, students must also attend to its details if they are going to remember it. One way to get them to do that is to have them name, spell, and rename the word once it has been identified. A note of caution about this, however. Used with beginners who are still struggling to remember letter names, the spelling turns their thoughts away from the word as they try to recall the names of the letters. Therefore, only when children are able to name letters *automatically* should they be asked to spell a word as a way of getting them to attend to its details.

Admittedly, some claim that children should never be asked to spell a word when learning to read is the goal. Their objection is based on the fact that able readers name words as quickly as they name letters, which means they hardly depend upon individual letters for identifying words. While nobody can refute this observation, counterclaims are still warranted. It is appropriate to point out, for example, that children who are learning to read are involved with a task that is different from that of a fluent reader. Further, the recommended attention to letters, combined with a number of opportunities to name a word, has as its *eventual* goal the ability to identify it automatically as well as correctly. A more general reaction to the claim that words should not be spelled (or traced) is a warning: Be wary of conclusions about children and reading that are drawn from research with mature readers.

Because the *distinctive features* of a new word (what distinguishes it from all other words) must be noted one way or another—and no assertion is made here about there being one best way to get children to notice them—some teachers rely on contrasts to foster the required attention. This means that if a new word is *soup,* it would first be written and identified. Next, a known and similar-looking word is shown:★

soup

soap

The children might next be asked to tell how the two words are both similar and different. If they know something about letter-sound relationships, comments about the vowel sounds and how they are recorded in the two words would be appropriate, too.

If no known words are available to serve as contrasts—and this is common with beginners—a new one can be listed with unknown words, once it has been identified. With a word such as *house,* for instance, children might be asked to tell which word says "house" in a list like the following:

1. dime

2. house

3. many

★ The use of print rather than cursive writing when words are introduced is recommended even when students are using cursive writing themselves. It is specifically recommended here because print helps to highlight differences and similarities. Helping, too, is the careful placement of the two words under each other.

A more demanding list follows:

1. mouse

2. dance

3. house

4. horse

Although a question like "Which of these words says 'house'?" is only dealing with word recognition, it is one step in the process of helping children identify *house*. (The earlier objection to the many workbook pages that deal with word recognition has to do with the fact that they do not go beyond recognition to identification.)

If you are now wondering how contrasts encourage students to attend to features of words that might otherwise go unnoticed, I can offer an explanation that has nothing to do with reading and goes back to my childhood. When I was in elementary school, identical twins moved into our neighborhood and eventually into my class. Because they dressed alike in every detail, it was impossible to tell them apart—or so I thought at first. For weeks I had to ask, "Are you Marjorie or Marie?" Each time I asked I resolved to try a little harder to learn to make a distinction, but to no avail.

All that changed the first time I was with the twins as they sat next to one another on the steps of their front porch. That provided the chance to make comparisons; with the opportunity, the two began to look unexpectedly different. (That is, the distinctive features of each became apparent.) One had a tiny scar on her forehead, something that I had not noticed previously. She also had a slightly crooked tooth that gave her mouth a somewhat different appearance from that of her sister. I saw that the hairlines at the foreheads were not identical. Once I noted such differences—and none was apparent until the contrast was made—the one job remaining was to fix in my mind which set of features went with the name "Marjorie" and which went with "Marie."

So it is with word learning. Contrasts help children become aware of the distinctive features of words. Once the children note these, they must learn to remember the response that goes with each set. And that is accomplished with practice.

Remembering New Words

The purpose of practice (repeated identifications) is to help students remember words permanently. Because of its critical importance for automatic identifications, practice is discussed in detail in later sections of the chapter. Now, a related topic that goes under the heading of *cues* will be considered.

Applied to word learning, a cue is what is used to help establish a connection between a given word (stimulus) and what it says (response). Or, to put it somewhat differently, one or more features of a written word are selected as a prompt for its identification. If what is selected fixes the correct identification permanently, it is a *relevant* cue. If it offers only temporary assistance and eventually fosters confusion and erroneous responses, it is *irrelevant*. With classroom illustrations, let me cite examples of the latter. (Subsequent chapters give ample attention to relevant cues.)

An abundant use of irrelevant cues occurred in a first-grade classroom close to the beginning of the year when the teacher was reviewing color words. As she wrote each on the chalkboard, she used a differently colored piece of chalk. The word *blue,* for instance, was written with blue chalk, *yellow* with yellow chalk, and so on. Predictably, when she finished writing the words, the children had no difficulty remembering them. Equally predictable is that those who did not know the words prior to this colorful lesson would not know them when they appeared later in books or written with white chalk or black ink. Why? The teacher had used an irrelevant cue (color) to help establish connections between visual stimuli (words) and correct responses to them.

To help children establish connections, some teachers outline the configuration of words. In introducing *funny,* to cite an illustration, they show:

The problem with explicit attention to contour is made clear below, and is the reason configuration is an irrelevant cue.

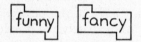

Another example of an irrelevant cue was heard in a classroom in which *look* was a new word. After writing it, the teacher commented, "This word says 'look.' It's easy to remember because it has two eyes in the middle—just what you use when you look at something." While this observation might help temporarily, dependence on two "eyes" in the middle for remembering *look* inevitably leads to confusion, specifically, when words like *book* or perhaps *foot* have to be learned. The child who later responded "see" when shown *look* points up another kind of confusion fostered by the teacher's comment.

In another classroom, the teacher was introducing new words in preparation for reading a story; one of the words was *monkey*. As with the other new words, the teacher wrote *monkey* on the chalkboard and identified it. She next told the students that they would be reading about a monkey; she also said there was an easy way to remember the word that said "monkey." At this point she explained that, like a monkey, it had "a tail at the end." If it happened that the only word in our language "ending with a tail" was *monkey,* the teacher's comment would help. However, other words not only end in *y* but also begin with *m* and, further, are about the same length as *monkey* (for example, *money*); thus the teacher's "help" called attention to a highly irrelevant cue.

Two further examples of irrelevant cues need to be cited because they were offered by two student teachers *after* they read an earlier version of this chapter. Their assignment was to describe practice to help children remember one high-frequency word. Correctly, one student chose *and;* the other, *the.* Correctly, too, each sample of practice presented the function word in contexts. Unfortunately, however, one student printed *and* in red—all the remaining words in each sentence were printed in black—while the other took the time to form *the* with yarn. In addition to using irrelevant cues, the two students demonstrated how easy it is to work hard on the wrong things.

To discuss (and, hopefully, to discourage) teachers' uses of irrelevant cues is not to deny that students use what is irrelevant quite on their own. Here I cannot help but recall a child who, when shown ten small word cards, quickly identified all ten words. Later, new cards were prepared for the same words, after which the child looked at *famous* as if she had never seen it before. In one sense, she had not. When the original card displaying *famous* was examined, it was found that a small piece of one corner had been torn off. Apparently, what this student had been responding to was a three-cornered card, not *famous.* What she had been relying on was an irrelevant cue.

Another irrelevant cue that children use is pictures—for instance, those in their readers. Because manuals often advise teachers to tell children to "look at the picture" when they cannot recall a word, pictures as cues for word identification requires further discussion.

Probably the best discussion can begin with a reference to what was heard in a classroom in which a child who was reading aloud was unable to recall the word *school.* His teacher suggested, "Look at the picture," which showed a building that was obviously a school. Immediately the puzzled reader said "school," not even looking at the written symbol for it.★ I believe it is safe to say that when he encountered *school* again, the same problem occurred.

This negative response to an unfortunately common practice is not meant to deny the significance of pictures for instruction. To the contrary, for pictures are *very* helpful at all grade levels in specifying word meanings and promoting oral discussions. Some that are in books also succeed in pricking children's curiosity to the point that they want to read the text that goes with the pictures. (In contrast, pictures that reveal the story reduce motivation.) I have also been in classrooms in which carefully selected pictures prompted students to write imaginative stories and descriptions. Nevertheless, as cues for word identification, pictures are irrelevant.

With all the attention that has now gone to irrelevant cues, you must wonder what could possibly be left that is relevant. To answer, let us first consider the

---

★ The frequency of this warrants repetition of an earlier reminder: Be sure students look at a word *when* it is being named.

meaning of relevant cue: permanent features that distinguish things. One permanent feature of a written word is the sequence of its letters. How significant
sequence is becomes apparent in words like *tap, pat,* and *apt.* The significance of
sequence prompted the earlier recommendation to have children name, spell,
and rename a new word, once it has been identified. To foster attention to
sequence was the reason another recommendation was made to provide children
with contrasts.

Other cues that are relevant for word identification are letter-sound relationships, which is why two subsequent chapters deal with phonics. The fact that
the structure of words is an additional source of relevant cues explains why a third
chapter will discuss structural analysis and how to teach it.

A Summary

Some of what has now been said about whole word methodology is pinpointed
below.

TEACHING NEW WORDS WITH WHOLE WORD METHODOLOGY

1. Write the new word either alone or in a context.
2. Pointing to the word, ask, "Does anyone know what this word says?" If nobody
   does, read the word, or, if it is in a context, read that and then reread the new
   word.
3. Pointing to the new word, have the students read, spell, and reread it.
4. Make sure the meaning(s) of the word is understood.
5. If the new word resembles known words, list some under it. Discuss similarities
   and differences.
6. At the end, erase all words except the new one, which the students will read,
   spell, and reread.

While the procedure just described should not be carried out in exactly the
same way with every new word, one detail should never be forgotten: *Make sure
that students look at the new word each time it is named.* Failure to recognize the
significance of this for learning is one reason why instruction with new words can
be both inefficient and unproductive.

WORD PRACTICE

Equipped with the ability to identify words automatically, students are free to
attend to the meaning of phrases, sentences, paragraphs, and more. Because the
aim of practice (repeated identifications) is automaticity, it is a most important
component of instructional programs *at all grade levels.*

What is done with word identification and practice before a selection is read ought to be sufficient to put all new words—or at least all those that are necessary for understanding the selection—into students' sight vocabularies. Checking up on their ability to identify them after the selection has been read is a wise procedure to follow too. (One way to do that was referred to earlier when work with basal reader vocabulary was depicted.) Responses may indicate a need for more practice; ways to provide for it will be described later.

If certain students consistently require more practice than others who are in the same instructional group, it is possible that they are being asked to cope with overly difficult material. If so, they should be given easier selections. On the other hand, extra practice may be all that is necessary to remedy the problem.

Need for Interesting Practice

While teachers should not think of themselves as being entertainers, superior ones do try to make word practice as interesting as possible. Making such an effort is important because involvement and achievement go hand in hand. That some small embellishment is all it takes to make practice attractive was brought home to me when I was visiting regularly in a fourth grade in which there were two boys with major deficiencies in reading. Although the teacher's desire to help was praiseworthy, the help itself was not. Day after day, nothing but a flash-card technique (word card is held up and one or more students name the word) was used. Day after day, it elicited little enthusiasm and, seemingly, little learning. What the teacher was demonstrating, in fact, was that *more* is not always a remedy—especially not more of the same.

To help, a slight alteration was suggested that created an unexpected amount of enthusiasm from the boys: List and number on the chalkboard brief phrases containing troublesome words. Have the boys take turns selecting number cards from a bag, which indicate the phrase they are to read. A correct response means the card can be kept; an incorrect one means it goes back into the bag.

In other classrooms, teachers have been successful with unadorned flash-card practice because, in these instances, it was presented as preparation for something interesting.* In one room, for example, flash-card practice served as a means for being successful with an attractive Halloween bulletin board:

- Among the materials displayed on the board was a large paper basket. A backing allowed for an opening at the top. Inside the opening was a pocket

---

* The need to extend a word of caution about all uses of flash-card practice was identified during a classroom visit. Individual words had been printed on cards but, unfortunately, as the teacher showed them she often covered the bottom parts of words with her fingers. With a word like *much*, no harm was done. With one like *great*, covering up the bottom part of the *g* made it look like a manuscript *a*. Be careful!

that held small paper pumpkins on which words and phrases had been printed. Students took turns picking pumpkins. Correct responses meant a pumpkin could be kept (temporarily); incorrect answers put the pumpkins back into the pocket.

This board was used under the teacher's supervision; children working in pairs could use it, too. At other times, different materials replaced the basket and pumpkins: cornucopia and fruit, net and fish, mailbox and envelopes, and jar and cookies.

Other Characteristics of Desirable Practice

In addition to being interesting, the most productive word practice is characterized by other features, four of which are discussed below.

Nonpunitive.   Children learning to read have to be willing to risk making mistakes, which is why practice ought to take place in a nonpunitive setting. That is, it should be seen by students as something that helps, not as a time for teachers to identify and punish errors. This indicates that a teacher comment like the following should be the rule rather than the exception: "I noticed yesterday that you were mixing up some words. Let's go over them, and then I'll ask you to do this sheet so that we can find out if they are still causing problems."

Matched to needs.   The teacher's comment underscores another characteristic of desirable practice: it is matched to needs. Depending on the need, a solution may simply be extra practice with certain words. Or, if there are students who appear to depend only on initial letters to identify words, a more specialized kind of practice should be planned. In this case, oral responses to lists of words like the following are appropriate:

best	best	beach
by	bell	bead
ball	bed	beak
but	beg	beast

Clearly described.   Directions for practice should be sufficiently clear that students know exactly what to do. As they advance in their ability to read, written directions should be used with increased frequency. This gives children something to refer to—a great help with long-term and multiple assignments. Reading the directions also provides extra reading practice.

Checked for correctness.   In one way or another, responses should be checked to make sure that what is being practiced, and therefore learned, is correct. Such checking is not done to seek out "offenders" but to provide information that should affect future instruction and practice.

The need to know whether a response is correct points up a shortcoming in group responses: a teacher can never be certain that all members are responding correctly or are responding at all. Some teachers minimize the problem by distributing pairs of small word cards to the members of a group. At various times, the cards might show *yes, no; true, false;* and *fact, opinion.* After silently reading sentence cards held by the teacher (each containing one or more troublesome words), students hold up an appropriate card. In response to a sentence like *The river in the story was deep,* the card showing *false* might be called for. Whether special devices are or are not used, all members of a group should be encouraged to respond. A total response is most likely to occur when the group is not too large.

EXAMPLES OF WORD PRACTICE

Responses from everyone are also likely to occur when the same thing is not always done in the same way. The following sections, therefore, show some of the variety that is possible for word practice.

Book Reading

Just recently, a day was spent in a school visiting first-, third-, fifth-, and sixth-grade classrooms. While each room showed commendable activities, in none were the children reading anything but basal readers, workbooks, and ditto sheets. That is why illustrations of word practice commence with book reading.

When a book is not overly difficult, reading it is one of the most ideal kinds of practice for a number of reasons. To begin, it provides for word practice in realistic settings—that is, in the context of sentences and more. When few words cause problems, reading a book also allows for exclusive attention to meaning, which, combined with a suitable rate, promotes comprehension. And with that comes such desirable by-products as enjoyment and self-confidence.

Teachers who appreciate the potential of book reading always make certain that they do not become so intent on teaching skills that they never develop readers. They also make certain that classroom libraries reflect students' interests. One observed teacher who kept interests in mind had a classroom collection that included series like the Nancy Drew books; cartoon, riddle, and joke books; other books dealing with such topics as judo; and still others that described simple experiments. Aware that some students are intimidated by length, this same teacher made sure that books with relatively few pages were available. Keeping difficulty in mind, she saw to it that free-choice materials allowed for selections that would foster confidence, not insecurity.

How to interest children in reading books is discussed in Chapter 14, starting on page 390. References listed at the end of this chapter offer additional ideas (24, 26), tell of books that children especially enjoy (7), and name still others that are easy to read (3, 8).

Bulletin Boards

Because bulletin-board displays can make practice appealing, let me continue with examples of word practice by describing a little of what has been seen in classrooms.

- In April, a board with a spring theme had been assembled; among its details was a large bushy tree. Red paper apples, on which words requiring practice appeared, were also ready. Each time a word was identified correctly, that apple went on the tree. To provide additional practice, all the apples were picked.

Starting with an idea like this one, a teacher is likely to think of others. For example, leaves might replace the apples or, in December, ornaments and a pine tree are appropriate. Appealing, too, would be the chance to build a pine tree. To do this, words and phrases could be printed on small, rectangular cards. As each is read correctly, that card would be thumbtacked to a board until a triangular tree is finally assembled. Later, the same rectangular cards can become bricks, now allowing for the gradual construction of one or more buildings—and, of course, for more word practice, too.

Children's interest in days like Halloween should also be put to good use:

- Every day starting on October 1, a paper ghost is added to a bulletin board. Appearing on each will be a word selected by the children as being especially difficult. Daily, all the ghosts on the board will be read until thirty-one have accumulated by the time Halloween arrives.

For variety, paper ghosts might also be placed in a "trick or treat" bag so that students can take turns pulling them out and reading them. Now the ghosts might show *the boy, an apple, these toys,* or, for more advanced readers, *the pranks, that symbol, my costume.*

Enthusiastic responses to "pulling things out" prompted one teacher to make a paper hat, now to be used as a magician's hat. Words were printed on small, rabbit-shaped cards that were pulled out of the hat by a magician and then identified by children in need of practice.

Games

Children's natural interest in games should be taken advantage of; a few more possibilities for word practice, therefore, are described below.

- Children can be soldiers as they march around a table on which small sentence cards have been placed face down. At the drill sergeant's command "Halt," the children select the closest cards and take turns reading them. An error results in a card going to the sergeant; success allows a private to keep his or hers. Then the marching resumes. The object is to keep the sergeant from getting more cards than any of the privates.

- Large sheets of tagboard can be ruled in squares that must be large enough to accommodate a written sentence. All squares are covered with number cards. A small spinner is needed too. For this game, each child gets a board. Each also takes turns spinning the pointer. The number at which it stops indicates which square to uncover. A student who can read the sentence now displayed keeps the number card. The student who cannot re-covers the sentence. The winner is the one with the largest number of cards.

- A football floor game can be made by drawing eleven vertical lines on a large, rectangular sheet of oak tag. Each line is numbered to correspond to the markings on a football field. The ends of the sheet are labeled "end zone." Two brown paper footballs and a stack of small cards on which sentences have been printed are needed too. Each member of a football team takes turns selecting a card. The student who can read the sentence moves a football from the fifty-yard line to the forty-yard line; if he cannot, he moves the ball back ten yards toward the opponent's end zone. The first team to make a touchdown is the winner. The game proceeds by placing the football back on the fifty-yard line.

Even though games can be highly successful in winning and keeping children's attention, certain reminders and guidelines are necessary if their educational significance is to be realized.

Games and Word Practice

1. The appeal of a game often interests students in making preparations for it. Such preparation can be unadorned flash-card practice.
2. A game and the details for playing it should be simple. Otherwise more time will go to teaching students how to play it than to the educational reason for having the game.
3. Participants should be students who will learn from the game. "Why am I using this?" is a good question for any teacher who relies on games to enliven practice.
4. If teams are required, the teacher should select members. When students do

the selecting, much time is wasted. Hurt feelings can be another undesirable consequence.

5. If a game is competitive, students who are frightened by competition should not participate, nor should those who do not have a chance to win.

6. The best games lose their appeal if they are around all the time or are played too often.

7. A game is not a game if students have to be coaxed to play it.

Phrase and Sentence Practice

When teachers keep in mind that most out–of–school reading is of connected text, not individual words, they make certain that most word practice concentrates on more than isolated words. What can happen to students when teachers make excessive use of isolated word practice has been effectively summarized by Hayes (17):

> They,
> read,
> as,
> if,
> every,
> word,
> were,
> followed,
> by,
> a,
> comma.

None of these observations is meant to discourage all uses of single word practice or to minimize the importance of isolating or, perhaps, contrasting words when confusion indicates a need for close scrutiny. Instead, the intention is to underscore the fact that using nothing but isolated word drill has undesirable consequences.

At the start, phrases foster attention to thoughts rather than to individual words. For example, after saying, "Put your hands . . . ," a teacher could show cards like the following:

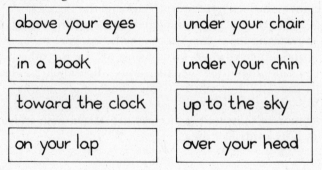

above your eyes	under your chair
in a book	under your chin
toward the clock	up to the sky
on your lap	over your head

Phrase cards like those shown next—the difficulty of the vocabulary depends on the students—go with the direction, "Think of a sentence that includes these words."

by the side of the house

above these buildings

over a mountainous road

into the huge cavern

among flowers and shrubs

Similar directions are appropriate for other types of processing units:

jumped up

quickly and quietly disappeared

an elderly man with thinning hair

the bulk of their problems

Other phrase cards with connected text can be attached to a bulletin board. This time, the teacher asks questions whose answers are on the cards. Other displays might be more elaborate—for instance, like what was seen in a classroom to highlight a much enjoyed story, "Jack and the Beanstalk." In this case, a tall, thick stalk had been made by rolling green paper. Long leaves, each displaying a phrase, grew along the stalk. Also on the board were paper figures of both Jack and the giant. Students took turns being one or the other, and with the selected figure in hand, they attempted the climb. Misread phrases brought a child crashing to the ground, after which it was someone else's turn to attempt the climb.

Early attention to sentence practice can get started with still another activity, now directed by cards like these:

Jump twice and stop.

Get a book from the table.

Carry a chair toward me.

Stand and then sit.

Close your eyes.

Look up here later.

At any grade level, word identification practice and sentence reading can take place with students who have two small cards displaying *yes* and *no*. In this instance, larger cards like the following are read silently by everyone, after which the appropriate small card is held up.

The color of grass is always green.

Men and women are called adults.

A square is a rectangle.

Useful information is in books.

Another way to use connected text follows:

Display pictures. Distribute phrase and sentence cards. The job for each student is to match a card with a picture. With some groups, a card might display *pretty child*. With others, cards might show *an evening of magnificent beauty* or, perhaps, *Anticipation was written on their faces*.★

The final example of word practice highlights meanings, which is important because unless students are encouraged to think about meaning, they might give

★ Notice how this use of pictures is essentially different from what was referred to earlier as being an irrelevant cue. Criticized earlier was the use of a picture to identify a word, often without giving attention to the word itself. In the suggestion above, content is being matched with content, a practice that relies on comprehension rather than on routine word drill.

all their attention to pronunciation. The same example also shows how one idea for practice can be adjusted to accommodate different levels of reading ability.

- Prepare envelopes, each labeled with a category—for instance, Size, Color, Sound. Print appropriate words on small cards, such as *large* (or *gigantic*), *blue* (or *azure*), *loud* (or *deafening*). Distribute envelopes and words. Each student in need of practice will be asked to read the words silently and to place them in the appropriate envelopes. (Preparation includes a discussion of the labels and a review of the words.) If a teacher cannot be available immediately to check responses, students can write their names on the envelopes to allow for a later check. By simply crossing out a name, envelopes can be reused with others.

WORD IDENTIFICATION AND NONSTANDARD DIALECTS

Before this chapter on whole word instruction and practice concludes, attention needs to go to nonstandard dialects. That topic is relevant because some believe that, for students who speak a nonstandard dialect, the meaning of "correct response" (to a written word) is different from what it is for speakers of standard English.

Nonstandard Dialects

One way to describe standard English is to say it is the language found in textbooks and spoken by well-educated people. Dialects described as nonstandard English are listed by Venezky (32) as follows:

> Northern urban Negro
> Southern Mountain (Appalachian)
> Spanish-American
> American Indian
> Hawaiian pidgin
> Southern rural (Negro and white)
> Acadian English

The nonstandard dialect called black English has received the greatest amount of attention, so I will use it to explain why questions have been raised about the meaning of "correct response."

Black English

Deviations of black English from standard English are usually categorized under the headings *phonological* (differences in pronunciation), *morphological* (differences in inflections), and *syntactic* (differences in sentence structure). Examples of each follow (19):

Category	Feature	Examples
Phonological	Stress pattern	The balloon got under the umbrella.
Phonological	Simplification of final consonant blend	Right behin' him . . .
Morphological	Loss of *-ed* suffix	It was a boy name' J. T.
Morphological	Loss of *-s* in plurals	He had bruise' an' . . .
Syntactic	Noun + pronoun = subject	The principal he . . .
Syntactic	Question inversion	An' his mother wonder why was he late.

The significance that nonstandard dialects have for those who teach reading depends on whether they subscribe to the *deficit* theory or to the *difference* theory, each of which will be explained.

Deficit Point of View

At one time, it was taken for granted that black English (and all other nonstandard dialects) was inferior and thus needed to be improved by being changed. This is the deficit point of view, which supports the notion that one responsibility of the school is to change the speech of nonstandard speakers to standard English. Whether it is capable of making such a change is debatable (29), but that does not have to be discussed here. What does require attention is the effect of the deficit point of view on teachers' expectations for reading.

The most noticeable effect has to do with word identifications. This is so because oral reading, which is so common in classrooms, centers attention on students' responses to each printed word. One consequence is that saying exactly what is on a page and pronouncing each word correctly are assigned as much importance as is comprehension. While those who hold to the deficit point of view would accept pronunciation variations associated with the well-educated Bostonian or, for example, the well-educated Philadelphian, they would be less likely to accept variations that reflect nonstandard dialects. Consequently, the latter would be corrected. One possible consequence of the corrections has been cited by Lipton:

> In forcing a child to call words accurately by continual references to his errors . . . we deny him the opportunity to read within the framework of his own language

development. This condition has caused many children to avoid reading and to become failures with the reading process. [20, p. 760]

Difference Point of View

Allowing a child "the opportunity to read within the framework of his own language development" sums up the *difference* point of view. From this perspective, differences in a given dialect are not equated with deficiency and inferiority. Prompting this more accepting stance has been the research of linguists (9, 30, 32) who have analyzed various back dialects and have shown that they are neither slang nor a sloppy, inferior version of standard English. Instead, they are ordered on the basis of highly developed principles and rules. While surface differences between standard English and such dialects do exist, nothing is lacking in the latter for successful communication.

Successful Reading

Although not all teachers subscribe to the difference point of view, it is imperative that all bear in mind the essence of successful reading so that distinctions are made between deficiencies in reading and differences in language.

Essentially, reading is comprehending. It is *not*—contrary to what practices like round robin reading seem to imply—a performing art. This means that whether students comprehend is *the* key matter. Whether they read with expression and in standard English is less critical.

To urge teachers to keep in mind the basic nature and purpose of reading is not to take the position that all deviations from what appears on a page are acceptable, that is, are "correct." Rather, the point being made is that what *is* acceptable for any given child is determined not only by what is printed but also by his dialect. If what he says when he reads aloud is what he would say were he speaking, should he be corrected? Wolfram, a sociolinguist, responds by saying, "If a child reads a passage in such a way that it systematically differs from standard English where his indigenous dialect differs, he has successfully read the passage" (34, p. 16). Kenneth Goodman, an educator, refers to these acceptable deviations as "dialect-based miscues" and maintains that:

> Rejection or correction by the teacher of any dialect-based miscue moves the reader away from using his own linguistic competence to the teacher's expected responses to the text. Word-for-word accuracy, in a narrow sense, becomes the goal rather than the meaning. . . . In encouraging divergent speakers to use their language competence . . . and accepting their dialect-based miscues, we minimize the effect of dialect differences. In rejecting them, we maximize the effect. [15, pp. 11–12]

If teachers of nonstandard speakers are going to be able to distinguish between dialect differences and word identification errors, they must be knowledgeable about students' speech patterns. Because of the extensive work that has been done with black English, existing publications provide a number of descriptions that are helpful (5, 14, 15, 33). What would also help is reduced attention to oral reading, since that fosters corrections by teachers whenever students do not say exactly what is on a page or when they pronounce words in their own dialect.

Surprisingly, a recent visit to a second-grade class while round robin reading was taking place uncovered one teacher who even felt obligated to correct "mispronunciations" by a bright, able child who had recently arrived from Australia. Clearly, the teacher was mistaken about the essential nature of reading. What its essence is (comprehension) needs to be kept in mind by all teachers as an increasingly large number of students whose native tongue is not English enroll in our schools.

SUMMARY

Identifying new words as wholes has been the subject of Chapter 5. Naming whole words, usually referred to as whole word methodology, was recommended as the way to get reading started.

When reading ability *is* getting started, all new words have to be directly identified since children lack the ability to decode them themselves. At that point, words that merit attention are those that (a) are of special interest and (b) appear in whatever material the children are expected to read. Inevitably, words from the second source will include service words.

Once children are able to use letter-sound relationships, word structure, and contexts to identify new or forgotten words, whole word methodology should enter into instruction only when a word is so irregularly spelled that the most advanced decoding ability will not help in getting it figured out.

Any teacher using whole word methodology at any grade level needs to decide whether to introduce a new word alone or in the context of other known words. Helpful with such decisions is the division of words that catalogs them as content and function words. While the former do not always require a context, the latter do since, by themselves, they are meaningless. Among the content words that need a context are homonyms, homographs, and homophones.

Just as the meaning of new words determines whether a context is needed, so too does it affect the amount of practice required for automaticity. Since the most meaningful words are the easiest to remember, a safe assumption is that function words will require more practice than content words. But both kinds will require some practice, a fact not always recognized especially in the middle and upper grades.

Essentially, practice (repeated identifications) allows for attention to relevant cues—that is, to those features of a word that distinguish it from all other words. The importance of relevant cues for permanently correct identifications is the reason Chapter 5 spent considerable time illustrating cues that are relevant and cues that are not. The importance of automatic identifications for comprehension is the reason the chapter also used a generous amount of space to describe ways to provide students with interesting practice because that is the kind that wins and keeps their attention.

Although for a long time, the meaning of "correct" response was taken for granted, recent years have witnessed a growing acceptance of responses that differ from an author's words in ways that match the reader's dialect. That is why Chapter 5 concluded with a discussion of nonstandard dialects and what they signify for the meaning of "correct" response. The need to make a distinction between successful reading (comprehending) and how a reader orally pronounces words was especially underscored not only for students who speak nonstandard dialects but also for those whose native language is not English.

REVIEW

1.   One recommendation in Chapter 5 was: Identify words for students only when there is no alternative. The chapter explained that the guideline is related to independence which, it said, is one important goal of an instructional program. In this instance, what is the meaning of *independence*?

2.   Let us say that students *are* able to figure out a new word by themselves with the help of what they know about letters and sounds and word structure. Will they still need to practice that word?

3.   A large number of terms were introduced in Chapter 5. See if you can define those listed below.

alphabetic writing system	function word
automaticity	high-frequency word
content word	practice
cue	service word
decoding	sight vocabulary

4.   Write down the first three sentences that come to mind. Next, underline all the structure words. Finally, what *is* a structure word?

5.   Explain the difference between word *recognition* and word *identification*. Which does reading require? Why?

6.   Color as an irrelevant cue for identifying words was discussed in Chapter 5. Are the following additional examples of a questionable use of color?

● A ditto sheet showed a list of sentences, each containing a word that named a color. Directions were to read each sentence and underline the color word with a crayon of the same color.

● Large chart paper to which a second sheet of paper had been pasted allowed for a board showing rows of window-like flaps that, when lifted, revealed a small square of colored paper. On each flap, the name of the color underneath was printed. By picking up a flap, children could learn whether their identification of the word was correct.

REFERENCES

1. Anderson, Clara F. "Black English Dialect and the Classroom Teacher." *Reading Teacher* 33 (February 1980): 571–577.

2. Barnitz, John G. "Black English and Other Dialects: Sociolinguistic Implications for Reading Instruction." *Reading Teacher* 33 (April 1980): 779–786.

3. Bissett, Donald J., and Moline, Ruth E. "Books in the Classroom." *Language Arts* 53 (May 1976): 504–509.

4. Bloomfield, Leonard. "Linguistics and Reading." *Elementary English Review* 19 (April–May 1942): 125–130, 183–186.

5. Burling, Robins. *English in Black and White*. New York: Holt, Rinehart and Winston, 1973.

6. Ceprano, Maria A. "A Review of Selected Research on Methods of Teaching Sight Words." *Reading Teacher* 35 (December 1981): 314–322.

7. Children's Book Council and IRA. "Children's Trade Books." *Reading Teacher* 30 (October 1976): 50–63.

8. Cunningham, Pat. "Books for Beginners." *Reading Teacher* 34 (May 1981): 952–954.

9. DeStefano, Johanna S. *Language, Society and Education: A Profile of Black English*. Worthington, Ohio: Charles A. Jones Publishing Company, 1973.

10. Dillingofski, Mary Sue. "Sociolinguistics and Reading: A Review of the Literature." *Reading Teacher* 33 (December 1979): 307–311.

11. Dolch, Edward W. *Problems in Reading*. Champaign, Ill.: Garrard Press, 1948.

12. Durkin, Dolores. "What Classroom Observations Reveal about Reading Comprehension Instruction." *Reading Research Quarterly* 14, no. 4 (1978–1979): 481–533.

13. Erdman, Loula Grace. "The Things They Write Me." *Elementary English* 51 (October 1974): 999–1002.

14. Fasold, R. W., and Wolfram, W. A. "Some Linguistic Features of Negro Dialect." In *Teaching Standard English in the Inner City*. Edited by Ralph W. Fasold and Roger Shuy, pp. 41–86. Washington, D.C.: Center for Applied Linguistics, 1970.

15. Goodman, Kenneth S., and Buck, Catherine. "Dialect Barriers to Reading Comprehension Revisited." *Reading Teacher* 27 (October 1973): 6–12.

16. Haber, Ralph N., and Haber, Lyn R. "The Shape of a Word Can Specify Its Meaning." *Reading Research Quarterly* 16, no. 3 (1981): 334–345.

17. Hayes, Alfred S. *Language and Reading: A Linguist's Views*. New York: Harcourt, Brace and World, 1969.

18. Karlsen, Bjorn, and Blocker, Margaret. "Black Children and Final Consonant Sounds." *Reading Teacher* 27 (February 1974): 462–463.

19. Lass, Bonnie. "The Relationship between the Oral Language of Black English Speakers and Their Achievement in Reading." Ph.D. dissertation, University of Illinois, 1976.

20. Lipton, Aaron. "Miscalling While Reading Aloud: A Point of View." *Reading Teacher* 25 (May 1972): 759–762.

21. Makita, Kiyoshi. "The Rarity of Reading Disability in Japanese Children." *American Journal of Orthopsychiatry* 38 (July 1968): 599–614.

22. Monteith, Mary K. "A Whole Word List Catalog." *Reading Teacher* 29 (May 1976): 844–847.

23. Paivio, Allan. "Mental Imagery in Associative Learning and Memory." *Psychological Review* 76 (May 1969): 241–263.

24.   Pillar, Arlene M. "Individualizing Book Reviews." *Elementary English* 52 (April 1975): 467–469.

25.   Rigg, Pat. "Dialect and/in/for Reading." *Language Arts* 55 (March 1978): 285–290.

26.   Ryan, Florence H. "Taking the Boredom Out of Book Reports." *Elementary English* 51 (October 1974): 987–989.

27.   Samuels, S. Jay. "Automatic Decoding and Reading Comprehension." *Language Arts* 53 (March 1976): 323–325.

28.   Samuels, S. J.; Begy, Gerald; and Chen, Chaur Ching. "Comparison of Word Recognition Speed and Strategies of Less Skilled and More Highly Skilled Readers." *Reading Research Quarterly* 11, no. 1 (1975–1976): 72–86.

29.   Shuy, Roger W. "Learning to Talk Like Teachers." *Language Arts* 58 (February 1981): 168–174.

30.   Shuy, Roger W. "Some Considerations for Developing Beginning Reading Materials for Ghetto Children." *Journal of Reading Behavior* 1 (Spring 1969): 33–43.

31.   Singer, Harry. "Sight Word Learning with and without Pictures: A Critique of Arlin, Scott, and Webster's Research." *Reading Research Quarterly* 15, no. 2 (1980): 290–298.

32.   Venezky, Richard L. "Non-Standard Language and Reading." Working Paper No. 43. Madison: Wisconsin Research and Development Center for Cognitive Learning, 1970.

33.   Wolfram, Walter. *A Sociolinguistic Description of Negro Speech.* Washington, D.C.: Center for Applied Linguistics, 1969.

34.   Wolfram, Walter. "Sociolinguistic Alternatives in Teaching Reading to Nonstandard Speakers." *Reading Research Quarterly* 6 (Fall 1970): 9–33.

35.   Yelland, H. L.; Jones, S. C.; and Easton, K. S. W. *A Handbook of Literary Terms.* Boston: Writer, 1980.

CHAPTER 6

WORDS IN CONTEXTS

PREVIEW

If every word that students either needed or wanted to read was identified for them, they would end up being anything but self-sufficient consumers of print. That is why teachers must provide instruction that will equip students with maximum skill in figuring out words themselves. One type of such instruction has to do with contexts—specifically, with using the context in which an unfamiliar word appears in order to make a decision about what it says. In this instance, context *refers to two or more words that relate to one another in a way that yields something meaningful. Thus, the* chair *is a context, but* chair the *is not. Similarly,* The baby fell off the chair *is a context, whereas* the chair off fell baby the *is not.*

Using contexts to get a word identified can be viewed as using known words to get help with an unknown one. For example, if clothes *was the only unknown word in the context* Put your clothes on hangers, *the four words that are familiar can (and should) be used to decide what* clothes *says.*

Although using contexts for help with troublesome words is a new skill for new readers, everyone—young and old—routinely uses them when attending to oral language. It is contexts, for instance, not mind reading, that allows for listening comprehension even when every word is not heard. The use of contexts also accounts for the ability to finish another's sentence when the speaker is slow or halting.

This routine, unconscious use of what is said to predict what is not heard or even spoken indicates that instruction with written contexts is not concerned with something that is totally foreign to children. Rather, it is an attempt to get them to transfer to written text what they do intuitively when attending to speech.

To promote the transfer, work with contexts should get underway before children even start to read. Exactly how it can begin is dealt with in Chapter 6. How the instruction progresses is described with a number of illustrations. As this work is described, certain terms are used that might be unfamiliar. All are in italics, so that can serve as a signal to read carefully and to ask, "Could I explain that term in a way that would be meaningful to someone who has not read the chapter?"

Before you read the chapter, why not see what you already know about using contexts by taking the fill-in-the-blank test in the Review.

Although classroom chalkboards sometimes display words in lists, everyday reading is rarely confined to single, isolated words. Instead, it is usually done to comprehend connected text that might be as limited as a phrase or as extensive as a book. Some type of verbal context, therefore, is commonly available to provide help whenever new or forgotten words are encountered. What can be done to ensure that students will be able to get maximum help from contexts is the subject of Chapter 6. (How contexts help with word meanings is discussed in Chapter 10.) Contexts viewed as a source of help with what words say can be divided into *general* and *local* contexts, each of which will be discussed.

GENERAL CONTEXTS

General context refers to the article, chapter, or book being read. General contexts are helpful in getting visually unfamiliar words identified because their content establishes expectations for certain words to occur. An article on golf, to cite one illustration, leads a reader who knows about that sport to expect such words as *course, tee, putting, penalty,* and *handicap*. Expecting them, the reader is in a better position to cope with them.

The value of anticipation for reading explains the importance of what is done before something like a basal reader selection or a social studies chapter is read. A story that takes place in Antarctica, for instance, calls for preparations that include asking students what they know about that part of the world. That it is very cold, that it is covered with snow and ice, and that penguins make their home there are some of the facts about Antarctica that may help students not only comprehend the setting, characters, and plot of the story but also deal successfully with individual words.

LOCAL CONTEXTS

Local contexts are connected, meaningful text that may be as short as *two shoes* or as long as the longest possible sentence. Since sentences are probably the most commonly used context, they provide the focus for much of the subsequent discussion.

Sentences

A *sentence* is a series of words that (a) are arranged in a way that says something meaningful and (b) have a subject and a verb. The structure of sentences plus the fact that they communicate something meaningful allow for the two sources of help with unknown words that are the concern of this chapter. One source is called *syntactic cues,* the other, *semantic cues.* Even though syntactic and semantic cues are so closely intertwined that readers commonly use them jointly, each will be discussed separately.

Syntactic Cues

Syntactic cues for identifying words are available only in *positional* languages. Like many others, English is positional because it relies on word order to convey meaning. The significance of word order explains why rearrangements of words commonly affect meaning or, in some instances, destroy it altogether:

> The man struck his pet.
> His pet struck the man.
> Struck man his pet the

Not to be overlooked is that word order can also have a pronounced effect on the meaning of individual words—one like *too,* for instance:

> They are too fat.
> They are fat too.

At times, the position of a word in a sentence may determine not only its grammatical function and meaning but also its pronunciation:

> One minute remains.
> One minute detail remains.

The two sentences above are useful in specifying how the arrangement of words in a sentence, which is referred to as its *syntax,* assists a reader in coping with unknown words. In this case, we will assume that *minute* is unfamiliar. In the first sentence, the position of *minute* in relation to the other words reveals that it can be nothing but a noun. Where it occurs in the second sentence, on the other hand, indicates that it is a descriptive word. In both instances, therefore, a prediction about grammatical function is possible because the word order of English sentences adheres to certain rules or patterns. Word order, used to determine the grammatical function of an unfamiliar word, is called a *syntactic cue.*

Admittedly, knowing its grammatical function is not the same as knowing what the word says. Nonetheless, having that information does narrow down possibilities to a considerable extent. The restrictions, coupled with additional constraints that come from semantic cues, may be sufficient to allow for a correct conclusion about the word even when the help that derives from spellings is withheld:

_____ her glass with milk.
A long time _____, few buildings were here.
Use the _____ to sweep the floor.

Semantic Cues

Whereas syntactic cues derive from word order, the origin of *semantic cues* is the meaning conveyed by words in the text that are known. Semantic cues function by helping readers make a meaningful selection from all the words they know that belong to the grammatical form class suggested by syntactic cues. To illustrate, in the sentence *Every* _____ *the leaves change color,* the position of the omitted word points to its being a noun. Although thousands of nouns exist, few make sense in relation to the message communicated by the five known words. In fact, *very* few are meaningful.

The combined assistance of syntactic and semantic cues is the reason why total spellings do not always have to be used to decide what an unfamiliar word says. This can be shown with the same sentence in which a single letter replaces the blank:

Every f_____ the leaves change color.

That minimal spellings may be sufficient when contextual cues are generous is important for students to know because the combined use of all available help fosters quick recognition of a word, which in turn facilitates comprehension.

Further Comments about Syntactic and Semantic Cues

Four other points about syntactic and semantic cues are important for teachers to keep in mind. The first is that contexts are helpful only if the word causing problems is known to readers in its spoken form. More specifically, if they have never even heard the word *limit* but encounter it in print, a context like *Limit your time on the phone to three minutes* will only indicate that the unfamiliar word at the beginning is a verb. In contrast, the same context is very helpful to readers whose oral vocabularies include *limit*.

The second point is that syntactic and semantic cues cannot be counted on to provide assistance if too many words in a context are not in a student's reading vocabulary. After all, who can hang on to the gist of a sentence if as many as half the words that comprise it are either unknown or can be identified only with considerable effort? This fact behooves teachers to provide ample practice with new words, whether they work with beginners or more advanced students. Only then will sight vocabularies be extensive, and only then can contextual cues function at their best.

Even when every word but one in a sentence *is* in a student's reading vocabulary, a context still may not be very helpful as is demonstrated by a sentence like *I have a* _____ . In this case, syntax does indicate that the troublesome word is a singular noun; semantically, however, not much is revealed since numerous singular nouns make sense. To be remembered, however, is that most reading is concerned not with individual sentences but with a series of related sentences. The illustrative context, for example, may be immediately followed by *My nose is running all the time.* Now, the singular noun *cold* makes a great deal of sense.

The fourth point about contexts that has significance for instruction can be made with the help of the following sentence:

The Spanish flag is red and _____ .

While the combined use of syntactic and semantic cues indicates that the missing word is the name of a color, the reader's knowledge of the Spanish flag specifies it. This dependence on background knowledge explains why most readers of this textbook could quickly fill in the blank in the following sentence, even though the blank in the previous sentence remains a puzzle:

The flag of the United States is red, _____ , and blue.

The importance of background knowledge is the reason why it is often said that successful reading depends as much on what readers bring to a page as on what the page offers them. This means that students who are successful with reading *are* successful not only because they have such assets as sizable sight vocabularies and ability to use contextual cues but also because they have a rich fund of knowledge to draw on as they try to make sense out of written discourse.

USING CONTEXTS

Making sense is exactly what using contexts is all about. Although young children are not consciously aware that making sense is the essence of language, they display an intuitive knowledge of that fact every time they speak. Such knowledge allows for attention to contexts even before children are able to read.

Oral Contexts

Prereading attention to contexts for help with words makes use of oral language. (Since not everyone seems to be cognizant of the relevance of work with contexts for reading, this is a good time to add one more goal to the list of readiness goals on page 72: Provide practice in using spoken contexts to supply a meaningful, unspoken word.)

How one kindergarten teacher who appreciates the value of contextual cues worked with eight children is portrayed below:

Teacher: Does anyone know what a detective is?

Jimmy: I do. He catches robbers.

Mary: Sometimes he gets shot, too.

Teacher: Yes, that's true, Jimmy. How is he able to catch a robber?

Jimmy: If somebody knows him, they can tell the police.

Teacher: But what if nobody does? Maybe he's wearing a mask, and nobody knows who he is. What then? Might he do something in the store he's robbing that will help a detective find him later?

Vivian: The other night on television a robber had wet shoes and left puddles in the store. That's how come he was caught.

Teacher: What do we call something like puddles—or maybe fingerprints. What do you call what a detective uses to catch a thief?

Jerry: I know. They're clues. He uses clues.

Teacher: Good for you. Have any of you ever heard the word *clue* before?

Mark: I have. I have a detective game at home.

Teacher: Good detectives know how to use clues, don't they?

Jerry: They use them to find people who kill people, too.

Teacher: Yes, they do. Today I want to find out if you'd make good detectives. I'm going to give you a clue by saying something. I won't say everything, though. I'll leave out a word at the end; and, if you listen, you'll be able to tell me the word I'm thinking of but don't say. Listen now. See if you can tell me the word at the end that I don't say. *In our room, we have fifteen girls and only nine*—who can finish it for me?

Group: Boys!

Teacher: Say, you really *are* good detectives. You certainly know how to use clues. I'll have to make it a little harder. This time if you think you know the word I don't say, raise your hand. Here goes. *When we draw pictures, we use crayons or* _____ .

Correctly, this kindergarten teacher started with brief sentences that dealt with what was familiar. She used the word *clue* rather than *cue* because the former has meaning for children. In addition, she provided maximum contextual help by omitting a word at the very end. On another day, both to shift the position of the omitted word and to vary how practice is carried on, the same teacher might deal with contextual cues by saying something like the following.

Sometimes mothers and daddies know so much about us that it seems they know what we're thinking even before we say it. They can almost read our minds, can't they? Let's see whether you can read my mind. I'll say something, but I'll leave out one word. I'll think of the word but won't say it. When I come to the word that I'm thinking of, I'll raise my hand. Listen. *Every Monday morning at ten, Mrs. _____ comes to our room for art.* What word did I leave out?

For still more variety, pictures are useful. Now, children select displayed pictures in order to complete sentences spoken by the teacher. For example:

An _____ can keep us dry. (picture of an umbrella)
My favorite pet is a _____ . (pictures of a dog, a cat, and a bird)
The children in the park are _____ . (picture of children on swings)

The last two sentences allow for attention to the guideline that should be used in evaluating children's responses: any response is acceptable as long as it is syntactically and semantically consistent with the rest of the context. In the third example above, acceptable responses include "swinging," "having fun," and "playing."

To provide contrasts of what is sensible and what is not, teachers should occasionally ask questions like, "Would it make sense to say, 'The children in the park are bicycles?'" Children who think that such a statement is funny clearly understand the essence of language. It is important that they continue to understand that print, too, must always be translated into something meaningful.

Oral Contexts and Minimal Graphophonic Cues

When children are dealing with written language and come across an unfamiliar word, they can get help not only from syntactic and semantic cues but also from the word's spelling. Since work with contexts is for the purpose of helping with reading, it should take spellings into account *as soon as possible.*

Help that derives from spellings is called a *graphophonic cue.* (The description highlights the connection between spellings—*grapho*—and pronunciations—*phonic.*) Even when students know just a few letter-sound relationships, use of minimal (one-letter) graphophonic cues in conjunction with contextual cues is both possible and desirable. Since the sounds that vowels record are affected by other letters occurring in the same syllable, incomplete graphophonic cues should be restricted to consonants.

To illustrate early use of oral contexts along with minimal graphophonic cues, let us see what one teacher chose to do with a group who knows the sound that *t* records:

Teacher: [Holds up card showing *t*.] We've just been talking about the sound that goes with this letter. Again, tell me some words that begin with that sound.
John: *Tell* starts with it.
Maria: So does *two* and *ten* and *tall*.
Teacher: Well, you certainly know lots of words that begin with the sound that goes with *t*. I wonder, though, if you can think of one certain word that starts with *t*. I'll think of it but won't say it. See if you can tell me

what it is. Listen. Right now we have two pets in our room. One is a
_____ . Which of our pets am I thinking of? . . . How did you
know I was thinking of the turtle? . . . Why did you know I *wasn't*
thinking of the gerbil? What if we had a tiger for a pet. Might I have
been thinking of that?

As more letter–sound relationships are taught, a teacher is able to vary
practice by (a) holding up a letter card, (b) speaking an incomplete sentence, and
(c) asking the children to finish the sentence with a word that starts with the sound
that goes with the displayed letter. The same cards can also be used with riddles
complemented with questions like, "Who can think of something that starts with
this letter—think of its sound—and that we wear on our hands?"

Written Contexts

Because the goal of the activities being described is to advance reading ability,
written sentences should replace spoken sentences as quickly as students' reading
vocabularies allow for the switch. At the start, written contexts like the following
are suitable.

I want to _____ the horse.

look   see

Jack _____ Sue are playing.

and   are

With sentences like these, children indicate which word makes sense by printing it
in the blank. (Printing a word is preferable to underlining or circling it because
the writing fosters attention to its details.) Systematic variation in work of this
kind ought to be provided; hence, variation like that illustrated below should
be common.

	Choices
Our _____ will help us. teach teacher	grammatically dissimilar
He _____ the wall. painted pained	graphically similar
Don't run so _____ . quickly fast	semantically similar
Can you _____ this? to in	nonsense

Another type of variation calls for underlining all sensible words:

> baby
> girls
> The boxes are on their way to school.
> boys
> children

>   us
>   up
> They are now on school.
>   in
>   at

Once students acquire spelling ability, filling in blanks with sensible words is possible. Now, some of the practice should allow for explicit attention to the fact that help with a word may lie in a sentence different from the one in which it is embedded:

That _____ was so funny. I want to go to the circus next year, too.

Greg forgot to water the plants. They _____ .

Filling in blanks with words that make sense grammatically and semantically is sometimes referred to as the *cloze* procedure. ("Cloze" comes from the word *closure,* a term associated with Gestalt psychologists, who maintain that human behavior is motivated by the need for wholeness or completeness.) You will probably recall taking comprehension tests that used cloze exercises. Sometimes teachers use them to help with comprehension, since filling in blanks encourages students to attend to the meaning of what they are reading.

When filling in blanks enters into work with contexts, it is *vitally* important that students see the connection between that work and real reading. That is, they must be helped to understand the link between (a) filling in blanks with the help of contextual information and (b) figuring out unfamiliar words while reading, using the same kind of help. Without such understanding, all these exercises may turn out to be nothing more than meaningless busy work.

Written Contexts and Minimal Graphophonic Cues

When children are not yet able to use the complete spellings of unfamiliar words in order to decode them, the use of minimal graphophonic cues, now coupled with written contexts, serves to move the focus still closer to reading. Again, the purpose is to show how contextual cues suggest sensible possibilities and how graphophonic cues determine which one is correct. Such a goal underlies what one classroom teacher was heard to say:

> I've written a sentence on the board and, as you can see, one word is missing. *[On Saturday we're going to _____ our car.]* Who would like to suggest what the missing word might be? . . . Okay. Tom thinks it's *sell.* Does anyone think it might be something else? . . . Let's see now. There have been four more very good suggestions—*buy, trade, wash,* and *clean* are good because they all make sense. However, the letter with which the missing word begins is on the back of this card. What letter is this? . . . Since it's *w,* what is the missing word? . . . Yes, only *wash* starts with *w.*

When written assignments are used, some should incorporate contexts like the following in order to demonstrate that important semantic help may appear after an unfamiliar word, thus suggesting the need to read to the end of a sentence before making a decision about the word:

> I can open the s_____ with this key.
> All three d_____ were barking.
> Don't r_____ or you might fall.

Written sentences that function in work with contextual and minimal graphophonic cues should show blanks of equal width since the concern is not for word length but for the help that derives from other sources.

Written Contexts and Additional Graphophonic Cues

As phonics instruction continues, students are able to use more and more graphophonic cues (plus contextual information) to make decisions about unknown or forgotten words. Now they are ready to learn how additional letters restrict even more what any unknown word can be. The more restrictive boundaries can be shown with written contexts like:

> The cars are going too f_____t.
> Th_____k you for helping me.
> I hope our t_____m wins.

To make exercises like these maximally meaningful and helpful for reading, probing is essential once students make a decision about a word. With the last context shown above, questions such as the following ought to be posed:

Why couldn't the word be *town?*	(Wrong last sound)
Why couldn't it be *room?*	(Wrong initial sound)
Why couldn't it be *tame?*	(Doesn't make sense)

Once phonics instruction clarifies the significance of syllables for decoding, written contexts in which the first syllable of a multisyllabic word is supplied can be used. For instance:

I'm going to use this box for a ta_____ .
O_____ your books to page 97.
Eating ap_____ is good for your teeth.

Contexts like those just shown should be used to remind students that when they are reading and come across an unknown word, it is possible that they will have to decode only its first syllable *if* they also consider the other words in the sentence. Such a reminder serves to show the connection between the exercises and real reading. And, as was mentioned before, unless students see the connection, what they do with exercises is not likely to transfer to what they do when they read.

Contexts and Complete Spellings

When students have acquired sufficient proficiency in decoding to use total spellings for word identifications, work focusing on sentences that include one unknown word is called for:

Cats and dogs are well-known <u>enemies</u>.
They are too <u>heavy</u> to walk on that ice.
It takes <u>practice</u> to be a good swimmer.
Their clothes are different because their <u>climate</u> is different.

With sentences like those just listed, students are told that the underlined word in each is not one they are likely to know but that if they read all the other words and then examine how the unknown word is spelled, they should be able to figure it out. At the beginning, attempts to figure out unknown words should be guided by a teacher's comments and questions. For example: "Read all the words that you know in the sentence. Think what they mean. What do they suggest the unknown word might be? Look at how the unknown word is spelled. With that spelling, what do you think it says? Now read the whole sentence. Does that make sense?"

Eventually, work with unknown words should center on connected sentences—a paragraph, for instance. Again, a balanced use of all available cues should be emphasized.

A Summary

What has now been covered is summarized in Figure 6.1. As you read each step, add to it by thinking of a context that illustrates the step.

Figure 6.1 Progression in Using Contextual Cues

> ### SPOKEN CONTEXT
> 1.   Spoken sentence with omitted word at the end.
> 2.   Spoken sentence with omitted word anyplace in the context.
>
> ### SPOKEN CONTEXT AND MINIMAL GRAPHOPHONIC CUES
> 3.   Spoken sentence with omitted word whose beginning letter is named or shown.
>
> ### WRITTEN CONTEXT
> 4.   Written sentence with omitted word. Children select suitable word from listed possibilities.
> 5.   Written sentence with omitted word. Children fill in the blank with a suitable word.
>
> ### WRITTEN CONTEXT AND PARTIAL GRAPHOPHONIC CUES
> 6.   Written sentence with initial letter of target word supplied.
> 7.   Written sentence with initial and final letters of target word supplied.
> 8.   Written sentence with first syllable of target word supplied.
>
> ### WRITTEN CONTEXT AND COMPLETE GRAPHOPHONIC CUES
> 9.   Written sentences with unknown word.

CONTEXTS AND BASAL READER LESSONS

Many of the exercises that have been described in the chapter offer ideas for written assignments. Their primary purpose is not to keep children occupied but to add to their ability to cope independently with unfamiliar or forgotten words. To ensure that the primary objective is realized, explicit attention to contextual help should enter into work with new vocabulary. Since basal readers are central to so many instructional programs, they will be used now to illustrate the recommendation. (This is a good time to reread the earlier description of a basal reader lesson in Chapter 5.)

A teacher's preparation for a basal reader selection (and for whatever else students are expected to read) has to consider what will be done with new words. Because what is done ought to reflect the importance of independence, the sentences in which the new words first occur should be examined in order to see whether the contextual cues they provide (plus what the students know about decoding) are enough to allow for independent identifications. If they are, those words should not be pretaught. Instead, after the selection has been read and it is time to check up not only on comprehension but also on new vocabulary, students' attention can be directed to each helpful sentence in the text so that a teacher can probe in order to learn (a) whether the new word was correctly named, (b) what was used to figure it out, and (c) whether its meaning in that particular context is understood. Questions about the possible help that may have come from other sentences or from information in the text should be posed too. All this is done to remind students in a very explicit way of the variety of help that is available whenever they find puzzling words.

Subsequently, all the new words can be displayed on phrase and sentence cards. Now, contexts should *not* offer generous help because the reason to have students read the cards is to see whether the new words are in their sight vocabularies. (This again points to the need for teachers to ask themselves, "*Why* am I doing what I'm doing?") If they are not, further practice is called for since the next time students encounter the new words, they may not be in helpful contexts.

SUMMARY

How the known words in sentences can be used to learn what the unknown words say has been the central concern of Chapter 6. These known words, referred to as *contexts,* are able to make this contribution because of two characteristics of English: it is a positional language, and it makes sense. Help that derives from the position of the unknown word in a sentence is called *syntactic;* help that stems from what the known words mean is called *semantic*. Together, the two sources of help are referred to as *contextual cues.*

How children gradually acquire skill in using contextual cues to get a word figured out was illustrated with many examples. As they indicated, initial activities with contexts make use of spoken language, which means that they can get started even before children are able to do any reading. The activities end when students demonstrate ability to use in combination all available sources of help whenever they come across new words.

Although careful, systematic attention to contextual cues will not eliminate misidentifications, it should do away with senseless responses. At least that will be the case when teachers make certain that students understand the connection between exercises with contexts and what they should do when they meet an unknown word during reading.

Because even the best use of contexts results in word recognition, not word identification, the chapter ended with another reminder about the importance of practice for developing sizable sight vocabularies. Such vocabularies are important because, after all, they account for contexts.

REVIEW

1. Since Chapter 6 deals with contexts as a source of help with unfamiliar words, it seems appropriate to review its content by asking you to fill in some blanks:

English is a (a) _____ language in which word order is critical for determining (b) _____ . The arrangement of words that makes up a sentence is referred to as its (c) _____ ; consequently, when the position of an unknown word in a sentence helps to identify it, that help is called a (d) _____ cue. Syntactic cues offer assistance by establishing the (e) _____ (f) _____ of an unknown word. For instance, in the sentence, "Many _____ were in the room," syntax signals that the omitted word is a (g) _____ (h) _____ functioning as the subject of the sentence.

Just as language as a whole makes sense, so too do individual phrases and sentences. The sense, or meaning, communicated by phrases and sentences offers a second type of contextual help. Because it has to do with meaning, it is called a (i) _____ cue. The sentence "Many _____ were in the room" provides minimal semantic help; one like "The swing went up and _____" provides (j) _____ semantic help.

Because the (k) _____ use of syntactic and semantic cues often provides considerable assistance with new or forgotten words, children should be encouraged to think about them whenever they have a problem with a word. Sometimes—as in "The swing went up and _____"— contextual cues will provide so much help that just about all words except one can be (l) _____ from consideration. Most of the time, however, contextual cues will have to be used in conjunction with the help that derives from the (m) _____ of the unknown word. That is why beginning instruction in (n) _____ goes along with early work with contexts.

2. Now that you've taken a cloze test, let us see how well you can do on a brief true-false test.

_____ (a) The larger a person's sight vocabulary, the more helpful are contexts with unfamiliar words.

_____ (b) A reader's background information does not enter into his or her use of contextual cues.

_____ (c) Contextual cues allow for inferences about unfamiliar words, assuming they are in the reader's oral vocabulary.

_____ (d) Whereas semantic cues are limited to the sentence in which an unknown word is embedded, syntactic cues are not similarly restricted.

REFERENCES

1. Barr, Rebecca C. "The Influence of Instructional Conditions on Word Recognition Errors." *Reading Research Quarterly* 7 (Spring 1972): 509–529.

2. Biemiller, Andrew. "The Development of the Use of Graphic and Contextual Information as Children Learn to Read." *Reading Research Quarterly* 6 (Fall 1970): 75–96.

3. Bormuth, John R. "Factor Validity of Cloze Tests as Measures of Reading Comprehension Ability." *Reading Research Quarterly* 4 (Spring 1969): 358–367.

4. Durkin, Dolores. "Listen to Your Children." *Instructor* 81 (February 1972): 87–88.

5. Durkin, Dolores. *Strategies for Identifying Words.* 2d ed. Boston: Allyn and Bacon, 1981.

6. Gomberg, Adeline W. "Freeing Children to Take a Chance." *Reading Teacher* 29 (February 1976): 455–457.

7. Juel, Connie. "Comparison of Word Identification Strategies with Varying Context, Word Type, and Reader Skill." *Reading Research Quarterly* 15, no. 3 (1980): 358–376.

8. MacGinitie, Walter H. "Contextual Constraint in English Prose Paragraphs." *Journal of Psychology* 51 (January 1961): 121–130.

9. Pearson, P. David. "A Psycholinguistic Model of Reading." *Language Arts* 53 (March 1976): 309–314.

10. Pflaum, Susanna W., and Pascarella, Ernest T. "Interactive Effects of Prior Reading Achievement and Training on the Reading of Learning-Disabled Children." *Reading Research Quarterly* 16, no. 1 (1980): 138–158.

11. Roberts, Marion A. "Reading Comprehension Breakthrough." *Language Arts* 56 (November–December 1979): 922–924.

12. Samuels, S. Jay; Dahl, Patricia; and Archwamety, Teara. "Effect of Hypothesis/Test Training on Reading Skill." *Journal of Educational Psychology* 56 (December 1974): 835–844.

CHAPTER 7

PHONICS: THE CONTENT

PREVIEW

Proficient readers use whatever help is available when they encounter an unfamiliar word that seems essential for comprehending what they are reading. With an alphabetic writing system, one important source of help is its spelling. Teaching students how to use spellings to work out pronunciations constitutes phonics instruction. What to teach for that purpose is the concern now.

Except for those who are thoroughly familiar with the content of phonics, this chapter needs to be studied. It is recommended that you go through the material slowly, carefully, and thoughtfully. Stop when something new is defined or explained. Do not go on until you fully understand what is said. In addition, commit the various generalizations (once they are understood) to memory; otherwise you will be unprepared to explain and discuss them with children.

Admittedly, efforts by neophytes to master the content of phonics sometimes prompt the question, "If I'm having so much trouble, how can children be expected to learn it?" This is natural puzzlement; however, it does not account for the fact that phonics is taught to children over a long period of time, which allows for a slow pace, repetition, and as much practice as is necessary. In contrast, Chapter 7 covers a great deal—fast. That is why it needs to be studied. As a result of such study, you will have the potential to teach phonics in a way that will turn it into a highly useful tool for students. And if what is taught is not useful, something is wrong!

What is wrong with some phonics instruction will be dealt with in Chapter 8, which concentrates on how to teach phonics. But before methodology is discussed, what is taught needs to be mastered. It is thus time to begin Chapter 7.

As the chapter on contextual cues showed, beginning instruction in phonics focuses on the sounds that letters record. At the very start, consonants are singled out for attention since they are more consistent than vowels in what they record. Even though some vowel sounds should be taught before all the consonants are covered, the discussion here will deal with all the consonants first. Afterward, vowels will be considered. Since the presentation is for adults who already know something about the alphabetic system of English, it is not meant to be a model for teaching phonics to children.

CONSONANTS

The discussion of consonants will divide them into (a) single consonants, (b) consonant clusters, and (c) consonant digraphs.

Single Consonants

The quickest way to identify the consonants is to say that they are all the letters in the alphabet except *a, e, i, o,* and *u.* Each word listed below begins with the sound commonly recorded by the initial consonant.

bell	how	lie	pie	to	yes
dog	jam	me	run	van	zoo
fun	kit	not	see	we	

The listed words include *yes* in which *y* functions as a consonant. The many times that *y* (as well as *w*) functions as a vowel will be discussed later. Now, the four consonants not listed *(c, g, q, x)* will be dealt with.

C and *g* each record two sounds, traditionally referred to in phonics as the *hard* and *soft* sounds. (When each is likely to occur will be explained later under the heading "Factors Affecting Consonant Sounds.") The hard sound for *c* is heard initially in *cut* and *can,* which indicates that it is the sound associated with *k.* The soft sound for *c* can be identified in *cell* and *city.* Again, this sound is associated with another letter, namely, *s.* To summarize:

C

Hard Sound	Examples
/k/★	cat, cob, cuff

★ Slash marks are used to make a distinction between letters and sounds. Thus, *h* refers to a letter, whereas /h/ symbolizes the sound that it represents in a word like *hall.*

156

Soft Sound	Examples
/s/	cent, cite, cyst

Like *c,* the soft sound for *g* is associated with another letter—in this case, *j.* The soft sound is heard at the beginning of *gym* and *gem.* In contrast, the hard sound for *g* can be heard at the beginning of *got* and *game.* (Sometimes *g* and *u* combine to record the hard sound, but this happens only when another vowel besides *u* is in the syllable. For example, *g* and *u* combine to stand for one sound in such words as *guess, guard,* and *guide* but not in others like *gun* and *gust* in which *g* records the hard sound while *u* stands for the vowel sound that every syllable must have.) The two sounds that *g* commonly represents are summarized below.

G

Hard Sound	Examples
/g/	gag, green, wig

Soft Sound	Examples
/j/	gem, gist, gypsy

Scrabble players know that the consonant *q* is always followed by *u.* Together, *q* and *u* record either a single sound or a blend of two sounds:

Qu

Sounds	Examples
/k/	bisque
/kw/	quit

In phonics, *qu* is treated as a unit—more specifically, as a single consonant.

Like *c, g,* and *qu, x* stands for sounds associated with other letters. This is illustrated in the following words, which show that *x* stands for a single sound, as well as for two different blends:

X

Sounds	Examples
/z/	anxiety
/ks/	sox
/gz/	exist

Since *x* occurs infrequently in words, attention to the sounds it represents can be delayed when phonics is taught to children.

Consonant Clusters

Fairly frequently, certain consonants appear as successive letters in a syllable. This is illustrated in such words as <u>st</u>ay, <u>bl</u>ue, wes<u>t</u>, and <u>br</u>is<u>k</u>. Dealing with each letter that comprises these pairs naturally takes longer than dealing with the two together. For that reason, the pairs are sometimes singled out for attention to promote efficiency. (The faster a word is figured out, the less likely it is to interfere with comprehension.) Pairs of consonants that frequently occur together are called *clusters*. Each cluster stands for two sounds, that is, for a *blend* of sounds. Pairs of consonants referred to as clusters are:

Consonant Clusters

bl	cr	fr	pl	sk	sn	sw
br	dr	gl	pr	sl	sp	tr
cl	fl	gr	sc	sm	st	tw

Rarely, three consonants occur in succession in a syllable—for example, in <u>scream</u> and <u>street</u>. For that reason, the term *cluster* generally refers to two consonants.

Consonant Digraphs

Whereas a reader can deal either with each letter in a cluster separately or with the pair, the same option is not available for consonant *digraphs*. That is the case because a consonant digraph is two letters that stand for one sound that is different from the sound associated with either letter. As the description suggests, decoders must treat a consonant digraph as if it were but one letter.

Consonant digraphs that are covered in phonics instruction are:

Consonant Digraphs
th (the, thin)
ph (phase)
gh (tough)
sh (shut)
ch (champ, chef)
ng (rang)

As the list shows, *th* stands for two different sounds. One, called the *voiced* sound, is heard in *the, there* and *feather*. The other, the *voiceless* sound, occurs in *thin, thirst,* and *both*. For any who have difficulty hearing the difference between the two sounds, the following contrasts should help, especially if each pair of words is read aloud:

Words with voiced sound	*Words with voiceless sound*
thy	thigh
bathe	bath
either	ether

breathe	breath
clothe	cloth
teethe	teeth

The next two digraphs listed, *ph* and *gh,* record the same sound, one associated with *f.* (When *gh* is in initial position as in *ghost* or *ghetto, g* records its hard sound while *h* is silent. Sometimes *gh* itself is silent, as in *high* and *caught.*)

Except in words of French origin, such as *chef, chauffeur, champagne, chaise,* and *chamois, ch* commonly represents the sound heard in initial position in *champ.*

The next digraph in the list, *ng,* does not occur in initial position but instead follows vowels *(rang, length).* The sound it records cannot be produced apart from the blends that are spelled *ang, eng, ing, ong,* and *ung.*

A comment also needs to be made about a pair of consonants that is not in the list: *wh.* Although some call it a consonant digraph, it was not listed because what *wh* records does not meet the criterion stated earlier for digraphs: two consonants recording a sound that is unlike the sound associated with either letter. In a word like *who, wh* stands for /h/. What it records in *which,* on the other hand, depends upon the speaker. In some dialect areas, *which* and *witch* are pronounced the same, indicating that *wh* stands for /w/. In other areas, *which* starts with /hw/. The three possibilities (/h/, /w/, /hw/) explain why *wh* was not included in the list of digraphs.

VOWELS

Like the discussion of consonants, the treatment of vowels divides them into single letters and pairs.

Single Vowels

The letters associated with vowel sounds are *a, e, i, o,* and *u.* Each of these five letters stands for what has traditionally been called a short sound and a long sound. The ten sounds can be identified in the following words:

Words illustrating short vowel sounds	*Words illustrating long vowel sounds*
at	aim
end	eat
if	ice
odd	old
up	use

The vowel sound in *up* is closely similar to what is called the *schwa* sound, the symbol for which is /ə/. The schwa sound enters into phonics instruction when words of more than one syllable are decoded because of the following pattern: *Vowel sounds in unstressed syllables are often (not always) reduced to the schwa sound.* Examples of words with the schwa sound appear below. To help identify it, the letters representing the schwa sound are underlined. To show the occurrence of /ə/ in unstressed syllables, stress marks are shown, too.

án<u>i</u>m<u>a</u>l   sód<u>a</u>   <u>a</u>lóne   ím<u>i</u>tate   <u>u</u>pón   háv<u>e</u>n

That the schwa sound does not occur in *every* unstressed syllable is illustrated in other words:

stampéde   brónco   éthnic   cálculate   maintaín

A second reason why decoders need to know about the schwa sound is found in multisyllabic words ending with a consonant followed by *le* (as in *purple, article*). In such words, the two final sounds are /əl/.

Vowel Digraphs

Like consonants, vowels may occur in pairs that must be treated as one letter. Like the consonants, too, the pairs are called *digraphs*. As the following list shows, certain vowel digraphs include *y* or *w*. In these instances, *y* and *w* are functioning as vowels.

Vowel Digraphs
oo (cool, cook)
ew (grew)
au, aw (auto, awful)
oi, oy (oil, oyster)
ou, ow (out, owl)

As the list points up, the digraph *oo* stands for two sounds. The one in *cool* (and in *boot, noodle,* and *raccoon*) is more common; thus decoders should try it first when they meet an unfamiliar word that has two successive *o*'s in a syllable. This sound is referred to as the long sound for double *-o* and is the same one that the digraph *ew* records. (This sound may also be represented by *u*, as in *flu, rude,* and *tumor*.) The second sound for *oo*, called the short sound, is heard in *cook, wool, foot,* and *stood.*

The vowel sound that both *au* and *aw* represent can be identified in words like *auto, paucity, awful,* and *law*. The two other vowel sounds that digraphs record are in initial position in *oil* and *out*. (These two sounds are called *diphthongs*.) The diphthong in *oil* is also recorded by *oy (oyster, toy)*; the diphthong in *out* can be recorded by *ow (owl, coward)*.

A Summary

The fifteen vowel sounds that decoders need to know are summarized below:

Words illustrating
the vowel sounds

1. at	6. aim	11. cool (stew)
2. end	7. eat	12. cook
3. if	8. ice	13. auto (law)
4. odd	9. old	14. oil (boy)
5. up	10. use	15. out (owl)

When teaching phonics to children, it is sometimes helpful at the beginning to use diacritical marks:

Long vowel sounds	*Short vowel sounds*
mē	mĕt
āim	ăsk
tōōl	tŏŏk

VARIATION IN SOUNDS

In beginning instruction, attention goes to individual letters and the sound each stands for. Nonetheless, it is the sequence of letters in a syllable that provides a decoder with information about the sounds that certain letters are likely to represent. Details about sequences are specified in some of the generalizations that are taught in phonics. Such generalizations, it is important to note, are not "rules" that always work. Our writing system hardly allows for that. Rather, their use should be thought of as a starting point in the decoding process that may or may not lead to a correct pronunciation. (What a decoder should do when what results is not correct is discussed later.) To illustrate all this, consider one generalization: *When there is one vowel in a syllable and it does not occur in final position* (for example, *mat*), *it usually stands for its short sound*.

If words like *bid, flak, stretch,* and *thrust* are unknown, a reader's use of this generalization will offer considerable assistance in getting them decoded. On the other hand, applying the same generalization to a word such as *ton* would not help. (Not to be overlooked is that if *ton* is embedded in a sentence like *A ton of coal won't last very long,* knowing the sounds that *t* and *n* stand for might be all that is necessary to get *ton* decoded because of the helpful context.)

Since vowels vary the most in the sounds they represent, generalizations about vowel sounds will be considered first. Afterward, variations in consonant sounds will get attention.

Factors Affecting Vowel Sounds

Fortunately, the sequence of letters in a syllable provides information (cues) about the sounds that certain of the letters are likely to represent. The following generalizations pinpoint cues for vowel sounds. (Each statement of a generalization is complemented with words that exemplify the specified pronunciation pattern.) Because teaching manuals sometimes deal with generalizations using spelling patterns, each generalization is summarized in that form. For the generalization that was discussed above, for example, the spelling pattern is (C)VC, where C stands for any consonant and V for any vowel. (The first C is enclosed in a parenthesis because the presence of an initial consonant is not essential to the pattern, a fact illustrated in words like *us* and *an*.)

Generalizations about long and short sounds.   The first group of generalizations suggests when long and short vowel sounds are likely to occur.

GENERALIZATIONS ABOUT LONG AND SHORT SOUNDS

When there is one vowel in a syllable and it is not the final letter, it usually stands for its short sound *(if, cent, stamp, bunch)*.

(C)VC

When there is one vowel in a syllable and it is the final letter, it usually records its long sound *(I, she, so, hi)*.

(C)V

When two successive vowels occur in a syllable and they are not special digraphs, the first generally records its long sound whereas the second is silent *(each, reel, tea, throat)*.★

(C)VV(C)

When two vowels are in a syllable, one of which is final *e*, the first usually records its long sound and the *e* is silent *(ice, chrome, brake, cube)*.

(C)VCe

When there are two vowels in a syllable, one of which is final *e*, and the two are separated by two consonants, the first will commonly stand for its short sound and the *e* will be silent *(fudge, prince, pulse, solve)*.

(C)VCCe

★ The digraph *ow* may record a diphthong *(owl, now)*, or it may follow the pattern described in this generalization *(own, low)*. In decoding a syllable that contains *ow*, children should try out both possibilities (starting with /ō/) in order to see which produces a recognizable word.

Generalizations about r-controlled vowel sounds.   In syllables in which a vowel is followed by *r* (for example, *car*) or *re* (for example, *care*), no attempt should be made to isolate its sound because, in these cases, the vowel sound is closely tied to the sound or sounds that follow it in the syllable. Generalizations about these *r*-controlled sounds follow.

GENERALIZATIONS ABOUT R-CONTROLLED VOWEL SOUNDS

When a single vowel is followed in a syllable by *r*, the vowel plus *r* record one of three blends that can be identified in *art, her,* and *for*. The most common of the three is heard in *dollar, her, fir, work,* and *fur*.
When a single vowel is followed by *re*, the vowel plus *re* usually stand for blends that can be identified in *care, here, fire, bore,* and *cure*.

Generalizations about y functioning as a vowel.   As was mentioned earlier, *y* functions as a consonant and as a vowel. As a consonant, it starts a syllable (for example, *yard, beyond*) and stands for the sound heard initially in words like *yes* and *year*. In all other positions, *y* functions as a vowel.

That *y* functioning as a vowel accounts for a vowel digraph was also mentioned earlier (for example, *coy, oyster*). The fact that *y* alone stands for three other vowel sounds is the subject of more generalizations:

VOWEL SOUNDS RECORDED BY Y

When *y* is in medial position in a syllable that has no other vowel, it commonly records the short *i* sound *(gym, myth, hymn)*.
When *y* records the final sound in a multisyllabic word, it stands for the long *e* sound *(penny, silly, fancy, autopsy)*.
In all other instances, *y* stands for the long *i* sound *(dye, my, dynamite, asylum)*.

When *y* functions as a vowel in such words as *day* and *galley*, it is silent, thus adhering to a pattern specified in a generalization stated earlier. (Which one?)

Graphemic bases.   Underscored in all the generalizations that have been listed thus far is that what a vowel records is affected by the position of letters in a syllable. That explains why teaching manuals sometimes give attention to *graphemic bases*. (They may also be called *phonograms*.) A graphemic base is a series of letters, starting with a vowel, that frequently constitute part of a word or a syllable. Examples are *-ain, -ipe, -ight, -ang,* and *-uck*. Since they do start with a vowel, each graphemic base can be pronounced. Dealing with a graphemic base rather than with individual letters is another way to speed up decoding.

Factors Affecting Consonant Sounds

Fortunately, consonant letters are fairly consistent in the sounds they represent. Two notable exceptions are *c* and *g*, which record sounds called *hard* and *soft*. When they are likely to occur is stated in two generalizations.

GENERALIZATIONS FOR C AND G

When *c* is followed in a syllable by *e, i,* or *y,* it usually records its soft sound *(cent, cite, cyst)*. Otherwise, the hard sound is common *(call, cot, cub, scrub, sac)*.
When *g* is followed in a syllable by *e, i,* or *y,* it usually records its soft sound *(gem, gist, gym)*. Otherwise, the hard sound is common *(gag, got, gum, glad, brig)*.

SYLLABLES

Beginning instruction in phonics makes no explicit distinction between *syllable* and *word*. For example, if *jam, jet,* and *jacket* are used in a kindergarten to teach the sound that *j* represents, only the initial part of the three words gets attention. That two of them are composed of one syllable whereas the third has two syllables is not dealt with. Eventually, however, students do have to understand that it is syllables, not words, that are worked on since it is syllables to which all the generalizations refer. (Reviewing the generalizations presented earlier will show this to be the case.)

Because it *is* syllables that are decoded, students need to know how to divide an unknown word into syllables before they try to figure out what the word says. Once again, generalizations that highlight visual cues (letters and their sequence) are available to provide guidelines. Before the generalizations are listed, what a syllable is needs to be discussed.

What a Syllable Is

A syllable is a vowel sound to which consonant sounds are typically added. This means that a syllable may be composed of only one vowel letter:

u   us   rus   rust   thrust

A syllable may also contain as many as three vowel letters:

lounge   seize   raise   voice   sleeve

Whatever the number of vowel letters, a syllable has but one vowel sound. This means that students are not ready to learn about syllables until they know some vowel sounds. The presence of a vowel sound in every syllable also explains the need to give attention to vowel sounds before all the consonants are taught.

Eventually, students must know there are five basic types of syllables that are differentiated by (a) number of vowel letters and (b) their placement. The five types are summarized below; they reflect the generalizations about vowel sounds that were listed earlier.

BASIC TYPES OF SYLLABLES

Description	Examples	Spelling pattern
one vowel, at the end	me, go, she, I	(C)V
one vowel, not at the end	met, an, chip	(C)VC
two successive vowels	meet, sea, ail	(C)VV(C)
two vowels, one a final *e*	mete, cube, ace	(C)VCe
two vowels, one a final *e*, with the two separated by two consonants	mince, bulge, else	(C)VCCe

---

Three other types of syllables occur in final position. One is a consonant plus *le,* which is found in words like *candle, icicle,* and *trifle.* The other two are spelled *ture* and *tion,* as in *puncture* and *notion.* (The syllable *tion* is usually pronounced "shun," but not always. In *question,* for instance, the pronunciation is "chun.")

Still another way of looking at syllables examines the placement of the sounds that compose them. More specifically, a syllable may have an *initial* sound, a *medial* sound, and a *final* sound. With a syllable like *rus, r* stands for the initial, or beginning, sound; *u* stands for the medial, or middle, sound; and *s* stands for the final, or last, sound. Since a syllable may be composed of just one sound—always a vowel—not every syllable has all three positions. Nonetheless, all three are possible.

Generalizations for Syllabication

Because decoding focuses on syllables (which, after they are decoded, are combined into a word), a reader's first consideration is the possibility that an unknown word may have more than one syllable. With unknown words, only visual cues are available to provide an answer; consequently, only visual cues should be featured in statements of generalizations.

GENERALIZATIONS ABOUT SYLLABICATION

When two consonants are between two vowels, a syllable division usually occurs between the consonants *(window, canteen, kindergarten)*.

When one consonant is between two vowels, a syllable division usually occurs between the first vowel and the consonant *(pilot, motel, aroma)*.

When *x* is the consonant that is preceded and followed by vowels, it and the preceding vowel are in the same syllable *(exit, oxen, taxi)*.

When a word ends in *le* preceded by a consonant, the consonant plus *le* comprise a syllable *(able, middle, purple)*.

The relevance for syllabication of two additional observations may not be immediately apparent. One was mentioned before: *Every syllable has a vowel sound*. With this basic fact in mind, a decoder should know that a string of letters like *fabric* can be no more than two syllables. Consequently, when he divides it into *fab* and *ric* with the help of a generalization just listed, he should know that it is time to stop insofar as syllabication is concerned and get on with decisions about sounds.

The second observation points out: *A final* e *in a syllable that contains other vowel letters records no sound*. This generalization (combined with the fact that every syllable must have a vowel sound) indicates that words like *exhale* and *stampede* should not be further divided after the syllables *ex* and *hale* and *stam* and *pede* are sorted out with the help of visual cues described in previously mentioned generalizations.

Once a decoder makes decisions about the likely syllabication of an unfamiliar word (or about the fact that it is one syllable), he is ready to consider graphophonic cues, syllable by syllable.★ Knowing how to use such cues results from instruction with letter–sound relationships and the factors that affect them. That is why the generalizations presented earlier covered the two topics.

STRESSED SYLLABLES

Knowing how a multisyllabic word is pronounced includes knowing which of its syllables is stressed. (Stress also enters into decoding in recognition of the fact that vowel sounds in unstressed syllables are usually reduced to the schwa sound.)

The fact that English words have come from a number of other languages means that consistent patterns for stress do not exist. The lack of them is the reason why students should adopt a trial–and–error approach when the time comes to decide which syllable of an unknown word is stressed. This approach is

★ To allow for concentrated attention to graphophonic cues, others (contextual and structural) are being laid aside temporarily. Even so, what was stressed earlier should not be forgotten: proficient readers use every available cue in their efforts to achieve the pronunciation of an unknown word. To keep the correct perspective in mind, reexamine Figure 6.1.

not as complicated as it might at first appear to be because decisions about stress are made after the pronunciation of each syllable is worked out. Therefore, if the word being decoded is familiar in its spoken form, the sounds of the syllables will be enough to indicate which is stressed.

To be more specific about all this, let us assume a student has heard the word *pendulum,* knows what one is, but has never come across the word in print. The first time he does, he will have to work out the pronunciation unless the context in which it is embedded offers generous help. But let us say that is not the case. Applying what he has been taught about using visual cues, first to get *pendulum* divided into syllables and then to make decisions about the sounds that the letters in each are likely to record, the student should be able to arrive at a correct pronunciation for each syllable. And that will be enough *when the word is familiar in its spoken form* to signal not only which syllable is stressed but also the correct, natural pronunciation. More specifically, "pĕn′ dū′ lŭm′" will suggest "pĕn′ jə lŭm."

FLEXIBLE DECODING

Because perfect consistency between spellings and pronunciations is not found in English words, generalizations about letter-sound relationships cannot be counted on to produce correct pronunciations every time they are used. On the other hand, what *can* be counted on to increase solutions are (a) the *flexible* application of generalizations and (b) the *combined* use of all possible sources of help. Here, let me elaborate on flexibility. Since flexibility means one thing for regularly spelled words and another for those with irregular spellings, a separate discussion of each type follows.

Generalizations Applied to Regularly Spelled Words

A *regularly spelled* word is one whose spelling and pronunciation match in a patterned way. It could also be defined as a word whose pronunciation can be predicted from the generalizations taught in phonics. By definition, then, phonic generalizations offer maximum help with unknown words that have regular spellings. It still must be noted, however, that if an *exactly* correct pronunciation is the criterion of success, the generalizations are successful only when applied to regularly spelled words that have but one syllable. This means that if you had never before seen such words as *shy, broil, cite,* and *stand,* you should be able to work out exactly correct pronunciations by applying certain of the generalizations that have been listed in the chapter. (See whether you can. It will serve as a self-check on your understanding of the generalizations.)

Phonic generalizations also offer reliable assistance with regularly spelled multisyllabic words; nonetheless, slight adjustments in pronunciations are required for two reasons. First, the decoding process makes syllables sound as if they were separate words. With a regularly spelled one like *canine,* for instance, decoding makes it sound like "ca′ nine′," just as it turns *carpenter* into "car′ pen′ ter′" and *notion* into "no′ tion′."

The second reason why adjustments with regularly spelled multisyllabic words are necessary has to do with the common occurrence of the schwa sound in unstressed syllables. In this case, adjustments change "brā′ zĕn′" into "brā′ zən′" "căn′ dī′ dāt¢′" into "căn′ də dāt¢" and "cŏn′ trīv¢′" into "cən trīv¢′." Expectedly, such adjustments are possible only when decoders are familiar with these words in their spoken form. When the same words are embedded in helpful contexts, adjustments can be made with considerable speed.

Generalizations Applied to Irregularly Spelled Words

How well phonics functions with irregularly spelled words depends upon (a) the decoder's knowledge of phonic generalizations, (b) his ability to apply them with flexibility, (c) the amount of assistance that the context offers, (d) the size of his oral vocabulary, and (e) his background knowledge. With examples, the significance of all five variables will be illustrated.

Let's say that a reader comes across the sentence *He could see the blood running through the vein.* Let's also say that this reader knows all the words except *vein* but soon identifies that because, after all, what else could it be but "vān" when the context is kept in mind, as well as the fact that the word begins with *v* and ends with *n?* (Notice how this conclusion assumes that the decoder's knowledge of the world includes an awareness of the connection between blood and veins.)

On another occasion, a reader needs to know what *push* says, which occurs in *The push is on. Push* immediately prompts this person to think of *rush,* a familiar word. Substituting /p/ for /r/, however, results in something that makes no sense. Well taught, this student persists. Knowing that it is vowel sounds that usually vary, he tries out the long *u* sound, but that results in more nonsense. He continues to try other vowel sounds and stops with /o͝o/, for that is a sound that produces a word that fits the context.

Still another reader has temporary problems with *magic,* which is in the sentence *He doesn't want to have anything to do with magic.* He first uses visual cues to arrive at the syllables *ma* and *gic.* Next, he applies generalizations about letter-sound relationships and arrives at the pronunciation "mā′ jĭk′"—something that fails to remind him of any word he has ever heard. He reexamines the context, but that does not help. He then remembers his teacher's discussing words that have the same syllable pattern *(mu sic, ba con; wa gon, li zard)* and of how the vowel letter in the first syllable of such words sometimes stands for a short rather than a long sound. He immediately tries /ă/ for the *a,* recognizes the word *magic,* rereads the sentence, and continues. (The rereading is important for comprehension.)

On another day, the same student has problems with *magazine.* At least he cannot immediately identify it. He divides it as *ma ga zine;* remembers about the short vowel sound in *magic;* and pronounces the word mă′ gā′ zīn̆′. Although incorrect, it is enough to allow this student (who knows about magazines) to shift to mă gə zēn′. After all, what else could it be in the context *They try to read at least one magazine every week?*

ORAL LANGUAGE AND DECODING

What the students just referred to readily demonstrate is that successful decoding is the product of much more than just phonics. Clearly in the picture is oral language. How that enters into decoding is explained effectively by the linguist Roger Brown:

> The usefulness of being able to sound a new word depends on the state of the reader's speaking vocabulary. If the word that is unfamiliar in printed form is also unfamiliar in spoken form the reader who can sound it out will not understand the word any better than the reader who cannot sound it. . . . The real advantage in being able to sound a word that is unfamiliar in print, only appears when the word is familiar in speech. The child's letter-by-letter pronunciation, put together by spelling recipe, will, with the aid of context, call to mind the spoken form. There will be a click of recognition, pronunciation will smooth out, and meaning will transfer to the printed form. [1, p. 69]

Teachers at all grade levels need to remember that adding to students' oral vocabularies is a contribution not only to their potential for decoding print but also to the likelihood that they will comprehend it.

SUMMARY

What needs to be taught to give students maximum skill in decoding unfamiliar words has been the subject of Chapter 7. What is taught centers on (a) letter-sound relationships, (b) factors that affect them, and (c) syllabication.

The chapter started by considering consonants because, except for *c, g, q,* and *x,* they are fairly consistent in the sounds they represent. This is true even for those special pairs of consonants called digraphs.

What the vowels *a, e, i, o,* and *u* (and *y* and *w*) record, both alone and in combination with other letters, was covered next. The discussion revealed both variability and patterns, and the latter were highlighted in generalizations. In this case, generalizations are statements about visual cues that signal the likelihood of certain sounds. For decoding, cues have to do with letters and the sequence in which they occur.

Because it is syllables, not words, to which the generalizations pertain, knowing about the syllabication of an unknown word is essential. That is why the chapter also offered generalizations for making decisions about syllables. Again, visual cues (letters and their sequence) were featured in these statements.

Together, all of the generalizations about vowel sounds, consonant sounds, and syllabication constitute an important source of help for decoders. Yet their full potential is realized only when they are applied with flexibility and in conjunction with contextual cues. That a reader's oral vocabulary and knowledge of the world also contribute to successful decoding was emphasized in the chapter too.

REVIEW

1. Explain (with some examples) how decoding ability is influenced by oral language.
2. A number of terms are associated with phonics. See whether you can define the ones shown below. Include an example in each explanation.

blend	graphophonic cue	schwa sound
cluster	"hard" sound	"soft" sound
digraph	phonogram	syllable
graphemic base	regularly spelled word	

3. Name fifteen one-syllable words that illustrate the vowel sounds taught in phonics.
4. Explain why this statement is correct:

In all of the following words, /n/ occurs in final position: *ten, line, maintain, mercantile.*

5. Using generalizations from this chapter, explain why *o* records a long sound in *hotel* and a short sound in *hot*.
6. Cite *all* the generalizations that contribute to decoding *act*.

REFERENCES

1. Brown, Roger. *Words and Things.* New York: Free Press, 1958.
2. Durkin, Dolores. *Phonics, Linguistics, and Reading.* New York: Teachers College Press, Columbia University, 1972.
3. Durkin, Dolores. *Strategies for Identifying Words.* 2d ed. Boston: Allyn and Bacon, 1981.

CHAPTER 8

PHONICS: INSTRUCTION

PREVIEW

Central to effective instruction in phonics is a teacher who is thoroughly familiar with what should be taught, knows how to teach it, and is as conscientious about promoting the use of phonics as about teaching the content. While all three characteristics are essential, it is necessary to stress the last one because of what is often found: schools spend considerable time (and money) teaching phonics in the primary grades and then do almost nothing to foster its use later. Instead, "Look it up in the glossary (or dictionary)" is the most prevalent direction heard whenever middle- and upper-grade students come across a new word or are baffled by an old one. Curious about this practice, I once asked a sixth-grade teacher if she could explain it. "I myself have never taught the lower grades," she began, "so I don't know enough about phonics to get involved with it. Maybe others feel the same way."

While the response of one person is hardly sufficient for reaching a conclusion about many, it is enough to prompt the reminder that the two chapters on phonics in this book are as pertinent for middle- and upper-grade teachers as they are for those at the primary level. The single response is also a reason to emphasize that instructional programs in phonics should be evaluated in relation to one criterion: students' ability to use spellings to identify words that are visually unfamiliar.

Because of the importance of use, Chapter 8 deals not only with how to teach phonics but also with how it functions in allowing students to work out pronunciations on their own. Self-reliance, then, continues to be the central theme. Of continuing importance, too, is the fact that:

- *Phonics is helpful only with words that are known in their spoken form.*

- *Phonics is maximally productive when the word that needs to be figured out is in a context.*

It also is a fact that Chapter 8 will be most helpful to those who know the content of Chapter 7.

Phonics instruction deals with letter-sound relationships, factors that affect them, and syllabication. As the chapter Preview stressed, instruction also shows how what is taught functions in getting unfamiliar words figured out.

In school, instruction with content and instruction with its use go on concurrently—or at least they should. That is, as soon as one piece of content is covered, how it enters into decoding should be demonstrated and practiced. Then more content is taught, after which its use is explained.

In contrast with desirable classroom procedures, the present chapter covers instruction with content first and then shifts to its use. The difference is pointed out in order to discourage anyone from concluding that classroom teachers should cover all possible content before they ever attend to how it functions with unknown words.

DEDUCTIVE VERSUS INDUCTIVE INSTRUCTION

Instruction with the content of phonics can proceed deductively or inductively. Since each way of teaching has merit, both will be described.

Deductive Instruction

As with any other deductive procedure, deductive phonics instruction moves from the general to the particular. That is, it starts with a generalization (about a letter-sound relationship, a factor that affects such relationships, or syllabication), which is then illustrated with particular words. To clarify, let me describe a deductive lesson.

A deductive lesson. The goal of the lesson is to teach a generalization about syllabication: *When two consonants are preceded and followed by vowels, a syllable division usually occurs between the consonants.* Because the lesson *is* deductive, the teacher starts with the generalization.

Prerequisites. The students are ready to be told about the generalization if they (a) know what is meant by "consonant" and "vowel," (b) understand what a syllable is, and (c) are aware of the significance of syllabication for decoding.

Teaching the lesson. Using a deductive procedure, a teacher might start by commenting, "I want to show you a way to divide unknown words into syllables so that you'll be able to figure out what they say. This is what to look for: two consonants with one vowel before them and one vowel after them. When you see that series of letters, vowel-consonant-consonant-vowel, the word probably divides between the consonants. You already know some words that have this arrangement of letters. I'll write them."

> picture
> window
> garden
> after

"Please look at *picture*. What two consonants are together? . . . What comes before the *c?* . . . What do you see after *t?* . . . Here is a word with two consonants that have a vowel before and after them, so the syllable break comes between *c* and *t*. I could write it like this." The teacher proceeds to print *pic ture*.

After discussing the other three words in a similar fashion, the teacher continues, "Now I'm going to write some words that I don't think you can read, but see if you can tell me where to divide them into syllables." (This part of the lesson is designed to help the teacher learn whether the generalization has meaning for the students. Unknown words, therefore, *must* be selected. This point is stressed because of the meaningless practice sometimes found in commercial materials: known words are used for what is supposed to be application of what was taught.)

> cancel
> halter
> surface

"Look at the first word. Does anybody know what it says? No? Where would it probably divide into syllables? . . . Why? . . . Can anybody tell me what it says now? No? It's *cancel*. Have you ever heard that word before? . . . Can someone tell me what it means?"

After attending to the remaining words, the teacher continues, "Now I'm going to write some words that you *can* read."

> happy
> candy
> hurry
> fancy

"Read these words out loud so that you can hear the syllables. . . . Tell me where to divide each, and I'll write the words to show the syllables."

> hap py
> can dy

> hur ry
> fan cy

"All of these words have two consonants together. The consonants have a vowel before them, and what letter comes after? [This line of questioning assumes the students know that *y* functions as a vowel at the end of a word. Were this not so, words like the four previous ones would be avoided until the dual role of *y* has been taught. Then they will be useful both to review the function of *y* as a vowel—which is what the teacher is doing now—and the generalization about dividing words into syllables.] I'm going to write some other words that have two consonants together. Tell me where to divide them into syllables."

> hump
> land
> free

Words like these three highlight the importance of all the details in the generalization being taught: two consonants that are preceded *and* followed by vowels.

While critical details like those just mentioned must always be accounted for in statements of generalizations, the statements themselves can be verbalized in any way that is meaningful for those being taught. Further, although teachers *must* be able to verbalize generalizations because they have to explain and discuss them, the same ability is desirable but not essential for students. What *is* essential is the ability to apply generalizations. Ronald Wardhaugh has written effectively about this:

> He [the child] may not be able to verbalize the rule any more than he could tell you how he ties his shoe laces; but just as he can demonstrate that he knows the rules for tying shoe laces by tying shoe laces, so he can demonstrate his knowledge of the rules for pronouncing *c* by reading *city* and *cat* correctly. His knowledge of the rules is demonstrated by his performance and it is unnecessary for him to learn to verbalize a statement about what he has learned, that is, about what he knows. [14, p. 136]

Inductive Instruction

As the deductive lesson pointed up, deductive procedures involve telling. In contrast, reasoning characterizes inductive instruction. Further, whereas a deductive lesson starts with a generalization and moves to particulars, inductive teaching begins with particulars (words), which, after being analyzed, allow for a generalization about them.

Applied to phonics, inductive instruction starts with words that have a visual-auditory feature in common—for instance, *down, day, do,* and *deep*. With the help of a teacher's questions about that feature, students are expected to reach a generalization that describes it. With the four words just cited, the generalization is a statement about *d* recording /d/. (Earlier chapters described inductive lessons with letter-sound relationships. See pages 57 and 82.)

An inductive lesson. The goal of the inductive lesson to be presented now is to teach about a factor that affects letter-sound relationships: *When there is one vowel in a syllable and it is in final position, it generally stands for its long sound.*

Prerequisites. Students are ready to learn the generalization if they (a) know the long and short vowel sounds, (b) know what a syllable is, (c) understand the meaning of "final position," and (d) can hear the individual sounds that make up a syllable.

Teaching the lesson. After reviewing the long and short vowel sounds, a teacher might begin an inductive lesson by listing on the board words like the following, all known to the students. (Words displaying the five vowels are preferable; however, suitable one-syllable words ending with *a* and *u* are nonexistent. At this point, one-syllable words are desirable to simplify the lesson.)

> me
> no
> she
> go
> hi

To help students induce the generalization from the five words, the teacher has them read aloud and then poses questions about certain visual and auditory features: "How many vowels are in *me?* . . . Which of its sounds does *e* stand for in *me,* the long or the short?" After asking similar questions about the remaining words, the teacher calls attention to the placement of the single vowel by asking, "Where is the one vowel in all these words?"

To bring the relevant details together, the teacher continues: "You've told me three things that are the same about all these words. You said they have one vowel, the vowel is at the end, and it stands for its long sound. Noticing all those things about words you don't know will help you figure out what they say. Now, whenever you see a word that you can't read and it has one vowel letter that's at the end, you'll know that it will have its long sound—or at least most of the time the vowel will stand for its long sound. I'm going to write all those things on the board to help you remember them." As the teacher writes, she reads:

1. one vowel letter
2. at the end
3. long sound

Pointing to each detail, the teacher helps the students verbalize the generalization getting attention. They will then be helped to use it to decode unfamiliar words like *be* and, later, *halo* and *silo*. The same generalization will also be helpful in decoding certain syllables in such words as *alto, tornado, cedar, erupt, cable, acorn, odor,* and *irate*.

WHICH METHODOLOGY TO USE

Whether to use inductive or deductive procedures to teach phonics is one of the many questions for which existing research provides no definite, unequivocal answer. Admittedly, books and articles have made positive claims for the special value of one or the other of the approaches (2, 4, 5, 11, 15); however, when the evidence is examined, it is found to be mixed with subjective interpretations, almost inevitably based on data that only describe beginning achievement in reading. Consequently, until studies are carried out that allow for fact-founded decisions, the best that can be done is to offer an opinion based on teaching experience and classroom visits. As you teach and gain your own insights, you may reach a different conclusion.

The conclusion recommended here is that an either-or choice is unnecessary. That is, teachers do not have to use one procedure *or* the other. Instead, in the day-by-day work of a classroom, moving back and forth between the two is the most natural and, in the long run, probably the most productive way to proceed. Nonetheless, it should be recognized that each way of teaching has distinct advantages.

For example, with children who are just beginning to read, the fact that words are composed of blended sounds represented by letters is totally new. At this stage, therefore, inductive instruction can make a contribution by helping them understand the very nature of our written language as known words are used to illustrate a letter-sound relationship.

Inductive instruction also has the potential of providing students with a strategy for independent learning by encouraging them to analyze written words in ways that can help them reason out phonic generalizations not yet taught. Inductive teaching thus gives them the opportunity not only to be independent learners but also to experience the delight of discovery. Of course, not all of this will happen with all children; still, inductive instruction does have this important potential. Used with beginners in phonics, it can also pave the way for a better understanding of what is being done when deductive methods are used later.

In spite of the potential, using only inductive teaching would slow down instruction to the point that a wide gap would soon exist between what is being taught and what students would find useful when they read. For the sake of efficiency, therefore, some instruction should be deductive. Emphasis on efficiency does not minimize the importance of careful explanations. Rather, it recognizes that there is neither the time nor the need to have students discover all the phonic generalizations inductively. Instead, once their basic meaning and useful-ness is understood, the details of each can be taught directly (deductively) and as quickly as students are able to learn and apply them to unknown words.

ISOLATION OF SOUNDS

Just as research offers no data-based guideline for using inductive or deductive instruction, so too has it failed to provide a reliable answer when the question, "Should sounds be isolated?" is posed. Once again, therefore, the recommenda-tion offered here is rooted in teaching experience and in what has been seen and heard in a large number of classrooms. ("Isolating sounds" refers to the explicit identification of a sound when a letter-sound relationship is taught. "The sound that *d* stands for in all these words is /d/" exemplifies an explicit identification.)

When letter-sound relationships are taught deductively, isolation of sounds is characteristic since this type of instruction starts with a generalization—for instance, with a statement like, "*S* stands for the sound /s/. You can hear it at the beginning of words like *see, so, saw,* and *six.*" With inductive instruction, on the other hand, sounds can be explicitly identified or not, depending on what a teacher chooses to do. Hence the question, "Should a sound be isolated from words and directly identified when it is taught?"

Some (3, 10) object to explicit identifications of sounds on the grounds that attempts to reproduce them apart from words distort them. Presumably, distor-tion is the reason why suggestions in the manuals of almost all the basal reader series deal with sounds as indirectly as they do. (See Figure 8.1 and the commen-tary about it.) In contrast, the recommendation here is that sounds should be explicitly identified whenever students seem to require direct identifications. An inductive lesson dealing with a letter-sound relationship will be described in order to clarify the recommended guideline.

The goal of the illustrative lesson is to teach the sound that *f* represents; therefore, the teacher begins with a list of known words that start with *f* and /f/. (To make it as easy as possible for students to hear /f/, each word begins with *f* followed by a vowel.)

> fast
> fun
> for
> five

After the children read the four words aloud, the teacher poses questions: "With what letter do all these words begin? . . . See if you can hear the sound that they start with. Read these words again and, as you do, listen for the begin-ning sound in each one. . . . Did you hear how each word began with the same sound? . . . That's the sound that *f* stands for. To be sure that you do hear its

Figure 8.1

DECODING

Phonemic analysis: The pupil will decode words containing the correspondence /e/e as in *get* (Introductory Activity).

Say the words: *Ted, get, Ben,* asking the pupils to listen for the sound in the middle of each word. Write the words on the chalkboard and have them read. Have pupils examine the words and find the one letter that is the same in all of them. Have the *e* in each word underlined. Elicit from the pupils that the letter *e* stands for the vowel sound heard in the middle of *Ted, get,* and *Ben.* Explain that the sound represented by *e* is called an unglided (short) vowel sound. Read the following words, asking the pupils to listen for the sound represented by *e* in each of the following words:

bed	set	wet	hem
fell	led	when	best

Then read each word again and have it repeated.

Now sketch a stick figure on the chalkboard. Explain that this is a drawing of a boy named Les.

Ask the children to help you describe Les. To do this, they will need to listen to some questions and be ready to answer them with words that contain the same vowel sound as in the word *Les.* Have pupils repeat this word; then continue. As each answer is given, write it on the chalkboard. Add details to the sketch as indicated by the answers to the questions. Be sure the children understand that each response must contain the same unglided (short) vowel sound as in *get* and *Les.*

Is this boy's name Larry or Les? (Les)
What shall we put in his hand—a bird or a net? (net)
What shall we put in his other hand—a bell or a ball? (bell)
What would be a good color for his shirt—red or blue? (red)
What numeral is printed on his shirt—nine or ten? (ten)
How old is he—six or seven? (seven)

Refer to the list of responses on the chalkboard, noting the vowel letter *e* in each word. Have volunteers reread the words and help the children make the generalization that the letter *e* in the words represents the unglided (short) vowel sound, the same sound as in *get.*

From Teacher's Edition of *Helicopters and Gingerbread* of READING 720, RAINBOW EDITION by Theodore Clymer and others, © Copyright, 1977, 1976, by Ginn and Company (Xerox Coropration). Used with permission.

●   *This manual segment illustrates how indirectly sounds will be taught by anyone who adheres to manual suggestions. What is recommended is so obscure, in fact, that some children may know no more about the connection between e and /ĕ/ at the end of the lesson than they did before it began.*

     Since isolating /ĕ/ from words does not seriously distort it, the reason for the careful avoidance of an explicit identification is unclear. Also unclear is why linguistic terminology (unglided sound) is used. Objections to the use of such unnecessary terms (which characterized the 1970s) are resulting in their absence in new materials.

sound, read the words again. . . . Can you think of another word that starts with the sound that you hear at the beginning of *fast* and *fun?*"

If responses are "food," "forest," "fire," and "fort" (all of which would be written to show that they begin with *f*), the children are offering evidence not only of having heard /f/ but also of having understood the meaning of "beginning sound." With such children, pronouncing /f/ is hardly necessary. Instead, the next step is to help them use their knowledge of the connection between /f/ and *f* to decode unfamiliar words. If they can read *sat,* for instance, they are ready to decode *fat.*★

But what about children who are unable to extract /f/ from words, even when many are used and numerous questions about them are posed? These students cannot be overlooked, for they are not uncommon. With them, pronouncing /f/ apart from words in which it occurs will not only *not* cause problems, it will be helpful. In fact, it will help not only in specifying the sound associated with *f* but also in clarifying the meaning of "beginning sound."

Still one more point needs to be made. To take the position that some students need to have sounds explicitly identified is not to support what has been heard in a few classrooms. I refer to unfortunate practices like having children go through daily recitations of "fuh-fuh-fuh" (an unnecessary distortion, by the way) even after they have demonstrated their knowledge of the sound that goes with *f.* I also refer to such obvious errors as associating *l* with "ul," *r* with "er," and *cr* with "cur."

USING PHONICS

On some occasions, what is seen and heard in classrooms points up how easy it is for conscientious teachers to get so caught up with teaching the content of phonics that they fail to highlight its usefulness. Consequently, how to get students to use what they know about letter-sound relationships, even when they know very little, will be described now. (The use of spoken sentences and minimal graphophonic cues was dealt with in the chapter about contextual cues. It illustrates a different, equally important early use of letter-sound relationships.) Later in this chapter, how a more advanced use of phonics is fostered will be described.

Early Use with Whole Word Methodology

In Chapter 5, whole word methodology was recommended for beginning instruction. If children know a few letter-sound relationships, they can enter into

---

★ Even when speech sounds are not explicitly identified—that is, are not isolated from words—this does not necessarily mean that students themselves do not isolate them. In other words, we cannot assume that what goes on in a student's mind mirrors what occurs during instruction.

efforts to teach whole words. To illustrate, if children need to learn the word *talk* and know the sound that *t* stands for, *talk* does not have to be immediately and directly identified. Instead, whole word instruction might begin by calling attention to three words, all unknown:*

draw
talk
room

Teacher comments start with: "I don't think you can read any of these words, can you? . . . One of them says 'talk.' Listen for the beginning sound in 'talk.' What letter stands for that sound? . . . Yes, the letter *t*. Which of these three words is the only one that could say 'talk'? . . . Yes [pointing to the second one], this says 'talk.' It's the only word up here that begins with *t,* so it's the only one that could say 'talk.' I'll erase the others. [This is important for reducing distractions.] Please look at *talk* so that you'll remember it when you see it in your story. What does this say? . . . Please spell it. . . . What's this word?"

Use in Spelling

In the course of a school day, a teacher will often want to write words on the board. A very wet morning, for instance, is a perfect time to discuss (and print) *rain*. Prior to writing it, comments like the following allow for the use of what is taught in beginning phonics: "Let me show you what the word *rain* looks like. What do you think is the first letter that I'll write? Think of the beginning sound in 'rain.' What letter stands for that sound? . . . Good. I'll write *r*. I have to add three other letters before it says 'rain.' Can anyone tell us what the last letter will be? Listen for the last sound in 'rain.' What letter stands for that sound? . . ."

Later, when children know about short vowel sounds, further attention to spelling and letter-sound relationships is possible. For instance: "The word that I just wrote says 'big.' What letter do I have to change to make it say 'bug'? What letter stands for the sound that you hear in the middle of 'bug'?"

Children can also work at the board. Now a teacher might direct each member of the group to write a word—for instance, *in*. Under *in,* the children can be asked to write related words like *on* and *an*. Other lists might include the following:

up	did	mop	mad	fun	not	sat	him
us	dad	map	mud	fan	net	set	ham
				fin	nut	sit	hum
							hem

---

* Every new word should not be taught this way because it is time-consuming. However, teaching some words this way is desirable since it helps children understand the usefulness of knowing about letters and sounds.

Earlier work at the board could dwell on having children add initial letters to make words:

and	all	ice	in	out
hand	tall	mice	win	bout
land	fall	nice	fin	pout
band	ball	dice	tin	shout
stand	wall	rice	pin	clout
brand	mall	lice	spin	
	stall	slice	thin	

As new words are written by the children—at the board or with pencil and paper at their desks—any whose meaning is unclear or unknown should be discussed. The activity, therefore, might also enhance oral vocabularies.

Use in Contexts

If a balanced use of all sources of help is to characterize students' strategies for dealing with unknown words, they must see instruction with phonics and instruction with contexts as being closely connected. How the connection can be stressed in written exercises was illustrated many times in Chapter 6. You will recall from that chapter a progression that went as follows:

Supplied	*Example*
Initial letter	I can open the s_____ with this key.
Initial/final letters	The cars are going too f_____t.
Initial syllable	Eating ap_____ is good for your teeth.
Total spelling	They are too *heavy* to walk on that ice.

How total spellings are used to figure out what a word says will be discussed later. Now, one additional way to show students how the combined use of contexts and partial spellings may be sufficient to figure out a word will be considered. It is illustrated below, first with separate sentences and then with a paragraph:

Don't j___mp in the house.
Can you c___tch this ball?
I can swim in the l___k___.

The morning was so c___ld that the children r___n to school. Wh___n they g___t there, it was too early to g___ inside. They played g___mes to k___p warm. At n___ne o'clock, the sch___l bell r___ng. They were gl___d to g___t inside the building.

What is absolutely essential with exercises like the preceding is that students see the connection between the exercises and what they should do and use when they come across an unfamiliar word while reading an assignment or something they themselves selected.

To show the usefulness of contexts (plus phonics) for reducing confusion with similar-looking words (for example, *show, shove; silver, sliver; where, there; tried, tired; lighting, lightning*), other written exercises are appropriate. As the following illustrations demonstrate, they can be adapted for different levels of achievement:

It _____ too big.
   saw   was

I want to _____ the picture.
         keep   peek

The _____ should slow down.
   terrific   traffic

Can you _____ this word?
    identity   identify

With sentences like these, the first job is to write the sensible word in the blank. The second one is to use the word not selected in a written sentence. Together, the two jobs allow a teacher to learn whether all the words were identified correctly. (They also keep students profitably occupied, thus freeing a teacher to work with a small group or an individual.)

Use in Substitutions and Additions

As more and more words and letter-sound relationships are learned, using phonics to figure out new or forgotten words becomes increasingly possible and productive. For instance, after children learn to identify *talk*—perhaps in the way that was discussed earlier in the chapter—and also know the sound that *w* stands for, they can use both learnings in what is called a consonant *substitution*. To demonstrate how replacing one sound for another produces a correct pronunciation, a teacher might write *talk* on the board, after which the instructional group would be asked to read it. The relationship between *w* and /w/ is reviewed next with known words like *will, was,* and *were.*

Once the necessary review of prerequisites is taken care of, the following can be written in a way that highlights the similarity as well as the single difference between the known *(talk)* and the unknown *(walk)*:

talk
walk

After the children read *talk,* the teacher should comment about the close visual similarity between *talk* and the word beneath it. She might mention that the second word not only looks very much like *talk* but also sounds something like it. At this point it is timely to say that it sounds like *talk* except that it begins with the sound that *w* stands for. Naturally, the next question is, "Can someone tell us what this second word is?" If someone can, the first of what will be many uses of substitutions has been demonstrated. If nobody can, the teacher will offer further help:

talk

I will <u>walk</u> home.

walk

In this case, all of the words in the sentence are known except *walk.* Now the teacher's question is, "What word would make sense in this sentence? Remember, it sounds something like *talk,* except it starts with the sound that goes with *w.*"

On those very rare occasions when even this amount of help is inadequate, the teacher can identify *walk* herself. ("This word is *walk.* I will walk home. Notice how much it sounds like *talk.* Talk, walk.") At this early point in instruction, answering one's own questions is fairly common; it also is helpful in clarifying their meaning. In time, responses will come quickly from the children.

Other types of substitutions are noted below, along with examples of *additions.*

Substitutions

Known word	*Decoded word*	*Process*
cage	page	(initial consonant substitution)
ice	ace	(initial vowel substitution)
and	ant	(final consonant substitution)
he	hi	(final vowel substitution)
act	ant	(medial consonant substitution)
shall	shell	(medial vowel substitution)

Additions

out	shout	(initial consonant addition)
an	ant	(final consonant addition)

A few observations about these processes are called for, beginning with the substitutions.

To begin, very simple and direct substitutions were listed since the purpose was to explain the process. It needs to be emphasized, therefore, that as students advance in reading they must learn to make more complicated substitutions; for instance, *handle* → *gamble.* Another type of substitution occurs when a reader uses *telephone* and *phonograph* to decode *telegraph.*

Looking at the additions, you will notice the absence of vowel additions. Why they are excluded can be explained with a word like *at*. To add a vowel—let us say *e*—to the beginning of *at* is to change the nature of the syllable and, as a result, to produce a word *(eat)* with an unrelated pronunciation. Adding *e* to the end of *at* has a similar effect. It results in a word—this time *ate*—with a different spelling pattern and thus an unrelated pronunciation.

Also to be noted in the lists is the possibility of decoding words (for example, *ant*) in different ways *(and → ant; an → ant)*. What readers will use depends both on what they know and on what they are able to recall.

For teachers, a most important point about the substitution and addition processes is that ability to use them does not happen automatically. Instead, it is achieved with explanations reinforced with practice. Some of the latter can be carried on with lists of words; for instance, if students can read *nine, best,* and *sit,* they are ready to read unknown but related words by substituting sounds. (See below.) If they know *ill* and are familiar with the pronunciation of the graphemic base *-ack,* they are ready to decode other unknown words by adding sounds:

Substitutions			Additions*	
nine	best	sit	ill	ack
mine	rest	sat	fill	back
fine	pest	set	pill	pack
pine	test		drill	black
dine	vest		still	stack
line	west		thrill	track
shine	crest		shrill	crack
			chill	shack

At more advanced levels, lists may be something like:

soda	candle	cottage
sofa	gamble	cabbage
toga	grumble	baggage

It is also important to remember that successful use of the addition and substitution processes with unknown words that are in a context (rather than in a list) is dependent upon the decoder's ability to recall relevant learnings at the time they are needed. More specifically, the child who comes across *mine* in a sentence and succeeds in decoding it through an initial consonant substitution *(nine → mine)* is successful because he (a) knows *nine,* (b) has learned about the sound that *m* represents, (c) mentally sees the connection between *nine* and *mine,*

* To provide for practice in additions, the letter whose sound is being added must be covered, then uncovered, so that responses to the first list would be: *ill, fill, ill, pill, ill, drill,* and so on. Unless this sequence is adhered to, the practice will be with substitutions *(fill → pill)* rather than with additions.

and (d) is able to recall all this when it is needed. The implication of the requirement is that phonics practice must provide students with ample opportunities to
decode words by recalling relevant learnings. This means that instead of completely monopolizing practice time with lists of words *(nine, mine, fine, . . .),* it
is far better to present an unknown word (for instance, *mine*) and then have
students try to read it by recalling on their own a known related word—*nine* or
some other. Still better is practice that places the unfamiliar word in a context so
that syntactic and semantic cues can function too. At the start, such practice will
be with written sentences, each containing an unknown word that is related to a
known one. With beginners, known words will be placed under the sentences.
(See the following examples.) The job for the reader is to figure out the unknown
word (which is underlined) with the help of the two known words:

The little boy sat on his mother's lap.
(let, cap)
What brand of gas does your car use?
(and, brown)

More advanced practice is similar except that helpful words are no longer provided. Instead, students are required to recall them on their own. All such practice
should be followed by a discussion of how the words were decoded and, if
necessary, of their meanings.

Not to be overlooked in this discussion is that substituting or adding sounds
does not always work. Knowing *one,* to be specific, is not going to help in getting
bone or *cone* decoded, just as *on* will not be directly helpful with *ton*—although it
will be with *Don.* Recognition of this makes it time to deal with a solution for
such problems. (How to solve them was illustrated in Chapter 7, starting on page
168. Because of the importance of such solutions, especially in the middle and
upper grades, please reread that material before proceeding.)

Flexible Use of Substitutions

Successful decoders at all grade levels apply what they have been taught *with
flexibility.* (They also keep in mind that written text, like oral language, makes
sense.) How flexibility helps when substituting a sound seems warranted but does
not produce a meaningful word will be discussed using *flood* as an example.

To start, let us say that the first time students see *flood* in print, it is embedded in the following context: *The rain keeps coming. It will flood all the basements.*
With this context, the sounds that *f, l,* and *d* stand for, combined with a reader's
knowledge of basements and of the fact that some get flooded when heavy rain

persists, should be sufficient to allow for a correct conclusion about the way *flood* is pronounced even though the double *o* has neither the long *(cool)* nor the short *(cook)* sound. (If the three sounds are not enough, more work with contexts and word fragments is called for.)

Let us shift now to a different situation in which *flood* is unfamiliar but appears in a less revealing context: *Nobody wants to think about a flood.* In this case, a reader should know from the words he can read that the unknown one is the name of something. However, since many nouns make sense in the context, the spelling of *flood* assumes importance. Therefore, noting *oo,* the reader should first try "flōōd," then "flŏŏd." He should also abandon both because neither is a recognizable word. What to do?

With one reader, trying the incorrect sounds for *oo* may be enough to suggest the correct one. With another, a trial-and-error process may be required in which other vowel sounds are tried until one clicks—that is, until a recognizable, sensible word results. More specifically, the second reader tries "flăd," "flĕd" (a real word, but it does not fit the context), "flĭd," and finally "flŭd."

The point of these illustrations is that successful decoders work differently but always with flexibility. The point for teachers is that flexible procedures do not just happen; they require practice. (The kinds of substitutions that were listed and discussed starting on page 186 mark the beginning of the trial-and-error processes being discussed now.) In this case, practice will focus on unknown, irregularly spelled words placed in contexts. It will be preceded by instruction in which a teacher *demonstrates* flexibility—that is, in which she herself models (verbalizes and acts out) flexible procedures by demonstrating the various routes that are available whenever initial efforts with irregularly spelled words fail to result in meaningful solutions. Such modeling merits far more time in middle- and upper-grade classrooms than is ordinarily assigned to it. Perhaps the scarcity reflects the fact that the need for both flexibility and modeling is not recognized in the content of teaching manuals.

Advanced Use of Additions: Blending Sounds

When procedures for working out the pronunciation of *flood* were discussed, a student's ability to combine sounds to produce a word was taken for granted. In practice, however, such an assumption will not always be accurate. This means that instructional time needs to go to blending sounds to produce syllables or words. Such blending, as illustrations will show, is an advanced use of the phonic additions discussed earlier, starting on page 186 (for example, *an* → *and*).

For the first illustration, let's do some mind reading. Let's also assume that the word *ramp* is not in a student's reading vocabulary; that she comes across it in the sentence *In place of stairs, a ramp was being used to get into the new house;* that she does not know (or does not recall) related words like *cramp* and *damp;* and, finally, that the following are her thoughts as she works on *ramp.**

> *There's only one vowel, so this is one syllable. One vowel not at the end probably means a short sound. That would be ă → ră → răm → rămp. Oh, sure. Ramp. Probably it's a board. In place of stairs, a ramp was being used to get into the new house.*

Admittedly, decoders who have heard the word *ramp* and know what one is are likely to use the three consonant letters plus contextual cues to achieve a swift identification. And, in fact, that is what ought to be done. The more detailed procedures just described are useful, however, in making several important points.

Decoding: Some Reminders

1. The initial step in decoding focuses on syllabication because generalizations about letter-sound relationships and the factors that affect them apply to syllables, not to words.

2. Decisions about the sounds that letters in a syllable are likely to record start with an examination of the *whole* of the syllable.

3. Once sounds are tentatively selected, they are blended to produce a syllable. If the syllable begins with a vowel, blending follows the sequence of the letters (ĕ → ĕn → ĕnd). On the other hand, when a consonant is the initial letter, the first vowel sound is produced, after which the initial consonant sound is added. In the case of *ramp,* therefore, the initial sequence is: ă → ră. The rest of the blending parallels the order of the remaining letters (ă → ră → răm → rămp, or ă → ră → rămp). This sequence is recommended in order to reduce distortions that result from isolated consonant sounds. In this case, the goal is to avoid a pronunciation that sounds like "ru-amp" because, although some children can switch from "ru-amp" to "ramp," many cannot.

Recommended sequences for combining sounds are further illustrated below.

Syllable	Blending sequence
shape	ā → shā → shāpe
owl	ow → owl

---

* One serious limitation in such a portrayal is the impossibility of describing thoughts that occur virtually simultaneously. What is given, then, is an approximation of what one decoder might consider. What any decoder is likely to think about depends not only on the word causing problems but also on (a) the words that are in his reading, listening, and speaking vocabularies, (b) what and how well he has been taught decoding procedures, (c) his prior experiences in working out other words, (d) the context in which the new word appears, and (e) the background knowledge that he brings to the context. All this indicates that each decoding experience is unique.

guard	ar → guar → guard
stem	ĕ → tĕ → stĕ → stĕm
	(or)
	ĕ → stĕ → stĕm

The last example illustrates the usefulness of being able to work with consonant clusters.

The following examples are designed to make the point that some students can leap to identifications (especially when contexts are used) with no need to proceed letter by letter, sound by sound.

Syllable	*Blending sequence*
throat	ō̸ → thrō̸ → thrōat
punch	ŭ → pŭnch
thrift	ĭ → thrĭf → thrĭft
brand	ănd → brănd
sulk	ŭ → sŭ → sŭlk
apt	ă → ăpt

Work with combining sounds into words will have chalkboards displaying something like the following:

ănt	part	ē¢l	brŭsh	rāng¢
ă	ar	ē¢	ŭ	ā
ăn	par	ē¢l	brŭ	rā
ănt	part		brŭsh	rān
				rāng¢

Blending is done aloud, first with guidance and demonstrations by the teacher and later with oral responses from students.

Decoding Multisyllabic Words

As students read increasingly difficult material, multisyllabic words become common. To illustrate how a decoder should go about figuring out multisyllabic words, more mind reading will be depicted. This time, the thoughts are those of a reader who has problems with *umpire*. It is in the context *An umpire is not always the best-liked person*. (As you read the thoughts, write whatever is suggested much as you would do on a chalkboard were you modeling the decoding for your students. This will make the processes being used more graphic.)

Let's see now. There's m *and* p *with vowels before and after. I'll try dividing it between them. One vowel not at the end. I'll try the short sound for* u. *I know the sound for* m, *so that's* ŭ → ŭm. *I can't think of any word that starts with "um." I better look at the second syllable. Oh, that looks like* fire. *Maybe it says "pire."*

Sure it does. Umpire. An umpire is not always the best-liked person. *Boy, that's for sure.*

Again, the thoughts of this decoder allow for important observations.

1. Once a word is divided into syllables, the pronunciation of one or more of them may result from a simple substitution—for instance, fire → pire. (Some decoders might have used another substitution for the first syllable: am → um.)
2. The pronunciation of each syllable, plus contextual cues, may be enough to bring to mind a multisyllabic word that is known in its spoken form. That automatically indicates which syllable is stressed.

A different decoder is unable to read *bacon* in the sentence *They had bacon and eggs for breakfast.* Following are his thoughts:

> *The c has vowels in front of it and in back of it, so I'll divide it between* a *and* c. *One vowel at the end might mean the long sound. That would be* ā → bā. *Oh,* bacon! *Bacon and eggs. They had bacon and eggs for breakfast.*

These brief thoughts prompt further observations about decoding:

1. When contextual cues are generous, highly restrictive constraints are placed on the word being decoded. Sometimes they are so restrictive that only one word is possible. At other times, as was true of *bacon,* constraints are enough to make partial decoding productive.
2. Life's experiences and the knowledge they bring always affect decoding. Thus, children who themselves have had a breakfast of bacon and eggs will find it easier to decode *bacon* in the context cited than will those who have not.
3. Decoding one word helps with others. Having figured out *bacon,* a decoder might find it fairly easy later to figure out *beacon.* And the decoder who successfully coped with *umpire* should encounter no major problems if he has to identify *empire* or *vampire.*

To allow for attention to other guidelines for teachers of more advanced readers, further work with a multisyllabic word will be discussed with a detailed explanation rather than with a reader's thoughts. This time the unknown word is *argue,* and it is the only unfamiliar word in the sentence, *She is one who likes to argue.*

As always, the decoder's first step is to consider the likely syllabication of *argue.* An inspection of *all* the letters shows two consonants *(r* and *g)* that are preceded and followed by vowels *(a* and *u).* This suggests the syllables *ar* and *gue.*

Might there be more than the two syllables? (Because you can read *argue,* the pronunciation indicates two. However, one who cannot read *argue* does not hear anything and must rely on visual help.) The first syllable, *ar,* cannot be subdivided because it has but one vowel. The second syllable, *gue,* has two vowels, but the second is a final *e,* which is not likely to be recording a sound. That being the case, *gue* is also one syllable. The syllabic division based on visual cues, therefore, is *ar gue.*

The decoder's next step is to consider the likely sounds in each syllable. With the first, there is one vowel, *a,* but it is followed by *r.* This suggests that *ar* probably represents the blend heard in *art.*

All of the letters comprising the second syllable, *gue,* are considered next. Because *g* is not followed by *e, i,* or *y,* it probably records its hard sound. At least that will be tried initially. The final *e* suggests a long sound for *u.* With all the likely sounds in *gue* now considered, the next step is to produce a syllable: ūe → gū¢.

Having arrived at possible pronunciations for the two syllables, the decoder is ready to consider which gets special stress. If *argue* is familiar in its spoken form, the sounds derived from the phonic analysis will suggest both the word (including its stressed syllable) and its meaning. And it is a word that makes sense in the given context.

What has been described in some detail can now be summarized as follows:

Focus		*Concern*
Word	1.	Syllabication
Each syllable, one at a time	2.	Letter-sound relationships
	3.	Blending
Word	4.	Stressed syllable?
	5.	Does the conclusion about the word make sense?

In addition to having a strategy for dealing with unknown words, students must also know how to try out different sounds. That skill was discussed earlier and is further illustrated in the next section because of the common occurrence of irregularly spelled words in more advanced materials.

Trying Out Sounds

To discuss trying out sounds, the thoughts of still another decoder will be presented. This time the baffling word is *prove,* and the context is *That doesn't prove a thing.*

The last e *probably means one syllable. Two vowels. The* o *has a long sound, so that's* ō → prōv¢. *Prōve? I never heard of that. I'll try the short sound:* ŏ → prŏv¢.

Gee, that's not a word either. Let's see. I'll try some other sounds: prāv, prēv, prīv, pr—I can't even say it with a long u sound. I better keep going: proov—oh, proov. Sure. That doesn't *prove* a thing.

The type of flexibility permeating this decoder's thoughts is so essential that it calls for elaboration.

1. When students start decoding a word, they use phonic generalizations. What results from the application of such generalizations must then be compared with what is stored in their auditory memory in order to determine (a) whether a real word has been produced and (b) whether the produced word makes sense.
2. Whenever the produced word is unsatisfactory, either because it is not a word or because it does not fit the context, the decoder should begin replacing one sound with another until a solution is found. Since it is vowels that frequently impede arriving at correct pronunciations, the decoder starts the substitution process with them.
3. Preparation for substituting vowel sounds begins with single-syllable words like those referred to in a previous section of the chapter (*fun, fan, fin; sat, set, sit*).

To allow for a final statement of guidelines and reminders, the efforts of one more decoder will be portrayed. In this instance, *giddy* is the word causing problems in the context *The children were too giddy to hear what the man said.*

I'll divide it between the d's. *The first syllable probably sounds like* kid *so that would be jid. The* y *has the long e sound so the last syllable is dē.* Jiddy. Jiddy? *I never heard of a word like that. Maybe g doesn't have the soft sound. I'll try the hard one. That would be* giddy. *That's okay.* The children were too giddy to hear what the man said.

The thoughts of this student underscore further reminders for teachers:

1. Although vowel sounds are usually the ones a decoder will have to "play with" to achieve correct identifications, different sounds for consonant letters may also have to be tried. This is certainly true of *g* and *c,* and also of *qu* and *x.* Syllables in which vowels are followed by *r* or by *re* are other signs of a possible need for adjustments (for example, *earn, barrel*).
2. While the adjustment made by the decoder just referred to (jiddy → giddy) proved to be correct, it must be remembered that "giddy" was recognized as being correct because the decoder (a) knew it in its spoken form and (b) found it to be a word whose meaning fit the context. What if this had not been the case? What if, after a number of trial-and-error efforts, nothing clicked? What then? That is the time for the decoder to seek help in a dictionary, both to check on the pronunciation and to learn the meaning of the unknown word.

PHONICS AND BASAL READER MATERIALS

All of the basal reader series give considerable attention to phonics starting in kindergarten; nonetheless, this and the previous chapter covered phonics instruction and practice in detail because what basal reader manuals recommend is not likely to produce superior decoders since so much is left undone. The following characterizes typical basal reader instruction:

1. The sounds that letters record are not explicitly identified. For example, /w/ may be referred to throughout a basal program as "the sound that *web* begins with."
2. Since sounds are not directly identified, blending them to produce words or syllables is not covered.
3. The process of trying out different sounds when the first one fails to produce something sensible is often ignored.
4. What is taught is frequently applied to words that students are already able to read.
5. Practice almost never focuses on unknown words placed in contexts.
6. Teachers are not encouraged to model the decoding process even though demonstrations are better than verbal explanations for teaching a skill like decoding.
7. While much attention goes to phonics in the primary grades, its use in subsequent grades is deemphasized even though that is when phonics should allow for independence in coping with unknown words.

The purpose of Chapters 7 and 8 is to equip teachers and prospective teachers with sufficient knowledge of phonics that they will be able to deliver instruction that is far superior to what most existing teaching manuals recommend.

PRACTICE

Whether instruction derives from manuals or a knowledgeable teacher's head, it must be complemented with practice. Examples of practice have already been described, and more follow.

Letter–Sound Relationships

How to instruct about the sounds that letters record has been illustrated. Although such teaching should always allow time for practice, the amount for some children may be insufficient to allow for the automatic recall that is necessary for decoding. For that reason, examples of additional practice with letter-sound relationships follow. All of the examples can be adapted according to the needs and abilities of particular students.

- Display cards on which a letter or digraph is printed. Distribute unlabeled pictures next. Let the children take turns naming a picture and finding the card that shows its initial (or final) letter(s).

- With children sitting at a table, have each select about five small letter cards. Call out words selected from a pile of word cards but do not show them to the participants. As each word is named, the child holding the letter that records its initial sound lays that card down. The first child out of cards is the winner. To encourage careful listening, an incorrect association results in the child's getting an additional card.

- Using small boxes labeled with a letter or a digraph and a collection of small objects and trinkets, let children take turns naming a trinket and the letter with which its name begins. As this is done, the trinket is placed in the appropriate box.

- Bingo-like cards can be prepared with letters printed in the boxes. As the teacher (or an able student) names a word, the children cover its beginning (or final) letter if it appears on their cards.

- To reinforce letter-sound connections and, in addition, to provide practice in hearing sounds in various positions in a syllable, a small sheet like the following is useful. To illustrate, if the letter of concern is *n,* its sound

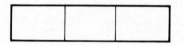

would be reviewed and then listened for in one-syllable words named by the teacher. If one is *pan,* the children should place a small marker in the right-hand box. Were another *not,* markers go in the left-hand box. Should *ant* be named, the marker belongs in the middle box. (Paper letters can be used as markers.)

- A sheet like the following allows for similar practice.

	Sounds		
	beginning	middle	end
1.	_____	_____	____
2.	_____	_____	____
3.	_____	_____	____

With this sheet, children put a check mark under the appropriate heading as the teacher again names one-syllable words in which a selected sound—the letter that records it could be displayed—occurs in various positions.

- To provide for periodic summaries, scrapbooks or sound books can be assembled by having children clip pictures of items whose names begin with a selected letter and sound. Sources for pictures are old magazines, store catalogs, newspapers, and greeting cards. If collections become large, individual books can be compiled with titles like "Vowels," "Consonants," and "Digraphs."

- Summaries can also be achieved with the help of large sheets of paper folded in accordion fashion. (Somewhere, the selected letter should be displayed. Without it, the practice would only be focusing on auditory discrimination.) Pictures whose names start with the selected letter and sound are pasted in the folds. To review a letter-sound association, a child pulls out each sheet and names the pictures.

- Have each member of a practice group attach a paper seal (with the child's name on it) to a bulletin board. In a box, place colored paper circles (balls) on which a letter or a digraph appears. The children take turns selecting a ball. If a child can name a word that begins with the sound that the selected letter stands for, he places that ball on top of his seal's nose. At the end, the one with the most balls being balanced is the winner.

- Table and floor games are useful for practice designed to solidify letter-sound relationships. One simple board is illustrated here:

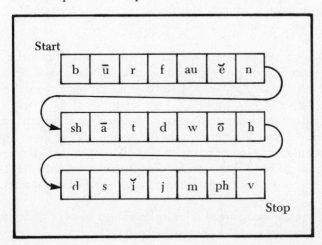

In this game, participants return to the starting point whenever they are unable to name a word that starts with the letter or digraph printed in a square.

When practice calls for students to think of, or name, words that start with a given letter or sound, some may not be able to recall even one. In such cases, riddles are helpful—for instance, "I'm thinking of a word that starts with the letter *m*. It's the name of something to eat."

One further observation needs to be made about practice with letter-sound relationships and, on the other hand, practice that is only concerned with auditory discrimination. It is necessary because when the latter is the focus, certain responses are correct even though they are incorrect when practice is with letter-sound associations. More specifically, if a teacher is providing practice in hearing /s/ and a child offers "Cynthia" as a word that begins with /s/, it is correct even though the teacher's own spoken examples were words like *see, Saturday,* and *six*. When instruction and practice shift to letter-sound relationships—specifically to the one between /s/ and *s*—and the teacher writes *see, Saturday,* and *six* as words exemplifying the relationship, a response like "Cynthia" is incorrect. It should not simply be rejected, however. Instead, the child proposing "Cynthia" should be told how it is correct (spoken form begins with the right sound), as well as how it is incorrect (written form does not begin with *s*). Luckily, responses like "Cynthia" provide opportunities for emphasizing that a speech sound is not always spelled with the same letter, and, further, for helping children begin to learn about the importance of flexibility for decoding.

Additions and Substitutions

By now, you should appreciate the value of a student's being able to add and replace sounds in syllables; hence you should value ideas for practice that supplement those mentioned earlier. Some possibilities follow.

- Make a fishing pond by painting a cardboard box blue inside. For a pole, attach a piece of string to a long, thin stick. To the end of the string attach a magnet. On small, fish-shaped cards print familiar words that allow for substitutions and additions. To each of these cards attach a paper clip. Finally, throw the fish into the pond. As children take turns catching a fish and naming the word printed on it (for example, *rock*), pose a question like, "What would it say if it began with *s* [or *bl*] instead of *r*?" If *ten* is caught, the question might be, "What would it say if you added the letter *t* to the end?" Correct responses allow children to keep their fish, temporarily.

Because the ability to *recall* relevant learnings is of critical importance for decoding, practice like the following is necessary:

- On small cards, write unfamiliar words that can be decoded with the help of known words plus substitutions or additions. Place the cards in a box (Surprise Box) or bag (Grab Bag). Let students select them and try to figure out what the words say. Each successful child will be asked to tell the word that helped with the new one. Both should then be written on a chalkboard to highlight the relationship.

Students in need of practice with additions and substitutions will enjoy working with bulletin-board displays. Descriptions of two follow.

- To the bottom of a board entitled "Iceberg Hop," attach white construction paper cut to look like icebergs. On the peaks print graphemic bases that have been studied. Make a set of letter cards and a small paper penguin. Children choose a letter and, holding the penguin, become one by hopping from iceberg to iceberg naming words by combining the selected letter with the graphemic base.

- A bulletin board in the spring might feature large daisies with petals that can be rotated. Single consonants and digraphs are printed on the petals; a graphemic base is printed on the center of each flower. Children take turns working with a daisy. By moving the petals, they can make and identify words formed by the rotating letters plus the graphemic base.

More ideas for practice with additions follow.

- Each participant receives a card showing six graphemic bases. For instance:

        _____ ap   _____ ock

        _____ ine   _____ ile

        _____ en   _____ ang

Children take turns selecting small letter cards from a deck. If a chosen letter forms a word with one of the graphemic bases and the child can say what the word is, he puts that letter in front of the base. Otherwise, the card is returned to the bottom of the deck. The first child to make six words is the winner.

- Cut out a small opening in the side of a shoebox. Immediately to the right print a graphemic base. On a narrow card that is longer than the box, print single consonants and consonant digraphs. By slowly pulling the cardboard strip through the box, children can practice adding sounds to make words.

- A written exercise allows for still more practice with additions. Now, columns of words like those shown below are used:

rake	oil	each
ark	ill	ink
rain	ripe	oats
pine	and	hare

By adding a certain consonant, cluster, or digraph to a row of three words (for example, *rake, oil, each*), new words can be formed *(brake, boil, beach)*.

More Advanced Decoding

Advanced decoding ability results from consistently excellent instruction over several years combined with numerous opportunities to apply what has been taught. As was mentioned before, even though instruction *and* application are both essential, far too many schools give excessive amounts of time to content and far too little to its use. It seems appropriate, therefore, to offer the following reminder:

INSTRUCTION IN A PRODUCTIVE
PHONICS PROGRAM

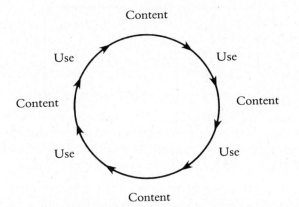

At advanced levels, use of phonics should concentrate on the flexible application of generalizations to irregularly spelled words. ("Advanced level" refers not to a grade but to a proficiency level. When it is reached depends not only on the students but also on the two other factors: the quality of instruction that has been available and the opportunities provided for use.) To make advanced practice both realistic and productive, irregularly spelled words should be (a) unknown in their written form and (b) placed in contexts. Available sources for both the words and the contexts are basal readers, content subject textbooks, and whatever else students need or want to read. Depending on the amount of practice that is required, other material can be teacher-composed sentences and what appears in sources like magazines and newspapers.

As advanced practice takes place, weaknesses may become evident. Certain students, for example, may have problems with blending. In such cases, exercises like those referred to earlier are appropriate:

bŭlk	urgȼ	quāįl	auk
ŭ	ur	āį	au
bŭl	urgȼ	quāį	auk
bŭlk		quāįl	

Since most decoding problems at this level lie with multisyllabic words, blending practice can include nonsense syllables if they are parts of multisyllabic words. That they *are* parts of words should be pointed out with illustrations (for example, *ruf* in *ruffle; vert* in *invert*). Whenever it seems appropriate, blending sounds to produce syllables can be followed by the question, "What would the pronunciation be if the vowel sound were the schwa sound?" (This is the time to remind students of the frequent occurrence of the schwa sound in unstressed syllables.)

As advanced practice takes place, inadequate knowledge of generalizations might be uncovered. To help with this deficiency, exercises like those shown next are useful. Now, *known* words are featured so that decisions can be made as to whether they are regularly or irregularly spelled. (A regularly spelled word is one whose pronunciation can be predicted from its spelling. Since phonic generalizations are the sources for predictions, these exercises offer a way to reinforce and review previously taught generalizations.)

	Regularly Spelled?				Regularly Spelled?		
	yes	no			yes	no	
done		X	dun	excuse	X		
port	X			double		X	dubble
your		X	yure	allergy			
since				cantaloupe			
fruit				sulpha			
once				chamber			
throat				erase			
get				eager			

When students are successful with one-syllable words, multisyllabic words can be included in "regularly spelled" assignments. When they are, many opportunities become available to call their attention to a most important prediction:

Vowel sounds in unstressed syllables are often reduced to the schwa sound. Multisyllabic words also offer opportunities to review that the first step in decoding is a consideration of syllables since generalizations concerned with sounds are applied to them, not to words.

Sometimes students themselves can hunt through dictionaries and compile lists for "regularly spelled" exercises. When they *have* been involved, they have come up with such observations as the following:

the frequency with which words end in silent e

> charge
> geese
> clique
> solve
> cause
> verse
> league

the frequency with which final e *signals information about the sound* c *and* g *will represent*

> bounce
> sauce
> chance
> edge
> cage
> barge

the variety of ways for spelling a final syllable containing /əl/

> purple
> symbol
> pencil
> cancel
> vocal
> careful
> hostile

Attention to connections between spellings and pronunciations can also spark interest in word origins. For example, the student who asks, "How come *one* and *once* are spelled the way they are?" is providing the perfect opportunity to help everyone discover the information that is available in unabridged dictionaries. Other spellings—for instance, *debt, doubt,* and *receipt*—offer the chance to discuss the influence of Latin on English. And many other words can pave the way to books that tell interesting tales both about individual words and about curious expressions. (Such books are discussed in Chapter 10.) What all this indicates is that even something like phonics can be a vehicle for letting students in on the fact that language is a fascinating topic.

SUMMARY

Chapter 8 discussed and illustrated ways for teaching (a) the content of phonics and (b) how it functions in getting words that are visually unfamiliar identified. Even though phonics *was* the concern, the significance of oral language and contextual cues for making identifications was not overlooked. Nor should they be in instructional programs.

As Chapter 7 explained, the content of phonics is about letter-sound associations, what affects them, and syllabication. The present chapter showed that all of this can be taught deductively or inductively. While the advantages of each were named, which procedure to use ought to be determined by how students respond. Or, as a maxim suggests, "If something works, don't fix it."

Whether presented deductively or inductively, phonics instruction is successful when students are able to use what is taught to figure out unknown words on their own. As Chapter 8 showed, use takes a variety of forms and includes adding, substituting, trying out, and blending sounds. That teachers need to demonstrate or model each of these processes was underscored. Ideas for practicing these skills were listed too.

REVIEW

1.   Explain the meaning of the following statements in a way that would have meaning for someone who has not read Chapter 8.

   (a)   The less prediction allowed for by the text, the more do visual features have to be used to figure out the identity of unknown words.
   (b)   Even though a child succeeds in working out the pronunciation of a word, it will not be in his sight vocabulary. Practice is still required.
   (c)   Known words should figure in phonics instruction. On the other hand, unknown words should be selected when the objective is applying what was taught.

2.   Whenever a child has to stop reading in order to figure out a word, he should reread the sentence in which it is embedded once he gets the word decoded. Why is the rereading important?

3.   We have all experienced the inability to recall something when it was needed. This happens all the time with phonics instruction. For that reason, many teachers keep a word notebook divided into sections for letter-sound relationships, factors that affect them, and syllabication. Each page in the most helpful notebook begins with a statement of a generalization. Two columns of words, each of which exemplifies the generalization, follow the statement. One column is comprised of easy words, the other of more difficult ones. The first are meant for instruction, whereas the second will be useful for application.

To get you started with some word lists, name four suitable words for each generalization stated below. The first two should be easy words; the last two, more difficult.

(a)   For purposes of syllabication, consonant digraphs function as if they were one consonant.

(b)   When y stands for the final sound in a multisyllabic word, it usually records /ē/.

(c)   Vowel sounds in unstressed syllables are often reduced to /ə/.

4.   See if you can complete the assignment sheet shown on page 201. Before responding to each word, divide it into syllables with the help of the generalizations discussed in Chapter 7. (Remember: The occurrence of the schwa sound in an unstressed syllable does not make a word irregularly spelled.)

5.   Chapter 8 recommended modeling procedures for working out the identity of irregularly spelled words. With that in mind, let us assume that *group* is unknown and is in the sentence *Schools group children by their ages.* Demonstrate how you would model for children the decoding of *group*.

REFERENCES

1.   Beck, I. L., and McCaslin, E. S. *An Analysis of Dimensions That Affect the Development of Code-Breaking Ability in Eight Beginning Reading Programs.* Pittsburgh: University of Pittsburgh, Learning Research and Development Center, 1978.

2.   Bliesmer, E. P., and Yarborough, B. H. "A Comparison of Ten Different Reading Programs in First Grade." *Phi Delta Kappan* 46 (June 1965): 500–504.

3.   Bloomfield, Leonard. "Linguistics and Reading." *Elementary English Review* 19 (April–May 1942): 125–130, 183–186.

4.   Chall, Jeanne. *Learning to Read: The Great Debate.* New York: McGraw-Hill, 1967.

5.   Cleland, Donald L., and Miller, Harry B. "Instruction in Phonics and Success in Beginning Reading." *Elementary School Journal* 65 (February 1965): 278–282.

6.   Durkin, Dolores. "The Importance of Goals for Instruction." *Reading Teacher* 28 (January 1975): 380–383.

7.   Durkin, Dolores. "Phonics: Instruction That Needs to Be Improved." *Reading Teacher* 28 (November 1974): 152–156.

8.   Durkin, Dolores. "Some Questions about Questionable Instructional Materials." *Reading Teacher* 28 (October 1974): 13–17.

9.   Durkin, Dolores. *Strategies for Identifying Words.* 2d ed. Boston: Allyn and Bacon, 1981.

10.   Fries, Charles C. *Linguistics and Reading.* New York: Holt, Rinehart and Winston, 1963.

11.   Gurren, Louis, and Hughes, Ann. "Intensive Phonics vs. Gradual Phonics in Beginning Reading: A Review." *Journal of Educational Research* 58 (April 1965): 339–346.

12.   Haddock, Maryann. "Teaching Blending in Beginning Reading Instruction Is Important." *Reading Teacher* 31 (March 1978): 654–658.

13. Samuels, S. Jay. "Comparison of Word Recognition Speed and Strategies of Less Skilled and More Highly Skilled Readers." *Reading Research Quarterly* 11, no. 1 (1975–1976): 72–86.
14. Wardhaugh, Ronald. *Reading: A Linguistic Perspective.* New York: Harcourt, Brace and World, 1969.
15. Weintraub, Samuel. "A Critique of a Review of Phonics Studies." *Elementary School Journal* 67 (October 1966): 34–40.

CHAPTER 9

STRUCTURAL ANALYSIS

PREVIEW

Chapter 6 pointed out that English is a positional language because it relies on word order to convey meaning. The forthcoming chapter exists because English is an inflected language, which is to say that it also communicates with affixes. This second characteristic is apparent when the meanings of pairs of words like door *and* doors, walk *and* walked, *and* common *and* uncommon *are contrasted.*

Because English is inflected, words vary in their structure. With some, it is simple (for example, mother*), whereas the structure of other words is more complex (for example,* mothers, motherly, unmotherly*). Simple or complex, the structure of a word that is unfamiliar to a reader in its visual form is another source of help for getting it figured out. Examining a word to determine its structure for that purpose is the subject of this chapter.*

Discussing such a topic requires certain terminology; consequently, the best preparation for Chapter 9 is a knowledge of those terms. It is recommended, therefore, that the following definitions be studied before the chapter is begun.

Word family. *Words having a common origin. They often share a base that is itself a word (*teach, teacher, teachable, *etc.) but not always (*spectator, inspect, spectacular, *etc.).*

Root. *That member of a family that has the simplest structure (for example,* teach*).*

Base. *A synonym for* root.

Compound word. *One composed of more than one root (for example,* doorknob, lifelong*).*

Prefix. *A unit of one or more letters placed before a root that alters its meaning (for example,* amoral, pre*school).*

Suffix. *A unit of one or more letters added to the end of a root that alters its meaning (for example,* treeless*) or grammatical function (for example,* trees*). A unit that affects meaning is a* derivational *suffix. One that alters grammatical function without changing the inherent meaning of the root is an* inflectional *suffix. Inflectional suffixes are also called* inflections.

Affix. *A prefix or suffix.*

Derived word. *One composed of a root plus a prefix (for example,* unlock*), or a root plus a derivational suffix (for example,* flawless*), or a root plus a prefix plus a derivational suffix (for example,* interchangeable*). A derived word is also referred to as a* derivative.

Inflected word. *One composed of a root plus an inflectional suffix (for example,* wants*).*

As you may have already inferred from the two previous chapters, the concern of phonics is unknown roots. The more specific concern is for their spellings, viewed as cues for their pronunciations.

As the Preview to this chapter suggested, the concern of structural analysis is the possibility that an unknown word may have one or more affixes, which are sources of help with both pronunciation *and* meaning.

To show how phonic and structural analyses function together (in conjunction with contextual cues), let's examine the thoughts of a reader as she decodes *flawlessly,* found in *All the children danced flawlessly.*

> *It tells how they danced (contextual cue), so* l, y *is an inflection (structural cue). Maybe* l, e, s, s, *is a suffix, like in* careless *(structural cue). That leaves* f, l, a, w. *The* a *and* w *go together because* w *couldn't be a syllable all by itself (phonic cue). That would be* aw → flaw *(blending).* Flaw. *That means something that's wrong with something (oral language), so* flawless *means without anything being wrong (structural analysis). There was nothing wrong with their dancing (context).* All the children danced flawlessly *(rereads to comprehend sentence).*

Read carefully, the thoughts of the decoder suggest (a) what needs to be taught for structural analysis and (b) how contextual, graphophonic, and structural cues (plus oral language) function jointly.

OBJECTIVES FOR INSTRUCTION WITH WORD STRUCTURE

If students are to acquire maximum skill in using structural cues for figuring out pronunciations and meanings, each lesson about an affix, starting with the very first one, must realize certain goals. Before they are specified, a review of the decoder's thoughts that were just described is in order since they reflect good, systematic instruction.

You will recall, first of all, that the decoder knew that *l, e, s, s* affixed to the end of a word (*flawless)* is likely to be a suffix. With that tentative conclusion, the four letters suggested not only how this suffix is pronounced (/ləs/) but also how it affects the meaning of roots ("without" or "doesn't have any"). Because *-less* had been taught well, the only part of the word that remained a puzzle was the root (*flaw),* and what had been taught in phonics allowed for working out its pronunciation. (With another decoder, *flaw* might have been identified as a familiar base word, once *-ly* and *-less* were temporarily separated from it.)

To make sure that all students can cope successfully with derived and inflected words, lessons must be planned so as to achieve certain goals:

OBJECTIVES OF EVERY LESSON WITH AN AFFIX
Student:

1. Knows the spelling and pronunciation of the affix.
2. Understands how the affix affects the meaning of roots.
3. Can transfer all this to a new situation—that is, to derived or inflected words that did not figure in the lesson.

Before lessons with affixes are described, the analysis of the decoder's thoughts about *flawlessly* will be continued in order to call attention to how the various types of cues functioned together.

SEQUENCE FOR USING ALL AVAILABLE CUES

Proficient readers use whatever information is available to get an unfamiliar word figured out both quickly and correctly. And they use that information not piece by piece but practically simultaneously. In contrast, children who are in the process of acquiring proficiency benefit from having a strategy that helps them use information that divides into contextual, structural, and graphophonic. How each functions was demonstrated by the decoder working on *flawlessly*. Reviewing her thoughts reveals a sequence that goes something like the following:

SEQUENCE FOR USING CUES

1. *Contextual cues:* looking for syntactic and semantic information.
2. *Structural cues:* looking for letters that indicate one or more affixes, which are mentally laid aside for the purpose of revealing the root.
3. *Graphophonic cues:* decoding the root if it is not familiar.
4. *Structural cues:* replacing affixes.
5. *Contextual cues:* checking to see whether the conclusion about the word makes sense.

The sequence just outlined might have raised two questions: (a) Why are structural cues considered before graphophonic cues, and (b) If structural cues *are* considered first, why is phonics dealt with in this textbook before word structure?

Why decoders should look first for structural elements (prefixes and suffixes) has to do with the fundamental importance of meaning. More specifically, because structural cues can help in getting an unknown word divided into *meaningful* units, the possibility of affixes' being part of the unknown word should be considered before thoughts turn to phonological units (syllables). The following comparison, using the derivative *disobey* as an example, illustrates the value of thinking about structure initially.

structural units	*phonological units*
dis obey	di so bey

Even though structural cues are considered initially, decoding phonological units was treated first in this textbook because when children are still beginners in reading, the majority of words are roots. When they are not, they will be inflected in simple ways (for example, *rooms, played*). At the start, such words are treated as wholes. If a kindergarten teacher, for instance, wants children to learn to read *girls* and *boys*, the two are presented as whole words ("This word says 'girls.' "). However, if this or any other teacher wants to begin work with structural analysis, comparisons and explanations are called for:

girl	boy
girls	boys

In either case, it still is a fact that beginning decoding is primarily concerned with base words, and thus with phonological units. Later, as children acquire more reading ability and words become more complex, decoding that makes use of both structural and graphophonic cues becomes increasingly necessary. That is when the sequence for using cues that was outlined on page 209 assumes importance.

BEGINNING INSTRUCTION

On the assumption that a framework for thinking about instruction with word structure has been established, it is time to see how affixes are taught. Since they divide into three kinds (prefixes, derivational suffixes, and inflectional suffixes), it also is time to inquire, Which of the three should be taught first?

To respond, two factors need to be taken into account. The first has to do with difficulty, thus with questions like, If a child can read *do*, would it be easier to deal with *redo* or *doing?* Since what is familiar *(do)* occurs at the beginning of *doing*, it is likely that *doing* will be easier. (It will also be easier because *doing* is a word that young children use in their speech, whereas *redoing* is not.) These considerations point up that some suffixes ought to be taught before prefixes are introduced.

The second factor that is relevant when sequence is the concern is the kinds of words that beginners need to learn. Even a quick look at easy material shows that inflected words like *toys* and *played* appear earlier than roots to which derivational suffixes have been added (for example, *playful, toyless*). The conclusion, then, is that lessons about word structure should be initiated with common inflectional suffixes (for example, *-s, -ing, -ed*).

Instruction with Inflectional Suffixes

Plural nouns occur early in written material; consequently, the first lesson to be described concentrates on the plural marker -*s*. It begins by calling the students' attention to familiar words:

black hat

After the children read *black hat* aloud, a teacher might say (as she holds up a picture of two black hats), "If I want to talk about these two hats, I can't say 'black hat.' Instead, what should I say so that you'll know I have a picture of more than one hat? . . . That's right. I have to say 'black hats,' not 'black hat.' Let me show you what 'black hats' looks like:

black hat
black hats

"What did I add to 'hat' to make it say 'hats'? . . . Yes, I added *s* at the end. I'll do the same with other words you know."

Now the teacher quickly prints *pet,* has the children read it aloud, next prints *pets,* and has them identify that. Eventually the board shows:

pet	top	girl	boy	cat	boat	car	room	dog
pets	tops	girls	boys	cats	boats	cars	rooms	dogs

Before another lesson with word structure is portrayed, a few comments about the lesson just described are in order. Probably the most important one has to do with the connection between oral language and instruction with inflections.* The teacher just described, you will recall, evoked oral language by asking, "What should I say so that you'll know I have a picture of more than one hat?" The children responded, "Black hats." Thus, to introduce a new learning in reading, the teacher made a natural shift from spoken to written language.

Spoken language entered the scene again, though covertly, when the children moved from plurals like *hats* and *pets* to one like *girls*. In this instance, it allowed them (unconsciously) to assign /z/ to the *s* in *girls* even though they had assigned /s/ to the *s* in *hats* and *pets*. While students do not need to have a conscious, verbalized understanding of what they do "without thinking," teachers should know about the following pattern:

When the final sound in a singular noun is /p/, /t/, /k/, or /f/, the inflection *s* stands for /s/, as in *caps, pets, tacks, puffs,* and *coughs*. Otherwise, *s* records /z/, as in *bells, toys,* and *wigs*.

* Nonstandard English and its effect on instruction are discussed later.

What students need to know and, in contrast, what teachers ought to know suggests an important guideline: Teachers should not teach everything they know; to do so invites unnecessary confusion. Another guideline is the reminder that everything cannot be accomplished at once. Eventually, different ways to form plurals will be taught: *box, boxes; pony, ponies; loaf, loaves; man, men.* Meanwhile, what was taught about the plural marker *-s* should enter into written assignments that allow for attention to both structural and contextual cues. For instance:

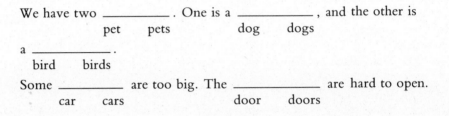

As was recommended in an earlier chapter, the correct word should be written in the blank rather than circled or underlined since the writing fosters attention to its details.

Other Instruction with Inflectional Suffixes

Because past-tense verbs show up in easy materials, a lesson for teaching the past-tense marker *-ed* will be described next. Notice how its features are similar to the lesson dealing with *-s*. In particular, notice how attention goes to the objectives identified earlier as being essential for any instruction (beginning or advanced) with affixes.

For this lesson, the following is on the board:

> Today we will play.

Once the children read the sentence aloud, the teacher inquires, "Did any of you play yesterday?" Responses are positive and include descriptions of a variety of activities. The teacher then comments, "I'm going to write a sentence that tells that you played yesterday."

> Today we will play.
> Yesterday we

After printing *we,* the teacher stops to ask, "Should I write 'play' again? Do we say "Yesterday we play,' or do we say something else? Today we will play. Yesterday we . . . What should I say here?" After the children tell her, the board shows:

Today we will play.
Yesterday we played too.

Once the two sentences are read aloud, the teacher suggests, "Look at this word (pointing to *played*). What did I add to the end of *play* to make it say *played*? . . . Yes, I added *e, d*. When I did that, I showed that we were talking about the way you played yesterday, not today. Let me add *e, d* to some other words you know." Eventually the board shows the following words, each of which is used in a sentence to make certain that the past-tense meaning is understood.

play	talk	jump	call	work	walk
played	talked	jumped	called	worked	walked

With inflected words like those above, children will display still more unconscious behavior. Automatically, they will shift from assigning /d/ to *-ed* *(played)* to assigning /t/ to the same inflection *(talked)*. Again, nothing has to be done to help children know what they did. What they did do, however, reflects another pattern:

When the sound preceding *-ed* is /p/, /k/, /f/, or /s/, *-ed* records /t/, as in *topped, asked,* and *passed.* Otherwise, *-ed* stands for /d/, as in *flawed, sealed,* and *tagged.*

What students *must* know about the past-tense marker *-ed* is described below.

When *-ed* is added to a verb that ends in *t* or *d*, it is a syllable (/əd/), as in *wanted, painted, needed,* and *landed.* Otherwise, *-ed* adds a sound (/d/ or /t/) to the verb but not a syllable, as in *washed, stayed,* and *helped.*★

In time, children must learn about other ways to indicate past tense (for example, *make, made; say, said; am, was; write, wrote*). But all this information is acquired gradually as the need for it arises. Gradually, too, other inflectional suffixes are taught—for instance: *plays, playing; smaller, smallest; quicker, quickly; child's, cars'.*

Nonstandard Speakers and Inflectional Suffixes

As has been illustrated, instruction with inflections is linked to oral language. When children's speech is standard English, the connection is helpful; when it is

---

★ All of the generalizations that should be featured in lessons for decoding are summarized at the end of the chapter.

not, references to oral language can create problems. With that in mind, teachers should adhere to the following guideline: Whereas references to spoken language ought to be made when standard speakers are being instructed ("If we want to tell about something that happened yesterday, what would we have to say? . . . Yes, we'd say 'burned,' not 'burn.' "), a similar reference may confuse nonstandard speakers who do not always pronounce inflections like -ed when they talk. For such speakers, therefore, instruction about inflections ought to be a direct, telling process in which it is advisable to make such pronouncements as, "When you're reading about something that has already happened—maybe it happened yesterday or last week or even last year—you'll often find the letters, e, d at the end of the word. That's why I put e, d at the end of *cook*. I wanted to show that we did that yesterday, on Thursday. Let's take a look at some other sentences that tell about things that have already happened."

> Last night I burned my finger.
> I walked in the park yesterday.
> I asked my mom for a dime this morning.

One further observation is important for teachers of nonstandard speakers: how they respond aloud to an inflected word like *burned* (whether with "burn" or "burned") is less important than is their correct understanding of the semantic significance of -ed (or whatever the inflection might be). That understanding is the key issue reflects still another fact: The primary concern of reading instruction lies with comprehension, not with what students say when they read aloud.

Samples of nonstandard deviations that have relevance for instruction with inflections are listed below (2, 8).

Written language	*Nonstandard speech*
I dropped it.	"I drop it."
He looks.	"He look."
She is coming.	"She is come."
They let us do it.	"They lets us do it."
He started crying.	"He stard cryin'."
Joe's bike.	"Joe bike."

LATER INSTRUCTION

A derived word, you will recall, may be a root and a prefix *(untie)*, or a root and a derivational suffix *(painful)*, or a root to which both a prefix and a derivational suffix have been affixed *(unconquerable)*. Some of the most common prefixes and suffixes are listed in Figure 9.1.

As was explained earlier, the left-to-right orientation of a word's spelling suggests that some derivational suffixes should be taught prior to prefixes. Before a lesson focusing on a derivational suffix is described, another role that oral language plays in work with word structure needs to be made explicit.

Figure 9.1 Some Common Prefixes and Derivational Suffixes*

Prefix	Meaning	Example	Suffix	Meaning	Example
un	not	unhappy	er	one who, doer of action	employer
ir		irregular	or		actor
il		illegal	eer		auctioneer
im		impatient	ee	object of action	employee
in		inactive	less	without	careless
a		atypical	able	capable of being	readable
non		nonhuman	ful	characterized by	careful
dis	not	disobey	y		oily
	remove	disarm	ous		joyous
re	again	remake	ful	amount that fills	cupful
	back	recall	ic (ical)	connected with	poetic, historical
mis	wrongly	miscount	ist		humorist
pre	before	preschool	ness	state of, quality of	softness
fore	before	forewarn	hood		childhood
	in front	foreword	ship		friendship
co	with	coauthor	ance		tolerance
counter	against	counteract	ence		dependence
anti	against	antiwar	tion (ation)		action, starvation
under	below	underage	ment		enjoyment
semi	half	semicircle	ty		loyalty
	partly	semitropical	ward	in the direction of	homeward
	coming twice	semiannual	ster	habit, occupation	trickster, songster

* This is an illustrative rather than complete listing. Instructional materials will identify other affixes. Also available to provide help are dictionaries in which you would learn, for example, that the prefix *un* means "not" (*unhappy*) and also "to do the opposite" (*untie*).

Like all other lessons concerned with word structure, those dealing with derivational suffixes and prefixes should help students cope with meanings as well as with pronunciations. Knowing about *-ful,* for example, should allow them to cope independently with the pronunciation *and* the meaning of derived words like *careful* and *doubtful.* All of this happens, however, only when the meaning of the base word is familiar. Specifically, if the meaning of *care* and *doubt* is unknown, awareness that *-ful* means "ful of" will help with neither *careful* nor *doubtful.* All this suggests that (a) proficiency in using structural cues to work out pronunciations and meanings is directly dependent upon the reader's oral vocabulary, and (b) if the meaning of the root in a derived word is not known and the context offers no help, a dictionary should be consulted.

Instruction with Derivational Suffixes

Like all other instruction with affixes, roots known to students are a starting point in lessons focusing on derivational suffixes. Such lessons also attend to the three objectives that ought to guide all work with word structure. When the focus is on the derivational suffix *-less,* for example, objectives are as follows.

Students will:

1.   Know the spelling and pronunciation of *-less.*
2.   Understand its effect on the meaning of roots.
3.   Be able to deal with *-less* when it appears in print as part of a derived word.

Let us see how these concerns are taken care of in a lesson focusing on *-less.* In this instance, the teacher has decided to use cleaning-up activities to teach about it. For that reason, she comments about the cleanliness of the classroom saying, "It's really spotless. Does anybody know what that means?" Let us assume that nobody does, so the teacher continues, "It means there isn't one spot in this room. It is completely without dirt or spots. Let me write the word *spot;* you know how to read that. Under it, I'm going to write the word I just used."

spot
spotless

"Let's take a look at the new part. Spell it. . . . How would you expect it to sound? . . . Yes, you'd expect it to have the short *e* sound, but we say it so fast at the end of a word that it sounds as if it were spelled with *u* instead of *e.* [If the children knew about the schwa sound, it would be referred to in order to identify the pronunciation of *-less* as /ləs/.] Let me say the new word again: *spotless.* Remember, this new part comes at the end of words and means 'without' or 'doesn't have any.' *Spotless* means 'without a spot'—like this room right now.

"I'll write some other words that you know to see what happens when *l, e, s, s* is added to them:

| mother | tree | shoe | head | tie | home |
| motherless | treeless | shoeless | headless | tieless | homeless |

"Everybody knows this first word, but what happens to *mother* when *l, e, s, s* is added? What does it say now? . . . What does it mean? Can somebody use *motherless* in a sentence?" And so the lesson about the new suffix continues.

As subsequent lessons concentrate on other suffixes, they will offer students considerable help with word meanings. Soon, for instance, they will allow for attention to antonyms in a form such as the following:

| careless | useless | painless | helpless | joyless |
| careful | useful | painful | helpful | joyful |

Systematic and frequent attention to word meanings through the vehicle of written derivatives is especially important for the following reason. Although derivatives appear regularly in written material, they are much less common in spoken language. To illustrate, while authors use descriptions like *treeless* and *mournful,* speakers—even well-educated speakers—are much more likely to say something like "bare" and "sad." The difference means that students can be *expected* to have problems with derivatives. Knowing this, teachers must make sure that ample, systematic instruction is provided—whether or not something like a basal reader manual suggests it.

Instruction with Prefixes

Earlier, a recommendation was made to teach derivational suffixes before attending to prefixes. That was not to say, however, that all such suffixes should be introduced prior to the start of lessons with prefixes. Why all of the derivational suffixes are *not* covered first is revealed in the entries in Figure 9.1, for they show that the meanings of a number of derivational suffixes are abstract and thus difficult to explain and understand (for example, "state or degree," "act or process"). With that in mind, instruction with some derivatives is soon followed by instruction with common, easily understood prefixes.

At one time, prefixes stood out in written material because hyphens separated them from base words. Since that is not always the case now, increased attention must go to prefixes to ensure that students can sort them out in unfamiliar derivatives. How a lesson with a prefix might get started will be described now.

In a discussion of the traits of characters in a story, *happy* is mentioned. Afterward, the teacher uses this adjective to introduce the prefix *un-* by saying,

"The word *happy* reminds me of another one. The word I'm thinking of is interesting because it has *happy* in it yet means just the opposite. It means 'not happy.' Can anyone tell me the word I'm thinking of?"★

If nobody can, the teacher answers her own question and then discusses both the pronunciation of *un-* and the effect it has on the meaning of *happy*. Using roots the children can read, she provides more illustrations. To highlight relationships, pairs are written as follows:

happy	tidy	hurt	even	fair
unhappy	untidy	unhurt	uneven	unfair

At another time, this same teacher will demonstrate that *un-* affixed to verbs means "to do the opposite" *(unbend, untie, uncover)*. Sometime, too, students will need to learn that *un-* at the beginning of a word may be part of another prefix *(underground, underfed)* or an integral part of a root *(uncle, unit)*.

One decoder who overgeneralized and reached a wrong conclusion about *u* and *n* in *unite (The soldiers need to unite if they expect to win)* went through the following trial-and-error process:

> *This word tells what the soldiers have to do to win. The* u *and* n *is a prefix, and there's nothing at the end that looks like a suffix. This means that* i, t, e *is the root. That says "ītĕ." I don't think there is such a word. At least I never heard of a word that sounds like that. Maybe* u, n *isn't a prefix. That would make the whole thing the root. If it is, there are two syllables:* u *and* n, i, t, e. *Oh, sure.* Unite. *You have to stick together to win. The soldiers need to unite if they expect to win.*

What these thoughts reemphasize is the significance of oral language for decoding. Specifically, competence in oral language led to the rejection of *ite* as a root and of *un* as a prefix. It also established the correctness of "unite."

To promote equally correct conclusions by other students, teachers should deliberately select words that look as if they may have prefixes and suffixes but in fact do not, and then act out decoding procedures similar to the one just portrayed. (Examples of such words are: *presto*, *remnant*, *antique*, con*stable*, raz*or*, and dig*est*.) By doing this on a number of occasions, teachers provide a model for successful decoding. Students will then be in a position to practice what they have observed.

Even with practice, they may still arrive at erroneous conclusions about a word's structure. This can be illustrated with the thoughts of a decoder who cannot identify *curly* in the sentence *Their hair is so curly*.

> *It tells about their hair. The* l, y *at the end is a suffix, so that leaves* c, u, r. *The* c *probably has the hard sound. That's:* ur → cur. *Oh, curly. Their hair is so curly.*

★ Once, another teacher was working with *un-* but phrased her comments differently: "I'm thinking of a word that means just the opposite of 'happy.' Can anybody tell me what it might be?" One child responded, "Sad." In this case, the response should—and did—tell the teacher about an important omission in her request. What *was* the omission?

To be noted in this decoder's thoughts is that an incorrect conclusion about *l, y* being a suffix did not interfere with the goal of decoding. That is, the decoder arrived at a recognizable word and comprehended its meaning.

SPELLING GENERALIZATIONS AND WORD STRUCTURE

Arriving at an understanding of a derived or an inflected word's structure is not too difficult when the root is unchanged. For example, even when students cannot automatically identify roots like *peer, harm, curb,* and *arch* but have learned about such suffixes as *-less, -ful, -s,* and *-es,* achieving an understanding of the meaningful parts of *peerless, harmful, curbs,* and *arches* would be fairly easy. On the other hand, sorting out structural units in unknown words like *penniless, plentiful, excitable,* and *making* is a more complex task because, in each case, the spelling of the root has been altered. With such words, spelling generalizations can be an important source of help. The recommendation, therefore, is to teach them not only to help students with spelling but also to provide a strategy for working out the structure of derived and inflected words in which the spelling of the root has been changed. When the generalizations receive attention for the second purpose, the connection between them and the job of working out a structure should be made explicit. Exactly how the spelling generalizations can help readers will be illustrated now.

Using a Spelling Generalization to Decode an Unknown Word

One spelling generalization goes as follows: When a root ends in silent *e (tape),* the *e* is usually dropped when a suffix beginning with a vowel *(-ed)* is added *(taped).* Even though a decoder might not know whether the final *e* in the root is or is not silent, the very common occurrence of silent *e*'s in English words means that the generalization just cited will point him or her in the right direction practically all of the time. Consequently, decoders who know about suffixes like *-ing, -ed, -est,* and *-able* should suspect that the roots in unfamiliar words such as *braking, cubed, finest,* and *solvable* are *brake, cube, fine,* and *solve.* Therefore, the steps for decoding the more complex words are:

braking	cubed	finest	solvable
brake	cube	fine	solve
braking	cubed	finest	solvable

More explicit attention will go to these recommended steps later in the chapter.

Statements of Generalizations

The spelling generalization just discussed, plus others, are listed in the next box. Like all other statements of generalizations, they ought to be memorized once they are understood to ensure that you will be ready to teach and explain them to children.

SPELLING GENERALIZATIONS

When a root ends in silent *e*, the *e* is usually dropped when a suffix beginning with a vowel is added. For example:

bake	starve	cube	bride	strange
baker	starvation	cubist	bridal	strangest

When a root ends in a consonant followed by *y*, the *y* is changed to *i* before most suffixes are added. For example:

cry	duty	merry	melody	history
cried	dutiful	merrily	melodious	historical

When a root ends in a consonant that is preceded by a single vowel, the consonant is usually doubled before a suffix is added.★ For example:

rob	mud	chop	run	bed
robbed	muddy	chopping	runner	bedding

The plural of nouns ending in *f* is formed by changing *f* to *v* and adding *es*. For example:

leaf	calf	loaf	self
leaves	calves	loaves	selves

As spelling generalizations are taught, they should figure in work that concentrates on uncovering roots in derived and inflected words:

merrily = merry + ly	merriment = merry + ment
miner = mine + er	graduation = graduate + ion
staring = stare + ing	melodious = melody + ous
witty = wit + y	wiry = wire + y
wisest = wise + est	enviable = envy + able

★ The doubled consonant is useful in signaling information about the sound of the previous vowel. Contrasts like the following illustrate the usefulness:

dinner	tapped	hopping	holly
diner	taped	hoping	holy

Since the need to sort out roots occurs with words in contexts, exercises like the following one ought to be common. In this case, students provide what appears in brackets.

I work puzzles *easily*.	[easy + ly]
The kittens ate *hungrily* from the bowl.	[hungry + ly]
Everyone danced *happily* around the room.	[happy + ly]
Angrily, the man pounded on the door.	[angry + ly]

Contexts can also be used to review statements of spelling generalizations:

She *slammed* the door.	I like the *coziness* of this room.
Don't be so *nosy*.	Their *facial* expressions were interesting.
He is the *tiniest* of all.	He *regretted* doing that.

Even though frequent, systematic work with derived and inflected words should be common in middle- and upper-grade classrooms, it often is not. Perhaps this is the time for teachers of older students to make a resolution to spend more instructional time on such words since they are the ones that cause problems.

COMPOUND WORDS

Just as derived and inflected words have a particular type of structure, so, too, do compounds. A compound word is composed of two or more roots—or, as one child was heard to explain, "It has two words hooked together."

Compounds divide into those that have little meaning in and of themselves and those with quite specific meanings. The first group are function words that are common (and important) as written material gets more difficult—for example: *nevertheless, anyhow, therefore, whereby, however, insofar, nonetheless,* and *moreover*. Like other function words, they should be introduced in a context. (In this case, more than one sentence is usually required to pinpoint meanings. With a compound like *nevertheless,* meaning could be taught with sentences like *I know the pool is open. Nevertheless, you can't go swimming.*) Although the parts of these compounds (for example, *never, the, less*) are aids to pronunciation, they signal nothing about meaning. Consequently, once the compound words are pronounced, attention should focus on each as a whole, not on its parts.

This is not true of the second category of compound words, which differ from the first in three ways. To begin, the second group is content words and thus are meaningful in and of themselves (for example, *blackberry, windowpane*). In addition, the inherent meaning of each root is retained, and those meanings help with the meaning of the compound word of which they are a part. (The last two characteristics tell why words like *notice* and *amuse* are not compounds.) Compound words in the second group are mostly nouns, but some are verbs (for example, *underline, overlook*) and others are adjectives (for example, *overdue, evergreen*).

What some children think about compound words has been described by Gleason (6) in a research report:

> They knew what the words referred to and how to use them, but their ideas about the words were rather amusing. One little boy said that an airplane is called an airplane because it is a plain thing that goes in the air. Another child said that breakfast is called breakfast because you have to eat it fast to get to school on time. Several subjects thought that Friday is called Friday because it is the day you eat fried fish. [p. 26]

If an awareness of compound words is to aid rather than deter decoding efforts, students must understand that examining an unknown word with the thought in mind that it might be a compound is to consider that the whole of it may be composed of two roots with a connected meaning. This, please notice, is essentially different from seeing *hot* in *hotel,* or *at* in *nation,* or *on* in *bonus.* The latter searching illustrates the highly *un*desirable practice of looking randomly for little words in bigger ones. It also shows disregard for the primary importance of syllabication *(ho tel)* for figuring out unknown words.

On the positive side, students should know that looking for little words in big words is helpful (a) only after the big one has been divided into syllables and (b) only when the little word contains all the vowels in a syllable. The significance of the two criteria for arriving at correct pronunciations is illustrated below:

helpful	*unhelpful*	*unhelpful*
amuse	amuse	amuse
a muse	a muse	am use
use	us	

A STRATEGY FOR COMPLICATED-LOOKING WORDS

The types of instruction and practice that have been illustrated in the chapter have as one of their goals a solution for a problem referred to by Lee Deighton: "Frequently, polysyllables composed by adding one suffix to another frighten the developing reader out of all proportion to their real difficulty" (1, p. 29). When students do have trouble decoding polysyllables—for instance, *carelessly, uncomfortable, foretelling,* and *plentifully*—teachers should be prepared to offer visual help that follows certain steps:

carelessly	uncomfortable	foretelling	plentifully
careless	comfortable	telling	plentiful
care	comfort	tell	plenty
careless	comfortable	telling	plentiful
carelessly	uncomfortable	foretelling	plentifully

Just as teachers should adhere to a certain sequence, first in decomposing a word into its structural parts and then in synthesizing them, so too must students. They should be taught, therefore, to use the following guidelines:

DECODING DERIVED AND INFLECTED WORDS

1. Lay aside the prefix first.
2. Lay aside each suffix, one at a time.
3. If the root is unfamiliar, decode it.
4. Put back the suffix immediately next to the root.
5. If there is a second suffix, add that next.
6. Add the prefix last.

Students who adhere to the guidelines when they are working with unknown words like *unwanted, worthlessness,* and *unenviable* will lay them out (mentally or on paper) as follows:

unwanted	worthlessness	unenviable
wanted	worthless	enviable
want	worth	envy
wanted	worthless	enviable
unwanted	worthlessness	unenviable

Why prefixes should be added last when the structural units of a word are being reassembled (and why they are removed first in the dismantling process) can be explained with the help of words like *unwanted, immeasurable,* and *indefinable,* for they demonstrate that a prefix will not always be attached to roots (*unwant, immeasure, indefine*) even though it will occur affixed to derived and inflected words containing those roots (*unwanted, immeasurable, indefinable*). Recognition of this fact indicates that the best sequence to follow for all derived and inflected words is one that removes prefixes first and adds them last.

To see how the guideline works with unknown words, the thoughts of another decoder will be considered, one who is having trouble with *unenviable* in the context *He was in the unenviable position of having to do it twice.*

> *It tells about position. Maybe* u, n *is a prefix, and* a, b, l, e *might be a suffix. The* i *before the suffix might mean that* i *really is* y. *If it is, the root is* e, n, v, y. *Oh sure,* envy. *You wish you had something, but* un *means you don't wish you had it. Let's see.* Unenviable. *That means you don't want to be in his place. That makes sense. I wouldn't want to have to climb into that icy water twice.* He was in the unenviable position of having to do it twice.

Students achieve the competence reflected in the decoding efforts just described only when all their teachers keep in mind the three objectives of every lesson dealing with word structure: (a) knowledge of how the affix is spelled and pronounced, (b) an understanding of its effect on the meaning of roots, and (c) ability to transfer these learnings to unknown words.

One further guideline for instruction underscores the importance of relationships among words: while attention to a single word is often justified, the importance of attending to one in relation to others should not be underestimated. Thus, when students are being taught *camp*, it might also be the time to call attention to *camper* and *camping*. ("Might" is stressed because too much of a good thing is still too much.) At a higher level, the need to teach *nation* might be a perfect time to list and discuss *national* and *nationality*. At still higher levels, words like *cent, century, centennial, centipede,* and *centigrade* might be listed to allow for a discussion of what they have in common both visually and semantically. At another time, it might be appropriate to ask about a possible connection between *audio, auditory, audible, audience, auditorium,* and *audition,* or between other words such as *puncture, punctuation,* and *punctilious*. However it is done, the point is that students should be helped both to appreciate and use the relationships that exist among English words.

Using relationships to cope with derivatives is especially important because of a pronounced difference between spoken and written language, which was mentioned previously. I refer to the fact that although derivatives appear frequently in written material, they are far less common in spoken language. The discrepancy is illustrated next. (In each example, the first sentence typifies what might be found in print; the sentence in the parentheses is how the same thought might be expressed in speech.)

The remains of that ship are unsalvageable.
　　(They'll never be able to save what's left of that ship.)
Reasonless fear kept her awake.
　　(She was afraid for no reason, and it kept her awake.)
The handwriting was undecipherable.
　　(You couldn't even read the handwriting.)
Humorlessness characterizes the man.
　　(The man has no sense of humor.)
Their tastes are indistinguishable.
　　(They have the very same tastes.)
He shows unquenchable optimism no matter what happens.
　　(He's always optimistic no matter what happens.)

That derivatives are much less common in spoken than in written language calls for restating what was said before: teachers working at middle- and upper-grade levels should feel obligated to allot *generous* amounts of time to derivatives. Most of their efforts should concentrate on meaning since that is what counts insofar as reading is concerned. Nonetheless, knowing how to pronounce derivatives is desirable; hence, correct pronunciations should not be completely bypassed. When attention does center on pronunciation, the need for trial and error in deciding which syllable is stressed will become clear, for often (but not always) a shift in stress occurs as a word lengthens:

nátion	pólitics	práy
nationálity	polítical	práyer
nationalístic	politícian	práyerfully

Examining the first two columns illuminates another characteristic of English: similarity in meaning is preserved by keeping the same letters even when the sounds they record change. To illustrate, the following words exemplify changes in consonant sounds.

reduce	bomb	medical	criticize	face
reduction	bombard	medicine	critical	facial

Other related words demonstrate alterations in vowel sounds:

child	athlete	sane	extreme	convene
children	athletic	sanity	extremity	convention

Unquestionably, the tendency to spell related words in similar ways, even when shifts in sounds (and stress) occur, complicates efforts to arrive at correct pronunciations. Not to be overlooked, however, is the contribution that the same characteristic makes to an understanding of meaning. And that, after all, is what is important for reading.

SUGGESTIONS FOR PRACTICE

Some of the most essential kinds of practice for structural analysis have already been described, but more suggestions follow. They begin with samples of written assignments.

- After the comparative and superlative forms of adjectives are taught, students can be asked to illustrate the meanings of descriptions like: *rich, richer, richest; busy, busier, busiest; clean, cleaner, cleanest.*

- Underline the correct answers:

  1. Which is the hottest?

     a lighted match   a summer day   a burning building

2.   Which is the greenest?

        a garden   tree leaves   grass

3.   Which is the smallest?

        a puppy   a bird   a kitten

With an assignment like the one just described, questions with indisputably correct answers are unnecessary; their absence, in fact, may lead to interesting discussions.

Responses to the next assignment tell if students understand what a root is. The assignment also allows for practice in following written directions.

- All of the following sentences include a word ending in *er*. Some of these words are roots. Others are not. Read each sentence. If the underlined word is a root, write *yes* after the sentence. If the underlined word is not a root, write *no*.

    1.   I <u>never</u> like to play that game. _____
    2.   Please pass the <u>butter</u>. _____
    3.   He is a very fast <u>runner</u>. _____

Similar written assignments can single out words ending in *or* (for example, *sailor, color*), *ing* (for example, *doing, bring*), and so on. Words can be easy or difficult depending upon the students' ability.

The next suggestion for a written assignment is indirectly concerned with roots and directly with word families.

- Which are in the same family? Look down each column of words. In each, underline all the words that belong to the same family as the first word in the column.

read	count	need	roast	skill	each
reader	counter	needy	toast	skillet	teach
ready	countless	needle	coast	skillful	teacher
reading	county	needing	boast	unskilled	teaching

- Prepare very small word cards, each showing a derived or inflected word. Sheets of incomplete sentences need to be typed too. Each sheet, along with the word cards, is placed in a large envelope. Directions for use are printed on the outside:

    1.   Read all the word cards.
    2.   Place cards in sentences to complete them.

If students are accustomed to self-checking, an answer sheet goes into the envelope too.

The primary concern for compound words has to do with students' ability to identify them in print and, in turn, to understand their meaning; consequently, little time ought to go to combining roots to form compounds, which is the writer's task. Therefore, only when the meaning of "compound word" is being taught are exercises like the following appropriate. In this case, students write the compound word that is defined.

> a coat for wearing in the rain   _____
> a bird that is black   _____
> a hole to peep through   _____

Just as soon as students understand the basic nature of a compound word, written assignments should have them perform tasks like the following.

- Read the sentences below. Underline all the compound words. At the bottom of the page, explain what each one means.

  1.   He hit the target the very first time.
  2.   I like pancakes for breakfast.
  3.   They cannot manage all that at once.
  4.   Use a bookmark so that you won't lose your place.

As was mentioned earlier, *much* attention should go to derivatives; consequently, written assignments dealing with them are described next.

- Directions: Write the base for each derivative. Then write a sentence that includes the derivative.

	Derivative	*Base*	*Sentence*
1.	imperfectly	_____	_____
2.	unsatisfied	_____	_____
3.	recaptured	_____	_____

- List words in random order, some of which are roots while others are derivatives. Selections should ensure that for every root (for example, *still*) there is a derivative with a similar meaning *(inactive)*. In a second column on the same sheet, children will write pairs of synonyms selected from the first column—for example: *clean, spotless; loyal, faithful; mad, insane; plain, unadorned.*

Bingo-like cards can be adapted for many different kinds of reading practice, including some for derivatives:

- Prepare cards showing such derivatives as *incorrect, uncooked, powerful,* and *unwatered.* Words called out will be roots: *wrong, raw, strong, dry,* and so on. The job is to match synonyms, this time by covering a derivative whenever a root with a similar meaning is called out. At another time, roots will be written and derivatives called out. Now the job is to cover a root if a named derivative includes it.

Other games for word structure follow:

- Make two sets of word cards, one for roots and the other for prefixes and suffixes. As in a card game, deal roots to players. Affix cards are the deck. Students take turns choosing a card. If a selected affix can be added to one of the roots and, second, if students can read and define the meanings of the root and the derivative, they lay that pair of cards down. If the affix is not usable, the card is returned to the bottom of the deck. The first player out of cards is the winner. (In some cases, students will have to consult dictionaries to see whether real words are being formed.)

- For a collection of word cards, select compounds plus other words that could be divided into two roots but are not compounds (for example, *notice, attack, father, target*). Shuffle all the cards and deal them to the players. Each studies his or her words and then lays down the compounds. A correct decision merits a point; wrong choices subtract points. The player with the most points is the winner.

- Sort derivative cards into "easy," "difficult," and "more difficult" piles, which will be placed face down on a table. Cards with the easiest derivatives are marked $1. Difficult ones are printed on $5 bills, and the most difficult of the derivatives go on $10 cards. Players take turns selecting a card from any of the piles. A correct identification, along with an explanation of the derivative's meaning, allows a player to keep the card. Otherwise it is returned to the bottom of the pile. The winner is the player whose cards add up to the most money.

When reading about these classroom activities and, most of all, when consideration is given to using them with students, it is essential to keep in mind the reason for having them. To lose sight of the goal—in this case, to increase knowledge of word structure in order to improve decoding ability—is to run the risk of having "fun and games" but not much learning. As with all other plans for instruction and practice, therefore, a teacher needs to ask, "*Why* am I doing this?" The answer is bound to provide guidelines for making an activity maximally productive. An honest answer might also indicate the activity has little educational value and should be forgotten.

TEACHERS' DECISIONS ABOUT NEW VOCABULARY

Before the chapter comes to a close, it might be helpful to synthesize what this and prior chapters have been recommending for ways to help students become self-reliant in coping with written words that are either new or have been forgotten. To do that, let us consider the question, How does a teacher decide what to do with new vocabulary? More specifically, if a teaching manual indicates that eight new words are in a selection that students will be asked to read, what should be done with them before the reading commences?

To answer, four factors need to be kept in mind:

FACTORS AFFECTING DECISIONS ABOUT NEW WORDS

1. Context in which new word appears.
2. Spelling and pronunciation of new word.
3. Students' ability to use contextual, graphophonic, and structural cues.
4. Words in their reading vocabulary.

The significance of each of the four factors will be clarified with illustrations.

When children are just beginning to learn to read, the lack of decoding skills requires that each new word be identified for them—unless, of course, a word is in a context that is so rich with cues that only one word is possible. A second reason for the frequent use of whole word methodology at the start reflects the fact that a number of the words that are necessary for sentences (for example, *the, was*) have irregular spellings, making decoding skills (assuming some exist) nonproductive. To be noted, however, is that as children acquire these skills, they will be able to figure out certain irregularly spelled words with help that derives from words learned earlier. For example, if *could* had been identified earlier with whole word methodology, the irregularly spelled words *would* and *should* can be decoded with help that comes from knowing *could* and the sounds associated with *w* and *sh*. Or, to cite one more illustration, if *shoe* was introduced earlier, it may provide assistance should the need occur to read *canoe*.

Implied in all this is that unknown words ought to be identified only when no alternative exists. (This is most important if students are to develop maximum independence.) Whether an alternative does exist depends upon the four factors listed above.

Applied to something like a basal reader lesson, what has now been said about new vocabulary offers the following guidelines for teachers:

1. Examine the new words in the selection as well as the contexts in which they first occur in order to eliminate any that students ought to be able to cope with because of their ability to use contextual, structural, and graphophonic cues.
2. Use whole word methodology with the words that remain. If any is a derived or an inflected word, present it in its root form first, then in the more complex form. For instance:

deny	patient	possess	syrup
denial	patiently	possession	syrupy
	impatiently		

3. If students can work out the pronunciation of a word (for example, *acme*) but are not likely to know its meaning, the latter should be clarified.

Once the basal reader (or any other) selection is read silently, additional attention should go to all the new words to make certain that each was identified correctly and, further, to provide for practice if it seems necessary. (Chapter 5 listed suggestions for word practice.) All this can be summarized as follows:

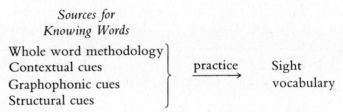

Sources for Knowing Words

Whole word methodology
Contextual cues
Graphophonic cues   practice   Sight
Structural cues   vocabulary

As was mentioned before, some of the attention that goes to new words can highlight their relationship to others. If one is *friend,* for example, it might be a time to write and discuss words like *friends, friendly, unfriendly,* and *friendship.* Should *permit* be a new word at later levels, more family members can get attention—for instance, *permission* and *permissive.* Connections like these have relevance not only for pronunciations but also for the topic to be discussed in the next chapter: word meanings.

SUMMARY

Like the earlier chapters on phonics, the present one considered what there is about unknown words that can help a reader arrive at correct conclusions about their pronunciation. In this instance, the focus was on structural cues, which also assist with meanings.

As the description "structural" suggests, structural cues are available to help readers because every word has a structure. In the case of roots, it is simple; with inflected, derived, and compound words, it is more complex. In all instances, however, the presence or absence of structural cues, referred to as affixes, indicates what the structure is. That is why instruction about word structure concentrates on affixes—more specifically, on how they are spelled, how they are pronounced, and how they affect the meaning or grammatical function of roots.

Since structural cues are of three kinds (prefixes, derivational suffixes, and inflectional suffixes), a question about the best sequence for introducing them was raised. When relative difficulty was considered, it was concluded that inflections ought to be taught first, followed by instruction with some of the more common, easily understood derivational suffixes. Afterward, attention can shift to the easiest prefixes.

Lessons for teaching affixes were described. How to help students systematically sort them out in unknown derived and inflected words was explained, too. Because proficiency in using structural cues is the result of both knowledgeable instruction and ample practice, suggestions for the latter were described.

REVIEW

1. The essential goals of every lesson dealing with affixes were listed in Chapter 9. Keeping them in mind, what should be accomplished in instruction about the prefix *mis?* Name derivatives that could be used both for instruction and for application.

2. Chapter 9 outlined what teachers need to consider when they are deciding what to do with new vocabulary. It recommended, for example, that regularly spelled words should be decoded by the students *if* they have the necessary prerequisites. Such a recommendation, however, assumes that teachers will know exactly what the prerequisites are for each word. With that assumption in mind, let us say that *faithfully* is among the new words in some material students need to read. List everything a student would need to know and be able to do in order to decode it correctly.

3. From your study of Chapter 9, you should be able to explain the following statement, which underscores a fundamental idea about syllabication.

    > In decoding, structural units are considered first, then phonological divisions. The structural units take precedence over the phonological units because of the fundamental importance of meaning.

4. What are the *structural* divisions of the following words?

1.	nation	4.	devilish	7.	roaster
2.	relish	5.	jealous	8.	auditor
3.	author	6.	dangerous	9.	inaccurately

5. If students have a problem identifying and understanding derivatives, teachers should be prepared to decompose and reassemble their structural parts in a way that will assist with both pronunciation and meaning. Guidelines for doing that were listed in Chapter 9. Using them, show how each derivative shown below should be taken apart, then put back together.

    iciness   unforgettable   momentarily   imperfectly

6. Looking for little words in bigger ones in order to get the latter decoded can create more problems than it solves—unless certain precautions are kept in mind. What, exactly, are those precautions? Explain them with examples.

GENERALIZATIONS FOR DECODING: A SUMMARY

SYLLABICATION

Structural Divisions

Most prefixes and suffixes are syllables *(un lock; care less; play ing)*.

When the inflection *-ed* is added to a verb ending in *d* or *t*, it is a syllable *(need ed; dent ed)*. Otherwise, it adds a sound to the verb but not a syllable *(marched, pulled)*.

When the inflection *-ion* is added to a root ending in *t*, the letters *tion* form a syllable *(act, ac tion)*.

Phonological Divisions

When two consonants are preceded and followed by vowels, a syllabic division usually occurs between the consonants *(win dow)*.

When a vowel precedes and follows a consonant, a syllabic division usually occurs after the first vowel *(si lent)*.

When *x* is preceded and followed by a vowel, the first vowel and *x* are in the same syllable *(tax i)*.

When a root ends in a consonant followed by *le*, the consonant and *le* are the final syllable *(pur ple)*.

For purposes of syllabication, consonant digraphs and vowel digraphs function as if they were single letters *(ath lete, au thor)*.

VOWEL SOUNDS

When a syllable has one vowel and it is in final position, it commonly stands for its long sound *(si lo)*.

When a syllable has one vowel and it is not in final position, it commonly stands for its short sound *(album)*.

When a syllable has two vowels, the long sound of the first is common *(meet, mete)*.

When a syllable has two vowels, one of which is final *e* and the two are separated by two or more consonants, the short sound of the first vowel is common *(pulse)*.

Vowel sounds in unstressed syllables are often reduced to the schwa sound *(random)*.

The digraph *oo* has both a long and a short sound *(cool, cook)*.

The digraph *ow* stands for both a diphthong and the long *o* sound *(owl, own)*.

When a vowel is followed by *r* in a syllable, three different sounds are possible *(art, her, for)*.

When a vowel is followed by *re* in a syllable, five different sounds are possible *(care, mere, hire, bore, pure)*.

Y FUNCTIONING AS A VOWEL

When *y* is in medial position in a syllable that has no vowel, it commonly stands for the short *i* sound *(myth)*.

When *y* stands for the final sound in a multisyllabic word, it usually records the long *e* sound *(fancy, quickly)*.

Otherwise, *y* is likely to stand for the long *i* sound *(try, style, cycle)*.

CONSONANT SOUNDS

When *c* and *g* are followed in a syllable by *e, i,* or *y,* they commonly stand for their soft sounds *(cell, cigar, cyst; gem, gin, gypsy).* Otherwise, the hard sounds are common *(can, talc, act; glad, pig, wagon).*

The letter *s* commonly stands for either /s/ or /z/ *(see, has).*

The digraph *th* records a voiced and a voiceless sound *(the, thin).*

The digraph *ch* commonly records the sound heard initially in *chop.* It may also stand for the sound heard initially in *chef.*

Together, *q* and *u* stand for either /kw/ or /k/ *(quit, antique).*

The letter *x* stands for /z/, /ks/ or /gz/ *(xylophone, sox, exact).*

STRESSED SYLLABLES

Primary stress falls on or within the root of a derived or inflected word *(feárless, rewárding).*

In a two-syllable root, the first syllable is often stressed *(kítchen).*

REFERENCES

1. Deighton, Lee C. *Vocabulary Development in the Classroom.* New York: Teachers College Press, Columbia University, 1959.

2. DeStefano, Johanna S. *Language, Society, and Education: A Profile of Black English.* Worthington, Ohio: Charles A. Jones Publishing Company, 1973.

3. Durkin, Dolores, *Strategies for Identifying Words.* 2d ed. Boston: Allyn and Bacon, 1981.

4. Gibson, Eleanor J., and Levin, Harry. *The Psychology of Reading.* Cambridge, Mass.: MIT Press, 1975.

5. Gleason, H. A. *Descriptive Linguistics.* Rev. ed. New York: Holt, Rinehart and Winston, 1961.

6. Gleason, Jean B. "Language Development in Early Childhood." In *Oral Language and Reading.* Edited by James Walden. Champaign, Ill.: National Council of Teachers of English, 1969.

7. Johnson, Dale D., and Pearson, P. David. *Teaching Reading Vocabulary.* New York: Holt, Rinehart and Winston, 1978.

8. Morgan, Argiro L. "A New Orleans Oral Language Study." *Elementary English* 51 (February 1974): 222–229.

9. Seymour, Dorothy. "Word Division for Decoding." *Reading Teacher* 27 (December 1973): 275–283.

10. Sustakoski, Henry J. "Some Contributions of Linguistic Science to the Teaching of Reading." In *Oral Language and Reading.* Edited by James Walden. Champaign, Ill.: National Council of Teachers of English, 1969.

11. Wardhaugh, Ronald. *Reading: A Linguistic Perspective.* New York: Harcourt, Brace and World, 1969.

CHAPTER 10

VOCABULARY KNOWLEDGE

PREVIEW

What is said and recommended in Teaching Them to Read *stems from one assumption: reading is comprehending. Admittedly, the previous chapters have spent many pages discussing how to teach students to figure out the pronunciation of words. Nonetheless, comprehension was still the concern since the value of knowing a pronunciation lies in the way it triggers meaning—if the word in question is in the reader's oral vocabulary. How oral vocabularies can be expanded and deepened is the focus now. Such a topic takes on an ever increasing significance as more and more bilingual children enroll in our schools.*

Because of the dependence of reading on oral vocabularies, some readers of this book may wonder why they receive attention as late as Chapter 10. The delay was deliberate and is rooted in two conclusions. The first, based on numerous visits to classrooms at all grade levels, is that surprisingly little is done with vocabulary development except to have students consult glossaries or dictionaries for meanings. The second conclusion is that more would be done were teachers truly convinced of the fundamental importance of vocabulary knowledge for reading. That topic is discussed now on the assumption that nobody could read the earlier chapters and fail to appreciate the significance.

Although it is the school's role in vocabulary knowledge that Chapter 10 looks at, the focus does not minimize nonschool sources of influence, for, after all, they often shape and reshape meaning. Who really understands the meaning of death, *for example, until a loved one dies? And who knows the meaning of* friendship *until a crisis occurs, and it is either experienced or sadly missed? Implicit in Chapter 10 is that word meanings change and grow as people change and grow and, second, that children have not lived long enough to have a full understanding of many words, including some fairly common ones.*

Even competent readers will fail to understand as little as a sentence if a key word is not in their oral vocabulary. A sentence like the following, for example, will be comprehended only by those who know what a spelunker is: *All are experienced spelunkers.*

While it is true that individual words give meaning to sentences, it is equally true that sentences give meaning to words. Look what happens to *run* in different contexts:

> Don't run so fast.
> She has a run in her stocking.
> Soon there will be a run on the banks.
> He batted in a run when it counted.
> The car will run better now.
> Everybody wants to run for that office.
> Would you run some errands for me?
> They run a risk every time they do that.
> She really knows how to run a business.
> Both roads run north and south.
> I hope I don't run into them at the store.
> The trucks seem eager to run us down.
> The contract will run for only one year.
> Those children run the streets day and night.

Although the previous sentences do not exhaust the meanings of *run,* they should succeed in demonstrating that the common practice of having students look up *the* meaning of a word in a dictionary is not the most correct, realistic, or interesting way to develop vocabularies. Better ways will be described. Because better ways are numerous, it might be helpful to start the chapter by considering how vocabulary development fits in with all the other things that require attention in a classroom.

WHEN TO WORK ON VOCABULARY

Finding time to attend to word meanings is mandatory whenever not knowing them would keep students from understanding required reading. A similar obligation exists when confusion about a word is apparent. In addition to meeting these responsibilities, superior teachers use special, preplanned activities and also take advantage of unexpected opportunities to work on vocabulary. All four circumstances will be discussed.

With Required Reading

Since so much required reading is of basal readers, they will be used to illustrate one time when attention to word meanings is necessary.

Typically, the segment of the teaching manual that suggests how to use a basal reader selection lists words that are not likely to be in the students' reading vocabularies. How to cope with their need to know what such words say was summarized at the end of the previous chapter. What they say, however, is less important for comprehension than what they mean.

When what a new word means is unknown, various procedures are available to clarify what it means in the selection that is about to be read. Which procedure to use depends on the word (its importance and difficulty), on the students, and on available time. Possible procedures to use with new words will be discussed later. (They are listed in the box below.)

WORD MEANINGS

Teaching meanings:	*Working out meanings via:*
Through experiences	Contextual cues
By reading to students	Structural analysis
With audiovisual aids	
With verbal explanations	

Meanwhile, it is relevant to note that in a study of basal reader programs, Beck et al. (5) divided word knowledge into three categories:

1. *established* (meaning is automatically accessed)
2. *acquainted* (deliberate attention required for recalling meaning)
3. *unknown* (not in semantic memory)

The researchers concluded that comprehending new ideas is facilitated when they are communicated with established words. This suggests that when students are asked to read a particular selection, enough time should go to vocabulary that few if any of the words will fall into Beck's second or third categories.

When Confusion Is Apparent

Even infrequent visits to classrooms would reveal a surprisingly large amount of confusion about the meanings of words and, going along with that, a greater eagerness on the part of students to be the first to respond with any definition than to take the time to think about an appropriate one. Some of the confusion will be described first:

In one fourth grade, a group of ten was beginning a unit of stories entitled "South of the Border." Asking, "What does *border* mean?" the teacher quickly heard, "It means somebody who lives with you, but he's not in your family." "No," continued the teacher, "it means something else." "I know," volunteered another child. "It means when you feel bored, like you're bored playing the same game."

Elsewhere, the meaning of *bold* (applied to the one who had burglarized a student's home) was getting attention in a discussion. One child explained its meaning by saying, "It's like when you go bowling." Disagreeing, another proposed, "It's like when a man doesn't have any hair on the top of his head."

In a third grade, the teacher inquired about the meaning of *idle* found in the sentence, *The children were idle*. Almost before the question was completed, one child said, "It means a statue."

These samples of confusion are cited not because they are humorous, which they are, but because none of the three teachers wrote any of the words being confused on the board. This calls for a reminder of the importance of *showing* words to students. Applied to the examples, showing means writing the following on the board as the first step in clarifying meanings. The next step is to put the words into contexts.

border	bold	idle
boarder	bowl	idol
bored	bald	

The final example of confusion is used to underscore the need to help students become consciously aware of the fact that words usually have more than a single meaning and, further, that contexts must be considered when a selection is made from possible meanings:

During a discussion of a character in a story, the teacher commented, "She certainly was a patient person, wasn't she?" Everyone agreed. The teacher then asked, "What does *patient* mean?" Immediately one child explained, "It means when you're sick and you go to the doctor and he tells you that you have to go to the hospital."

With these illustrations in the background, a review of some guidelines for handling confusion about words is in order.

To begin, show students the words. In addition, put the words in a sentence or, better yet, in the larger context in which they occurred so that the dependence of meaning on context can be underscored (for example, "But the story wasn't about anyone being sick. Remember, I used *patient* to describe the kind of person that Abigail was. I said she was patient. What does that say about her?"). Finally, in addition to reminding students with examples that a word usually has more than a single meaning and that contexts affect meanings, encourage thoughtful responses by not calling on anyone immediately. As another writer has observed, "Students often perceive the discussion of a story as a contest to see who can answer the teacher's question first" (15, p. 145).

With Unexpected Happenings

Just as confusion about word meanings is inevitable, so too are unexpected opportunities to teach and clarify them. How observed teachers have taken advantage of such opportunities is instructive. For instance, one teacher whose classroom had been vandalized the night before used the context of an exceedingly untidy room to teach about *vandal, vandalism,* and *vandalized.* (At first, one child thought *vandal* was the name of the person who had done the damage.) Since acoustical tiles had been torn from the ceiling, the meaning of *acoustics* and *acoustical* was not overlooked, nor was the need to write the words for all to see, say, and discuss.

In another classroom, the Monday following a four-day weekend revealed a half-empty fish tank. "Did the fish drink all the water?" wondered one child. In response, the teacher filled two plates with water and by Wednesday was able to use them to explain the meaning of *evaporate* and *evaporation* in a way that reinforced an observation made by Anderson and Freebody: "Every serious student of reading recognizes that the significant aspect of vocabulary development is in the learning of concepts, not just words" (2, p. 8).

Teachers who appreciate the need to narrow the gap between what goes on in school and what happens outside always try to realize the potential of current events for expanding vocabularies. Once more, let me illustrate this commendable practice.

Worldwide attention to gasoline shortages prompted one teacher to help students understand *ration, depleted,* and *emergency,* using contexts taken from newspapers. Another teacher used heavy rains and nearby rivers to teach *flood, crest,* and *tributary*. Still another teacher, this one of younger children, recognized the forthcoming spring vacation as an opportunity to contrast *solid* and *hollow* as these concepts are realized in chocolate bunnies. One more teacher used an attractive bulletin-board display of Halloween masks made by students to extend the meaning of *mask* by relating its use in activities like skiing, scuba diving, surgery, and keeping warm.

Through Planned Activities

Although the use of unexpected happenings and current events and holidays is highly desirable for expanding vocabularies, so too are *planned* activities. How some observed teachers planned for vocabulary growth will be described now to illustrate possibilities.

One teacher has a Nym Center that features two decorated boxes, each with a slit in its cover. One box is labeled *synonym;* the other, *antonym.* Every Monday morning, the students take turns selecting "the word of the week." Once it is chosen and its meaning discussed, the word is printed on a small card that goes into the *synonym* box. Another card, this one displaying a word with an opposite meaning, is tucked into the one for antonyms. At any time during the week, students are free to add to either box. Should a selected word be *end,* for example, students might add cards with words like *stop, cease,* or *conclusion.* Everyone is also encouraged to add to the *antonyms.* On Friday, all of the cards are read and checked for correctness. Correct cards go on a bulletin board, and their contributors (students print their names on the cards) are acknowledged. This teacher continues the weekly practice until interest wanes. With some groups, this has meant about a month; with others, the routine continues all year.

Another teacher uses a selected theme to feature word meanings. Again, an attractive box is used that might display a label like *People Words.* If it does, possible words are *twin, parent, roofer, tailor, quarterback, cousin,* and *senator.* Still one more teacher uses a jar for words encountered in free reading whose meanings are unfamiliar. (The sentence in which each occurred is written and deposited in the jar.) Later, they are discussed and, if necessary, someone looks up their meanings in a dictionary to see which fits the context.

WAYS TO FOSTER VOCABULARY GROWTH

Having considered the various times for attending to word meanings, let us turn now to a more systematic look at the methods for fostering vocabulary growth, which were listed on page 237. Although possible methods are numerous, explaining the meaning of one word with other words is, without question, the most commonly used method. It must be recognized, nonetheless, that its frequency is not matched by its effectiveness. Why this is so has been explained well by Dolch:

> The average adult tries again and again to tell children with words what things are. . . . The child asks, "What is a snake?" The adult says, "An animal that crawls along the ground." The child imagines such an animal and asks, "But his legs will be in the way." The adult says, "Oh, he hasn't any legs." So the child takes off the legs and sees a legless body lying there. "But how does he crawl around without legs?" "He wiggles," says the adult. The child tries to make the legless body wiggle. "How does that get him to go forward?" The adult loses his temper. The peculiar way in which part of the snake pushes the other part cannot be described. It has to be seen. Let us go to the zoo. [9, p. 309]

What Dolch effectively points up is the special significance of experiences for word meanings:

$$\text{Experiences} \rightarrow \text{Acquisition of} \rightarrow \text{Vocabulary}$$
$$\text{(direct or vicarious)} \quad \text{knowledge and}$$
$$\text{concepts}$$

TEACHING WORD MEANINGS THROUGH EXPERIENCES

As with all other experiences, those conceived to be a means for developing vocabularies divide into direct and vicarious. Direct experiences will be treated first.

Direct Experiences

Each of us has already learned that one product of experiences, be they connected with occupations, hobbies, sports, or whatever, is a growth in vocabulary. In some instances, experiences even account for variation in the way a word is defined. Take *stock* as an example; then consider how it might be explained by a chef, an investor, a farmer or rancher, a horticulturist, a gun owner, and a merchant.

While it is true that no teacher needs to be told about the relationship between experiences and vocabulary, classroom observations do uncover the need to remind some that vocabulary does not *automatically* develop as a result of an experience. Rather, experiences must be deliberately linked with language, which means that when teachers decide to take students out to see the world, they should have made some decisions *beforehand* about the concepts and vocabulary that ought to come alive as a result of the experience.

When taking students out to see the world is being considered, it is important to remember that the world includes such ordinary places as a grocery store, a drugstore, or a block in the neighborhood and that the ordinary can be as fruitful for vocabulary as the more dazzling and exotic. A grocery store is a good place to acquire meaning for *kale, parsley,* and *yams;* and a walk in the neighborhood might be the best of dictionaries for *dormer, gutter, cupola, shutter,* and *antenna.* On the other hand, a trip to an airport—if that is possible—can change the meaning of *airplane* from a noisy spot in the sky to a structure of unexpected size, while a trip to a zoo can transform *snake* from an unbelievable creature into a starkly simple reptile.

One teacher learned that weekly trips to something as close as the new auditorium being built at his school is productive not only for vocabulary but also for promoting an interest in reading among sixteen children (ages seven through eleven) with serious reading problems. As a result of careful planning, dictionaries, stories, and pictures gradually came into existence, along with an understanding of words like *crowbar, wheelbarrow, cable,* and *bolts.*

Ordinary materials as well as ordinary places can also be productive. One teacher, for example, used tiny trinkets and toys to teach the meaning of *miniature.* This prompted a boy to talk about miniature golf; it prompted his teacher to discuss the prefix *mini* and to refer to words like *minibike* and *miniskirt.* Another teacher used cups to contrast the meanings of *opaque, transparent,* and *translucent,* after which an interesting discussion took place about when it is necessary to have transparent glass and when opaque or translucent materials are better or even necessary.

Still another teacher used a nature walk in which rocks were collected to give meaning to *pointed, pale, speckled, striped, rough, flaky, crumbly,* and *rounded* (19). She also used the students' budding interest in rocks to give them practice in both reading directions and carrying them out through pantomime:

> Move a big rock.
> Walk with rocks in your shoes.
> Fall like a rock.
> Carry a heavy bucket of rocks.

What began as a rock collection with older students ended with an interest in the meaning and origin of such expressions as:

> "A rolling stone gathers no moss."
> "People who live in glass houses shouldn't throw stones."
> "A stone's throw from here."

Descriptions like "stone cold," "rock bottom," "heart of stone," and "stone deaf" were discussed, too.

Even while the value of taking students out to see the world is being highlighted, what must be acknowledged is that excursions may be either impossible or overly time-consuming. Since finding ample time for everything *is* a problem, it probably is a good policy to bring the world into the classroom when that can be done and to bring students out to see the world when no alternative exists. Either way, deliberate steps must be taken to ensure that students acquire more concepts, knowledge, and vocabulary as they learn more about their world. Minimally, this makes pretrip preparations and posttrip discussions mandatory.

Vicarious Experiences

For both practical and pedagogical reasons, experiences that schools offer will often be vicarious. But that does not mean they must also be dull. To make sure that they are not, superior teachers make frequent use of two good sources of vicarious experiences: audiovisual aids and books that they read to students.

Figure 10.1

From *My Picture Dictionary* by Hale C. Reid and Helen W. Crane, of the GINN ELEMEN-
TARY ENGLISH SERIES, © Copyright, 1977, 1971, 1965, 1963, by Ginn and Company
(Xerox Corporation). Used with permission.

Audiovisual aids.   It does not take very long for teachers to learn the value of pictures for clarifying concepts. At times, pictures can even portray the meanings of words that might at first seem nonpicturable. (The reproduced page from a picture dictionary shown in Figure 10.1 demonstrates this.) I have also seen magazine pictures, this time in a scrapbook assembled by fifth graders, that pinpointed meanings with an accuracy that could not be matched by verbal explanations. I recall pictures that portrayed with great specificity and feeling such words as *sparkling* (sun shining on hoar frost), *vast* (large, empty beach), *affection* (young child hugging his grandmother), *serenity* (country snow scene), *anticipation* (dog awaiting his master), *vanity* (teenager looking in a mirror), and *neglect* (old shanty).

Whatever the visual or audio aid might be (pictures, photographs, models, graphs, charts, maps, diagrams, films, slides, recordings), it is important for teachers to be consciously aware of what needs to be said or done to realize their full potential for developing vocabularies. At times, what is necessary may be as basic as helping students learn how to look at pictures so that the common practice of only seeing what is already familiar will be replaced by something more productive. Making the most of another audio or visual aid might require a carefully planned discussion before using it, or afterward, or both. Sometimes it means selecting slides instead of a film in order to allow for a more careful, slow-paced study of individual objects. Regardless of what the specific requirements are, the general point is: Audiovisual aids help with concepts and vocabulary to the extent that teachers consciously plan for this to happen. Such a reminder is prompted by a recently observed sixth-grade teacher whose only preparation for a social studies film was: "Now if you'll get to your seats and keep still, we'll have a movie."

Reading to students.   When teachers remember the importance of vocabulary knowledge, reading to students will be more than a pleasant pause in a day's activities—and without diminishing the pleasurable feature. Of relevance now is the way it can promote interest in words, as well as an understanding of their meanings. Somewhat surprisingly, one way to promote interest is by reading the same book more than once. At least my own experiences have shown that children like to have certain material read and reread and that it is the multiple readings that lead to an interest in particular words. It is as if different features of a book or story catch the listeners' attention with each reading, eventually leading to a special awareness of, and curiosity about, certain words. With the curiosity, of course, comes the perfect time to discuss them.

Reading to students can also be productive for vocabulary development when books are selected with that goal in mind. The reproduced material in Figures 10.2 and 10.3 shows what might be read to (or read by) both young and older students. Worthy of attention, too, are the many informational books now available that introduce and explain—typically with the help of illustrations—terms related to a particular theme: space, light, sound, weight, size, shape, color,

Figure 10.2

Words from the names of famous people

Sometimes, too, somebody's name becomes a word for every-day use.

Sandwich comes from the name of an English nobleman, the Earl of Sandwich. The Earl was a very busy man and he hated to interrupt what he was doing to have a meal. So he invented a new and convenient kind of food. He put two pieces of bread together with meat or cheese between them, and made what is now called a sandwich.

Pasteurize comes from the name of a famous French scientist, Louis Pasteur, who first proved that some diseases were caused by germs. He invented a system of heating milk and quickly cooling it again, in such a way that all the harmful germs in it were killed. Almost all the milk that is drunk in this country today is safe because it has been treated in this way. It is pasteurized.

40

Figure 10.3

Thoburn, Tina. *Discovering Shapes,* art by James Caraway. Copyright © 1970, 1963 by The Bobbs-Merrill Co., Inc.

time. Some among them are very helpful in supplementing textbooks used in content fields like social studies and science.

In one classroom, the teacher's frequent reading of fiction helped students notice (and comment about) the tendency of authors to replace *said* with more descriptive terms. It also led to a list of words on the board:

	said	
responded	called	commented
inquired	shouted	warned
repeated	answered	wondered
asked	reported	whispered

A list in another room resulted from frequent contacts with books about animals:

A herd of _____
A flock of _____
A nest of _____
A school of _____
A hive of _____

In another classroom, a book that was supplemented with colorful illustrations culminated in a summary:

In still another room, a fifth-grade teacher who wanted to interest her students in mythology began by reading about the winter Olympics, an event of current interest. How mythological names enter into other facets of modern life came next: Atlas tires, Venus pencils, Hercules fencing, the Pegasus symbol for gasoline, the figure of Hermes to symbolize flowers-by-wire. All this was enough to make the teacher's weekly reading of myths an eagerly anticipated event. It also accounted for constantly growing vocabularies.

DIRECT TEACHING OF VOCABULARY

When word meanings are viewed as a subject for study, instruction can be organized around topics like synonyms and antonyms, or like word histories and etymology. Which focus is better depends on the words requiring attention and, in the case of word histories and etymology, on what a teacher knows.

One way to categorize direct instruction with vocabulary is shown in Figure 10.4. Please study the list before proceeding.

Synonyms, Antonyms, and Homophones

The category "synonym" is the one that is probably used most often in classrooms. However, that the study and use of synonyms is more complex than is

Figure 10.4

SOME CATEGORIES FOR ORGANIZING INSTRUCTION WITH VOCABULARY

Synonyms: words of similar meaning *(board, plank; clear, lucid).*

Antonyms: words of opposite meaning *(slowly, quickly; lazy, industrious).*

Homophones: words with the same pronunciation but different spellings and meanings *(would, wood; fowl, foul).*

Homonyms: words with the same pronunciation and spelling but different meanings.
Let's *rest* now.
The *rest* of the month was cold.

Homographs: words with the same spelling but different pronunciations and meanings.
It is made of *lead.*
Lead me to the table.

---

commonly realized is something that Albert Harris has effectively explained (18). Reacting to the routine practice of explaining one word with another, he cautions:

> One difficulty with this procedure is the danger of relying on superficial verbalizations. Words that are clear to the teacher may be quite hazy to the child. Many of the classical boners are due to a superficial and inadequate grasp of word meanings. It is not sufficient to tell a child that *frantic* means *wild,* or that *athletic* means *strong;* he may try to pick *frantic flowers* or pour *athletic vinegar* into a salad dressing. [p. 409]

Another complicating yet interesting facet of synonyms is the way they demonstrate that words often mean more than they say. At one level, *thin* and *slender* communicate something similar, but at another, the message is entirely different. Differences in what synonyms communicate are further illustrated in sentences like:

They will eat at seven o'clock.	She is a housewife.
They will dine at seven o'clock.	She is a homemaker.

These sentences illustrate one reason why synonyms are defined not as words having identical meanings but as words with similar meanings. The same sentences also demonstrate that words have both direct (denotative) and implied (connotative) meanings. Further examples of denotative and connotative uses of language follow, all concerned with occupations.

Denotative	*Connotative*
psychologist	shrink
garbage collector	sanitary engineer
mechanic	grease monkey

The preceding list shows the value of contrasts for teaching meanings, whether the words are *cry* and *wail,* or *transparent, translucent,* and *opaque,* or *and* and *or.* One way of dealing with contrasts is through work with *antonyms:* words of opposite meaning.

In Chapter 9, antonyms were used to illustrate negation by prefix:

tidy	perfect	active	typical
untidy	imperfect	inactive	atypical

regular	legal	human	obey
irregular	illegal	inhuman	disobey

Roots also enter into a study of antonyms, whether students are beginning or advanced readers:

up	inner	add	ancient	lucid
down	outer	subtract	modern	vague

Because of the helpfulness of contrasts in clarifying meaning, times when the dictionary gets attention should be occasions for dealing with antonyms as well as synonyms.

As was mentioned before, *homophones* (words with the same pronunciation but different spellings and meanings) call for the use of chalkboards. Another reference to a teacher who failed to use one might help reinforce the importance of allowing for *visual* distinctions when homophones are the concern. At the time of the visit to this teacher's third-grade classroom, she was discussing *hole* and *whole* and inquiring about the difference in their meanings. (Neither word had been written. Instead, the teacher simply said there are two different words, both pronounced "hole," and they have different meanings.) The distinction was to be communicated through sentences that the students suggested. The first sentence offered was both interesting and revealing. "Hold your hand up," said one girl. More surprising than her contribution was the teacher's response. "No," she said, "that's the word *hold,* not *hole.*" Still, nothing was written.

What should have been done? More specifically, what would the teacher have done if the guidelines referred to earlier had been followed? She not only would have written *hole* and *whole* right at the start but also would have written contexts like:

The surprised man fell into the *hole.*
That is why his *whole* body hurts.

Were this done and a student's response still used *hold,* the following contrast would be the next *visual* step.

hole
hold

Once the single-letter and single-sound differences were noted, a written sentence would add further help:

The cover over the hole was too heavy to hold.

All this can be summarized with the statement: *Reading instruction should give students the chance to see as well as to hear what is being taught and discussed.*

Homonyms and Homographs

The extent to which contexts—verbal or nonverbal—influence the meaning we assign to words is not always appreciated. Take the following sentence as an example: *This is the time when people want their pasts forgotten and their presents remembered.* Stated in the context of December holidays, the sentence has obvious meaning. Apart from that season, however, the meaning is much less clear. Totally unclear is the meaning of homonyms and homographs, except when they are in contexts. That the meaning of a homonym like *lost* is text dependent is illustrated next:

	wallet.
	mind.
Paul lost his	place.
	sight.
	touch.

While the meaning of homonyms must be deciphered from context, both the meaning *and* pronunciation of homographs are text dependent:

She has a tear in her dress.   The content is very interesting.
She also has a tear in her eye.   They are totally content now.

The existence of homonyms and homographs is the most apparent reason why dictionary assignments like one seen recently on a fourth-grade chalkboard are *un*acceptable. The assignment pertained to a list of ten words.

1.   Write each word three times.
2.   Using a dictionary, write a definition for each word.

Far superior (if not used repeatedly) is an assignment that starts with words placed in sentences and then asks for definitions that fit those contexts.

WORD HISTORIES

Like ourselves, every word has an origin and a history. To know about them is to know a word better. That is why superior teachers do not overlook word histories when their intent is to expand vocabularies and, at the same time, foster an interest in language.

One sure way to get students interested in word histories is to use their own names. Reference materials like *Dictionary of Given Names with Origins and Meanings* and *A Comprehensive Etymological Dictionary of the English Language* (21, 23) will tell them that some family names (for example, *Baker*) indicate an occupation, some (for example, *Hill*) a place of residence, while others (for example, *Johnson*) reflect an ancestor's given name. Their own given names also have meanings: Annette ("little Ann"), Dolores ("sorrow"), Donald ("proud chief"), Charles ("strong"). They might also learn that, in other countries, *John* is *Johannes, Juan,* or *Ivan*. In one classroom, an interesting scrapbook grew out of a two-week study of students' names.

Whereas people's names may have long histories, other words are evidence that vocabulary is being constantly added to English. Portmanteau words (word formed by combining parts of two other words) are appropriate for discussing additions:

motel	motor + hotel
smog	smoke + fog
brunch	breakfast + lunch
tangelo	tangerine + pomelo
telecast	television + broadcast
heliport	helicopter + airport
guesstimate	guess + estimate
happenstance	happen + circumstance

To provide a starting point for any teacher who appreciates the value of word histories but who is a neophyte with this facet of language, the following books are recommended as being informative, interesting, and easy to read:

Mathews, C. M. *Words, Words, Words.* New York: Charles Scribner's Sons, 1980. Starting out by noting "Human beings are talkative creatures," Mathews goes on to tell in seven chapters how words become available for humans to use. In the telling, he relates some history of the English language, as well as interesting accounts of how certain words made their way into English.

Miller, Casey, and Swift, Kate. *Words and Women.* New York: Anchor Press, 1979. Linguistic sexism is the underlying theme of this book. That it has existed in English for centuries is documented with interesting examples.

McCormack, Jo Ann. *The Story of Our Language.* Columbus, Ohio: Charles E.

Merrill Books, 1957. Written for intermediate-grade students, this paper-back traces the roots and development of what became American English. A section in the back lists references that will be useful to anyone who wants to supplement this brief history.

Nelson, Francis W. *The History of English*. New York: W. W. Norton and Co., 1963. This is a forty-one-page account of our language by a professor of linguistics. Its straightforward style makes it an interesting, easily read description of the beginnings of American English.

Funk, Charles E. *Thereby Hangs a Tale*. New York: Harper and Brothers, 1950. This is a book for adults in which the author tells about words that "acquired their meanings in an unusual manner."

Lambert, Eloise. *Our Language*. New York: Lothrop, Lee and Shepard, 1955. Like so many of the other books that deal with the history of our language, this one could be read by middle- and upper-grade children, yet the content is interesting enough for adults to enjoy. For many adults, in fact, it will provide new information about American English in general and about certain words in particular.

Laird, Helene, and Laird, Charlton. *The Tree of Language*. New York: World Publishing Company, 1957. This is written for children with middle- and upper-grade reading ability. Some of its most interesting pages tell how individual words came to mean what they do now. Prior to these accounts, other chapters recall some of the early history of English.

INDEPENDENCE IN WORKING OUT WORD MEANINGS

As has been stressed a number of times, effective teachers do whatever they can to help students become self-reliant readers. Self-reliance with word meanings is fostered with attention to two topics already discussed: contexts and word structure. At the time they were discussed, independence in arriving at correct pronunciations was the concern. How contexts and word structure provide help with meanings will be considered now.

Using Contexts

When children are still in the early stages of acquiring reading ability, knowing the pronunciation of a written word commonly suggests its meaning because most words in easy materials are in their oral vocabularies. As these same students advance, however, and are expected to read more difficult material, words that are unfamiliar both visually and orally become common.

Fortunately, the context in which such words appear often provides help with their meaning—at least to readers who are aware of such help and know how to use it. To make certain that students will know how to take advantage of contextual cues to get assistance with word meanings, instruction over the years should explain in exactly what forms the help might come.

How contexts reveal meanings has been cataloged in various ways (1, 3, 24). Eight categories will be discussed here. That they are not always distinctly different from each other is recognized; nonetheless, the categories do permit specificity both for this discussion and for instruction with children. This contrasts with many teaching manuals and practices whose "help" is as vague and circular as "Sometimes the sentence tells the meaning of the word. Sometimes the meaning of a word will be found in the sentence in which it occurs" (11). In all the illustrative sentences that follow, the word in italics is presumed to be one whose meaning is unknown.

1. Definition. The most obvious source of help is the context that acts like a dictionary and defines a word. This direct type of assistance characterizes textbooks because, at least in theory, their function is to explain and clarify. The following context, which might appear in a science text, is used now to show that sometimes a definition helps only if other key words are understood:

> The *nucleus* is the center of the atom.

The next context is less like a dictionary than the previous one, yet is more helpful. It also demonstrates that a context may be more than a sentence.

> After they crossed the mountains, they flew over the *desert*. It was very dry because a desert doesn't get much rain. There were no rivers or even creeks, and the soil looked like dry dust and sand.

2. Synonym. Providing a reader with a synonym is another way in which contexts help with meanings:

> I wish I was *ambidextrous*. Then I could use both hands equally well.

Whether the help in this context ought to be categorized as synonym or definition is debatable but also unimportant. What *is* important is how the second sentence explains the meaning of *ambidextrous*.

The next context shows another example of synonym help and, further, reveals the significance of the word *too* for reaching a conclusion about the meaning of *surrendered*.

> When the major *surrendered,* the others gave up too.

3. Summary.   Sometimes a troublesome word is one that an author used to summarize what preceded it. And what comes first may help with its meaning:

When John heard the noise, his knees began to shake. His hands were wet and
    cold. He felt as if he couldn't move. He was *terrified*.
Charlie is interested in everything and everybody and is always asking questions.
    He is a very *inquisitive* person.
People are being encouraged to combine modern, traditional, early American,
    French provincial—and all in the same room. The style is toward the *eclectic*.

4. Simile.   A simile is a figure of speech that compares things. For this discussion, the important point is that the comparison may clarify a word's meaning. The following contexts illustrate this.

> The cat's eyes *glowed* in the dark as if they were little lights.
> The sports car *lurched* forward like a dog starting out to chase a cat.
> The speaker's voice *droned* on like the humming of a bee.

At times, neither *as* nor *like* is in a context, although a simile is still available to help with the meaning of a word:

> He took the money with the *deftness* of a pickpocket.

While similes can help with meanings, the illustrations continue to underscore the importance of experiences and world knowledge for comprehension. Specifically, if a reader knows nothing about the characteristics of successful pickpockets, the context just referred to will hardly define *deftness*.

5. Example.   More prosaic than the simile but more explicitly helpful are examples:

The letters *un* are a common *prefix* in our language, as in *unhappy, unclean,* and
    untrue.
Joan was a very *selfish* child. For instance, she would never let any of the others
    play with her toys or look at her books.

6. Appositive.   Enclosed with commas, an appositive is another direct source of help with meanings:

The *minutes,* a written record of the meeting, were kept by the secretary.
Etymology, a branch of language study dealing with word origins, ought to be
    viewed as one way to help children expand their vocabularies.
The natives believed that *demons,* or evil spirits, lived beyond the river.

7. *Antonym*.   As the term *antonym* suggests, this contextual aid comes through contrasts, which are communicated in a variety of ways:

There is a great difference between the *tumult* on the outside and the peace inside.
She always is so disorganized and disorderly. She never does anything in a *methodical* way.
At the beach, some parts are deep and others are *shallow*.
I wonder whether the money will be a blessing or a *bane*.
Sue and Mary were eager to leave, but their brother was *reluctant*.
The boys slowed down, then drove *rapidly* again when they saw the others coming.

8. *Groupings*.   The appearance of a word in a series assigns it at least a general classification. For instance:

He used many different forms for writing poems, *essays,* plays, and short stories.
I had to shop for dinner and bought bread, meat, tomatoes, and *yams*.
The wallpaper was so colorful that I can only remember seeing yellow, *aqua*, and black.

All three of the contexts above demonstrate an important point: Knowing what a word means in general (for example, knowing that an essay is something somebody wrote) may be sufficient for comprehension, depending on the reader's purpose.

Depending on a teacher's purpose (and on students' abilities), categories of contextual help that are different from the ones listed here might be selected. Actually, how help is cataloged is much less important than that some type of scheme be used to give students a strategy for examining contexts should they include a word critical for comprehension but whose meaning is unfamiliar. Knowing how to do that in some systematic way not only fosters improved comprehension but also adds to vocabulary knowledge. It thus is an important contributor to a student's growing independence as a reader.

Classroom observations indicate that the last point merits attention because (as was mentioned before) starting at about third grade, teachers tend to have students use glossaries and dictionaries to learn about meanings. While students do need to learn how to use these reference materials, they have equal need to know how to use contexts because when they read on their own—in school or at home—they are more inclined to make a guess about a meaning than to break the continuity of what they are reading by going to a dictionary (assuming one is available). Instruction in using contexts can replace the guesswork with a more productive strategy. It should begin early, therefore, and eventually focus on categories like those described. Some categories (appositive, definition, examples) offer more apparent help than others (simile, groupings, antonym) and thus should get attention first. Any such attention ought to include illustrations offered by the teacher, followed by others that students themselves find in textbooks and such materials as newspapers. Eventually, instruction should also include examples of unhelpful contexts, for to avoid them is to avoid reality. These contexts demonstrate when a dictionary *ought* be be consulted, assuming the word in question is impeding comprehension.

When students know about contextual help for word meanings, they should be given the chance to use what they know with required reading. To be specific, if certain of the new words in a basal reader selection first appear in sentences that reveal what they mean, preparation for reading the selection should bypass them. After the selection is read, however, students should be questioned about the meanings of those words and, equally important, about how they arrived at them.

Using Word Structure

The previous chapter showed how students can use the structure of derived and inflected words to work out pronunciations on their own. At the same time, it showed how structure helps with meanings, thus allowing for more independence. The parallel attention to pronunciation and meaning was natural because, when unfamiliar derived and inflected words are dismantled and reassembled in the way that was explained in Chapter 9, both pronunciation and meaning can be achieved. The twofold contribution of the recommended procedure was demonstrated recently in a third grade in which a child was unable to do a workbook page because he did not understand *unaccented*. With correct guidance from the teacher, he worked out both the pronunciation and meaning by decomposing and reassembling its structural parts in the recommended way:

unaccented
accented
accent
accented
unaccented

In another classroom, the hero of a basal reader story happened to be a retriever. Although everyone in the instructional group appeared to know about retrievers, nobody was able to explain the meaning of the first word that the teacher wrote on the board:

retrieve

This led to a discussion of what retrievers do and of the meanings of:

retrieve
retriever
retrieval
retrievable

Word relationships and what they signify for meaning received attention in another classroom with numerous poster displays similar to the one following:

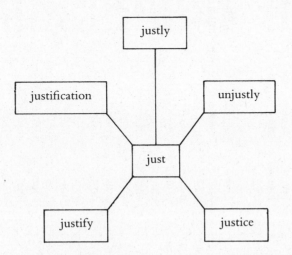

Elsewhere, a student's broken glasses prompted a discussion of a different word family:

spectacles   inspect
spectacular   inspector
spectator   inspection

Word structure as an aid for meanings is especially productive when students are knowledgeable about Latin and Greek roots and prefixes like those in Figure 10.5. To make etymology interesting, something like a word tree might be assembled on a bulletin board (17) so that words originating in different languages can be placed along different branches. Word cards display the English word (such as *evolve*) followed by, in this case, the Latin word *evolvere,* meaning "to unroll."

Since the likelihood of attention to origins depends on teachers' knowledge of etymology, references for word origins are listed next. Together with those named earlier under the heading "Word Histories," they provide a starting point for bringing to life a language that is far more fascinating than many realize.

Figure 10.5 Some Latin and Greek roots and prefixes: Common meanings*

Root	Meaning	Example
audire	to hear	audience
calor	heat	calorie
folium	leaf, sheet	folio
		foliage
dicere	to speak, tell	predict
gram	letter	monogram
graph	writing	autograph
logos	speech	monologue
	reason	logic
	study of	geology
manualis	of the hand	manual
mare	sea	marine
meter	measure	thermometer
mimeo	imitate	mimic
mittere	to send	transmit
mobilis	moveable	mobile
pedis	foot	pedestrian
phobia	fear or hatred of	phobia
phonos	sound	phonics
portare	to carry	portable
	doorway	portal
scribere	to write	postscript
sonus	sound	sonorous
spectare	to see, look at	spectacles
tenere	to hold, have	tenacious
visio	sight	television

Prefix	Meaning	Example
auto	self	autograph
bi	two	biped
bio	life	biography
geo	earth	geology
heter(o)	different, other	heterogeneous
homo	man	homicide
homos	same, equal	homogeneous
hydro	water	hydroelectric
inter	between, among	international
mal	bad, badly	maladjusted
micro	small	microfilm
minimus	little, small	miniskirt
mono	one, alone	monogram
omni	all, everywhere	omnipresent
photo	light	photograph
poly	many	polysyllable
post	after	postscript
sub	under	submarine
	further division	subcommittee
super	above, beyond	supersonic
tele	distant	television
therm	heat	thermometer
trans	across	transmit

* Suffixes are not included because so many indicate part of speech rather than meaning. Some that do suggest meaning were presented earlier in Figure 9.1.

Epstein, Sam, and Epstein, Beryl. *The First Book of Words*. New York: Franklin Watts, 1954. The simplicity of this book is disarming, for it offers accurate and interesting information about many aspects of words: prefixes, suffixes, compound words ("struck-together words" it calls them), and brand names. Not many adults will read it without learning more about etymology; yet its simple style, combined with many illustrations, makes it suitable for middle- and upper-grade children.

Ernst, Margaret S. *Words*. New York: Alfred A. Knopf, 1954. The subtitle summarizes the content: *English Roots and How They Grew*. But it does not point out that this book resulted from classroom instruction with middle- and upper-grade students. The content is written directly to children and includes assignments that make it self-instructional.

Brown, James I. *Programmed Vocabulary*. Chicago: Lyons and Carnahan, 1965. Prepared for high school students, the content in this book will also be instructive for most adults. It uses a programmed approach (small steps at a time with written responses required) and deals with a selected list of prefixes and roots, tracing them back to original language sources.

Quinn, Jim. *American Tongue and Cheek*. New York: Random House, 1980. A very current look at English by a less than serious author, this book defends the use of a number of words and phrases that scholars have been "trying to stamp out." In the process, it provides much information about English and its history.

Sperling, Susan K. *Tenderfeet and Ladyfingers*. New York: Viking Press, 1981. This account of the sources of selected words and expressions in English divides the content on the basis of body parts. Under "finger," for instance, the following expressions are dealt with: *thumbs down, rule of thumb, keep one's fingers crossed, knuckle down,* and *all thumbs.*

When teachers are knowledgeable about etymology, they are able to instruct about words like:

autograph	auto	(self)
biography	bio	(life)
autobiography	graph	(writing)
geography	geo	(earth)
geology	logy	(study of)
biology		

They are also prepared to explain the origin of such words as:

portable	script	telegraph	telegraph	automobile
porter	manuscript	telegram	autograph	automatic
portfolio	scripture	telephone	photograph	autonomy
export	scribble	television	mimeograph	autocrat
report	inscribe	teletype	phonograph	automation

How etymology gets students interested in language, underscores relationships between words, and helps with meanings can be demonstrated by an account of one fifth grade. On the day I was observing, political trials in Washington, D.C., were everyone's concern; as a result, the students were discussing *indict*. Questioned about its meaning, they offered wordy definitions, all vague. The teacher, therefore, told of the many languages from which English words have come and explained that *indict* was from a Latin word *dicere*, meaning "to speak," and from the Latin prefix *in*, whose multiple meanings included "against." She then concluded, "The word *indict* means to speak against someone." The discussion next moved to the connection between that meaning and what was happening in Washington, D.C.

Subsequently, the teacher redirected the students' attention to *indict* (which she had printed on the board), reminded them that it had to do with speaking or speech, and asked whether they could think of other words that contained *d, i, c, t*. One child immediately proposed *dictionary*, eventually defined as a book containing words people use when they speak. Another student, whose mother was a secretary, added generously to the examples by offering *dictate, dictation*, and *dictaphone*, all of whose meanings were clarified. Writing *dictator*, the teacher asked why it was correct to call someone who ruled without asking for advice a "dictator." One student promptly explained, "What he says goes." "Yes," the teacher added; "his word is law."

To show how attention to etymology is possible even at a first-grade level, let me describe what was seen when a small group was being instructed in the use of a typewriter. As the teacher typed, the children watched what appeared on the paper. "What's that?" one child inquired as soon as he saw an asterisk. In response, the teacher typed *asterisk*, pronounced it, and explained that it meant "little star." Directly under *asterisk* she typed *aster*, read that, and explained it was the name of a flower that evidently had reminded someone of a star because that was what *aster* meant. After promising to bring in pictures of asters, the teacher continued with the typing; the children, with their looking.

INSTRUCTIONAL MATERIALS

As was just demonstrated, the best of instructional materials for extending vocabularies is what is in a teacher's head, since that knowledge allows for on-the-spot instruction. Next on the list of effective materials is whatever is close at hand,

Figure 10.6

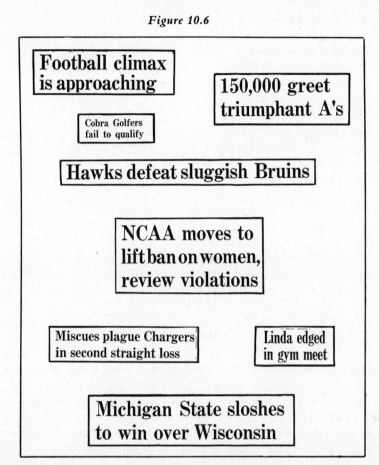

because that interests children. In this case, shoes serve as a good example because they allow for attention to many words, such as: *arch, strap, leather, canvas, rubber, oxford, sandal, moccasin, tight, loose, comfortable,* and *uncomfortable.* Shoes might even be used to introduce homophones *(pair, pear, pare; sole, soul; heel, heal)* and homonyms *(tie, tongue, lace, pinch, buckle).*

Newspapers are other close-at-hand material. In this case, ads illustrate the persuasive use of language, and thus of hyperbole and the kinds of words that go with that. Because sports writers seem to want to avoid using *win* and *lose* at all costs, headlines in the sports section of newspapers are helpful too (see Figure 10.6). And so is the terminology of the newspaper industry itself: *beat, by-line, caption, circulation, copy reader, correspondent, dateline, dummy, edition, editor, editorial, features, morgue, teletype, wirephoto.*

Why teachers should never think that work with vocabulary requires purchasing special materials is further reinforced by illustrations like the following.

Display at gasoline station
> "Courtesy is contagious.
> Let's start an epidemic."

Sign at gasoline pump
> "Prices do not exceed maximum allowable price."

Stamped on pieces of lumber
> "Kiln dried"

Stamped on hotel key
> "If carried away inadvertently, please drop in any mailbox."

Advertisement on pencil for new furniture store
> "Don't gamble on quality. See us first."

Calling attention to the great potential of the language that literally surrounds us is not meant to deny the value of commercially prepared materials. In fact, much help is available commercially in the form of books, worksheets, pictures, films, filmstrips, cassette tapes, and phonograph records. Meriting repetition, nonetheless, is that in ordinary, inexpensive, and close-at-hand sources lies much material for enhancing students' oral vocabularies.

PRACTICE

Justifiably, teachers wonder about finding time to give vocabulary development the attention it deserves. Since one opportunity lies with assignments that students complete on their own, ideas for independent work follow.

- On tongue depressors, print words whose meanings have been studied. Print synonyms (or antonyms) on other depressors. Put them all in a box. The student's job is to match words by putting appropriate depressors together (back to back) with a clip-type clothespin. Decisions can be checked with a typed list of correct pairs.

- On the cover of a file folder, draw four rows of rectangles, three per row. Number them. Cut three sides of each rectangle to make booklike openings. On each rectangle print a derivative. Open each and, on the inside of the back cover of the folder, print roots that are synonyms. Close the folder. A student works with an alphabetical listing of the roots and with a sheet numbered from 1 through 12. From the list, he selects and writes synonyms for each derivative, later checking responses by opening each book.

- Cover two empty juice cans or ice cream containers with gift-wrapping paper. Attach a card to each, one displaying *fast,* the other *slow.* On other cards print expressions that have been studied (for example, *like a streak of lightning, at a snail's pace, lagged behind, poked along, make a beeline for*). The goal is to put each expression in the appropriate container.

Prepare a sheet showing two columns of words. Direct students to read each pair of words and to think about their meanings. If the two have a similar meaning, they write *s* in the parenthesis that separates each pair. If meanings are opposite, *o* is written. If they are neither similar nor opposite, parentheses are left blank.

Prepare a sheet showing groups of words:

egg	wood	window	red	shoes
bread	iron	table	white	watch
dish	paper	lamp	yellow	coat
milk	book	cabinet	rainbow	hat

Direct students to read each group of four words, to think about the meaning of each word in a group, and to draw a line through the one that does not belong with the other three. They then write one or two sentences to explain each decision.

On the back of large, colorful pictures, print descriptive adjectives. (For a baboon, one teacher printed *hairy, huge, terrible, ugly, scary, fierce,* and *strong*.) Students select a picture and write about the content, using as many of the words as possible. With newly acquired pictures, students can suggest appropriate descriptions themselves.

Interest in games can be taken advantage of. For example:

On a chalkboard, list twenty words whose meanings have been studied. Direct students to write the numbers 1 through 10 on their papers in a vertical column. After the numbers, they write any ten of the twenty words. In random order, call out synonyms (or antonyms) for the twenty words. As this is done, students circle a word on their paper whenever a synonym (or antonym) is named. The first to circle all words is the winner.

Shuffle a set of word cards and deal them to members of a small group. The deck for the game is other cards on which homophones appear. Students take turns selecting a card from the deck. If they choose one that is a homophone for a card they hold and if they can define the two words, those cards are discarded. If not, the card is placed on the bottom of the deck. The first one out of cards is the winner.

Print sentences on cards, each containing a word (underlined) whose meaning is not likely to be known but can be inferred from contextual cues. (Correct definitions are on the backs of cards.) Four students select sentence cards from the deck. Time is allowed for the four to study contexts and decide on meanings. Each then reads his sentence, explains the meaning of the underlined word, turns the card over, and reads the definition. If the explanation is correct, he advances one space upward on a board like the one shown here.

I am the winner!

(Various markers can be used: paper squares, corn, buttons, and so on.) All cards are returned to the deck. The game ends when a player gets to the top of the board.

- Cover a potato chip can to make it look like a firecracker. Put small, cardboard strips in it, each displaying a sentence with an underlined derivative. On a few cards of similar size, print *Bang!* The game proceeds as players take turns selecting a card from which they read the sentence aloud. The card is kept if they can name a root with a meaning similar to that of the derivative. (Whenever a *Bang* card is selected, it is automatically kept, and the player gets another turn.) The winner is the one with the largest number of cards.

CONCLUDING COMMENTS

Admittedly, the treatment of vocabulary development in this chapter has been extensive. Although it is possible that the length and detail may be overwhelming rather than helpful, they were prompted by two facts. The first is that reading ability is dependent upon oral language to such an extent that overlooking the latter automatically places limits on the former. The second fact is that school activities rarely reflect the fundamental importance of oral language, even when bilingual children are in the classroom. With all the possibilities for enhancing vocabularies that have now been discussed in Chapter 10, it is hoped that the content will foster not only more attention to vocabulary development but also better, more interesting attention. While bilingual children *need* this, all students *deserve* it.

SUMMARY

As Chapter 10 considered how to extend oral vocabularies, it was reflecting the fact that readers must bring meaning to a page if they are to get meaning from it. The chapter was thus underscoring the importance of both vocabulary development and comprehension.

Typically, problems with vocabulary increase as students advance from one grade to the next. This does not mean that word meanings should be of concern only to middle- and upper-grade teachers but that carefully planned instruction ought to begin as soon as children start school and ought to continue until they graduate.

As Chapter 10 concentrated on vocabulary knowledge, it identified many ways to promote it. Early sections in the chapter dealt with the value of experiences, both direct and vicarious. Especially stressed was the need for teachers to *plan* for experiences to enhance vocabularies; otherwise, their potential might not be realized.

From there the chapter moved to a discussion of more direct and systematic means for adding to vocabularies. Attention thus went to synonyms, antonyms, homophones, and word histories. The fact that words have multiple meanings was especially underscored when the discussion shifted to homonyms and homographs, which are always text-dependent words. Connotative and denotative meanings were illustrated too.

Recognizing that the ability to cope independently with word meanings is important, Chapter 10 explained how students can be taught to work out meanings on their own. This accounted for a section on use of context and for another one on word structure.

What was covered, then, can be summarized as follows:

ENHANCING ORAL VOCABULARIES

Through experiences	*Instruction with:*
direct	synonyms, antonyms, homophones
vicarious	homonyms, homographs
audiovisual aids	*Instruction to foster independence*
reading to students	use of context
Through word histories	use of word structure

Chapter 10 pointed out that attention to word meanings is mandatory whenever they are likely to cause problems with required reading. Other help is essential when students are confused about a meaning. The best of teachers also take advantage of unexpected happenings, and complementing the unexpected is their generous use of planned attention. All four times for focusing on vocabularies were discussed and illustrated. Together, they can make for a varied and interesting program for enhancing students' oral language.

REVIEW

1. Explain the following: *We must not teach word meanings as a substitute for genuine understanding*.
2. Why are these two statements both correct?

    Pronunciations without meaning are useless for reading.
    Meaning without pronunciation is useful for reading.

    What is the implication of the truth of both statements for instructional programs?
3. Although it is unnecessary for children to be able to define terms like *homophone* and *homograph*—what they need to be able to do is comprehend homophones and homographs—teachers should be able to define them so that they can explain these kinds of words to students. With that in mind, define the following: *homographs, homonyms, homophones*.
4. As students advance in their ability to read, they need to know about denotative and connotative meanings. With examples, distinguish between the two.
5. At a number of places in this book, the dependence of reading on oral vocabularies has been illustrated. With examples, review the various ways in which the dependence shows up.

REFERENCES

1. Ames, Wilbur S. "The Development of a Classification Scheme of Contextual Aids." *Reading Research Quarterly* 2 (Fall 1966): 57–82.
2. Anderson, Richard C., and Freebody, Peter. *Vocabulary Knowledge and Reading.* Reading Education Report No. 11. Urbana: University of Illinois, Center for the Study of Reading, August 1979.
3. Artley, A. Sterl. "Teaching Word Meaning Through Context." *Elementary English Review* 20 (February 1943): 68–74.
4. Askov, Eunice N. "Context Clues: Should We Teach Children to Use a Classification System in Reading?" *Journal of Educational Research* 69 (May–June 1976): 341–344.
5. Beck, Isabel; McKeown, Margaret G.; McCaslin, Ellen S.; and Burkes, Ann M. *Instructional Dimensions That May Affect Reading Comprehension: Examples from Two Commercial Reading Programs.* Pittsburgh: Learning Research and Development Center, University of Pittsburgh, 1979.

6. Boatner, M. T., and Gates, J. E. *A Dictionary of American Idioms*. Woodbury, N.Y.: Barron's Educational Services, 1975.

7. Dale, Edgar. *The Word Game: Improving Communication*. Bloomington, Ind.: Phi Delta Kappa Educational Foundation, 1975.

8. Deighton, Lee C. *Vocabulary Development in the Classroom*. New York: Teachers College Press, Columbia University, 1959.

9. Dolch, Edward W. *Psychology and Teaching of Reading*. Champaign, Ill.: Garrard Press, 1951.

10. Donlan, Dan. "Teaching Words Through Sense Impressions." *Language Arts* 52 (November–December 1975): 1090–1093.

11. Durkin, Dolores, "Reading Comprehension in Five Basal Reader Series." *Reading Research Quarterly* 16, no. 4 (1981): 515–544.

12. Eisiminger, Sterling. "Using Name Origins in the Elementary Classroom." *Language Arts* 53 (October 1976): 753–754.

13. Funk, Wilfred. *Six Weeks to Words of Power*. New York: Pocket Books, 1955.

14. Funk, Wilfred, and Lewis, Norman. *30 Days to a More Powerful Vocabulary*. New York: Wilfred Funk, 1942.

15. Gambrell, Linda B. "Think-Time: Implications for Reading Instruction." *Reading Teacher* 34 (November 1980): 143–146.

16. Gipe, Joan. "Investigating Techniques for Teaching Word Meanings." *Reading Research Quarterly* 14, no. 4 (1978–1979): 624–644.

17. Gold, Yvonne. "Helping Students Discover the Origins of Words." *Reading Teacher* 35 (December 1981): 350–351.

18. Harris, Albert J. *How to Increase Reading Ability*. New York: Longmans, Green, 1961.

19. Hucklesby, Sylvia. "A Nature Walk." *ERIC/ECE Newsletter* 5 (June 1971): 1–2.

20. Johnson, Dale D., and Pearson, P. David. *Teaching Reading Vocabulary*. New York: Holt, Rinehart and Winston, 1978.

21. Klein, Ernest. *A Comprehensive Etymological Dictionary of the English Language*. New York: Elsevier, 1966.

22. Kurth, Ruth J. "Building a Conceptual Base for Vocabulary Development." *Reading Psychology* 1 (Spring 1980): 115–120.

23. Loughead, Flora H. *Dictionary of Given Names with Origins and Meanings*. Glendale: Arthur Clark Company, 1974.

24. McCullough, Constance M. "Context Aids in Reading." *Reading Teacher* 11 (April 1958): 225–229.

25. McKenna, Michael. "Portmanteau Words in Reading Instruction." *Language Arts* 55 (March 1978): 315–317.

26. Morris, William. *It's Easy to Increase Your Vocabulary*. Rev. ed. New York: Penguin Books, 1975.

27. Nurnberg, Maxwell, and Rosenblum, Morris. *How to Build a Better Vocabulary*. New York: Popular Library, 1961.

28. Past, Kay C.; Past, Al; and Guzman, Sheila B. "A Bilingual Kindergarten Immersed in Print." *Reading Teacher* 33 (May 1980): 907–913.

29. Pincus, A. R. H., and Pincus, R. E. "Linguistic Sexism and Career Education." *Language Arts* 57 (January 1980): 70–76.

30. Yelland, H. L.; Jones, J. C.; and Easton, K. S. W. *A Handbook of Literary Terms*. Boston: Writer, 1980.

PART IV

INSTRUCTION: CONNECTED TEXT

CHAPTER 11

COMPREHENSION

PREVIEW

Many parents (and even some teachers) appear to equate good reading with an effective oral delivery. As a result, helping children is equated with listening to them read aloud. This textbook disavows those conclusions and, instead, equates reading with comprehending.

That prior chapters dealt with topics that are important for comprehension is reinforced in a report in which Golinkoff (8) compares students who are successful comprehenders with others who are not. Characteristics of the latter are summarized below.

Poor comprehenders . . .

make more decoding errors.
take more time to decode.
ignore contextual cues while decoding.
are more concerned with pronunciations than with meanings.
read word by word.
are less adaptive in the type of reading they do.
are less aware of what it means to comprehend.

Chapter 11 now looks at comprehension more directly. It begins by showing what a complex process comprehension is by referring to some of the multiple variables that enter into and affect it. On the assumption that instruction should affect it positively, examples of comprehension instruction are given. How such instruction fits in with the use of basal readers is also covered, since they are usually at the center of the time set aside to teach reading.

Because of the need for practice, three kinds are dealt with in Chapter 11: practice that is part of comprehension lessons, practice that is realized when students read a selection, and practice that comes in the form of written assignments based on needs.

The chapter following this one supplements Chapter 11 by considering comprehension within the framework of subject matter textbooks.

The ability to comprehend written discourse is determined by many factors, some of which are not the product of instruction. One student, for example, may cope successfully with a certain passage not so much because of what he learned in school but because of background information that he acquired on his own. In another case, unusual interest in the content may contribute substantially to success. The point is that reading comprehension is too complex to be classified "school responsibility." Nonetheless, much can be done in classrooms to help students develop into able processors of print.

FACTORS THAT AFFECT COMPREHENSION

Before instruction is considered, a closer look at some of the variables that enter into comprehension should be helpful. For convenience, they are divided into factors that are on the page and factors that are in the reader's head.

On the Page

Our own experiences as readers tell us that some pieces of text are so poorly written that trying to comprehend them is as much a guessing game as it is a reading task. Poorly organized content, obscure explanations and descriptions, pronouns with ambiguous referents, unwieldy sentences—all these defects and more make some selections almost incomprehensible no matter what the reader's ability.

It has to be recognized, however, that the most gifted of writers cannot guarantee success for readers because it is not always possible to avoid sources of difficulty like technical or uncommon words, abstract ideas, complex relationships, and unstated but important details. What those who write informational text *can* do is offer headings, subheadings, definitions, summaries, pictures, graphs, and tables, all of which help readers who know how to use them when they are involved with expository material. On the other hand, writers of narrative text help out by relating their tales in what Pearson and Johnson (16) call a "more-or-less cause-effect to cause-effect fashion." All this points up that whether readers comprehend depends on a sizable number of variables, some of which include what an author puts on the page.

In the Reader's Head

Other variables have to do with what is in the reader's head. Part of what teachers can put into students' heads has already been discussed: large sight vocabularies, expertise in using all available cues to get words decoded, extensive knowledge of word meanings. Since what is known about a topic before reading about it commences also exerts considerable influence on comprehension (1, 2, 3), the knowledge of the world that is in a reader's head can hardly be overlooked. In fact, world knowledge has been, and continues to be, a very popular topic with linguists, psychologists, psycholinguists, and educators whose current research is an effort to learn exactly what constitutes the comprehension process (6). Since reading *is* thinking, the reader's intelligence is still another piece in a very complicated picture.

One way to summarize all this is to say that comprehension is achieved when a match exists between the demands of the selection and the abilities, knowledge, and effort of the reader. Within that framework, comprehension instruction is one means for ensuring that a match will be the rule for students, not the exception.

LISTENING AND READING COMPARED

Long before children come to school, they are successful comprehenders of speech. The obvious similarities between spoken and written language have led some to conclude that the only new task for beginners in reading is to learn to translate the symbols they see into words they know (7). For these individuals, then, the major concern is decoding, not comprehension instruction.

Recently, analyses of spoken and written language (17) have raised questions about this position because more careful comparisons of listening and reading highlight differences that have significance for defining what one must know and be able to do in order to become a reader. Hence, a discussion of some of the more pertinent differences between listening and reading follows.

To begin, a great deal of listening takes place in the context of conversations, which makes what is heard different from what is typically found in written material. Specifically, the content of speech is likely to be more personal and to deal with the immediate environment and shared experiences, all of which facilitate communication. Now, for example, the referents for *their, his,* and *I,* or for *tomorrow* and *yesterday* are rarely ambiguous. What also helps is the habit of speakers to monitor the effects of what they are saying. In this case, a listener's facial expression or direct question may bring about helpful changes in the form of repetition, elaboration, or examples.

Not to be overlooked is how the nature of speech itself makes communication easier. Features like intonation and stress help, and so does the way in which speakers segment sentences (with pauses) into meaningful units like phrases and clauses.

When the focus switches to reading, a different picture emerges. Now it is the recipient of the message—that is, the reader—who must make adjustments. In this case, they have to be made not only to the writer's perspective (which may be very different from the reader's) but also to his or her use of long or uncommon words and of sentences with complex structures. Further adjustments have to be made to content because, more often than not, it will have one or more of the following characteristics: dense, unfamiliar, detailed, technical, nonrepetitive.

Fortunately, readers who know enough to do so can help themselves. If they are trying to acquire information from text, for example, they can preview the material first in order to pick up the general gist of the content. Whether reading fiction or fact, they can also make adjustments if problems occur once the reading begins. More specifically, they can slow down, or stop and ponder, or, if necessary, reread. Meanwhile, they can use punctuation marks to chunk the text into meaningful units. But, it should be noted, all this will be done only by those who appreciate that reading is an *active* process, one likely to require more conscious effort than does listening.

What these various comments suggest, then, is that any who claim that decoding ability (plus oral language comprehension) is all that is required to be a proficient reader have reached an unrealistic conclusion. From a teaching perspective, a more accurate, but still incomplete, one is:

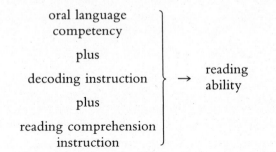

SOME CONCERNS OF COMPREHENSION INSTRUCTION

Since readers must adapt to what authors do, knowing what they do points up subject matter for comprehension instruction. Although not everything that authors do will be discussed, the partial description that follows will at least illustrate topics and goals for instruction.

Before attention goes to the illustrations, two important points must be made because of deficiencies in teaching manuals. The first follows: When the goal is to improve reading comprehension, teachers must make certain that students see the *significance* of what authors do *for reading*. That manuals overlook this can be illustrated with one that suggests teaching that rhetorical questions are something authors use to attract readers' attention. The same manual, however, says nothing about the possibility—and this is what is important for readers to know—that such questions may be followed by the answers (4).

The second point is that while definitions of terms may be one essential part of comprehension instruction, in and of themselves they do not constitute such instruction. Take the case of *fact* and *opinion* as an example. While readers do need to know the difference between the two, they must also understand how such knowledge should affect the way they read something like an editorial or an advertisement.

All this underscores (again) the need for teachers to keep asking, "*Why* am I doing this?" When the answer is, "To advance students' ability to comprehend," manual suggestions will often have to be changed, enlarged, or skipped. Certainly this is the case when they deal with what authors do.

Graphic Signals

One thing that authors do to communicate is to use certain visual properties of written language. Since these features of print provide information to readers who understand them, they are referred to as *graphic signals*. The common graphic signals and their functions are listed next:

GRAPHIC SIGNALS

Capital letter

    shows beginning of sentence
    indicates proper name, title

Period

    signals end of sentence
    indicates abbreviation

Question mark

    shows end of question

Exclamation mark

    conveys excitement, emotion

Comma

    shows beginning and end of thought unit
    sets off person addressed
    separates items in list or group
    sets off appositive

Colon

> indicates something will follow that is related

Italics, underlining, all caps

> indicate stressed word, which may affect meaning

Boldface type

> shows heading, subheading, emphasis

Parentheses

> may enclose explanation, extra thought

Quotation marks

> show what someone said
> indicate title, nickname

Indentation

> start of new paragraph

Signal Words

Just as the physical properties of written language offer information that is significant for comprehension, so, too, do certain words. Samples of these *signal words* are shown next, along with descriptions of their function.

SIGNAL WORDS

What, Who, Why, When, Which, Do, Can, Will

> at start of sentence indicate possible question

And

> links words, phrases, sentences

Or

> indicates alternative or appositive

First, next, while, later, afterward, finally

> point up sequence

The next week, a year later

> indicate passing of time

Because, since, so, therefore, consequently

> signal cause-effect relationship

For example

   signals illustrations, instances

Like, as

   signal comparison

Think, probably, believe, possibly

   suggest opinion

For that reason, that is why

   refer to previously mentioned idea or event

Language Functions

Commonly, authors do certain things to achieve certain goals. They may use a title, for instance, to announce the subject, theme, or main idea of what they are writing, or they may use a pronoun to avoid needless repetition. Since knowing about these means and ends assists readers, instruction with what will be called *language functions* also contributes to students' ability to comprehend. Samples of what writers do and why they do it follow.

LANGUAGE FUNCTIONS

Title, headline

   used to announce subject, theme, main idea, or to attract attention

Descriptive words

   used to form mental picture

Details

   used to communicate clear idea or picture

Pronouns

   used to stand for person, place, thing, idea, event

Adverbs

   used to stand for other words that tell where

Repetition

   used to emphasize a point

Comparison

   used to clarify or contrast

Definition, appositive, footnote

> used to add information or to explain

Sentences

Readers who know about the nature and form of sentences are in a better position to process them than are others who do not. Sorting out the subject and predicate in a troublesome sentence, for example, might be the first step in working out its meaning. Topics like the following, therefore, provide additional subject matter for comprehension instruction.

SENTENCES

Nature of sentence

> has subject and predicate
> may have compound subject and/or compound predicate
> may be two sentences combined

Kinds: declarative, interrogative, exclamatory, imperative

Word order

> distinguishes between telling and asking sentence
> may affect meaning

Verbal

> gerund construction referring to subject

Adjectives, adverbs, phrases, clauses

> make kernel of sentence more descriptive, informative

Placement of comma, phrase, clause

> may alter meaning of sentence

Intersentence Relationships

If comprehension is to be achieved, readers must understand not only how the words comprising a sentence relate to one another but also how the sentences that make up a paragraph are interrelated. Topics concerned with intersentence connections follow.

INTERSENTENCE RELATIONSHIPS

Nature of paragraph

> may communicate details about a main idea
> one sentence may express main idea

Cause and effect

> may be told in separate sentences

Simile

> may extend beyond one sentence

Meaning of word

> may be explained in another sentence

Referent for pronoun, adverb

> may be in previous or following sentence

Sequence

> may be revealed in series of sentences

Elliptical sentence

> requires reference to previous sentence to be understood

Text Structure

Other topics meriting classroom time pertain to structure—that is, to the way a piece of text is put together. The need to teach about structure arises from two facts. The first is that the structure of written discourse varies from one genre to another. That is, stories (narrative discourse) are put together in a way that differs from the structure of both expository discourse (explanations, descriptions) and procedural discourse (directions). The second fact is that knowing about the structure of whatever is to be read facilitates both comprehension and retention. This is so because such knowledge establishes expectations about content, about the likely sequence in which it will be developed, and about the author's method of delivery.

Since expository text is the subject of the next chapter, sample topics about structure pertain to narrative material.

STORIES

Structure

> setting
>
> > characters
> > location
> > time
>
> episode(s)
>
> > initiating event
> > main character's response and formation of goal

attempt(s) to achieve goal
outcome of attempts
resolution

Other information about stories also helps to comprehend them. For example:

Characters

traits revealed through

direct descriptions
what characters say, do, think
what others say about them

Perspective

first person

revealed through use of *I, we*
told from one perspective, therefore limited

third person

revealed through use of *he, she, they*
gives total picture
characters' thoughts/behavior can be explained

Kinds of stories

real
make believe
folk tale
fable
tall tale
myth
epic

NEED FOR COMPREHENSION INSTRUCTION

Even though possible topics for comprehension instruction are numerous, research indicates that it is unexpectedly scarce in both classrooms and basal reader manuals (4, 5). On the other hand, what classrooms and manuals provide in abundance is comprehension assessment, typically carried out with *many* questions. Why comprehension is constantly tested but rarely taught has no obvious explanation. Perhaps as more is learned about the comprehension process, more suggestions for teaching it will get into manuals. And if they do, increased instruction is likely to show up in classrooms.

NATURE OF COMPREHENSION INSTRUCTION

Before examples of what ought to be going on in classrooms are offered, some definitions will be provided, the first of *comprehension instruction* itself.

Comprehension Instruction

> Teacher does/says something that ought to help students understand, or work out, the meaning of connected text.

The "doing" and "saying" referred to in the definition are assumed to be some combination of definitions, explanations, descriptions, illustrations, demonstrations, and questions. With the last, only those that deal with the *process* of comprehending meet the demands of the definition; questions focusing on its *products* are considered to be assessment.

To make certain that the distinction between the two types of questions is clear, let us consider the following text: "The new factory polluted the water. Many of the trees were cut down. More people lived there, too. For that reason, the Canadian geese never returned to Chesapeake Bay."

Questions viewed as being instructive for comprehension (in particular, for showing the dependence of the last sentence on the previous ones) might include: "What do you need to know to understand that last sentence? . . . Read the whole paragraph to see what *For that reason* means. . . . What are all the things to which *that* refers?" An assessment question about the same text might ask, "Why didn't the geese return?"

Also to be noted about the definition of comprehension instruction is that the concern is for efforts to teach students how to comprehend, not for the multiple factors that facilitate comprehension (for example, world knowledge, motivation, sizable sight vocabulary, proficiency in decoding). To be stressed, then, is that a distinction is being made between (a) facilitating comprehension, (b) testing comprehension, and (c) teaching comprehension.

Because basal reader series and other commercially prepared materials often equate (rather than distinguish between) comprehension instruction and comprehension assessment, two pages from manuals are reproduced in Figures 11.1 and 11.2. Please examine the two and the comments about them before proceeding.

As the first chapter in this book indicated, any preplanned instruction—whether with comprehension or something else—should be complemented with application and practice. What those two facets of a lesson are is reexplained on page 285.

Figure 11.1

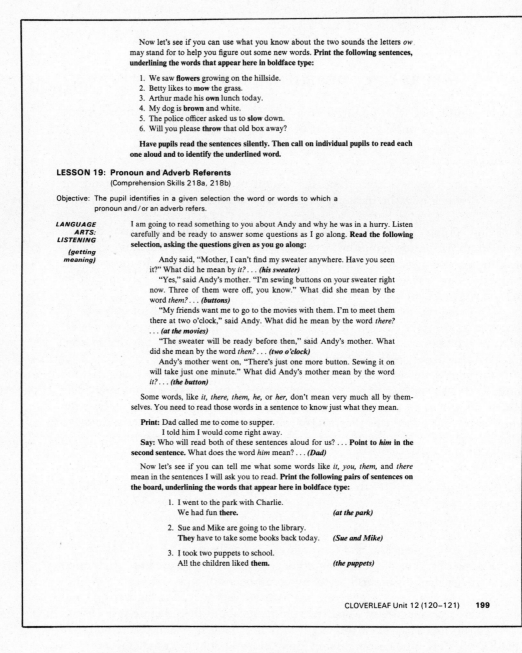

Now let's see if you can use what you know about the two sounds the letters *ow* may stand for to help you figure out some new words. **Print the following sentences, underlining the words that appear here in boldface type:**

1. We saw **flowers** growing on the hillside.
2. Betty likes to **mow** the grass.
3. Arthur made his **own** lunch today.
4. My dog is **brown** and white.
5. The police officer asked us to **slow** down.
6. Will you please **throw** that old box away?

Have pupils read the sentences silently. Then call on individual pupils to read each one aloud and to identify the underlined word.

LESSON 19: Pronoun and Adverb Referents
(Comprehension Skills 218a, 218b)

Objective: The pupil identifies in a given selection the word or words to which a pronoun and / or an adverb refers.

*LANGUAGE
ARTS:
LISTENING*

*(getting
meaning)*

I am going to read something to you about Andy and why he was in a hurry. Listen carefully and be ready to answer some questions as I go along. **Read the following selection, asking the questions given as you go along:**

Andy said, "Mother, I can't find my sweater anywhere. Have you seen it?" What did he mean by *it?* . . . *(his sweater)*

"Yes," said Andy's mother. "I'm sewing buttons on your sweater right now. Three of them were off, you know." What did she mean by the word *them?* . . . *(buttons)*

"My friends want me to go to the movies with them. I'm to meet them there at two o'clock," said Andy. What did he mean by the word *there?* . . . *(at the movies)*

"The sweater will be ready before then," said Andy's mother. What did she mean by the word *then?* . . . *(two o'clock)*

Andy's mother went on, "There's just one more button. Sewing it on will take just one minute." What did Andy's mother mean by the word *it?* . . . *(the button)*

Some words, like *it, there, them, he,* or *her,* don't mean very much all by themselves. You need to read those words in a sentence to know just what they mean.

Print: Dad called me to come to supper.
     I told him I would come right away.
Say: Who will read both of these sentences aloud for us? . . . **Point to *him* in the second sentence.** What does the word *him* mean? . . . *(Dad)*

Now let's see if you can tell me what some words like *it, you, them,* and *there* mean in the sentences I will ask you to read. **Print the following pairs of sentences on the board, underlining the words that appear here in boldface type:**

1. I went to the park with Charlie.
   We had fun **there**.   *(at the park)*

2. Sue and Mike are going to the library.
   They have to take some books back today.   *(Sue and Mike)*

3. I took two puppets to school.
   All the children liked **them**.   *(the puppets)*

CLOVERLEAF Unit 12 (120–121)   **199**

● *This "Lesson 19" appears under the heading "Instruction for Basic Reading Skills." However, as the reproduction shows, what is suggested is assessment, not instruction. That is, the concern is to see whether students can cope with referents, not to teach them how to cope.*

Preceding this "lesson" is another that deals with two sounds that ow records. This is mentioned because it typifies another common tendency in basal reader manuals (4). Not only do they deal with assessment when they promise instruction, but they also flit from one topic to another that is unrelated.

Figure 11.2 shows that, on some occasions, manuals offer excellent comprehension instruction in a way that relates it directly to the reading that students do on their own. Unfortunately, Figure 11.2 also reinforces a point made above: that manuals shift from one topic to another, unrelated one. In this case, dealing with personification is immediately followed by a manual segment called "Locating Information Quickly."

Why manuals for basal series commonly (a) offer assessment but call it instruction and (b) flit from one topic to another—many of which have nothing to do with the selection in the basal reader—has no obvious explanation.

Figure 11.2

INSTRUCTION: Recognizing and Understanding Personification

LANGUAGE ARTS: WRITING

(style elements)

● Pupils should understand that if they can determine what human qualities an author has given to something that is nonhuman, they will be able to picture the thing more vividly.

Write the following sentences on the chalkboard:

1. The ringing telephone insisted upon being answered.
2. A broken shutter slapped the side of the house.

You know that writers use figures of speech to make what they say more interesting. What are two kinds of figures of speech that you have already studied? . . . *(metaphor and simile)* A third kind of figure of speech is called personification. **Write the term on the chalkboard.** Do you see the word *person* in the word *personification?* . . . *(yes)* **Underline *person* in *personification.*** Personification is talking about an object or a thing as if it were a living person. When writers say that the sky cries, the horn wails, or the wind sings, they are using personification. The sky, horn, and wind are all nonhuman things, yet they are spoken of as crying, wailing, and singing, which are things that people do.

Look at the first sentence on the chalkboard. . . . What is being talked about as if it were a person? . . . *(the telephone)* What did the telephone do that a person does? . . . *(insisted)* Now read sentence 2. . . . What is talked about as if it were a person in that sentence? . . . *(a shutter)* What did the shutter do that a person does? . . . *(slapped)*

When you come across personification in your reading, be sure that you know what object or thing is being talked about as if it were a person. Then decide in what particular way that object or thing is said to be like a person.

Write the following numbered sentences and lettered statements on the chalkboard:

1. The wind chimes sang in the gentle breeze.
   a. The wind chimes made musical sounds.
   b. The wind chimes were singing a song.
2. The moon painted a yellow stripe across the still water.
   a. The moon was using watercolors.
   b. The reflection of the moon made a yellow stripe on the water.
3. The furniture spoke of its owner's bad taste.
   a. The furniture talked to someone about bad taste.
   b. The owner of the furniture had bad taste.
4. Bright candles marched down the center of the long dining table.
   a. The candles were in a parade.
   b. There was a row of candles in the center of the dining table.

Number a sheet of paper from 1 through 4. Each numbered sentence on the chalkboard contains personification. An object or a thing is talked about as if it were a person. Decide which of the statements following the sentence gives the meaning of the sentence. Write the letter of that statement next to the number of the sentence. **When pupils have finished, discuss the answers with them. Correct answers are as follows: (1) *a* (2) *b* (3) *b* (4) *b.***

APPLICATION AND MAINTENANCE OF BASIC READING SKILLS

Locating Information Quickly   (Reference and Study Skill 315)

● Pupils should be reminded that if they can locate information quickly on a page, they will save themselves a great deal of time.

KEYSTONE Unit 14 (303–317)   **273**

Reprinted from *Keystone,* Level L, The Houghton Mifflin Reading Program. Copyright © 1979 by Houghton Mifflin Company. Used by permission.

Application

> Teacher does/says something that allows for the use of what was featured in instruction. This is done under her supervision.

Practice

> Teacher gives an assignment to see whether students can use on their own what was taught.

Application and practice both yield information that helps a teacher know if more (or different) instruction is needed. They are an important part, therefore, of diagnostic teaching.

SAMPLES OF COMPREHENSION INSTRUCTION

To illustrate what comprehension instruction is, two lessons will be offered in an abbreviated form, one dealing with unstated information, the other with similes. Like all other meaningful lessons, they should stem from a preestablished goal based on needs.

Although what will be described are preplanned lessons, what is needed to improve comprehension abilities may be identified (and should be attended to) at unexpected times. For example, students' failure to understand a sentence generous with adjectives and adverbs calls for on-the-spot teaching in which it is shown that sorting out the kernel (subject, predicate, object) of such a sentence is helpful in arriving at its meaning. This point is made to underscore the fact that the subsequent descriptions of preplanned lessons are not meant to deny the value of on-the-spot teaching.

Implied Information

Budding readers need to know that authors do not tell everything directly and, as a result, they themselves may have to add information—that is, read between the lines. To meet that need, a lesson like the following is appropriate.

Goal. *To teach that information may be implied rather than stated directly.*

Instruction. Sentences like the following are displayed on cards.

> Those children are afraid of dogs.

> Dad is very tired tonight.

> Maria is an unselfish person.

Students in the instructional group read each sentence silently, after which the teacher asks one to tell what it says about the children (Dad, Maria). To illustrate that writers do not always say directly what their characters are like or how they feel about something, different but related sentences are displayed next:

> When they saw the dog, the children ran away.

> Dad's eyes were closing as he watched TV.

> Even though Maria was hungry, she fed the cat first.

With the help of probes and comparisons, the teacher uses the three additional sentences to show that they say something directly but, *in addition,* they also imply what was stated directly in the three original sentences.

Application.   A sheet with a list of sentences is distributed to each member of the group, the first two of which are:

1.   Beth asked her mother how she felt as soon as she got home.
2.   At dinner last night, my brother really cleared his plate.

Again, the teacher asks what each sentence says about the person named and, second, what that information reveals about the person that is not mentioned in the sentence. Further probing encourages the students to tell exactly how they arrived at the unstated conclusions. Finally, the teacher reminds them that when they are reading a story, the author might not say exactly what characters are like but that what they are like becomes clear by what they say and do and by what others in the story say about them.

Practice.   A sheet entitled "What Does That Tell You about the Person?" is distributed next. More sentences are listed. Now, a blank to be filled in is listed under each one. For example:

> 1. David tossed his hat on the table and left his coat on the floor.
>   (David _____)

With a sentence like this one, correct completions could be something like "is careless," "is sloppy," or "is in a hurry." A discussion of responses allows for calling attention to the fact that different readers may reach different conclusions about identical material.

Subsequent instruction.   If students do well with the practice assignment, subsequent instruction for the same goal can shift to paragraphs. For instance:

The man was in a big car driven by a chauffeur. When the car stopped in front of the airport, the chauffeur got out quickly and opened the back door. Out stepped a well-dressed man.

Once more, the teacher's probing will focus on (a) what is said and (b) what is implied by what is said. The possibility that the reader's inferences may be wrong (especially when a writer provides insufficient information) will be considered, too. With the preceding paragraph, for instance, one inference might portray the man as being an important executive, whereas another might point to the possibility that he is a mobster. Different conclusions allow for explicit attention to the fact that judgments sometimes have to be suspended until more information is supplied. For example, what does the well-dressed man do when he gets to his destination?

Once instruction focuses on more than single sentences, the best of application and practice will make use of stories, chapters, articles, and so on. This is *essential* if students are to see the relevance of school exercises for real reading.

Similes

A selection that students will be reading that contains similes provides a suitable time (and suitable examples) for initiating instruction with this type of comparison. If all the similes in the selection have the *as . . . as* construction, the goals of the lesson are as follows.

Goals.   *To teach the function of a simile. To teach that* as . . . as *signals the use of one.*

Instruction.   The teacher begins by writing the following on the board:

> The boy jumped high.
> The boy jumped very high.

With questions and discussion, the point is made that *very high* indicates a height greater than *high*. Then the following dialogue takes place.

Teacher: I'm going to write some words that mean higher than *very high*. What do you suppose they'll be?

Group: Very, *very* high!

Teacher: No, better than that. [Writes *The boy jumped as high as the sky*.] When I say that the boy jumped as high as the sky, do I mean that he was up in the clouds?

Group: No!

Teacher: No, I'm just trying to impress you with the fact that his jump was *really* high. To do that, I compared it with something that all of us know is about the highest thing around. With the comparison, I hoped you'd get the feeling that this was a person who could *really* jump. Let me write another sentence that uses a comparison to make a point. This time I want to tell you that somebody came and went very, very quickly. [Writes *They came and went as quick as a wink.*] In this case, why is a wink a good comparison?

Child: It's about the fastest thing you do. You do it so fast, you don't even know you do it.

Teacher: Right. I can wink so quickly that it would be hard to know how long it takes. I certainly wouldn't want to have to time it. Here's another good comparison [Writes *She ran as fast as a deer.*]

Once the quickness of deers is discussed, the teacher writes the following in order to call direct attention to the use of *as . . . as* in all the comparisons.

> as high as the sky
> as quick as a wink
> as fast as a deer

Afterward, the teacher summarizes: "Authors use these kinds of comparisons to give you a better feeling for what they're trying to say. They want to make sure you get the point. For the comparisons, they use the word *as* twice— for instance, 'as blue as the sky' or 'as green as grass.' Now when you see those words, you'll know that the writer is making a comparison. He or she may be comparing two very different things, yet the comparison really makes the point. For example, if I wanted to tell you how tough the meat was that we had for dinner last night, I might say something like, 'It was as tough as leather.' When I say that, I don't really mean leather. What I *do* mean is that eating the meat was pretty much like trying to chew leather. In other words, I want to be sure that you know just how tough that meat was."

Application.   To reinforce what the teacher said about similes, each child receives a list of sentences for supervised practice:

1.   That tree is as tall as a skyscraper.
2.   Her dress was as colorful as a spring garden.
3.   Their hands were as cold as ice.
4.   All the children are as busy as bees.
5.   The baby's skin felt as soft as silk.

Guided by the teacher, the children (a) read each sentence silently, (b) identify the simile and explain why the comparison is a good one, (c) underline the simile, and (d) draw a second line under *as*.

Practice.   In this case, practice is carried out with a basal story since all members of the group have a copy. Once the students read the story silently and are prepared to respond to the five questions that were posed before the reading

began, they will read the story a second time in order to find similes with the *as
. . . as* construction. The sentences that are found will be listed. The similes
themselves will be underlined so that they can be checked and discussed later.

Subsequent instruction.   Material containing similes that are signaled by *like*
provides the next opportunity to deal with comparisons. Now, examples such as
the following are appropriate.

> They fought like cats and dogs.
> The kitten looked like a ball of fur.
> She works like a beaver.

Once the two types of similes are dealt with, the word *simile* will be introduced as a way of synthesizing what has been studied. To be emphasized, however, is that it is far more important for students to recognize and comprehend
similes than it is to know what the comparisons are called. This point is made
because teaching manuals often show more concern for defining terms (for example, first-person narration and third-person narration) than for explaining to students the significance for reading of what is being defined (4).

TWO REMINDERS FOR COMPREHENSION INSTRUCTION

Before the focus shifts to other matters concerned with comprehension, two
reminders will be offered. The first has to do with what the outcomes of comprehension instruction should always be:

> Students will:
>
> > *understand* what is taught.
> > see the *relevance* of it *for reading*.
> > *use* what is taught *while reading*.

Admittedly, teachers cannot stand over students while they read in order to
make certain that what was taught is affecting what they do. However, they *can*
make sure that each instance of comprehension instruction is executed in a way
that clarifies the link between what is being taught and what should be done while
reading. Stated differently, teachers should let students in on the training process.
This suggests that even though written exercises are likely to enter into attempts
to teach students how to comprehend, getting the exercises done should not be an
end in itself. Instead, each assignment should be seen by teachers and students
alike as a means for improving what students do and think when they are reading
a book, a chapter, an ad, or whatever.

The second reminder for comprehension instruction can be communicated
with a reference to what was recently seen on the bumper of a small truck:

> Love thy neighbor.
> Tune thy piano.

Although it is true that reading instruction will contribute to the ability to understand the sticker, it is not sufficient. In this case, only the person who knows about the sound of untuned pianos will be able to make the inference that connects the two lines of text. And this brings us back to a topic that continues to receive considerable attention in discussions and studies of comprehension: world knowledge.

WORLD KNOWLEDGE AND COMPREHENSION

All of the experiences that we ourselves have had as readers verify the fact that the more we know about a topic, the better are we able to comprehend written material that deals with it. This explains why interest in a topic (which means that the reader already knows something about it) and success in reading about it go hand-in-hand (10). Or, to cite another illustration, physicists are better comprehenders than we are of physics textbooks not so much because they have superior reading skills as because they have greater knowledge about their specialization. But it does not take a scholarly field like physics to verify the relevance of background information for comprehension; seemingly easy sentences such as the following are sufficient:

> Ruth fell. She hurt her knee.

What might be overlooked with "simple" sentences like the two above is that it is our knowledge of the consequences of falling (based, perhaps, on personal experience) that gives us the ability to link the two sentences into a cause-effect relationship. Stated differently, what we know allows us to add (infer) information that the writer only implies. Realization of the amount of inferencing that reading demands is one reason a reader is now conceived to be anything but a passive recipient of an author's message. Peter Johnston reinforces this when he observes (14):

> . . . reading comprehension is [now] viewed as the process of using one's own prior knowledge and the writer's cues to infer the author's meaning. This involves a considerable amount of inferencing at all levels as one builds a model of the meaning of the text. [p. 16]

While it may seem that the importance of experiences (and of the concepts, knowledge, and vocabulary they build up) is so obvious that it is unnecessary to use space in this book to highlight it, what has been heard in a few classrooms points to a different conclusion. Notice in the following dialogue, for example, how one student's efforts to use his experiences went unrewarded during a social studies discussion even though it is just such use that teachers should be promoting.

Teacher: Who can give us an example of a group?
Child 1:   A fight.
Teacher: When we find out the four reasons that make a group, you'll see that a fight isn't a group.
Child 2:   When you're on a bus in Chicago.
Teacher: Once we read about the rules of a group, that will fit.

This brief conversation shows why it is necessary to emphasize that teachers who are genuinely interested in improving students' ability to read not only should encourage them to use their experiences to help with comprehension but also should make an effort to relate what students experience outside school to what goes on inside. Otherwise, what goes on inside will lack that element of reality that makes attending school an authentic rather than a contrived, "bookish" experience.

It has to be acknowledged that the questioning that goes on in classrooms is sometimes bookish, especially when the source of questions is a teaching manual. When answers also come from manuals, other less-than-desirable discussions are inevitable. For instance:

Teacher: Who can tell us what a continent is?
Child 1:   A really big place with states and countries and stuff.
Teacher: Could anyone give us another description?
Child 2:   It's a large land mass.
Teacher: Fine. Good.

What this teacher needs to remember is that it is when comprehension breaks down that the exact words of a text tend to be used in responding to questions.

QUESTIONS AND COMPREHENSION

Whether the goal is to facilitate, teach, or test comprehension, the use of questions by teachers is both common and expected. How questions enter into instruction was illustrated earlier when lessons concerned with implied information and similes were described. How questions function to facilitate comprehension and, later, to test it will be dealt with now.

Prereading Questions

One way to characterize the act of reading is to say that it is a purposeful pursuit. In everyday life, a purpose for reading often comes into existence first (for example, to dye a shirt), after which certain material takes on significance (instructions on a box of dye). At other times, material comes first (for example, newspaper), and that prompts the purpose (for example, to learn about spring fashions).

When the focus shifts to classrooms, the same two sequences are possible. A purpose may exist first (to learn facts about penguins), after which certain types of materials become appropriate to read (for example, encyclopedia article); or the material might come first (for example, a story about penguins), after which one or more purposes for reading it will need to be established. One way for teachers to do that (and, at the same time, to facilitate comprehension by encouraging students to attend to what is important) is to pose prereading questions. Because prereading questions are meant to signal what is important, teachers should select them *with care*. Asking questions about trivial details, for example, must be avoided because, if done routinely, it encourages students to reach erroneous conclusions not only about what proficient readers do but also about the very nature of reading itself.

Since what is important to attend to varies from one selection to another, so too should the types (and number) of prereading questions. In one case, for example, the setting of a story may be extremely important; at other times, it is insignificant. In another instance, the development of one particular character is what counts, whereas in another selection certain details about the plot merit special attention because they figure in the resolution of a problem. The point to be made, then, is: Don't ask questions just to ask questions.

Whether literal or inferential comprehension is required of a reader also varies, this time according to the way an author develops content. Specifically, if the writer of a story states directly what a given character is like, literal comprehension is sufficient. On the other hand, if the author of a fable only implies its moral, knowing what it is requires inferential comprehension.

Another way to think about requirements is in the framework of types of information that result from comprehension—for instance, details, main ideas, and so on. Classifying them this way may help in formulating prereading questions:

SOME READING REQUIREMENTS

Literal or inferential comprehension of:

> details
> main ideas
> sequence of events
> cause-effect relationships
> comparisons
> character traits

Depending on the selection and on what students' reading needs might be, different requirements might affect prereading questions:

OTHER REQUIREMENTS

Evaluation of or judgments about:

> fact or opinion
> adequacy
> appropriateness
> worth
> correctness

Since carefully selected prereading questions are designed to guide readers as they move through a selection, they should be put in writing so that students have an opportunity to refer to or review them. Students should know that the ability to answer the questions is a sign that the reading has been done satisfactorily; thus it is time to switch to something else—perhaps to a written assignment dealing with sequence that was given because sequence was important in the development of the plot or because following the sequence of events in a previous selection caused problems.

Postreading Discussions

Students' responses to the questions posed before they read (and to any other question that seems essential to ask during a postreading discussion) allow teachers to learn what was comprehended. Periodically, postreading discussions should also allow time for teaching students how to go about answering questions. (Reading to find a certain date, for instance, calls for a type of reading that is very different from what it takes to sort out facts from opinions.) When the extra goal is added to a discussion period, an altered sequence is necessary. Instead of (a) prereading questions, (b) silent reading, and (c) discussion, there will be:

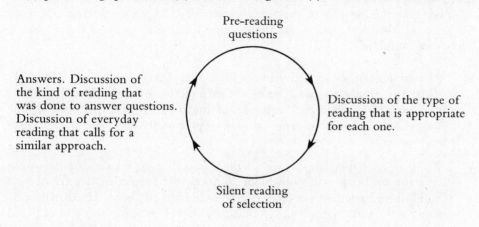

Pre-reading
questions

Answers. Discussion of
the kind of reading that
was done to answer questions.
Discussion of everyday
reading that calls for a
similar approach.

Discussion of the type of
reading that is appropriate
for each one.

Silent reading
of selection

Periodically, postreading discussions can include time for making distinctions among (a) questions that are answered directly in the selection, (b) questions whose answers are only implied, and (c) questions that are not answered at all.

Sometimes still other procedures are called for. With slower children, for instance, there might be a need to explain what it means to answer a question. One third-grade teacher with such children often lists prereading questions in the order in which a selection answers them. She takes one question at a time, asking the children to stop their silent reading when they think they have the answer. After a child proposes one, other probes follow: What made you think you found the answer? Did you think you had found it earlier, then decided you hadn't? Why do you think that *is* the answer? Is it a complete one? Can it be shortened and still be correct?

Whatever procedures are used in postreading discussions, the end product should be students who will be able to establish their own goals and then read in a manner that ensures their realization in the most efficient way possible. Meanwhile, before such a point is reached, students should be given intermittent opportunities to raise their own questions about what they will be reading (13). This introduces some ego involvement, and thus the likelihood of working harder to find the answers. Student questions are both possible and suitable when the content deals with what is somewhat familiar and when it has high interest appeal.

PRACTICE FOR COMPREHENSION

Two kinds of comprehension practice have now been considered. The first was in the samples of comprehension instruction. (You will recall the cycle: instruction, application, practice.) The second is the silent reading of a selection, which may be the best practice of all. To complete the picture, samples of a third kind will be given now. This third type is helpful when comprehension deficiencies are uncovered. Like the samples of practice that were in Chapters 5 through 10, they illustrate what students can do on their own while a teacher gives time to small groups or individuals.

- Assemble a scrapbook collection of magazine pictures with similar content. Write paragraph-long descriptions of each picture on cards. Put all of them in a pocket attached to the inside of the back cover of the book. The assignment calls for inserting the appropriate card into the slot beneath each picture.

- Write a paragraph that describes something. (For young children, it might be a toy or an animal; with older students, the subject matter could be a building, a group of people, or a scene.) Dittoed copies are distributed, along with written directions: "This paragraph tells about something. Read it carefully. Then draw what is described." Later, finished pictures will be discussed in order to look for both omitted and added details.

- Paste newspaper ads (or ads from children's magazines) on cards, numbering each one. Students working with the cards write corresponding numbers on a sheet of paper. After each number they note information that a potential buyer would like to have but is omitted from the ad. Later, notations will be compared and discussed. One result might be generalizations about the kinds of information that are both included and excluded in advertisements.

- Assignments with a focus established by a question (for example, Could you hear this? Could you feel this?) can take the following form.

Could You Hear This?

		yes	no	maybe
1.	an ant walking on dirt	_____	_____	_____
2.	a fence running around a yard	_____	_____	_____
3.	a clock telling time	_____	_____	_____

- Written assignments for details related to *who, what, where, when, why,* and *how* might start as follows.

  1. This little puppy ran <u>into the yard.</u> _____

  2. Trying his best, the boy <u>was able to win.</u> _____

  3. The art museum is located <u>in the center of a large metropolitan area.</u> _____

  4. <u>It was at least a decade ago</u> that this community got its start. _____

With the previous assignment, the job is to indicate with one word *(who, what, where, when, how, why)* what the underscored part tells about. With the following assignment, the job is to indicate with one word *(same* or *different)* whether each pair of sentences communicates similar or dissimilar messages.

- 1. The cat was napping on the kitchen floor.
     The cat naps after lunch in the kitchen. _____
  2. Even though Susan was late, the teacher didn't say anything.
     The teacher was silent as Susan, who was late, walked into the room. _____
  3. The very shy child said nothing.
     The child, who is very shy, remained silent. _____

An assignment like this one (and many others, too) will be most fruitful for comprehension if time is taken to discuss answers, not with a concentration on "right" or "wrong" but with one that considers "Why do you think so?"

The next assignment provides practice in following directions. (Practice for directions is also illustrated in Figure 11.3.)

Figure 11.3

Finger Puppets

To make each puppet you will need pieces of felt or cloth. For a pattern you use your own fingers. Make the pattern on paper. Make it about 2 inches wider all the way around than your finger. Be sure to make it wider at the bottom than at the top. Make the top square.

Now cut out your paper pattern. Pin it to the felt, or draw the pattern on the felt with an ink pen. Cut two pieces of felt this size. This is the body of the puppet. Glue the two pieces together leaving the bottom open. Now cut 2 arms, a head and 2 hands. Glue these pieces on the body.

You can now add eyes, and all other items to make your puppet real. These are easy to make and you can have many, many different characters.

25

How to Have Fun Making Puppets. Mankato, Minn.: Creative Education, Inc., 1974, p. 25. Copyright © Creative Education, Inc.

● Draw on a ditto master a picture of a man. Under the picture, type directions for finishing and coloring it. For instance:

    1.   Give the man a brown hat.
    2.   Color his suit to match his hat.
    3.   Put a walking cane in his right hand.

With more advanced readers, more complicated directions should be used. The bare outline of a row of store fronts, for instance, might be drawn. What to make each store—drug, fruit, hardware, and so on—will be indicated in writing.

At times, sequence is important for comprehension; ideas for written assignments concerned with that follow.

● Have a group read a story that they can handle on their own for the purpose of following the sequence of events involving the main character. Afterward, each member of the group picks up five slips of paper (or whatever number is suitable) at some designated place, each with a sentence describing an event. The task is to arrange the sentences in correct order by pasting them on a sheet:

    1. _____
    2. _____
    3. _____
    4. _____
    5. _____

Adapted for more able readers, the assignment uses a more difficult story and signal words.

Initially _____
Then _____
Subsequently _____
After that _____
At the end _____

● Another written assignment that calls attention to signal words for sequence concentrates on sentences like those shown next. The first answer is given in order to explain what students are to do.

    1.   *Walk* to the door. When you get there, *turn around*. Before *sitting down, smile.*

l. walk 2. turn around 3. smile 4. sit down

    2.   Just before you *bend down, stand up*. At the end, *sit down* again.

● One other assignment for sequence focuses on semantic equivalence:

Do they say the same thing?

(a)   Prior to arriving at the theater, the boys bought candy.

(b)   The boys went to the theater. When they arrived, they bought candy.

(a)   Sue picked up her shoes at the shoemaker's. Then she went home.

(b)   On her way home, Sue got her shoes at the shoemaker's.

● Words that substitute for others may cause comprehension problems. The start of one assignment that deals with substitutions is shown next. Again, answers are given to explain what students are expected to do.

1.   I shoveled the snow so park *here*.

> **where it's shoveled**

2.   *He* will starve if someone doesn't feed that puppy.

> **puppy**

● Many stories have an underlying theme. An assignment for reaching conclusions about one is described next.

Have a group read two stories, both written at their independent level (can read it without help) and dealing with the same moral (for example, telling one lie leads to more lies). The job is to read the two in order to decide on one title that is suitable for both.

● The final illustration of independent comprehension practice also deals with stories.

Type words describing character traits at the top of a ditto master (for example, *curious, shy, patient*). After reading a story, students will write under *curious* the name of any character who displayed that trait. A similar procedure will be used with the other descriptions. (Characteristics not displayed by anyone can be included.)

CONCLUDING COMMENTS: PUTTING IT ALL TOGETHER

What has now been said about developing comprehension ability divides into three parts:

Teaching comprehension	*Silent reading*	*Practice*
goal	prereading questions	independent assignments
instruction	postreading discussion	
application		
practice		

The following comments about the parts are meant to clarify how they fit together in an instructional program.

Part One: Teaching Comprehension

As the chapter pointed out at the start, time in classrooms should be allotted to lessons that focus on a preestablished goal (for example, to explain hyperbole and its function). Practice designed to promote mastery of what is taught is provided when the instruction takes place. Still more might be provided with the silent reading of a selection. For example, should hyperbole be the concern, the very best of practice is reading a tall tale.

The importance of comprehension lessons means that they should be offered as often as possible. If what they teach can be applied to something like a basal reader selection, instruction should precede the reading. At other times, a comprehension lesson may replace what is usually thought of as a basal lesson.

Part Two: Silent Reading

Much of the directed silent reading that goes on in classrooms during the reading period is of basal reader selections. As was pointed out, making the reading purposeful can be accomplished with carefully selected prereading questions. The same questions also allow for opportunities to make explicit to students the connection between the nature of a question and the kind of reading that ought to ensue to get it answered. Such connections should be discussed as often as the need for explicit explanations exists.

Once the reading is done, discussions should deal with the questions posed earlier and with any others that seem necessary. A confused or wrong answer to a prereading question may identify a focus for future instruction or for on-the-spot assistance and explanations, in which case students are helped to reexamine that part of the text that pertains to the question.

Postreading discussions may also be a time to return to the text for review. More specifically, if one or more earlier lessons dealt with first-person perspective and the selection is told from that point of view, it could be used to review how such a perspective limits what can be revealed. Now, illustrations will be in the selection. What the consequences might be had a third-person perspective been used might be considered, too.

Even though—as the examples demonstrate—no single formula exists for handling the silent reading of a selection, any desirable procedure sees to it that students who do the reading are better comprehenders in one or more ways because of what was done with the selection.

Part Three: Practice

Typically, individualized instruction is not usually realized when a teacher works with an entire class. Working with less than everyone means that students who are not with the teacher need to be profitably occupied. Obviously, being occupied with an assignment designed to improve some aspect of comprehension is all to the good. At times, the occupation may be with extended reading; at other times, with shorter written exercises. Both are helpful as long as students see the relationship between the latter and real reading.

SUMMARY

Chapter 11 started by considering the large number of factors that determine whether a reader will be able to comprehend a given piece of text. Some of the variables have to do with the text itself, others with variables related to the reader.

The chapter then explained important differences between listening comprehension and reading comprehension. That was done to show that reading comprehension ability requires more than listening ability plus decoding ability. Since it does, a need exists for reading comprehension instruction.

Because what constitutes a suitable topic for comprehension instruction is vast, the chapter listed only sample topics. Those mentioned were dealt with in the framework of what authors do, since what they do has relevance for readers. The need to help students see that relevance was especially emphasized. Two lessons were then presented in order to demonstrate comprehension instruction. For each, instruction, application, and practice were described.

Since so much of what students are asked to read in school originates in basal readers, the chapter went on to consider what needs to be done with basal selections (or any other assigned reading). To make reading a purposeful activity, a recommendation was made to pose carefully selected prereading questions, which ought to be written. Later, students' answers will allow for information about their comprehension ability insofar as those questions and that selection are concerned.

What the chapter should have succeeded in underscoring is that whether students comprehend a selection is hardly a simple matter. Complex though it may be, providing more comprehension instruction than now exists should allow more and more students to cope successfully with more and more selections. What will help, too, is relevant practice. Chapter 11 listed samples of practice and, more than once, emphasized the need for students to see the link between practice exercises and the reading that they do on their own.

REVIEW

1.   One way to learn whether students have comprehended a selection is to have them formulate questions about its content after they read it. With that in mind, see whether you can write three questions about the content of Chapter 11, one having to do with an important detail, one with a main point, and one with an evaluation of some part of the content.

2.   Name some of the topics for comprehension instruction that were referred to in Chapter 11. Name others that were not listed and explain why they, too, are significant for improving comprehension ability.

3.   Before reading Chapter 11, did you think that comprehension was less complex or more complex than how it is portrayed in the chapter? Why?

4.   Explain why the following equation is questionable:

> oral language comprehension + decoding
> ability = reading comprehension

Why is the following more accurate but still incomplete?

> oral language comprehension + decoding
> ability + comprehension instruction =
> reading comprehension

5.   Chapter 11 discussed what teachers can do with a selection after it has been read by an instructional group. Should oral reading ever enter into post-reading activities? If yes, for what reason(s)? If no, why not?

6.   Reading is now said to be a *constructive* process in the sense that the reader is an active participant in producing meaning. Reading is also said to be an *adaptive* process because one type of reading is insufficient. With examples, explain the exact meaning of the two descriptions.

7.   The chapter illustrated the difference between a question that assesses comprehension and, in contrast, questions that are instructive for comprehension. What are other examples of the two different types of questions?

REFERENCES

1.   Anderson, R. C.; Reynolds, R. E.; Schallert, D. L.; and Goetz, E. T. "Frameworks for Comprehending Discourse." *American Educational Research Journal* 14 (Fall 1977): 367–381.

2.   Anderson, R. C., and McGaw, B. "On the Representation of Meanings of General Terms." *Journal of Experimental Psychology* 101 (December 1973): 301–306.

3.   Anderson, R. C.; Pichert, J. W.; Goetz, E. T.; Schallert, D. L.; Stevens, K. V.; and Trollip, S. R. "Instantiation of General Terms." *Journal of Verbal Learning and Verbal Behavior* 15 (December 1976): 667–679.

4.   Durkin, Dolores. "Reading Comprehension Instruction in Five Basal Reader Series." *Reading Research Quarterly* 16, no. 4 (1981): 515–544.

5.   Durkin, Dolores. "What Classroom Observations Reveal about Reading Comprehension Instruction." *Reading Research Quarterly* 14, no. 4 (1978–1979): 481–533.

6.   Durkin, Dolores. "What Is the Value of the New Interest in Reading Comprehension?" *Language Arts* 58 (January 1981): 23–43.

7.   Fries, Charles. *Linguistics and Reading.* New York: Holt, Rinehart and Winston, 1963.

8.   Golinkoff, Roberta M. "A Comparison of Reading Comprehension Processes in

Good and Poor Comprehenders." *Reading Research Quarterly* 11, no. 4 (1975–1976): 623–659.

9. Goodman, Kenneth S. "Reading: A Psycholinguistic Guessing Game." *Journal of the Reading Specialist* 4 (November 1967): 123–135.

10. Guthrie, John T. "Reading Interests." *Reading Teacher* 34 (May 1981): 984–986.

11. Guszak, Frank J. "Teachers' Questions and Levels of Reading Comprehension." In *The Evaluation of Children's Reading Achievement.* Edited by Thomas C. Barrett. Newark, Dela.: International Reading Association, 1967.

12. Hansen, Jane. "The Effects of Inference Training and Practice on Young Children's Reading Comprehension." *Reading Research Quarterly* 16, no. 3 (1981): 391–417.

13. Hunkins, Francis P. *Involving Students in Questioning.* Boston: Allyn and Bacon, 1976.

14. Johnston, Peter. "Implications of Basic Research for the Assessment of Reading Comprehension." Technical Report No. 206. Urbana: University of Illinois, Center for the Study of Reading, May 1981.

15. Kachuck, Beatrice. "Relative Clauses May Cause Confusion for Young Readers." *Reading Teacher* 34 (January 1981): 372–377.

16. Pearson, P. David, and Johnson, Dale D. *Teaching Reading Comprehension.* New York: Holt, Rinehart and Winston, 1978.

17. Rubin, A. D. "A Theoretical Taxonomy of the Differences between Oral and Written Language." Technical Report No. 35. Urbana: University of Illinois, Center for the Study of Reading, April 1977.

18. Sanders, N. M. *Classroom Questions: What Kinds?* New York: Harper and Row, 1966.

19. Stein, N. L., and Glenn, C. G. "An Analysis of Story Comprehension in Elementary School." In R. O. Freedle, ed., *New Directions in Discourse Processing.* Hillsdale, N.J.: Erlbaum, 1979.

20. Whaley, Jill F. "Story Grammars and Reading Instruction." *Reading Teacher* 34 (April 1981): 762–771.

CHAPTER 12

CONTENT SUBJECTS AND STUDY SKILLS

Reasons for Difficulty of Textbooks
    Vocabulary
    Graphics
    Content
Research with Expository Text
    Student Variables
    Text Variables
    Processing Variables
    A Summary
Implications of Research with Expository Text
Readying Children for Textbooks
    Reading to Children
    Using Homemade Materials
Beyond the Primary Grades
A Teacher's Preparation for a Chapter
    Content Objectives
    Display Centers
    Reading Objectives
Preparing Students for a Chapter
Scheduling Activities
Accommodating Poor Readers
Reading Instruction and Textbooks
    Teaching Students How to Study
    Other Kinds of Reading Instruction
Concluding Activities for a Chapter
Rate of Reading
    Skimming
    Scanning
Locating Information
    Using a Dictionary
    Using an Encyclopedia
Summary
Review

PREVIEW

It would be difficult to dispute the contention that students should be asked to read only what they are capable of understanding. Nonetheless, observations in middle- and upper-grade classrooms commonly reveal that textbooks for such content areas as social studies and science are beyond the grasp of many who are supposed to learn from them (11). An obvious solution for the mismatch is better—that is, more appropriate— textbooks; however, since it continues to be a largely ignored solution, teachers need to know what to do with the books they are expected to use.

To help them with what often seems like an impossible task is the purpose of this chapter. Because teaching students how to cope with expository (informational) text ought to begin early, the chapter does not bypass the primary grades.

One suggestion in the forthcoming chapter for helping with textbooks is similar to what was recommended much earlier for your own study of Teaching Them to Read. *It seems appropriate, therefore, to have you read again the advice offered in the Preview of Chapter 2:*

1. *Skim the chapter in order to get a general picture of the content. Headings and subheadings will help with the overview, as will the summary that concludes the chapter.*
2. *Examine the questions at the end and then keep them in mind to guide a second, more careful reading. Now give attention to important terms, which will be in italics, and to the recommended teaching procedures. Why they are recommended (and why something else is not) should be noted too.*

In recent years, researchers have been documenting what teachers have known for a long time, namely, that students who can read stories do not always have equal success when they read to acquire information. What classroom teachers also know is that most of the textbooks that supply information are very difficult.

REASONS FOR DIFFICULTY OF TEXTBOOKS

The sample paragraphs shown on the next page illustrate some of the reasons why students' efforts to understand content subject textbooks often result in frustration, not information. The following sections discuss three variables that contribute to the difficulty of such books.

Vocabulary

That vocabulary commonly impedes comprehension is accounted for by the fact that content subject textbooks are characterized by a generous use of hard-to-pronounce, difficult-to-understand terms. One researcher has reported that over five hundred specialized words and phrases appeared in eight sets of mathematics textbooks prepared for grades 1 through 3 (34). Since elementary school mathematics requires fewer specialized terms than social studies and science, and further, since specialized vocabulary increases in materials written for grades beyond the first three, the only possible conclusion is that students face major vocabulary problems in subject matter textbooks.

Compounding the technical-term problem is the frequent appearance of familiar words used in unfamiliar ways. Easy to find in textbooks, for example, are words like *bank, shrink, bed, neck, school, foot,* and *farming,* now functioning in a way that could impede comprehension:

> river bank
> shrinking world
> bed of rock
> neck of land
> school of fish
> foot of a hill
> farming the seas

SAMPLE PARAGRAPHS FROM TEXTBOOKS

Grade Three Social Studies

Big cement canals carry water from the dams. Smaller ditches go from the canals to the farmers' fields. There are gates in the ditches. When the farmers need water, they open the gates, and water flows through furrows beside the plants and trees (33, p. 232).

Grade Five Social Studies

The soil of the Great Plains is not their only resource. They have riches under the soil. The one that brings in more money than any other is oil. Natural gas, also, earns much money. You read about both in the chapter on the South. Another gas, helium, lies underground in parts of the Great Plains. Most of the helium taken from the ground comes from the Texas Panhandle, the part of the state that extends northward. This gas is lighter than air and, because it will not burn, it is safe to use. It is therefore good for inflating balloons and airships (25, p. 406).

Grade Four Science

As the layers of sedimentary rock are forced upward, they crack. Cracking takes place at the domes and forms ridges. As rain falls on the domes and flows over the ridges, rock is washed away. The different levels of sedimentary rock are exposed. These exposed layers of sedimentary rock make up the rock you see in older folded mountains (31, p. 116).

Grade Six Science

Spongy bone may be thought of as a network of bone combined with a network of spaces. The network of bone contains cells which contact each other through tiny canals. The network of spaces, as we have seen, contains blood vessels which nourish these cells. This network of spaces also contains a soft, light tissue called *marrow*. Long bones, like the humerus, have large central cavities in which there is no bony structure at all. These cavities are filled with marrow (30, p. 240).

Vocabulary per se is not the only problem. Another is the rapid rate at which unfamiliar words appear. Because some refer to concepts and relationships that are completely foreign, a typical result for students is the need to cope with unfamiliar content that is communicated with unfamiliar words. One further result, therefore, is a large number of textbooks that are incomprehensible to a large number of students.

Graphics

Another reason why textbooks present problems is their reliance on graphics (for example, charts, graphs, tables, diagrams, and maps) to communicate important information. Just how numerous graphics can be is revealed in a comparison made of two textbooks:

> In two widely used fifth-grade texts—one in social studies and one in science—1096 graphic devices are used for instructional purposes. Of this total, 962 are either photographs or illustrations, the remaining visuals including 130 maps, seven charts, and seven tables. Only nine two-page spreads in the 358-page science book are without a visual, and in the social studies text of 495 pages only twenty-one spreads have no illustrative material. [7, p. 647].

At this point you might be thinking, But doesn't a generous use of graphic material simplify a textbook? Such a conclusion overlooks the fact that children must first learn how to read each type of graphic before they understand its concentrated content. Only then can it function either to supplement or complement the verbal text.

Content

What has now been cited as some of the problems inherent in reading textbooks can be both summarized and extended by saying that a considerable amount of what is found between their covers goes beyond what students have experienced, requiring them to visualize what they have not seen and to understand what is foreign. When it is also kept in mind that it is prior knowledge of a topic that often allows a reader to make inferences as well as distinctions between what is important and what is not, it has to be concluded that learning from existing textbooks is no ordinary task for most elementary school students.

RESEARCH WITH EXPOSITORY TEXT

While any proficient reader could look through a content subject textbook and quickly discern why it would be difficult for children, researchers are more helpful to teachers because what they have pinpointed as being potential sources of problems have more specific implications for instruction. According to researchers like Thomas Anderson, for example, interdependent factors that determine whether expository text is likely to be understood divide among student, text, and processing variables (1, 2).

Student Variables

You should not be surprised to learn that research reports underscore the dependence of comprehension on a reader's having one or more clearly defined purposes for doing the reading. As was mentioned in the previous chapter, purposes in school usually come into existence with questions or assignments that are made explicit before the reading begins. (Questions might also be dispersed throughout a textbook chapter.) Either way, these researchers say, students ought to know exactly what they are supposed to learn from their reading. Otherwise, they might wander aimlessly through a text and end up learning little or nothing.

Expectedly, the same researchers also stress the significance of a reader's knowledge of the world for comprehension as well as his or her interest in reading the material.

Text Variables

What the text deals with—in particular, how its content relates to what the reader already knows—is yet another factor that has to be taken into account when potential comprehension problems are considered. If what the author has assumed the reader knows about a given topic *is* known, an increase in vocabulary, concepts, and information is likely to result from the reading. Increase in knowledge is also likely to occur when the text is characterized by overall coherence; that is, it is well organized with pieces that fit together in some clearly apparent way.

Processing Variables

Processing variables are defined as what is required for getting information from the page into the reader's head (1, 2). They include the attention that readers must give to whatever information is relevant to their goals, the encoding of the information attended to, and the retrieval from memory of whatever is relevant.

What is now called *metacomprehension* (or *comprehension monitoring*) is also thought to contribute to the successful processing of print. This refers to those mental processes whereby readers evaluate and regulate their own comprehension (or the lack of it) by asking themselves as they read such questions as, What is the meaning of this sentence? Does it make sense? How does this relate to what I just read? Is this consistent with what I know? *Fix-up strategies* (4) for those times when comprehension breaks down include rereading, slowing down, or even seeking outside help when the meaning of a critical word is unclear or unknown or when an essential piece of information is missing.

Comprehension monitoring is likely to occur only when readers need (or want) to attain certain goals. In fact, it is the goals that help them know when all is not well. Johnston makes the same point when he says that monitoring progress requires readers to decide "on the basis of their purpose for reading when to remove their processing from 'automatic pilot,' take conscious control, and instigate the appropriate alternative strategies. This is a very important part of reading comprehension" (21, p. 27).

A Summary

What has now been said about variables that have a positive effect on comprehension of expository material can be summarized as follows:

READER
1.   Has essential background information.
2.   Is aware of the goals for reading and keeps them in mind while reading.
3.   Is motivated to do the reading.

TEXT
1.   Content is not completely foreign.
2.   Content is organized in a way that makes it clear and easy to follow.

PROCESSING
1.   Reader gives appropriate attention to content that is related to goals.
2.   Reader encodes whatever information is necessary for attaining goals.
3.   Reader is able to retrieve whatever information is necessary for understanding relevant content.
4.   Reader monitors his own comprehension to identify problems so that they can be remedied during the reading process.

What clearly emerges from the picture of effective studying sketched by researchers is a type of reading that could be described as a flexible and purposeful activity in which knowledge of preestablished goals determines what is attended to and remembered. Clearly bypassed, on the other hand, is a concept of reading that sees it as an attempt to take in everything at one unchanging rate of speed.

IMPLICATIONS OF RESEARCH WITH EXPOSITORY TEXT

Research with expository text suggests that what is done with content area text-books ought to be viewed as an effort to help students learn how to learn from text. Within that framework, it is again meaningful to divide teachers' efforts into three categories: (a) facilitating comprehension, (b) testing comprehension, and (c) teaching comprehension. Before the categories are discussed and illustrated, let us first consider how what is done in the primary grades can pave the way for learning from text in later years.

READYING CHILDREN FOR TEXTBOOKS

Without question, having children take turns reading stories aloud consumes a great deal of time in the primary grades. As should now be clear, that practice, coupled with the one of asking questions about every detail, hardly constitute the most effective preparation for acquiring information from text.

Admittedly, an increasing amount of expository and procedural discourse is being offered in basal programs (see Figures 12.1 and 12.2). Nonetheless, the major emphasis continues to be on narrative discourse and on getting children to read it aloud with much expression. One consequence is that the large number of primary-grade teachers who use basal readers must supplement them with other materials and activities in order to prepare students for later tasks. High on the list of helpful activities is to read to children.

Reading to Children

One reason why good readers get better is that what they read increases their knowledge of the world. The importance of that by-product explains why teachers should never let a day go by without reading something to their students. When adding to what is known and understood about the world is one goal for the reading, selections ought to provide information about a topic that is of interest. If a basal story tells about beavers, to cite one illustration, what a teacher reads might be a factual account of the same animal in order to allow for a comparison of real beavers and story-book versions. What is not acceptable in the latter can be highlighted, too.

The day that a child brings a cocoon that she found on the way to school is another time for reading informational material. It might also be the time to find books in the library so that even more can be learned about the stages of development that eventually lead to butterflies and moths. Or, to cite one more illustration, what better time to read about evaporation than when it is suddenly discovered that all the pictures that the children just painted are dry?

Figure 12.1

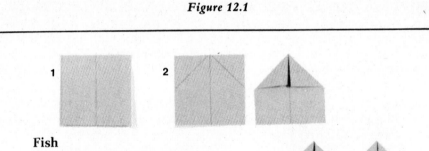

Fish

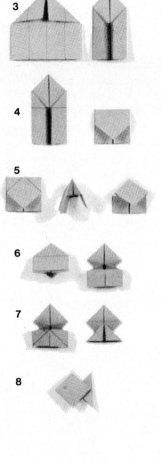

1. Fold a paper square down the center, open it, and lay it flat.

2. Fold the top two corners down to meet at the center line.

3. Fold the sides in to meet at the center line.

4. Fold the paper so that the point at the top touches the bottom of the paper.

5. Fold the top corners down and then *in* so that they are tucked inside between the pointed flap and the back. The corners should meet at the center line under the flap.

6. Turn the paper over. This is how the back should look. Fold up the back flap to meet the top point.

7. With the back facing you, fold up the lower corners of the flap to meet at the center line.

8. Turn your fish over to the right side, draw an eye on it, and decorate it.

36

Mitchell, Joanne Robinson, and Ryle, Anne Libby. "Paper Folding: The Art of Origami," in *Reflections*. Lexington, Mass.: D. C. Heath and Company, 1975, p. 36. *Reflections* copyright © 1975 by D. C. Heath and Company. Permission granted by the publisher.

Figure 12.2

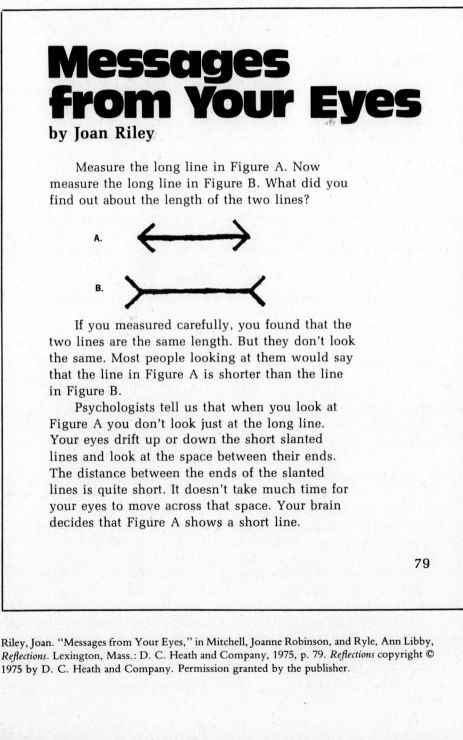

Messages from Your Eyes

by Joan Riley

Measure the long line in Figure A. Now measure the long line in Figure B. What did you find out about the length of the two lines?

A.

B.

If you measured carefully, you found that the two lines are the same length. But they don't look the same. Most people looking at them would say that the line in Figure A is shorter than the line in Figure B.

Psychologists tell us that when you look at Figure A you don't look just at the long line. Your eyes drift up or down the short slanted lines and look at the space between their ends. The distance between the ends of the slanted lines is quite short. It doesn't take much time for your eyes to move across that space. Your brain decides that Figure A shows a short line.

79

Riley, Joan. "Messages from Your Eyes," in Mitchell, Joanne Robinson, and Ryle, Ann Libby, *Reflections*. Lexington, Mass.: D. C. Heath and Company, 1975, p. 79. *Reflections* copyright © 1975 by D. C. Heath and Company. Permission granted by the publisher.

Depending on the children's own ability to read, other informational books should be part of a classroom library from which selections can be made at free-choice time. (See Figures 10.2 and 10.3 for examples of easy-to-read material.)

Using Homemade Materials

Whereas it would be unusual to see subject matter textbooks in kindergarten, finding homemade informational material there should be customary. One teacher who thought it was none too early to bring kindergartners into contact with nonfiction conducted a number of experiments with water; then, following each one, she and the children wrote about it. (Some of what was written constitutes Figure 12.3.) End results of the experiments included an understanding of new concepts and the vocabulary that goes with them (for example, *liquid, freeze, solid, steam, boil, evaporate*). Additions to reading vocabularies were other results, as was some understanding of sequence and how a reader keeps track of it.

Preparation for reading the various kinds of graphics that are in textbooks was seen in another kindergarten in which the eye color of the children was the topic of interest. Eventually, colors were summarized in a chart like that in Figure 12.4. At a later grade, the same data could be summarized with a bar graph. Still other graphics that have been seen in first- and second-grade classrooms include:

A diagram showing the placement of furniture in the classroom.
A pie graph depicting how children spend a twenty-four-hour period of time on school days.
A map showing the route the children will take to get to the high school auditorium where they are to hear a band concert.
A line graph showing temperature variation over a two-week period.

BEYOND THE PRIMARY GRADES

All the preparation in the world at primary-grade levels does not eliminate the need for teachers in middle and upper grades to provide systematic help with content subject textbooks. Help viewed as facilitating comprehension begins when a textbook that is unfamiliar to students is first distributed. The purpose of this help is to acquaint them with the book in a way that will make it easier to learn from it.

Examining a new textbook can begin by calling attention to the title, author(s), and copyright date. Whether the date is relevant can be discussed in relation to the types of topics covered, which creates the need to examine the table of contents. What is done with that will be affected by its organization and clarity; generally, however, it is best to focus the examination with questions: Have you read about some of these topics in other books? Does this book deal with the present or will it take us back to people who lived a long time ago? Which chapter tells about the South? On what page does Chapter 7 begin? Now that you've

Figure 12.3   Summaries of Kindergarten Experiments with Water

```
                    Ice

1.   We put water into the freezer.

2.   The water is a liquid.

3.   The water is freezing.

4.   The water is a solid.

5.   The water is ice.
```

```
            Float and Sink

Some things float.

Some things sink.

Things heavier than water sink.

Things lighter than water float.
```

Figure 12.4   Categories for Summarizing Eye Coloring

Eye Coloring			
hazel	blue	brown	gray

looked at the names of the chapters, do you think the title of this book is a good one? Why?

If students' responses point up special interests or dilemmas, the index can be examined. Again, questions should guide the looking: Is this book going to tell us a great deal about tornadoes and hurricanes, or just a little? Are these two types of storms dealt with only in the one chapter, or do the authors refer to them elsewhere? On what pages do the authors discuss hydroelectric power? Which gives more information—an index or a table of contents? When should each be used?

Getting acquainted with a textbook also calls for attending to its graphic features. Once more, probing is helpful: If you were having breakfast in California, what meal might a New York friend be eating? If you like to live where there aren't too many people, what states would make a good home? If you lived in _____, during what months would your raincoat get lots of use? Examining graphics should be supplemented with comments about the author's use of color, italics, boldfaced type, brackets, boxes, indentations, underlining, summaries, and questions. Later, when individual chapters are studied, more attention should go to such devices, in particular to how they function to facilitate comprehension.

If a glossary is included, that should be examined. Now, appropriate questions would be something like, "How do you pronounce the word that's spelled *q, u, a, y*? What does it mean?"

While everything that has been recommended for acquainting students with new textbooks is important, a word of caution about doing too much is warranted by a few classroom observations that revealed such detailed introductions that students tired of a book before they began to study it.

A TEACHER'S PREPARATION FOR A CHAPTER

Teachers are hardly in a position to help students learn how to get information from a textbook chapter if they have not read it themselves. Consequently, the first step for anyone seriously interested in providing help is to read whatever the students will be reading. Other parts of a teacher's preparation are listed in the box. Since textbooks are usually studied a chapter at a time, what is listed focuses on that unit.

PART OF A TEACHER'S PREPARATION

1. Reading the chapter
2. Deciding about:
   (a) important content and vocabulary
   (b) procedures for dealing with both
   (c) display center
   (d) reading objectives
   (e) procedures for attaining reading objectives

Some of what a teacher needs to do will be discussed, starting with decisions about important content and vocabulary.

Content Objectives

Not everything in a chapter needs to be learned. This means that teachers must decide ahead of time what merits close scrutiny by considering factors like importance, relevance, and students' abilities and interests. (It is doubtful that a certain fourth-grade teacher followed these guidelines, since one bulletin board in his room displayed students' highly technical descriptions of moths, each sounding very much like a reference book. Accompanying the reports were equally detailed diagrams of the insects. Seeing the board made it natural to wonder whether these same students could answer questions like, Why do moths like wool? What can be done to protect woolen clothing from being damaged by moths? Why is it effective? Although these reflections are not meant to suggest that only what is practical is valuable, they *are* intended to point out that too much of what students are expected to learn from textbooks bears little relationship to their lives or interests. As a result, it is quickly forgotten—assuming it was ever learned.)

Once essential content has been separated from what is less important, objectives for the chapter should be written. Written statements are recommended for several reasons. To begin, writing them requires a clarification and preciseness not always achieved when one simply thinks about them. The written account will also serve as a reminder when subsequent decisions are made about how the selected objectives will be reached. And, finally, written objectives indicate what should be evaluated later on.

Sample objectives for various topics are shown next; other examples are in the reproduced material in Figure 12.5.

An awareness of how magnets are useful to people.
An understanding of thunder and lightning in relation to their causes and dangers.
A knowledge of how gravity works on humans and their environment.
An understanding of the connection between the physical features of an area and
     the occupations of its people.

Which terms in a chapter need to be understood becomes apparent as essential content is identified.

Display Centers

After decisions are made about important content and vocabulary, a teacher is in a position to know what should be placed in one or more display centers. Ideally, a

Figure 12.5

comes less dense, and is pushed upward. As a result, air currents are formed which flow in a circular pattern.

3. A psychrometer consists of two thermometers, one of which has its bulb covered with a wick that is kept wet. Since evaporation from the wet wick lowers the temperature reading of the wet-bulb thermometer, the reading of the wet-bulb thermometer is lower than the reading of the dry-bulb thermometer. The difference between these two readings depends upon the relative humidity of the air. The lower the relative humidity, the greater the evaporation will be from the wick; the greater the evaporation from the wick, the lower the wet-bulb thermometer reading will be. With a special table, the readings of the two thermometers can be used to determine the relative humidity.

Check Your Information

Assign this activity as an independent self-evaluation. The answers are as follows:

1. Nitrogen   3. saturated
2. bottom   4. wind

Things to Do

Encourage the pupils to conduct these activities on their own. Then the results may be discussed in class.

The following activity is included for use at your own discretion. To determine the volume of oxygen in air, place a candle upright in a dish of water. Light the candle, and then quickly but carefully place a glass tumbler or large test tube over the lighted candle. Make certain that the mouth of the glass tumbler or large test tube is below the level of the water. As the candle burns beneath the glass tumbler or large test tube, the flame will consume the oxygen from the air trapped within the container. Then the water will rise in the glass tumbler or large test tube in proportion to the volume of oxygen removed by oxidation. (Approximately one-fifth of the tumbler or test tube will be filled with water at the time the flame burns out.)

Teacher's Overview of Chapter 8, THE OCEANS AND THE WEATHER, pages 114–129

PURPOSE

This chapter is designed to make the pupils aware of the weather and how the ocean of water and the ocean of air interact to affect the weather—for example, by developing clouds which might result in rain.

APPROACH

Chapter 8 begins with a definition of *weather*. Then techniques of observing and describing the weather are investigated. The pupils also consider various concepts which aid in understanding and forecasting the weather. Finally, some recent research on the weather is considered. This chapter contributes to the overall development of the unit by emphasizing the interaction be-

tween the earth's two great oceans—the ocean of air and the ocean of water.

BEHAVIORAL GOALS

After the pupils study this chapter, they should be able to:

1. Construct and use instruments for making weather observations and measurements.

2. Make and use charts for recording weather observations and measurements.

3. Use weather reports and weather maps to trace the movements of air masses, fronts, highs, and lows.

4. Describe the importance of air masses in determining the weather.

5. Inquire and read about research on the weather.

T86

Smith, Herbert A., Blecha, Milo K., and Pless, Herbert. *Modern Science,* Level Six, 1972, p. T86. Reprinted with permission of Laidlaw Brothers, a Division of Doubleday & Company, Inc.

● *Teachers' editions of subject-matter textbooks include a manual or guidebook like those provided for basal readers. As with basal manuals, they should be viewed as offering suggestions, not prescriptions.*

This reproduction shows a page from a manual for a sixth-grade science book. The top half of the page deals with concluding activities for one chapter; the bottom half is the beginning of multiple suggestions for the next chapter. For all the chapters, suggestions are offered for objectives, vocabulary study, questions, discussions, experiments, and end-of-chapter reviews and evaluations. In a section called "Science Background," teachers receive additional information about each topic covered.

Even with the best of manuals, teachers need to keep in mind that no author knows their particular students. As a result, it is the teacher's responsibility to choose from among a manual's recommendations only those that are appropriate for the students.

center includes trade books⋆ whose difficulty matches students' abilities and with content that repeats, clarifies, or extends what is to be studied. Textbooks might also be available, some of which could be easier or more difficult than the one being used. (Textbooks with old copyright dates might be deliberately included since they invite both comparisons and critical reading.)

Depending on what was selected for study, collateral material might be historical novels, biographies, and autobiographies. Still other possibilities are magazine and newspaper articles, pamphlets, travel brochures, and maps. Realia, pictures, and other audiovisual aids also make helpful contributions, especially when one or more content objectives are about something that is totally new. For science, equipment necessary for conducting experiments is appropriate.

Display centers can be assembled just prior to the introduction of a new chapter, thus exciting interest right at the start. At other times, it is better to delay their appearance because the later arrival can reexcite interest after more mundane but necessary jobs have been done. In some instances, assignments will deal with the display materials; at other times, students should be free to make their own selections. However it is used, a display is an important adjunct to work done in the content areas.

Reading Objectives

After decisions have been made about important content, vocabulary, and one or more display centers, others need to be made about how the chapter will be used to advance the students' ability to deal with expository text. In this case, guidance comes not only from existing abilities but also from the nature of the chapter itself. If the content is characterized by cause–effect relationships, they might be a focus for instruction. Or if following a sequence is essential for understanding all or some of the content, that could figure in reading objectives. Still more possibilities will be described later.

PREPARING STUDENTS FOR A CHAPTER

Having made her own preparations for a chapter, a teacher is ready to prepare students to read it. Well-done prereading procedures will not only facilitate comprehension but will also provide a model for students of what should be done whenever they need to read difficult, expository material on their own. That even the best of students need a model was uncovered in a study of Harvard and Radcliffe freshmen. After examining their reading habits, the researcher wrote:

> The typical approach of 90 percent of these students was to start at the beginning of the chapter and read straight ahead. No attempt was made to survey the chapter,

---

⋆ A trade book is one written for library and bookstore markets rather than for instruction.

note marginal headings, or first read the recapitulation paragraph in which the whole structure and summary of the chapter was given. Thus, none of the clues and signals provided as a basis for raising questions were used to identify specific purposes for reading. [24, p. 196]

No one best way exists to establish cognitive readiness for a chapter. What follows, therefore, is a possible series of steps whose purposes should be explained to students. Or, as Ann Brown and others have learned from their research (6), "Children should be fully informed participants in any training enterprise" (p. 16).

PREREADING PREPARATIONS FOR A CHAPTER

Step One: Title and Introductory Paragraph

Direct students to read the title silently. The introductory paragraph might then be read aloud either by the teacher or an able student who had a chance to look it over. Just this small amount of material is likely to elicit responses, especially if a teacher probes with questions: Does anyone know something about this already? Does it remind you of anything we talked about earlier? (Questions such as these are important because they activate prior knowledge and help students see the connections between what they already know and what they are about to learn. They might also spark interest in reading the chapter.)

Step Two: Structure of Chapter

To help students see how the chapter is put together, headings and subheadings should be examined next. (Awareness of the author's organizational scheme makes the content more comprehensible and memorable because students now have a framework into which pieces will fit in a way that shows their relationships.)

Step Three: Graphics

Students might next be asked to leaf through the chapter to look at graphic material. Again, questions should provide a focus so that students do not view what is being done as aimless browsing. Questions about pictures can call attention to details that might be overlooked, or they can assist in estimating the actual size of what is pictured. Queries about other graphics might elicit responses that suggest a need for help—for instance, How are certain lines and arrows to be interpreted? If the chapter introduces a new type of graphic aid, more careful consideration of that is necessary.

Step Four: Summary

To wrap up the overview, the summary at the end of the chapter should be read. If questions are included, they should be examined too, after which the students can be asked if they themselves have questions that they hope the chapter will answer. (Student contributions provide an observant teacher with information about interests, which might be useful in suggesting topics that can be researched by individuals or small groups.) When questions originate with students, they are more likely to want to read the chapter in order to get answers.

Step Five: Help with Vocabulary
Attention to selected vocabulary comes next. Exactly what should be done varies according to factors like the importance of a word to the content being studied, its pronunciation in relation to its spelling, its meaning and general usefulness, and the interest that it might hold for students. Minimally, the pronunciation and meaning of all *important* words should be dealt with. Sample procedures for attending to vocabulary follow:

- Have children decode the words. Then discuss meanings. If appropriate, ask for both examples and nonexamples.

- After a word is pronounced, put it into a sentence that suggests its meaning. (Ideally, sentences should come from the chapter.) Direct students to read the sentence silently to see if they can figure out the meaning from the context.

- Once the pronunciation and meaning of a word have been dealt with, related words might be written and discussed. If the word is *colony*, for instance, *colonist, colonize, colonial,* and *colonization* can get attention, perhaps with a visual display:

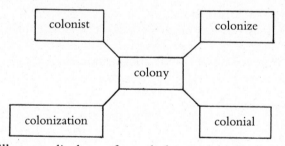

Still more displays of vocabulary might be organized around one word. For instance:

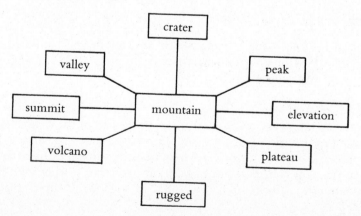

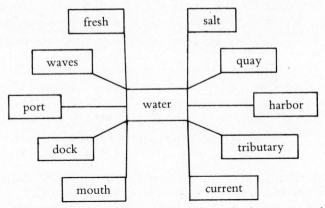

- Another possibility is to have students list words in a word book, once pronunciations and meanings have been taken care of. In this case, they write a sentence that includes the word and, following that, the definition of the word in that context.

- Self-help cards can be prepared for each word. On one side, the word will be written. (With especially hard-to-pronounce words, diacritical marks can be used.) On the second side, a definition is written. Later, students can work with a partner to see if they can pronounce each word and explain its meaning.

Step Six: Questions

Once important vocabulary has received attention, it is time to pose questions (in writing) that pertain to the selected goals. (Time should be taken to make sure that all the questions are understood.) The fact that these and other questions will be discussed once the chapter has been read should be made clear.

Occasionally, able students might be asked to read the chapter in order to write their own questions about its content. Predictably, some will deal with trivial details, which provides a teacher with the opportunity to make distinctions between important and less important content. Simultaneously, it gives the students an opportunity to learn that it is unnecessary—even undesirable—to give careful attention to everything. It is important for them to be reminded of this because the numerous questions often posed about basal reader selections can be misleading about what it means to be a proficient reader.

What has now been described as preparation for reading a chapter can be reviewed with the following headings:

1. Title and Introductory Paragraph
2. Structure of Chapter
3. Graphics
4. Summary
5. Help with Vocabulary
6. Written Questions

Much more could be added to the steps just described. If followed as given, however, they are enough to demonstrate to students that preparing for a chapter involves more than counting the pages to see how long it is. For teachers, the same steps demonstrate that meaningful help involves far more than directing students to read a chapter and to answer questions listed at the end. (What one social studies manual suggests for a chapter is shown in Figure 12.6.)

SCHEDULING ACTIVITIES

Exactly what should to be done to achieve the goals established for a chapter depends upon a variety of factors that always include the students, the content of the chapter, and the nature of the goals themselves. What never varies, however, is the need for teachers to think about how the various activities will be scheduled. One way to think about a schedule is shown here:

	Possible simultaneous activities	*Concluding activities and evaluation*
Preparation	Silent reading of the chapter	
(1) by the teacher		
(2) of the children	Special assignments	
	Small group instruction	
	Assistance to individuals	

As the progression of procedures indicates, at least some students will get special assignments (in addition to reading the chapter) for such purposes as providing additional information or preparing summary material. Whenever one student or a group does have a special project, responsibilities should be recorded on a job sheet. If more than one student is involved, teachers need to keep in mind that a group responsibility works best:

1. When one student is designated as the group leader.
2. When each member knows exactly what he or she is to do.
3. When a stipulated amount of time is allocated for fulfilling the responsibility.
4. When the group's efforts result in a physical product—for example, a report, a list of suggestions or questions, a booklet, a picture, a tape recording, or a demonstration of an experiment.

Classroom observations reveal that special assignments for able readers commonly include reporting to other students what they learned from supple-

Figure 12.6

compare with the statement made earlier that one out of five families move each year?

4. Read *Farmer Boy* by Laura Ingalls Wilder. Discuss ways our living has changed in less than a century.

CHAPTER 3···MAPS AND GLOBES
pages 25–27

SUGGESTIONS and PROCEDURES

INTRODUCTION

The focus in Chapter 3 is on uses of maps and globes. No new terms are introduced. Nevertheless, some of the map and globe skills emphasized may be difficult enough to require extended practice for some children. The meaning of the terms *symbol, legend* or *key,* and *scale,* is developed in this chapter although the terms themselves are not used.

Before beginning work on the chapter, see that each child is provided with a road map of your state and that some air maps are available. Road maps may be secured free at filling stations or state highway departments, and air maps from airline offices.

pages 25, 26

USING MAPS AND GLOBES

Have the children read the first two paragraphs about maps and globes, then pause for discussion. Explain that men found maps useful even before they knew the shape of the Earth. For example, a man who knew nothing of the Earth beyond the area of his home could show his family where he had killed a large animal by drawing a map. Draw on the chalkboard a crude map of a clearing encircled by trees. Put a mark behind a large boulder to show where the hunter stood and an arrow near the tallest tree to show where

the animal fell. Here the children can see an image of an area which is described only by symbols. Point out that any large map of a very small area can show many details, such as single trees or a large boulder.

Ask why the globe can show no details. Help the children to verbalize what they know about the globe's inaccuracies. Ask: Is the Earth really smooth like most globes? Explain that just as the globe does not show all the high and low places of the Earth, it does not show the Earth's exact shape. Scientists are not sure about the exact shape of the Earth. They are now studying and measuring it, and globes of the future may be shaped a bit differently to reflect new knowledge of the wider and narrower areas. Establish the basic point that a globe shows the whole Earth, but a map may show either the whole Earth or some very small part of it. Ask the children what kinds of maps they have used, and for what purposes.

page 26

COMPARING MAPS AND GLOBES

How is the world map, which shows the whole Earth, different from the globe? Emphasize: The map is flat, the Earth is round. Since a map is not bulky like the globe, it is easy to carry with you. You can see more of the Earth at one time on a map. You can also see small details on a map if it is a large map of a small area.

At a later discussion period, use half an orange shell or half an old hollow rubber ball to let a child show what happens when we must make a flat map to represent half the round globe. Let the children discuss the mapmaker's problem in putting together the broken edges. Help them to see that this cannot be done exactly. Lead to the generalization that in this kind of map the most distortion occurs at the edges.

Have the children look at their road maps of their state and get some familiarity with the symbols used. Locate rivers, lakes, mountains, highways, and important cities. Discuss the uses children have seen others make of maps and globes.

27

mentary reading. Unfortunately, two outcomes are typical: reports taken word for word from whatever was read and, second, reporting that is done so poorly that only children blessed with an abundance of good manners listen.

While these negative reactions are not meant to discourage the use of oral reports, they *are* designed to remind teachers that even superior readers of high intelligence need to be taught how to translate something like an encyclopedia article into their own words and to give reports that are not deadly dull.★ To avoid dullness, only certain kinds of oral reporting should be done. For instance:

- Interest in people can be used to advantage by having able readers tell what they learned in a biography or an autobiography. If biographies of the same person written by different authors have been read, oral reports could stress similarities and differences in the two accounts. What the textbook told about the person also enters into the postreport discussion.

- Histories of some words are sufficiently interesting that brief oral reports about them are both appealing and educationally significant.

- If a display table includes realia or pictures, plus cards that ask questions about them, oral reports can provide answers.

- Interesting newspaper or magazine articles might deal with topics relevant to a chapter's content, and able readers could report on them. Later, all members of the class would be free to select the articles from the display table.

- If able readers are asked to study (with the help of guideline questions) textbooks that were chosen because of old copyright dates, they can prepare oral reports featuring differences or even contradictions in what the older publications said as compared to what the students' own textbook related about a given topic.

ACCOMMODATING POOR READERS

When teachers provide adequate preparation for reading a chapter, average and better-than-average students should be able to do the silent reading on their own and, in addition, work on some special project or assignment. Even with the best of preparation, however, students with reading deficiencies will need additional help. Some ways to offer it are shown in Figure 12.7. What is listed shows how teachers can help slower children learn important content (thus add to their knowledge of the world) while, at the same time, they are helping them become better readers of expository text.

★ More is said about these problems and their solutions later in the chapter.

READING INSTRUCTION AND TEXTBOOKS

Once students have been prepared for a chapter, variation in activities should be characteristic. For example, some students might begin the reading right away; simultaneously, others will receive information about their special assignment(s), typically begun *after* they read the chapter. When everyone is occupied, the teacher is free to work with small groups or individuals. Since the typical basal lesson does relatively little with content like that found in textbooks (10), some of the work should be reading instruction—at times, something like that described earlier under the heading "Accommodating Poor Readers." Further examples of instruction designed to improve ability to read expository text will be covered now.

Teaching Students How to Study

One important kind of reading instruction was implied when how to preview a chapter with students was described since the goal of the procedures was to teach them how to study. Achieving such a goal is facilitated when teachers take the time to explain to students *why* they are being asked to do certain things—for instance, to read the summary of a chapter before the chapter itself is begun. Some teachers organize such explanations within the framework of SQ3R (survey, question, read, recite, review). Originally used to improve the reading of servicemen (28), the sequence of behaviors to which SQ3R refers is one way to systematize and explicate studying.

Following are directions for each part of the SQ3R scheme. As you read about certain parts, you may be reminded of what was referred to earlier in the chapter as metacomprehension or comprehension monitoring.

STUDYING A CHAPTER

Survey: Skim through the chapter to get a general picture of the organization and content. Attend only to headings and subheadings, captions, graphics, and summaries.

Question: Return to the start of the chapter. Taking one section at a time, turn the headings and subheadings into questions. How do people use magnets? would be asked if the heading was "Man's Use of Magnets."

Read: Read the section to answer the question(s).

Recite: Looking away from the book, recite to yourself what was learned to answer the question.

Review: After following the above procedures with each section, review all the questions to see whether they can still be answered. If any cannot, reread the troublesome section.

Figure 12.7

Possible Accommodations for Less Able Readers

Teach Content	Improve Reading Ability
Leaf through the chapter with the children, stopping to highlight and summarize key points. At the end, write major headings on the chalkboard (simplified if required) in outline form. Have the children review content with the help of the headings.	As you go through the chapter, ask the children to read certain words and explain their meanings. Write the roots of derivatives to help with meanings and to show relationships.
If graphic aids are important for a chapter, go over each one. Call attention to important details. Ask a volunteer to tell in a few words what the graphic is communicating.	As graphic materials are examined, write key words on the board. Check to see if the children can identify them and explain their meanings.
When questions for a chapter are assigned, hold these children responsible only for those that depend upon direct, literal comprehension. If necessary, the sheet that lists *their* questions can indicate the page number on which the answer is located. Have the children read the paragraph silently; then check answers. Do this one or more times to provide a model for their independent efforts to answer other questions.	
If certain topics covered in a chapter are to be further researched by children working in small groups, assign less able readers to a topic for which easy-to-read books are available. Again, prepare simply worded questions to guide and focus their reading.	
Select important or especially difficult sections of the chapter and read them to the children. Following each section, ask questions about the content. Whenever possible, relate the content to the children's own lives and interests.	Show key terms by writing them on the board. Make sure that the children understand their meaning.

Select sentences from the chapter that may be difficult to understand because of complicated structure and list them on the board. Ask questions about the content of each. If necessary, point out subjects and predicates in order to begin to show how the meaning of long sentences can be worked out.

Select sentences from the chapter that may be difficult to comprehend because they include uncommon words or idiomatic expressions. Help the children understand each one by explaining the words or expressions. If contextual cues are available, bring them to the children's attention.

Use pictures, slides, a filmstrip, or a simplified graph as a focus for a discussion of important terms and content. Write key words and phrases on the chalkboard. Discuss meanings.

If a film (or some other audiovisual aid) was used to introduce the chapter, reshow it. Afterward, discuss the content in greater detail. Raise questions. Encourage the children to ask other questions.

Same as above.

If a filmstrip (with captions) helps to clarify the material being studied, show it to these children. As this is being done, have a more able child read the captions aloud.

Assign a simply written book that deals with one or more of the topics selected as being important for the chapter under consideration. Prior to the reading, pose (in writing) a few simply worded questions about its content. Later, discuss answers to see if the book was adequately understood.

Assign a simplified account (teacher written) of the important content presented in the chapter, along with questions about it. Discuss answers later. Raise other questions if necessary.

Under a teacher's supervision, only a small group should participate in the initial use of SQ3R. Material that is less than a chapter ought to be the focus. Still other reminders are listed next:

REMINDERS TO TEACHERS ABOUT SQ3R

Survey: To foster the kind of reading that a survey calls for, only a given amount of time should be allowed. Otherwise, students will read too slowly for the stated purpose.

Question: Typically, children will require help when headings are first turned into questions. A few examples are usually sufficient to specify transformations.

Recite: When a group is involved, the recitation is done aloud by individuals. When students use SQ3R themselves, it is done silently.

Review: Comments about the recitation part of the pattern apply equally to the review.

Other Kinds of Reading Instruction

In addition to teaching students how to study in some systematic way, other reading objectives are both appropriate and necessary for expository material. Therefore, four illustrative goals and how they might be realized will be described. To show when attention can go to a reading objective, part of what was shown earlier is presented next:

Possible Simultaneous Activities	Concluding Activities and Evaluation
Silent reading of the chapter Special assignments Small group instruction Assistance to individuals	

Goal: *To teach about ways to comprehend complicated sentences.*

For this goal, a teacher should scan the chapter to find sentences whose complicated structure is likely to cause problems. One social studies text (27) includes sentences like the following:

This ended the old system by which a congressman who was not re-elected in November could continue in office until March even though he had been defeated. [p. 329]

Then another man made a cotton gin and patented it, or gained from the government the sole right to make and sell it. [p. 271]

To help students work out the meanings of complicated sentences, a teacher might show something like the following:

Subject	*Verbs*	*Objects*
another man	made	cotton gin
	(and)	
	patented	it

How *or* functions in the sentence should be considered next. Afterward, it is time to write on the board: *patent = permission from government to make and sell something.*

Once the pieces of a sentence are dealt with, they can be reassembled with a request like, "Tell us in your own words what this sentence says."

Goal: *To teach about using contexts to get help with word meanings.*
Authors of content subject textbooks usually provide help with word meanings; nonetheless, teachers cannot take it for granted that students will know how to use it. That is why time should be taken either to teach or to remind them of how contexts help with meanings. (This topic, you will recall, was discussed in Chapter 10.) Sentences like the following, all taken from one social studies textbook (25), are appropriate for the goal. (The italicized words, the ones now getting attention, were not italicized in the textbook.)

What really happens, though, is that heat waves are *reflected* or bounce back into the air. [p. 54]

We build high *dams* behind which water is stored. [p. 20]

Eskimos have several kinds of homes, each of which is an *igloo*. [p. 201]

Hunting for *caribou* and other land animals is hard work when the ground is not frozen. [p. 204]

Using the last sentence as an illustration, a teacher's directions might be: "Read the first seven words. They hint at what a caribou is. What *is* a caribou? . . . What word suggested that it is an animal? . . . Do you know anything else about a caribou? . . . Let me hear you pronounce it."

Goal: *To teach about distinctions between expository and narrative text.*
After certain students read a chapter, they can be asked to read narrative material (story, poem) about a topic covered in the chapter (for example, fog, life on a

farm, person of historical importance, an animal, a flower). Postreading probes might include: Did the information in your textbook help you understand _____ ? Did anything in _____ contradict what the textbook said? Which was easier to read? Why? Did this change the way you read it? When is it a good time to read a textbook and when is it better to read _____ ?

Goal: *To teach about appropriate reading rates.*

This goal, first discussed in Chapter 11, requires use of contrasting questions: What were the direct and indirect causes of World War I? When did World War I begin? (Whenever possible, questions should be selected from those posed before the chapter was read.) With this goal, answers are not required. Instead, the discussion centers on the rates of reading that are appropriate for each question. The discussion should also point up (with examples) that some answers are not in the chapter but instead are the reader's own ideas and opinions.

CONCLUDING ACTIVITIES FOR A CHAPTER

What ought to be done to conclude the study of a chapter depends on instructional objectives. Always, however, the three main reasons to have concluding activities need to be kept in mind.

The first is to synthesize all the bits and pieces that were studied in a variety of ways. This ensures that students are left with a picture whose pieces are put together. There will be times, of course, when missing pieces are discovered. Depending on their importance, the discovery might lead to further study or, possibly, to the need to read the next chapter.

From a teacher's perspective, concluding activities are opportunities to see what students have learned insofar as the selected objectives are concerned. As with all other assessment efforts, the aim is not to put dents into the students' self-esteem but to collect information that will be useful when plans are made for a subsequent chapter.

In addition to allowing for a synthesis and an assessment of learnings, concluding activities should give students the chance to communicate to others what they have learned, discovered, or enjoyed. Although some children have much less need for sharing than others, all (including the teacher) can profit from it, if it is done well.

Regardless of which of the three aims is being considered (synthesis, assessment, or sharing), concluding activities should allow time for students' responses to the questions assigned before the chapter was studied. A few comments about responses follow.

To begin, should students have to write answers? In this case, age needs to be taken into account because younger children get tired if they have to write for long periods of time. Also to be kept in mind is that requiring written answers fosters brevity, which is relevant when it is remembered that some of the best questions call for long answers.

Some teachers avoid written responses by directing students to note the page number on which they find an answer. If necessary, pages can be referred to when answers are being discussed. Other teachers bypass written responses by teaching students how to take brief notes that can serve as prompts in the course of discussing a chapter. At the same time, they work at getting students to paraphrase an author's words, which is useful whenever the need to report on reference materials occurs. (The importance of these two abilities suggests still other important goals for reading instruction carried on in conjunction with the study of content subjects. Both will be discussed.)

While prereading questions usually figure in concluding activities—although not always in the original order or with the same wording—they should not be thought of as the only way to terminate the study of a chapter. Other questions should also be entertained, especially those stemming from students' interests and curiosity and from the special assignments and projects. Important, too, are questions that are designed to take students beyond the content of the chapter and, whenever possible, to help them see its relevance for their own lives.

Student-made materials such as charts, posters, murals, maps, diagrams, and time lines are especially helpful in summarizing material; consequently, they may also figure in concluding activities. Since vocabulary is always an important part of subject matter instruction, something like a dictionary of new terms is appropriate. And so, too, are oral reports, when their topics are of interest and when the reporter is well prepared.

To sum up, then, no one best way exists for bringing the study of a chapter to a productive close. Whatever is chosen, however, should allow for a synthesis and assessment of learnings. It should also give students the chance to share with others what they have been doing and learning.

RATE OF READING

Unlike oral reading, silent reading allows for great variation in rate. Since the successful comprehension of textbooks requires purposeful variation, rate of reading is an appropriate topic to cover both in the present chapter and at any time when students are dealing with expository material.

Skimming

Skimming is the quick type of reading that is done to get the general gist of material. A skimmer can thus be compared to an eavesdropper who tries to pick up just enough of a speaker's words to learn what in general is being said. Because previewing a chapter is done to uncover in a general way what the content is about, previews exemplify skimming. However, when skimming is first attempted under a teacher's supervision, material that is both shorter and easier than a textbook chapter should be used. Questions like the following are appropriate for promoting this type of reading.

If you wanted to learn about caring for a pet dog, would this page help?
What would be a good title for this paragraph?
Read the page; then tell us if the title says what it is about.
Read this paragraph; then see if you can tell us what it's about in just one sentence.
Will this section help to answer the fourth question?

When practice in skimming is the goal, a small group of students who are similar in reading ability should be the participants. This allows for sufficient but not overwhelming challenge and, in time, for reminders like, "I'll give you just a couple of minutes to look it over to answer the question."

Scanning

As important as skimming is the process called *scanning*. Scanning is faster than skimming and is used when something in particular has to be found—a word, a number, a name, a certain fact, a certain phrase. It can be described, therefore, as a deliberately focused and searching type of behavior. Figuring prominently in its use are such materials as a dictionary, timetable, index, menu, or list of baseball scores. Questions that begin like the following go along with scanning:

> Where did . . . ?
> How many . . . ?
> In what month . . . ?
> How large . . . ?

Unlike skimming, scanning is a novel process in the sense that spoken language cannot be scanned. Since scanning ability is not likely to develop automatically, students have to be helped not only to carry it on efficiently but also to know when scanning is appropriate.

When it *is* appropriate can be illustrated in a variety of ways. The easy-to-manage telephone directories of small communities, for example, are useful in demonstrating that finding a classmate's address so that a get-well card can be sent does not require a careful reading of each name listed but, to the contrary, a quick search until a certain one is found. The need to use a dictionary to find an appropriate meaning offers another opportunity to demonstrate a time for scanning, as does the need to look up an item in an index or to learn from a television schedule when a certain program starts. The fact that it is not difficult to find materials and occasions that call for scanning indicates its importance.

Instruction with scanning can get started by using lists like those found in directories, timetables, dictionaries, and the like. These materials are recommended at the beginning because their narrow width facilitates the straight-down-the-middle eye movements that are the mark of a mature scanner. While children will not be able—at least not at first—to employ a similar pattern with wider pages, lists do give a teacher the chance to point out that a left-to-right, line-by-line approach does not always characterize reading.

Whether lists or normally spaced material is used, students should know that scanning follows a certain sequence:

SCANNING

1.   It begins with a definite purpose.
2.   It proceeds quickly in search of whatever relates to that purpose.
3.   When the objective of the search seems to have been found, it is double-checked to see if it is pertinent.
4.   If what has been found *is* related to the purpose, it is read carefully.

To ensure success when students first attempt scanning, questions that will facilitate their search should be posed. With material no longer than a paragraph, a teacher can ask pointed questions like: What is the weight of a full-grown blue whale? Who was the first Soviet astronaut? When was the Fourteenth Amendment passed? What color are the coins? If we do this experiment, will we need string or wire?

If, in the process of scanning, children pick up more information than is required for the stated purpose, it means they are searching too carefully and slowly. This can be discouraged with a comment like, "I'll give you just thirty seconds to find out how many children are allowed to ride on a school bus." (Recommending time limits to foster more rapid reading assumes the students in question have enough ability to allow for scanning but need a prompt to get them out of the undesirable habit of reading everything at the same rate.)

With practice like that described, most children find it relatively easy to locate something when questions directly suggest the form in which it will appear (a date, an amount, a color, a name, and so on). This allows not only for the use of longer material but also for questions that do not offer direct help and might even require answers found in different places. Scanning at this level can be initiated with questions like: Are there any rocks on the moon that are not found in the United States? What is the coldest and the warmest that it gets in Mexico City?

Since proficient reading may include both scanning and skimming, practice with the two eventually should be combined. For this purpose, questions can be distributed to an instructional group (for example, the prereading questions for a textbook chapter) and then examined to see the kind of reading that each calls for.

Later, other lists of more varied questions can be studied to reinforce the idea that reading ranges all the way from rapid scanning to slow, methodical plodding. In this way, students will come to realize that flexible rates are an essential attribute of mature reading. To specify this, a poster like the following is useful after all the points have been discussed.

SLOW DOWN!

When material
    is related to your purpose
    has new ideas
    has important details
    is a long, complicated sentence
    includes an important word or expression that is not known

SPEED UP!

When material
    is not related to your purpose
    is easy
    is familiar
    repeats what was said before

LOCATING INFORMATION

Whether offered during the time set aside for reading or when a content subject is being studied, the bulk of reading instruction with expository material should concentrate on helping students learn how to acquire information. They also need to know how to locate information for various purposes: to clarify what they are attempting to learn, to extend it, to verify it, or to answer a specific question. This means that they should be taught how to use reference materials like dictionaries and encyclopedias.

Using a Dictionary

Often, the first contact with alphabetical order occurs when young children have alphabet books. Initial contact with dictionaries themselves usually comes through picture dictionaries, which are now available in grocery stores as well as bookstores and as part of basal reader series (see Figure 10.1).

    The use of pictures to explain words provides a natural transition to the more customary type of dictionary. So, too, do dictionaries whose authors write definitions that are appropriate for children. In one series,* a dictionary described as being for ages six to eight includes such suitable explanations as:

teeth	more than one tooth
telephone	something that carries your voice through wires so that you can speak to someone far away

For ages eight to ten, another dictionary in the same series includes definitions like:

canal	a very big ditch across land and filled with water so that ships and boats can move along it
canary	a small yellow bird kept as a pet because of its sweet song

Dictionaries such as the ones just referred to are in striking contrast to what was once seen in a third grade. It was the "customary" dictionary for that grade even though the definitions were as difficult as the words they were supposed to explain. The fact that dictionaries are helpful with meanings was *not* the lesson these third graders were learning. Nor was the lesson taught in a recently observed fifth grade. When a group of students were directed to look in their basal reader glossary for the meaning of *furrow,* they found "a groove."

To be useful, even the best dictionaries (and glossaries) require an understanding of alphabetical order as it relates to finding something. What it takes to find a word goes under the heading *Location Skills.*

Location skills.   Knowing alphabetical sequence is one piece of this collection of skills; knowing how to put that sequence to use is another. Teaching use might get started with an alphabetical listing of kindergartners' names and the need to know whose turn it is to hold the flag when the pledge of allegiance is recited. Making a class telephone directory also relies on alphabetical order. Later, its more technical features can be emphasized with procedures like the following.

- Name a letter. Ask for the two that come next in the alphabet. Or name a letter and ask for the letter that precedes it. (When this is first done, children should be allowed to use something like alphabet cards for assistance.)

- Divide the alphabet into parts *(a–f, g–l, m–s, t–z)*. Then write them on the board. Name a letter and ask in which part it is found. Later, similar questions can be posed about words—for instance, "Would this word be found at the beginning of a dictionary, in the middle, or toward the end?"

* This series of four dictionaries (Primary Dictionary Series) is available through Pyramid Publications, New York.

- Write pairs of words that have the same first letter but a different second letter. Ask which word in a pair would be listed first in a dictionary. Later, similar questions can focus on pairs in which the first two or three letters are identical.

- Introduce guide words by pointing out a few. Then have students examine others in their own dictionaries in order to consider the question, How are guide words selected? How they function when searching for a word should be considered next.

The most advanced location skills for dictionaries require knowing about word structure. This is so because entries are roots, even though it is the meanings of derived and inflected words that are often puzzling. This suggests that instruction about roots, prefixes, and suffixes should be supplemented from time to time with practice in finding the meanings of derived or inflected words by looking up their roots in a dictionary.

Pronunciation skills.   One reason why a reader might use a dictionary is to learn the correct pronunciation of a word. Or if an attempt was made to decode it but the result was not a word that was familiar in its spoken form, he may consult a dictionary to see if the product of his efforts is correct. In either case, the reader has to know how a silent dictionary communicates about speech sounds.

If diacritical marks figured in phonics instruction, the type of assistance offered in pronunciation keys will not be unfamiliar. Students who know about phonics will also know about the schwa sound, and they will be aware of the great variability in what vowel letters stand for. This means they will not be surprised to find that pronunciation keys in dictionaries give far more attention to vowel than to consonant sounds. Having experienced the consistent way in which most consonants represent sounds, these same children will understand why many of the consonants in words listed in dictionaries have no special markings.

Even though phonics instruction makes sizable contributions to a student's ability to use a pronunciation key, some practice with the latter generally is necessary. To be realistic, it should center on words whose pronunciations are unknown. To make it easy, initial practice should be with short words. Eventually, however, children will need to work with longer words and be reminded of the function of stress marks.

Selecting a meaning.   For reading, knowing what a word means is much more important than knowing its pronunciation. Since knowing what it means in a specific context is more important than knowing what it means in general—assuming there is such a thing as "general meaning"—another of the goals of dictionary instruction is the ability to select one meaning from a range of possibilities.

Since dictionaries list meanings according to grammatical function, children are helped in making selections when they know how a given word is functioning grammatically. This means that practice designed to help with correct selections must center on unfamiliar words placed at least in the context of a sentence.

While the ability to choose appropriate meanings is of primary importance, other features of dictionary information should not be overlooked. Attention to antonyms as well as to synonyms, for instance, adds to understandings. And knowing about the origin of a word promotes retention of meaning. Fortunately, most of the new dictionaries for children are giving increased space to etymology, which makes them more interesting as well as more informative (22).

Providing for practice. To add interest to the practice that is essential if students are to become proficient users of dictionaries, teachers should do more than make such questionable assignments as: "Look up these words, write definitions for all, then write sentences that include each one." Better activities to which children have responded with enthusiasm are described next.

- With the help of a dictionary, have children illustrate various meanings of a single word—for instance, *Don't run so fast, She has a run in her stocking, The colors will run, He scored a run.*

- On small cards type questions that a dictionary answers (for example, What do the initials A.M. and P.M. mean? What is the origin of the word *lieutenant?*) Let each student search out answers, which can be read and discussed later.

- Distribute a question like the following: How would you feel if someone said you were:

  1. huge
  2. precocious
  3. witty
  4. gregarious
  5. sly

Students look up the meaning of each word and then write a sentence describing how they would feel were it applied to them.

- Prepare groups of words whose meanings can be acted out. For example:

People: supercilious, grim, perplexed, serene, hospitable
Movements: strut, stroll, plod, stomp, jog, prance, march

- Using categories like those shown in the previous exercise, distribute one group of words to an instructional group. After looking up the meanings in a dictionary, members can plan ways to demonstrate them.

- Have children look up the meanings of words like *pleasant, pheasant, peasant,* and *present;* or of pairs like *medal, metal; pebble, petal; cattle, kettle;*

amiable, amicable; eminent, imminent. Discuss the meanings, including the spellings, to make certain that each word is understood and distinguished from the others.

- Have students look up the origin and original meaning of their own first names. Each should be given the chance to report her or his findings to the class.

- Clip newspaper articles that would be of interest, and underline any word whose meaning might be unknown. Have students select suitable definitions by looking up the words in a dictionary.

- If dictionaries with old copyright dates are available, ask the students to compare them with newer ones. Comparisons can highlight differences in pronunciation aids and types of definitions. The older dictionaries might also include words no longer listed in more recent editions. The more recent dictionaries, on the other hand, will show additions to our language.

- Prepare questions like these:

  Have you ever eaten with <u>gusto</u>?
  Did you ever find yourself in a <u>dilemma</u>?
  Did you ever <u>regale</u> anybody?
  Would you like to be <u>eradicated</u>?

  Direct students to look up the meanings of the underlined words and then answer the questions.

- For advanced students, lists of foreign words and phrases can be prepared (for example, *status quo, bon voyage, élan*). With a dictionary, they can learn both pronunciations and meanings. By using them in written sentences, they can show what they learned.

- For the enlightenment of their teacher, students can prepare a dictionary of current slang expressions. Following the form of more orthodox types, this dictionary would include correct spellings; division of words into syllables; diacritical markings; various meanings that are listed according to grammatical function; and, if available, information about the origin of each word or expression. A pronunciation key should be supplied, too.

One final comment about school attention to dictionaries is necessary, namely, it should never be so overriding as to deemphasize the amount of help with pronunciations and meanings that is available to readers who know how to use contextual, graphophonic, and structural cues. This is important for practical reasons: children will not always have dictionaries in their pockets, but they can carry in their heads a knowledge of the three kinds of cues. This needs to be stressed because, as was stated before, once glossaries appear in textbooks, teachers are much more likely to say (and teaching manuals are more likely to suggest),

"Look it up in the glossary" than to comment, "Let's see if you can figure out this word. What does the sentence tell you about it? Look at the spelling. What about that suffix?" Until probing like this becomes the rule rather than the exception— which it often is by the middle grades—what is taught about contextual, graphophonic, and structural cues becomes an end in itself rather than a very productive means for developing independent readers.

Using an Encyclopedia

Much that is taught about dictionaries contributes to the ability to use encyclopedias since both rely on alphabetical sequence for organizing the information they contain. Nonetheless, encyclopedias present new tasks and therefore new problems, and it is with those that the forthcoming discussion deals.

Readability.   A common problem with encyclopedia articles is their difficulty. After examining eight multivolume encyclopedias, one researcher concluded:

> Viewing the intermediate grades as a whole, these measurements revealed that students in the upper reading levels were generally able to comprehend approximately one out of three social studies articles, while students in the lower reading levels could comprehend only approximately one in fifty encyclopedia articles. [8, p. 151].

Even though some like to think of work with encyclopedias as "enrichment," the findings just referred to reinforce what visits to middle- and upper-grade classrooms commonly reveal: students are asked to use encyclopedias written at a level that makes them incomprehensible. Among the undesirable consequences is what one author calls "naive plagiarism" (9). To discourage this, classrooms and libraries should have encyclopedias whose difficulty matches students' abilities.

For all the reasons that make the expository material of textbooks difficult, what is presented even in carefully matched encyclopedias will not always be easy to comprehend. This means that what is done to help students cope with textbook reading is pertinent when they are being taught to use encyclopedias. In fact, encyclopedia articles offer excellent opportunities to apply what has been taught about how to study—for instance, to apply the SQ3R strategy.

Instruction with encyclopedias.   Since motivated students are the easiest to teach, instruction with encyclopedias might profitably begin with questions likely to pique their curiosity. Don Wolfe (35) suggests using riddles, plus information about the topics under which answers can be found. (Adding such information simplifies the task, making success more likely. This is important at the start, since success breeds not only more success but also interest.) Appropriate riddles might be something like:

A lady bug is not a bug. What is it? (Look under *Bugs*.)
A jumping bean is not a jumping bean. What is it? (Look under *Jumping Beans*.)
A starfish is not a fish. What is it? (Look under *Fish*.)

Curiosity might also be sparked by requests to check on the accuracy of such statements as:

All birds can fly. (Look under *Birds*.)
A snake cannot close its eyes. (Look under *Snakes*.)

Even with simple tasks like these, students should get assistance when they put forth initial efforts to get answers. At the start, they should be reminded of the question or statement that is to guide their reading. ("Remember now. We don't want to know everything about snakes. We only want to know if it is true that they cannot close their eyes.") Students should also be encouraged to scan an article until they find what appears to be related to the task. ("Why don't you read through this quickly until you see something about a snake's eyes. In fact, look for the word *eyes*. Then read that part carefully.") Later, each question should be repeated and, in turn, each response listened to attentively. ("Let's see now. The statement said that a snake cannot close its eyes. What did the encyclopedia say about that, Carol?") If irrelevant information is offered, it should be identified as such and separated from the rest.

Further practice in selecting pertinent material can be guided by steps like the following:

Helping Students Find Pertinent Material in Encyclopedias
1.   Pose a question.
2.   Help students decide under what topic the answer is likely to be found.
3.   When the article is located, have them read it silently, paragraph by paragraph. After each paragraph ask, "Does this deal with the question? . . . Why (not)?"
4.   At the end, repeat the question. Ask students to answer, using their own words.

Gradually, more difficult encyclopedia tasks are possible. For example, a question like "What is wheat germ?" could initiate the need to coordinate the content of several articles. To get students involved with this, a teacher might pose a series of related questions and, in the process, end up with a simple, written outline to which they can refer when they read and, later on, when they report.

What is wheat?
What is a germ?
Is wheat germ either wheat or a germ?
If not, what is it?

For a while, results of encyclopedia reading should be reported orally and briefly to small groups. Later, when students have acquired some facility with writing, they need to be helped to retain what they learn by preparing brief, written accounts. Again, this should be initiated with definite assignments or questions. If more than one set of encyclopedias is available, something like the following is possible:

Pilchard			
	What is it?	Where does it live?	Value to people?
Source #1			
Source #2			
Source #3			

At other times, questions like the following can be posed for reading encyclopedia material:

How does a camel keep from getting thirsty as it takes long journeys across hot and dry deserts?
What is the difference between a hare and a rabbit?

Initially, written answers should be kept brief. With questions like those preceding, restrictions can come through a direction such as "Write no more than four sentences."

When written answers are first required, they should be checked to see if students are using the words of the author or their own. This concern is justified not only because plagiarism should be discouraged but also because word-for-word-out-of-the-book answers usually indicate that the material went from the encyclopedia to the student's paper without ever passing through his head.

If the words of the article *are* being used, a return to oral reporting is called for because with oral responses, there is less of a tendency to use an author's words. When the oral response is acceptable, a written account of it can follow. In this way, students are being helped to paraphrase rather than to copy. More than that, they are being helped to sort out and to think.

Note taking and outlining.   Often the best written answers will take the form of brief notes or, if the material lends itself to this, an outline. Both are helpful when material has to be retained or reported to others. At times, questions that prompted the reading will provide a framework for the note taking or the major points of the outline. When an assignment is less well defined or when the job is to report briefly on the whole of an article, students can be taught how to take notes by having them do the following:

GUIDELINES FOR TAKING NOTES

1. Read the material until a shift in focus occurs.
2. Stop reading, think about what was read, and write a sentence or two that summarizes it. (If necessary, reread.)
3. Continue reading until there is another shift. Follow the same procedure.

At first, a teacher will need to work on these steps with a small group; much of the initial work, in fact, will be done aloud. Summary sentences, for instance, will be spoken first, then written. In time, and with sufficient practice, some students will be able to use the procedure independently and might even be able to substitute brief, partial sentences, or even an outline, for the sentence summaries.

When students are first introduced to outlines, a table of contents can provide a model. Headings and subheadings in chapters also illustrate topics and subtopics. Whatever is done to help students pick out main ideas and related details will contribute to understanding outlines, too.

When outlining is first attempted, the material should be brief with content that lends itself to outlines. Content about black widow spiders, for instance, might divide into three categories:

Black Widow Spider		
Description	Habits	Life History

Students receive a copy of this outline both to guide their reading and to introduce them to outlines. Later, group-composed outlines of more complicated material might begin with a display of headings and subheadings, printed on cards of different colors to distinguish between the two.

Still later, the more usual type of outline has to be introduced. At first, something like the following could be distributed with the direction to fill in subordinate ideas as material on birds is being read.

```
                       Birds
   I.  What birds have in common
       A.
       B.
       C.
       D.
  II.  Uses for feathers
       A.
       B.
 III.  Other contributions to man
       A.
       B.
       C.
```

Eventually, some elementary school students may reach the point where they are highly competent in preparing simple outlines; with others, such competency takes a little more learning, a little more reading, and lots more practice.

Oral reports.　Sometimes, what is learned from encyclopedias or supplementary textbooks is sufficiently important or interesting that an oral report to the entire class is called for. Before oral presentations are given, however, the requirements of effective reporting should be discussed. Steps like the following, displayed for all to see and think about, might be one product of such discussions.

```
                    Reminders

   1.  Stick to the topic.
   2.  If necessary, use brief notes or an outline
       but do not read a report.
   3.  If possible, illustrate material by using
       pictures, objects, diagrams, and so on.
   4.  Don't talk too long.
   5.  Try to be interesting.
```

At first, an oral report should be given to a small number of students; in fact, only when students achieve proficiency in reporting should they be allowed to take up the time of an entire class.

SUMMARY

Chapter 12 attests to the fact that reading stories and reading textbooks are essentially different tasks. Evidence of the difference shows up repeatedly when students who comprehend stories with relative ease encounter major obstacles when the need arises to learn from one or more textbooks.

As Chapter 12 pointed out, much that characterizes the content of textbooks explains the difficulties. Commonly, for instance, it will deal with information that is not only new to students but also far removed from their everyday lives and interests. Compounding these problems is the fact that writers of textbooks communicate information with specialized vocabulary and complicated sentences. Frequently, too, what they say about a topic moves along fairly quickly, making for content that is dense and thus difficult to process and remember.

Although these same authors provide aids for readers in the form of headings, subheadings, graphics, definitions, examples, and summaries, they function as such only for readers who know enough to use them. That is why Chapter 12 concentrated on ways for making these aids not only known to students but also something that will affect what they do when they study on their own.

What they do at such times should always be affected by the reasons for studying; consequently, Chapter 12 also discussed how teachers can bring purposes for reading a chapter into being and, further, how they can help students see the link between a purpose and the type of reading that ought to follow. Since the types that are called skimming and scanning should be part of a student's repertoire of reading skills, they were considered in the chapter, too.

Although Chapter 12 was mostly concerned with ways for helping students learn how to learn from text, it still covered ways for teaching them how to locate information found in such sources as dictionaries and encyclopedias. That was done because use of reference materials commonly enters into work with content area textbooks.

REVIEW

1.   To start, see whether you can explain the following:

adaptive reading	fix-up strategies	procedural discourse
comprehension monitoring	metacomprehension	scanning
expository discourse	narrative discourse	skimming

2.   Why is it helpful to leaf through a chapter in a textbook before reading it?
3.   What is the connection between (a) purpose for reading and (b) comprehension monitoring?
4.   Chapter 12 recommended using display centers. What contributions can they make to the study of a chapter?

5. Explain the meaning of: From a student's perspective, "learning how to learn from text" is an apt description of part of what is done with textbooks in the classrooms of knowledgeable, competent teachers.

6. Using the content of Chapter 12, compose three questions (or describe assignments) that call for (a) skimming, (b) scanning, and (c) slow, careful reading.

7. How to teach dictionary skills is one of the topics that Chapter 12 covers. Now, to synthesize what has been said about dictionaries throughout *Teaching Them to Read,* please answer the question, When should students be encouraged to use dictionaries, and when should such use *not* be encouraged?

8. How would you respond to those who believe that a comprehension score from a reading achievement test tells how well (or how poorly) a given child comprehends written text?

REFERENCES

1. Alessi, Stephen M.; Anderson, Thomas H.; and Goetz, Ernest T. "An Investigation of Lookbacks during Studying." Technical Report No. 140. Urbana: University of Illinois, Center for the Study of Reading, September 1979.

2. Anderson, Thomas H., and Armbruster, Bonnie B. "Studying." Technical Report No. 155. Urbana: University of Illinois, Center for the Study of Reading, January 1980.

3. Applebee, Arthur N. "Looking at Writing." *Educational Leadership* 38 (March 1981): 458–462.

4. Baker, Linda. "Do I Understand or Do I Not Understand: That Is the Question." Reading Education Report No. 10. Urbana: University of Illinois, Center for the Study of Reading, July 1979.

5. Broudy, Eric. "The Trouble with Textbooks." *Teachers College Record* 75 (September 1975): 13–34.

6. Brown, Ann L.; Campione, Joseph C.; Day, Jeanne D. "Learning to Learn: On Training Students to Learn from Texts." *Educational Researcher* (February 1981): 14–21.

7. Burton, Albert. "Purple Marbles and Little Red Hula Hoops." *Reading Teacher* 24 (April 1971): 647–651.

8. Dohrman, Mary H. "The Suitability of Encyclopedias for Social Studies Reference Use in the Intermediate Grades." *Journal of Educational Research* 68 (December 1974): 149–152.

9. Dohrman, Mary H. "Stopping 'Copy-catting.' " *Elementary English* 52 (May 1975): 651–652.

10. Durkin, Dolores. "Reading Comprehension Instruction in Five Basal Reader Series." *Reading Research Quarterly* 16, no. 4 (1981): 515–544.

11. Durkin, Dolores. "What Classroom Observations Reveal about Reading Comprehension Instruction." *Reading Research Quarterly* 14, no. 4 (1978–1979): 481–533.

12. Durkin, Dolores. "What Is the Value of the New Interest in Reading Comprehension?" *Language Arts* 58 (January 1981): 23–43.

13. Edfeldt, A. W. *Silent Speech and Silent Reading*. Stockholm: Almquist and Wiksell, 1959.

14. Garner, Ruth, and Reis, Ron. "Monitoring and Resolving Comprehension Obstacles: An Investigation of Spontaneous Text Lookbacks among Upper-Grade Good and Poor Comprehenders." *Reading Research Quarterly* 16, no. 4 (1981): 569–582.

15. Gaskins, Irene W. "Reading for Learning: Going beyond Basals in the Elementary Grades." *Reading Teacher* 35 (December 1981): 323–328.

16. Gibson, Eleanor J., and Levin, Harry. *The Psychology of Reading*. Cambridge, Mass.: MIT Press, 1975.

17. Gonzales, Phillip C., and Hansen-Krening, Nancy. "Assessing the Language Learning Environment in Classrooms." *Educational Leadership* 38 (March 1981): 450–452.

18. Guthrie, John T. "Purpose and Text Structure." *Reading Teacher* 32 (February 1979): 624–626.

19. Herber, Harold L. *Teaching Reading in Content Areas*. Englewood Cliffs, N.J.: Prentice-Hall, 1970.

20. Ireland, Robert J. "Let's Throw Out Reading!" *Reading Teacher* 26 (March 1973): 584–588.

21. Johnston, Peter. "Implications of Basic Research for the Assessment of Reading Comprehension." Technical Report No. 206. Urbana: University of Illinois, Center for the Study of Reading, May 1981.

22. Laughlin, Rosemary M. "The State of School Dictionaries." *Language Arts* 52 (September 1975): 826–830.

23. Locke, E. Q. *A Guide to Effective Study*. New York: Springer, 1975.

24. Perry, W. G. "Students' Use and Misuse of Reading Skills: A Report to the Faculty." *Harvard Educational Review* 29 (Summer 1959): 193–200.

25. Preston, Ralph C., and Tottle, John. *In These United States*. Boston: D. C. Heath, 1965.

26. Readence, John E., and Moore, David. "Strategies for Enhancing Readiness and Recall in Content Areas: The Encoding Specificity Principle." *Reading Psychology* 1 (Fall 1979): 47–54.

27. Rickard, John A., and Ray, Rolor E. *Discovering American History*. Boston: Allyn and Bacon, 1961.

28. Robinson, Francis P. *Effective Study*. New York: Harper and Row, 1961.

29. Smith, Frank. *Understanding Reading*. New York: Holt, Rinehart and Winston, 1971.

30. Smith, H. A.; Blecha, M. K.; and Pless, H. *Modern Science*. Level Six. River Forest, Ill.: Laidlaw Brothers, 1972.

31. Smith, H. A.; Blecha, M. K.; and Sternig, J. *Science 4*. River Forest, Ill.: Laidlaw Brothers, 1966.

32. Taylor, Barbara. "Children's Memory for Expository Text after Reading." *Reading Research Quarterly* 15, no. 3 (1980): 399–411.

33. Wann, K. D.; Vreeland, J. D.; and Conklin, M. A. *Learning about Our Country*. Boston: Allyn and Bacon, 1963.

34. Willmon, Betty. "Reading in the Content Areas: A 'New Math' Terminology List for the Primary Grades." *Elementary English* 48 (May 1971): 463–471.

35. Wolfe, Don M. *Language Arts and Life Patterns*. New York: Odyssey Press, 1961.

PART V

INSTRUCTIONAL MATERIALS

CHAPTER 13

BASAL READER PROGRAMS

PREVIEW

As was pointed out in Chapter 1, instructional materials can be anything that displays print: textbooks, trade books, magazines, comic books, signs, labels, menus, calendars, newspapers, billboards, stamps, greeting cards, license plates, telephone directories, candy wrappers, and so on. That materials ought to function by assisting, not dictating to, teachers was also underscored with the help of a comparison:

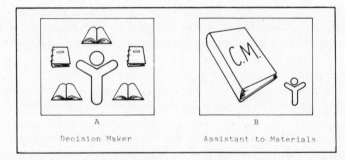

Many references have already been made to the best known of materials: basal readers. Such references are impossible to omit in a realistic account of school and reading, for it would be difficult to find an elementary school classroom that does not use one or more basal series. In recent years, pieces of basal programs have even made their way into kindergartens.

Because of the special influence that basal reader materials enjoy, they will now be discussed more directly, not for the purpose of promoting greater use but to describe a professional use. Or, to put it somewhat differently, Chapter 13 will show how Teacher A might use basal readers, manuals, and workbooks. To complete the picture, the chapter that follows this one discusses other kinds of materials, since even the best use of basals will not result in the best possible instructional program.

Even though teachers might not always verbalize their philosophy regarding instructional materials, each has one. Even the teacher who uses whatever happens to be on the shelves has a philosophy, questionable though it may be.

This text, too, has a philosophy. Some of its tenets are based on facts—for instance, that no single material is best for all students. Others are the result of classroom visits during which reactions to materials were observed. Part of the philosophy is also personal taste and therefore anything but scientific.

That very little about instructional materials *is* scientific has been emphasized in many publications but never so clearly as in Jeanne Chall's report, *Learning to Read: The Great Debate* (4). From a three-year study she concluded that even the most widely used materials are more the product of convention and market demands than of research findings and that the claims and guarantees that publishers make are rarely backed up by carefully collected empirical data. Now, almost two decades later, the conclusions still remain accurate.

That the perfect material does not exist naturally raises questions about using something like a basal reader manual as if it were divinely inspired. It should also highlight the need for teachers to be constantly searching for the combination of materials that seems best for a particular group of students or for certain children within the group. It is to help with just such a search that the present chapter and the next one were written.

Unintentionally, a reference to the need to be searching might have conveyed the idea that in every school the question of what materials to use is wide open. To those who would relish such a possibility and to those who would find it threatening, let me point out that such freedom is rare. In some schools, many restrictions are placed on what can be used; in others, certain materials are required, but opportunities to choose supplementary materials are available. In a very few schools, on the other hand, restrictions are practically nonexistent. Because of the variation, the descriptions of materials in this and the following chapter are designed, first, to help teachers use better whatever it is that must be used and, second, to help them choose more wisely whenever choices are possible. When choices can be made, certain guidelines are helpful in ensuring that all or at least most of them will be wise.

The most basic guideline is that nobody is ready to decide on instructional materials until other decisions are made about what is to be accomplished with them. If what needs to be accomplished with a particular group is a clearer understanding of the difference between fact and opinion and of what it implies for reading, the editorial in yesterday's newspaper could be not only the least expensive but also the best choice. If, with another group—or an individual—the need is to provide help in noting important details, appropriate choices of materials include a menu or directions for playing a game. On the other hand, if certain students have learned to dislike reading because of unsuccessful efforts to master it, one obvious need is material that is of interest *to them* and that they can read successfully. With that in mind, a wise choice may be simply written but hardly elegant books about motorcycles or drag racing.

Attention to the important sequential connection between identifying goals and selecting materials suggests the correct role for materials: assisting a teacher in reaching as yet unachieved goals that are educationally significant. While no teacher is likely to quarrel with such a role assignment, undergraduates enrolled in my reading methods course forgot it when they were tutoring children. Even though the importance of selecting materials in relation to goals had been stressed and restressed, subsequent discussions of the tutoring showed that something else had been done. Repeatedly, students explained their selection of materials—they had a rich source to choose from in a materials center—with words like, "Oh, it looked interesting," or "I had heard about them and thought I'd see how they worked," or "I remembered you had talked about that in class." Rarely heard were professional explanations like, "I knew Jimmy had trouble remembering the different short vowel sounds, and I thought this practice material might help." Together, all the explanations demonstrated that a wealth of material does not automatically result in good instruction. They also were a reminder of the failure to get across a basically important guideline: *Instructional goals ought to be selected before thoughts turn to materials.*

Apparently other instructors are also less than totally successful in establishing the means-end connection between materials and goals because visits to classrooms do uncover teachers who, instead of letting materials assist them in realizing unmet needs, have allowed themselves to become subordinate to materials. Clearly in a subordinate role, for example, is the teacher who has a group read a story both silently and orally simply because that is what a manual said to do. So, too, is the one who decides what to teach on any given day by looking at what is required to fill out the next few pages in a workbook even if what they focus on will make little or no contribution to reading ability. The same questionable role is played by teachers who do not do something—for instance, do not give enough attention to word meanings—not because they think they are unimportant but because the commercially prepared materials they use do very little with vocabulary development.

In contrast with these illustrations is the teacher whose first priority is student needs, which, in turn, define goals. Among the means available to help attain the goals are materials, some of which will be described in this and the subsequent chapter. Emphasis on "some" is not an apology but a recognition of the fact that the marketplace is so filled—even cluttered—with materials, it is impossible to provide anything that even comes close to being a complete inventory.

Figure 13.1

The Fox and His Bag

One day a fox
 found a great big bee.
He put the bee in a big bag.
Then he took the bag
 and began to go along.
He went along and went along.
At last he came to a house.

61

Ruddell, Robert B., Taylor, Mark, and Adams, Phylliss, *Upside and Down,* Pathfinder Basal Reader Program, 1978, p. 61. Used by permission.

●   *This is from a reader labeled "Level 9," which contains first-grade material. Like all other easy basal readers, this one has an illustration on practically every page. While colorful illustrations do make a book attractive, they can take attention away from the text. Too many pictures of the wrong kind can also reduce (or eliminate) the need to read the text. What is attractive, therefore, is not necessarily desirable for teaching reading.*

Figure 13.2

John Muir,
Earth Planet, Universe

by Sam Leaton Sebesta

On a hill in the middle of the University of Wisconsin, a large rock bears the words MUIR KNOLL. It overlooks the soundless sailboats and tiny waves of Lake Mendota. Thousands of kilometers away, giant sequoias stand above a murmuring, pebbled stream. They are part of the Muir Woods of northern California.

About two days' journey north of Muir Woods, in the state of Washington, rises Mount Rainier. Climbers who are brave enough to try this peak stay overnight at Muir Camp. Farther north still—near Sitadaka, Alaska—Muir Glacier moves slowly down a mountain slope.

251

Ruddell, Robert B., Sebesta, Sam Leaton, and Ahern, E. Jeanne, *The Widening Path,* Pathfinder Basal Reading Program, 1978, p. 251. Used by permission.

● *This reader, Level 19, is from the same series and is said to be at the sixth-grade level. Like other advanced basal readers, it includes both prose (fiction and nonfiction) and poetry. It also has a short diary. If students are to learn how to read different kinds of material, the variety is essential.*

WHAT IS A BASAL READER SERIES?

It is almost taken for granted in elementary schools that one or more basal reader series will figure prominently in their instructional program. In many, in fact, they *are* the program. Originally, readers and workbooks for students and manuals for teachers made up a series; but, with the passing of time, the number of series as well as the makeup of each has expanded considerably. Now every publisher includes not only the core materials (readers, workbooks, and teaching manuals) but also such supplements as letter and word cards, ditto masters, tests, taped recordings, games, and pictures. (The amount of materials requires numerous authors, which is why each series is identified with a reference to the publisher's name.) The present discussion of basals concentrates on the core materials.

Basal Readers

Since it is an exceptional person who was not taught to read with basal materials, a detailed description of the readers seems unnecessary. Figures 13.1 and 13.2 show, first, what they are like now and, second, how the readers advance from simple text to more difficult selections. (Some series [17] print readers and workbooks in both braille and extra-large type.)

Prior to 1969, a basal program was composed of readers that divided as follows:

Text	Number of readers
Preprimer	3
Primer	1
First Reader	1
Second Reader	2
Third Reader	2
Fourth Reader	1
Fifth Reader	1
Sixth Reader	1
Seventh Reader	1
Eighth Reader	1

Starting in about 1969, publishers began to switch from grade to level markings. Since the numbering systems were not uniform, "Level 11" in one series might be what was previously called a Fourth Reader, whereas in another series the same level might be a Third Reader.

Presumably, one reason for the change in markings was to foster individualized instruction. That is, it was hoped that schools would now select readers not in relation to students' grade placements but on the basis of their reading ability. Another reason for the change to level markings was that kindergartens began to teach reading. Such an innovation created problems for publishers when the easiest materials in their series had first-grade labels. Problems also existed when schools employed a nongraded organization.

For unexplained reasons, a switch back to grade-level markings began in about 1980. (It is a generally accepted fact that the best-selling series have noticeable influence on others. Whether this accounts for the more recent change is unknown.) Now, therefore, descriptions like *primer* (rhymes with "swimmer") and *sixth-grade reader* are being used again.

Whether referred to by level or grade, the readers in each basal program are made up of content that gradually becomes more difficult. Difficulty is controlled, first of all, by vocabulary. That is, compared to more difficult readers, the easier ones in a series use fewer new words and repeat them more frequently. New vocabulary in the easier readers also includes more words that are common. On the assumption that content and sentence length also affect *readability*—a term referring to the difficulty of text—the easier readers have both shorter sentences and shorter selections, which have content assumed to be appropriate for younger children.

For at least half a century, reading specialists and researchers have tried to be scientific about measuring the difficulty of written text. One result is a number of readability formulas, the best known of which have been offered by William Gray and Bernice Leary (13), Irving Lorge (14), Rudolph Flesch (12), Edgar Dale and Jeanne Chall (6), and George Spache (15). To illustrate a formula, the one that Spache proposed is shown below.

Grade level of text = .141 average sentence length per 100 words + .086 percent of words outside the Dale 769 Easy Word List + .839.

The time required to use readability formulas prompted the development of other ways for assessing difficulty. For example, the Fry Readability Scale, shown in Figure 13.3, simplifies calculations considerably.

Recent complaints about readability formulas are more serious than the large amount of time required to use them, for they stem from more advanced conceptions of the comprehension process (11). The increased importance now being assigned to world knowledge, for instance, makes it natural to wonder how a formula can determine the difficulty of a given piece of text for particular readers since none accounts for what each reader already knows (or does not know) about the content. The fact that short sentences may contain less direct information and thus require more inferencing than longer, more explicit sentences is still another reason to wonder about the value of mathematical formulas that use sentence length as one variable. All this is to say that how to assess readability is among the many questions in reading that remain unanswered and thus continue to win researchers' attention. Meanwhile, individuals continue to use readability formulas with a trust that is not merited. It is possible, in fact, that

Figure 13.3

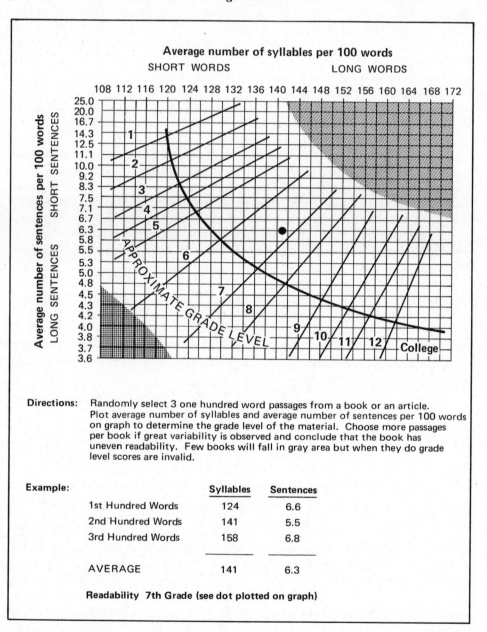

Directions: Randomly select 3 one hundred word passages from a book or an article. Plot average number of syllables and average number of sentences per 100 words on graph to determine the grade level of the material. Choose more passages per book if great variability is observed and conclude that the book has uneven readability. Few books will fall in gray area but when they do grade level scores are invalid.

Example:

	Syllables	Sentences
1st Hundred Words	124	6.6
2nd Hundred Words	141	5.5
3rd Hundred Words	158	6.8
AVERAGE	141	6.3

Readability 7th Grade (see dot plotted on graph)

From Edward Fry, *Reading Instruction for Classroom and Clinic* (New York: McGraw-Hill Book Company, 1972), p. 232. Copyright © 1972 by McGraw-Hill Book Company and used with their permission.

an experienced teacher's judgment about difficulty may be as accurate (or more accurate) as answers from existing formulas.

Basal Reader Teaching Manuals

Directions for using each selection in a basal reader, presumably to advance students' abilities, make up the manual that accompanies every reader. In some ways, then, the most important part of any basal series is its manuals, especially when teachers view them as something that should be followed closely. Unfortunately, what close adherence leads to has been identified in some analyses of manuals (1, 2, 9):

SOME OF WHAT TEACHERS WOULD DO IF THEY FOLLOWED MANUALS CLOSELY

Primary-grade level	*Middle- and upper-grade levels*
Give too little time to new vocabulary and word practice	Give too little time to new vocabulary and word practice
Teach phonics in a way that is overly obscure and indirect	Forget that phonics was taught earlier, and encourage students to use glossaries and dictionaries for help with troublesome words
Provide decoding practice using words children can read	
Divide selections in readers into parts even though the division makes comprehension more, not less, difficult	
Give more attention to expressive oral reading than to comprehending text	Do more to help students locate information (for example, in dictionaries and encyclopedias) than to teach them how to understand it
Ask an excessive number of assessment questions	Ask an excessive number of assessment questions
Assign too many brief, written exercises without ever clarifying the connection between the exercises and real reading	Assign too many brief, written exercises without ever clarifying the connection between the exercises and real reading

What needs to be done to compensate for flaws in basal manuals will be described later. Now it might be helpful to consider what the guideline referred to earlier (goals should be selected before thoughts turn to materials) signifies for teachers who are required to use a basal series.

When a school (or school system) chooses a certain series, it commits itself to the overall goals of that program. [Since teachers are an important part of selection committees, questions to consider when selecting a series constitute Figure 13.4. They are based on what was learned when the manuals of basal programs were analyzed (9).] In effect it is saying, "We need to provide instruction that results in large sight vocabularies, proficiency in decoding, comprehension abilities, flexible rates of reading, and students who like to read; and of all the series that are available, we think this one does the best job." What is important to note about such a commitment is that it does not bind any teacher to manual suggestions for each lesson. In fact, the responsibility of the truly *professional* person is to select from manual recommendations (a) only what will advance reading ability and (b) only what is needed by the particular group of students to whom the lesson will be directed. At any given time, therefore, what is suggested may be used, altered, shortened, lengthened, or skipped. What is important but *not* in a manual will have to be added by the teacher.

Figure 13.4   Selecting a Basal Series

SOME THINGS TO THINK ABOUT

Assumption: The most important piece of a basal series is the manual. Questions about manuals that ought to be considered are listed below.

New Vocabulary

1.   Do the selections in the readers contain an excessive number of new words?
2.   Do the manuals provide specific and ample help for teaching them?
3.   Are suggestions for word practice sufficient—and sufficiently varied and interesting?
4.   Are provisions made for periodic review of vocabulary?

Phonics

1.   Is the identification of sounds sufficiently explicit that all children will know exactly what is meant by expressions like "the sound that *f* stands for"?
2.   Does blending sounds to produce a syllable or word get attention?
3.   When something is taught, is it applied to *un*known words?
4.   Do middle- and upper-grade manuals encourage *use* of what has been taught by fostering periodic practice and review? Or is the solution for word problems, "Look it up in the dictionary or glossary?"

Structural Analysis

1.   Do the manuals give as much attention to the meaning of affixes as they do to their pronunciation?

2. Is instruction about word structure correct?

3. Do the manuals teach a specific strategy for dismantling and reassembling word parts that will allow children to work out the meaning and pronunciation of unknown derived and inflected words?

Contexts

1. Do manuals provide suggestions for teaching children exactly how to use contexts to arrive at the identity of an unknown word?

2. Is specific help offered for teaching the various ways in which a context may help with the meaning of a given word?

Vocabulary Knowledge

1. Does the series have a grade-by-grade plan for enhancing vocabulary knowledge?

2. Does the plan include procedures that are varied and also of interest to children?

Comprehension

1. When suggestions are made for advancing comprehension ability, are they of a kind that do deal with instruction, or are they merely an attempt to learn whether children are able to do something?

2. Are at least some of the many questions that appear in all the manuals of a kind that will advance children's ability to comprehend, or are they only concerned with finding out whether something in fact *was* comprehended?

3. If certain children have difficulty comprehending all or parts of a selection, does the manual provide helpful suggestions, or does it just offer more questions to ask them about the content?

Provisions for Individual Differences

1. What kinds of suggestions are made for coping both with children who require extra help and with those who need extra challenge? Does "Give them *more* of the *same*" characterize these suggestions or, on the other hand, are real alternatives offered?

Irrelevant Concerns

1. Do the manuals allot too much space to matters that will not contribute to reading ability—for example, to topics like career education and "creativity?"

The senior author of a basal series makes the same points about manuals:

The manual is not a recipe book—and it should not be used as one. You cannot add thirty-five children, fold in one teacher, slowly blend eight units from a basal reader, and get good reading by the end of the year. [5, p. 160]

Basal Reader Workbooks

Anyone brought up on basal readers knows about basal workbooks, since the latter always accompanies the former. Typically, workbook pages (coupled with ditto sheet exercises) are completed by students working alone, after they finish a selection in a reader.

If workbook pages always dealt with instructional goals not yet attained by the students who are being asked to do them, nobody could ever quarrel with such assignments. Nor would anyone question basal reader workbooks (and ditto sheet exercises) if all their content dealt with something that contributes to reading ability. However, since neither criterion is met consistently, questions do have to be raised about the automatic use of every page in every workbook even when they show no relationship to selections in the readers.

That a page does not match what students need or are ready to learn can be corrected simply by skipping it—perhaps to return to it later. That the content of pages does not always reflect the requirements of reading ability is a more serious shortcoming that can only be remedied by those who publish and write the workbooks. Meanwhile, superior teachers are sensitive to the possible lack of relevancy and devise their own practice whenever necessary. (The need to do that is the reason prior chapters list ideas for practice.)

Admittedly, providing for better practice than is sometimes found in commercially prepared materials is a tall order for new teachers who have not had the chance to accumulate better alternatives. With that in mind, the best advice for them is, first, be alert to flaws in the content of workbooks and ditto masters, and, second, substitute something better whenever that is possible. Other advice goes as follows: Even if you have neither the experience nor the time to be Teacher A right away, never allow yourself to be content being Teacher B.

One faculty that I am acquainted with was not about to let itself become a collection of Teacher B's and thus turned a summer workshop into a productive two weeks by tearing apart hundreds of old basal workbooks in order to organize pages according to the type of practice they provided. (Pages failing to deal with what is relevant for reading were discarded.) Eventually, all the pages were filed in a materials center on the basis of what they dealt with and at which level. When the school year began, teachers were free to make selections from the files whenever the regular classroom materials were inadequate.

Workshop time the following summer was spent on an evaluation of the organized pages and on presentations from each teacher about the way she or he had supplemented them with other ideas. Later, the best ideas were described on cards, also filed in the materials center. The product of this very cooperative effort on the part of a total faculty was an abundance of ideas for assignments and, as a result, new opportunity to develop a program marked by excellence.

To provide a contrast for this ambitious, professional faculty, a graduate student's account of what took place in a primary-grade classroom in another school system is given below. It depicts what can happen when basal materials are allowed to run a program.

> No attempt was made to ease the children into the lesson. Instead, once they were seated in the reading area, the teacher immediately began to review words printed on cards. Following that, she listed new words on the board and read them. There was no discussion of meanings, nor was any attempt made to put them into contexts. (It is possible that the teacher thought the children knew the words; however, if that was the case, why introduce them at all?) While this was being done, a number of children looked around the room rather than at the board.
>
> Next came an example of a teacher who followed a manual to the letter. (The close attention reduced eye contact with the children, making the whole procedure highly impersonal.) Predictably, the selection was read in round robin fashion. Since little had been done to prepare for the reading, it was not good. In fact, nobody really seemed to pay much attention to the oral readers—not even the teacher since she was busy reminding other children to follow in their books what was being read aloud. After a page was finished, questions were asked about every detail. The page-by-page approach made for disjointed content; it is possible, therefore, that the intermittent interrogation impeded rather than aided comprehension. (When the story was finished, I'd like to have asked the children to retell it to see whether they were able to grasp the wholeness of the tale.) When the oral reading ended, the teacher asked the group to open their workbooks so that three pages could be assigned, none of which pertained to the selection just read. As the children got up to leave, each received two ditto sheets.

WHAT ACCOUNTS FOR THE WIDESPREAD USE OF BASAL READER MATERIALS

Even though superior teachers have remedies for flawed materials, the shortcomings of basal reader series make it natural to wonder why their use is taken for granted practically everywhere. One explanation is the human trait known as habit. Another has to do with the risk involved in changing to something else when basal materials (plus other factors that contribute to achievement) result in adequate reading ability—or at least adequate test scores—for most students. Still another explanation is found in the question, But what else is there?

In theory, the best alternative to dependence on a basal reader series is an instructional program tailor-made for a particular school. In such a case, the faculty would (a) define instructional goals for all the facets of reading ability that were discussed in Chapters 5 through 12; (b) order them in a sequence that goes from what is easy to what is more difficult; and (c) decide on the best materials for attaining each goal. Because, in practice, faculties have neither the time, the interest, nor the competence to do all that such a mammoth undertaking requires, it has become customary for schools to rely on one or more basal series not only to provide for the core of their instructional programs but also to ensure coordination of efforts from one grade to the next. All this would have better results if teachers remembered that basal manuals offer suggestions, not prescriptions, and that any series must be complemented (and enlivened) with other kinds of materials—not necessarily commercially prepared.

Since how a basal series is used is critical, that topic is discussed next. First, though, consider what some teachers have done to supplement basal selections:

- A series of stories in a third-grade basal reader dealt with jungle animals. To introduce the unit, one teacher prepared a display of colorful *National Geographic* photographs of the same animals. Each was accompanied by a one-paragraph description followed by questions whose answers were not in the paragraph. Books that had the answers were also displayed.

- The next selection in a second-grade basal reader was about a cat. One teacher developed interest in reading the story by bringing in pictures of her own two cats, which resulted in a discussion about cats in general. By the next day, the teacher had prepared a bulletin-board display of cat pictures along with a table display of books about cats written at various levels of difficulty.

- In one fourth grade, students were ready to read a story about a boy who was discontented because he was not as big as his older brother and sister. How he learned that being big is not necessarily desirable constituted the plot. To provide some variety in what is done with basal material, the teacher asked the group to read the basal story, plus another very easy book about a young hippopotamus who wanted to be a bird but learned through a variety of experiences that being a bird is not all he had thought it would be. For the two books, the one assignment was as follows:

  > Even though "A Sad Little Hippo" is about an animal, it's very much like the story in your basal reader. In fact, the two stories are so much alike that the two could have the same title. Read both stories; then think of one title for both. So that you won't forget it, write your title below. Later, we'll discuss your suggestions to see which is the best for the two stories.

- Before a group began to read a basal story about penguins, the teacher read aloud a short, interesting, factual account of penguins. The preestablished purpose for reading the basal story was to decide whether its author was knowledgeable about penguins. Once the story was read, discussed, and compared with the factual account, fiction and nonfiction books about penguins would be added to the classroom library.

HOW BASAL MATERIALS OUGHT TO BE USED

Although minor variations are found from one basal series to another, the outline of a basal lesson presented earlier in Chapter 2 gives a fairly accurate picture of how manual suggestions in all the series are organized. Since the ensuing discussion of a professional use of basal materials reflects that outline, it is repeated in Figure 13.5 in a different form and with oral reading omitted. What Teacher A might do to make a basal reader lesson maximally productive will now be considered.

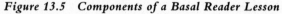

Figure 13.5   Components of a Basal Reader Lesson

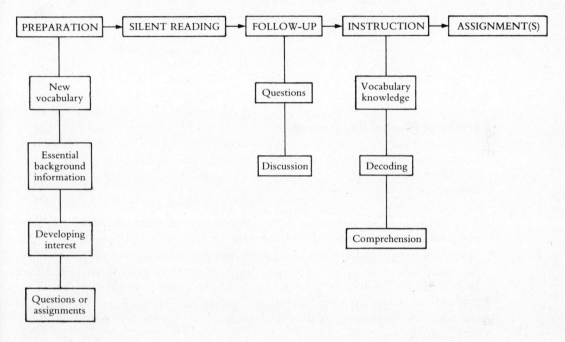

Read the Selection

Even though manuals often summarize what students will be reading, teachers should read the whole of a selection so that the kinds of comprehension problems the students may encounter can be identified. Unusual uses of language (for example, figurative expressions, similes, metaphors, sarcasm, hyperbole), long, complicated sentences, and short ones with much implied content illustrate possible sources of difficulty, which should be dealt with before students start to read. (Dealing with teacher-identified problems may be far more beneficial than following manual directions, since what the latter suggest for comprehension is more often concerned with testing it than with teaching it.)

Reading the selection beforehand also allows a teacher to identify the background information that is required to comprehend it. For example, if a plot makes sense only because the speed of airplane travel was not available when the story took place, students need to know that forms of available transportation now taken for granted were not always in existence. At other times, bilingual students may require certain preparatory information because of cultural differences.

The third reason for a teacher to read a selection ahead of time is to learn what is in it that *must* be comprehended. That, in turn, allows for a judicious selection of prereading questions.

To summarize:

> *Teachers should read a selection ahead of time*
> *in order to identify:*
> > potential sources of comprehension problems.
> > necessary background information.
> > what is important to comprehend.

Examine Manual Suggestions

Having read the selection, a teacher is ready to decide which manual suggestions to follow, ignore, or change. Comments designed to help with such decisions follow.

Preparation.   What is done before students read a selection is meant to facilitate comprehension without reducing interest in reading it. Minimally, attention should go to new vocabulary,★ necessary background information, and prereading questions, some of which may be in the manual. (Ideally, questions should both guide and motivate the reading. Ideally, too, some should come from the students so as to increase interest in reading the selection.) Depending on the selection, instruction with some aspect of comprehension might be necessary, too.

Silent reading.   At the very beginning, primary-grade manuals recommend page-by-page reading, each of which is preceded by questions and followed by discussion. At later levels, manuals may suggest dividing a selection into one or more parts, in which case each section is again preceded by questions and followed by discussion.

In contrast to a piecemeal approach, the recommendation here is to have students read a selection as a whole without interruption unless it is unusually long or difficult. If excessive difficulty is common rather than exceptional, it is possible that students are in the wrong reader. When basals are used, they should be at their *instructional level*. To clarify "instructional level," two additional descriptions are defined below:

★ What to do with new words was discussed in Chapter 9 under the heading "Teachers' Decisions about New Vocabulary."

Independent level. Material written at a level of difficulty that allows a child to read it without help.

Instructional level. Material that is difficult enough for a child that it will add to his abilities if used with an instructor.

Frustration level. Material that is so difficult that it cannot be understood even if help and instruction are available.

Postreading discussion.   Even though authors of primary-grade manuals seem to take it for granted that every selection should be read aloud, the recommendation for all grades is to follow the silent reading of a selection with discussion, either immediately or soon afterward. As the discussion proceeds, a teacher's concern should not just be for right or wrong answers; what lies behind the answers should be considered too. Erroneous responses, for example, may be evidence of the need for a certain kind of comprehension instruction. They may also indicate a need to return to the text to examine the source of the problem.

Instruction.   How well children read anything depends on what else they have read and on what they know and have experienced. It also depends on what they have been taught about the topics covered in Chapters 5 through 12. One time to offer this instruction is when basal reader selections get attention, since they generally provide suitable subject matter. Their vocabulary, for instance, might include examples for decoding instruction; certain sentences might serve to demonstrate a new use of contexts for help with word meanings; or the inclusion of certain signal words might allow for explicit attention to cause–effect relationships and how they are communicated.

If what is in a selection was used for comprehension instruction before the children read it, postreading time should allow for a check to see whether what was taught entered into the reading. This is important for bridging the gap between lessons and applying what they teach to actual reading.

Independent assignments.   Even a quick look through manuals makes it clear that all of them are generous with suggestions for written exercises, usually originating in workbooks and ditto masters. Since students do need to practice and use what they are learning, no teacher should apologize for giving written assignments—assuming that doing them *will* advance reading ability. When that is the criterion, written assignments usually are a combination of basal reader exercises and teacher-composed practice. In all instances, students should be able to see the connection between what they are asked to do and real reading. Otherwise, assignments inevitably end up being little bits and pieces that are not likely to have much effect on reading ability. In contrast, they may be highly effective in fostering negative attitudes toward reading.

Anyone giving assignments should also bear in mind an observation made by Spiegel (16):

Children deserve to be treated as thinking participants who do something not just because the teacher tells them but because they are aware of the purpose and nature of the task. [p. 325]

Outline Decisions

Once decisions are made about what will be attempted in a basal lesson, the results can be written on an index card (5″ × 8″) in outline form. (Teaching experience leads to increasingly brief outlines; however, even a new teacher should aim for brevity to avoid getting lost in details.) Use of a card during the course of a lesson helps with questions like, What do I do next? What examples should I use to explain this? Have I done everything? While adjustments will always have to be made for different groups of students, the outlines provide a good base from which to work.

If children are expected to do *their* work, it is advisable to give them copies of an assignment sheet, at the top of which prereading questions can be listed. (As has been mentioned, students should understand that they are not finished with a selection until they are able to answer the questions.) Next on the sheet comes very brief descriptions of other assignments—for instance, "workbook, pp. 38–39" or "fact-opinion sheet." The use of assignment sheets provides not only reminders of responsibilities but also practice in following written directions. At the same time, they allow teachers to give uninterrupted attention either to individuals or to small groups.

SUMMARY

Chapter 13 described what was referred to many times in earlier chapters: basal reader series. These materials warrant generous coverage in a methodology textbook because they not only influence but, at times, even shape teachers' behavior.

Core materials in a series are readers, workbooks, and ditto-sheet exercises for students, and manuals for teachers. Presumably, the readers provide instructional-level material while the workbooks and ditto sheets allow for various kinds of practice. How and when to use both the selections in the readers and the pages in the workbooks is explained in manuals.

Whereas a somewhat dependent use of basal materials may be justified in the case of new teachers, its continuation is not. Instead, each year of experience should find a teacher moving a little further away from manual prescriptions and a little closer to an instructional program that directly reflects the instructional needs (and interests) of a particular group. While some parts of the program will originate in basal manuals, others should stem from a teacher's knowledge of both her students and what it takes to be a proficient reader.

Because proficient readers are successful with all kinds of materials, the next chapter looks at some that can contribute not only to supplementing basal readers but also to making school reading more authentic than it can ever hope to be when a basal program is *the* program.

REVIEW

1.   When Chapter 13 described basal readers, it implied but did not state directly the meaning of *controlled vocabulary*. What *is* the meaning? How does a controlled vocabulary enter into the development of basal readers?
2.   (a) What is the meaning of *readability?* Why are traditional ways for measuring it being questioned? (b) How does readability differ from, yet relate to, the terms *independent level, instructional level,* and *frustration level?*
3.   Chapter 13 stated that some pages in basal reader workbooks should be bypassed because doing them will not advance students' ability to read. Find one such page and explain why it provides little more than busy work.
4.   What was not stated in Chapter 13 is that some workbook pages are so relevant for reading that they should be not only assigned but also expanded. Find one of these pages, explain the relevance of its content for learning to read, and tell how it could be expanded.
5.   What is meant by, "A truly professional teacher never allows herself to become merely an assistant to materials"?
6.   After reading Chapter 13, you should be able to explain the following sketch, which was referred to in Chapters 1 and 3.

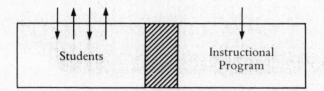

What is the connection between the message inherent in the sketch and basal materials?

REFERENCES

1.   Beck, I. L., and McCaslin, E. S. "An Analysis of Dimensions That Affect the Development of Code-Breaking Ability in Eight Beginning Reading Programs." Pittsburgh, Penn.: Learning and Development Center, University of Pittsburgh, 1978.

2.   Beck, Isabel L.; McKeown, Margaret, G.; McCaslin, Ellen S.; and Burkes, Ann M. "Instructional Dimensions That May Affect Reading Comprehension: Examples from Two Commercial Reading Programs." Pittsburgh, Penn.: Learning Research and Development Center, University of Pittsburgh, 1979.

3.   Broudy, Eric. "The Trouble with Textbooks." *Teachers College Record* 75 (September 1975): 13–34.

4.   Chall, Jeanne S. *Learning to Read: The Great Debate*. New York: McGraw-Hill, 1967.

5.   Clymer, Theodore. "The Structured Reading Program," in *Readings on Reading Instruction*. Edited by A. J. Harris and E. R. Sipay. New York: David McKay Company, 1972.

6.   Dale, Edgar, and Chall, Jeanne S. "A Formula for Predicting Readability." *Educational Research Bulletin* 27 (January 1948): 11–20.

7.   Durkin, Dolores. "The Importance of Goals for Reading Instruction." *Reading Teacher* 28 (January 1975): 380–383.

8.   Durkin, Dolores. "Phonics: Instruction That Needs to Be Improved." *Reading Teacher* 28 (November 1974): 152–156.

9.   Durkin, Dolores. "Reading Comprehension Instruction in Five Basal Reader Series." *Reading Research Quarterly* 16, no. 4 (1981): 515–544.

10. Durkin, Dolores. "Some Questions about Questionable Instructional Material." *Reading Teacher* 28 (October 1974): 13–17.

11. Durkin, Dolores. "What Is the Value of the New Interest in Reading Comprehension?" *Language Arts* 58 (January 1981): 23–43.

12. Flesch, Rudolph F. *Marks of Readable Style: A Study of Adult Education*. New York: Bureau of Publications, Teachers College, Columbia University, 1943.

13. Gray, W. S., and Leary, Bernice E. *What Makes a Book Readable*. Chicago: University of Chicago Press, 1935.

14. Lorge, Irving. "Predicting Readability." *Teachers College Record* 45 (March 1944): 404–419.

15. Spache, George. "A New Readability Formula for Primary-Grade Reading Materials." *Elementary School Journal* 52 (March 1953): 410–413.

16. Spiegel, Dixie Lee. "Desirable Teaching Behaviors for Effective Instruction in Reading." *Reading Teacher* 34 (December 1980): 324–330.

17. Ward, Marjorie. "Reading Instruction for Blind and Low Vision Children in the Regular Classroom." *Reading Teacher* 24 (January 1981): 434–444.

CHAPTER 14

LANGUAGE EXPERIENCE AND OTHER MATERIALS

Language Experience Materials
> Guidelines for Using Language Experience Materials
> Use of Language Experience Materials with Younger Children
> Use with Older Students

Trade Books

Still More Materials

Concluding Comments
> Basic Skills, Abilities, and Understandings
> Special Instructional Needs
> Usefulness of Reading
> Literary Experiences

Summary

Review

PREVIEW

As was pointed out in the previous chapter, the need for sequential, coordinated instruction from grade to grade is one major reason why basal reader programs are found everywhere. Since they are, it is essential for all who use them to keep in mind that even if their manuals and practice materials were better than they now are, using nothing but a basal program has built-in limitations. One lies in their inability to teach in ways that relate what is done to particular children. Another limitation when basals are used exclusively (and by Teacher B) is their failure to connect what is done with reading in school with what might be called real reading. Too often, in fact, how a basal series functions results in a portrayal of reading that equates it not with pleasure and usefulness but with doing exercises. What all this points up is the need to complement basal materials with others that (a) personalize learning to read, (b) allow for reading just for the sheer fun of it, and (c) make reading seem relevant to life outside school. Materials that help realize these goals are the main concern of this chapter.

Chapter 14 starts with language experience materials because they are uniquely equipped to add both a personal touch and relevancy. The fact that they can also be a means for advancing reading ability is illustrated.

Since the use of language experience materials usually leads to creative writing, Chapter 14 goes on to describe how teachers can stimulate that, which is pertinent for a book about reading because what one student writes provides others with something to read. Also providing students with something to read are trade books; thus they are considered, too.

The chapter concludes with descriptions of a few additional commercially prepared materials, selected because they are helpful when older students have limited reading ability.

To put all materials into a correct perspective, what is a means and what is the end needs to be distinguished and kept in mind:

Means	*End*
Decisions about:	Individualized
objectives and procedures	instruction
for lessons	
materials	
assignments	

While individualized instruction is the best way to ensure that students learn to read, it cannot guarantee that they will want to read. Teachers who appreciate the importance of interest and motivation naturally think of language experience materials because they are one of the most effective ways to relate what is done to students' interests. They can also make a special contribution to work with bilingual children.

LANGUAGE EXPERIENCE MATERIALS

Superior teachers have never had to be told that children are interested in their own experiences and that a written account of them is as much a reader as is a textbook. Over the years, however, some professional educators (2, 6, 13) have proposed a more formalized rationale for using language experience materials:

1. By the time children enter school, they have had a large number of experiences.
2. They have sufficient ability in oral language to tell about them.
3. When what they say is written, the accounts can be used to teach reading.

The conception of language experience materials in this book is broader than what is implied above, for it sees them as encompassing any noncommercial text that deals with the interests and experiences of an individual or a particular group. Whether the words are identical or only similar to what one or more children said is also thought to be less critical than that the content be current and relevant. Within that framework, material like that in Figures 14.1 and 14.2 is "language experience" and so, too, are invitations, thank you notes, messages for greeting cards, a letter to parents; reactions to pictures, books, or a walk in the

Figure 14.1

NARRATIVE CHARTS

Gingerbread Boys

Each of us made
    a gingerbread boy.

They were brown.

They were good
    to eat.

A cooking experience

Wild Flowers

We went for a walk.

We looked for wild flowers.

We found many kinds.

They were many colors.

They were many shapes.

An excursion

Sandra's Cat

Sandra's cat came to school.

Her mother brought it.

It was hungry.

We fed it some milk.

It slept in a basket.

We liked the little white
    kitten.

A visit from a pet

54

Lee, Dorris M., and Allen, R. V. *Learning to Read through Experience,* 2nd ed. Copyright ©
1963. Reprinted by permission of Prentice-Hall, Inc., Englewood Cliffs, N.J.

Figure 14.2

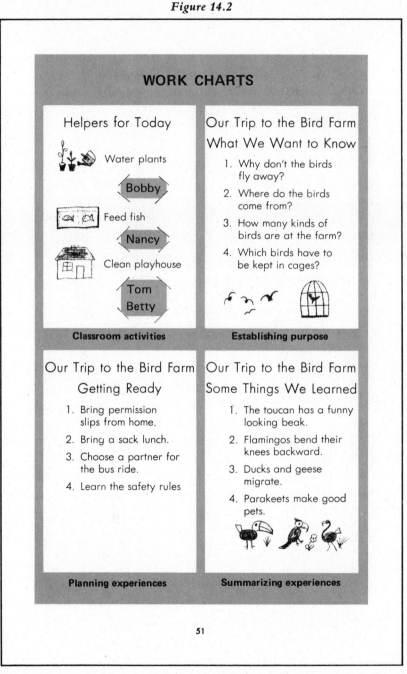

WORK CHARTS

Helpers for Today

Water plants

Bobby

Feed fish

Nancy

Clean playhouse

Tom
Betty

Classroom activities

Our Trip to the Bird Farm
What We Want to Know

1. Why don't the birds fly away?
2. Where do the birds come from?
3. How many kinds of birds are at the farm?
4. Which birds have to be kept in cages?

Establishing purpose

Our Trip to the Bird Farm
Getting Ready

1. Bring permission slips from home.
2. Bring a sack lunch.
3. Choose a partner for the bus ride.
4. Learn the safety rules

Planning experiences

Our Trip to the Bird Farm
Some Things We Learned

1. The toucan has a funny looking beak.
2. Flamingos bend their knees backward.
3. Ducks and geese migrate.
4. Parakeets make good pets.

Summarizing experiences

51

Lee, Dorris M., and Allen, R. V. *Learning to Read through Experience,* 2nd ed. Copyright ©
1963. Reprinted by permission of Prentice-Hall, Inc., Englewood Cliffs, N.J.

neighborhood; questions to pose to visitors; directions for making something, getting somewhere, or carrying out an experiment; and captions composed by students for their art (see Figure 14.3)

Guidelines for Using Language Experience Materials

Guidelines for using language experience materials are given below in the form of answers to frequently posed questions.

Should they be used with an entire class? The most ideal use involves one child, which means that classrooms in which there are teacher aides can (or should) offer numerous opportunities for highly personal uses of language experience material. Reality being what it is, unassisted teachers usually work with a small group since a whole class should be involved only when an experience is of great interest to everyone. (Also placing limits on whole class work is that differences in reading ability increase as students move from one grade to the next. What is productive for some, therefore, will be too difficult or too elementary for others.)

How does a teacher decide when to use the children's words, when to modify them, and when to do the composing herself? This question brings the discussion back to the dependent relationship between goals and teaching procedures, because some goals (for example, to show the connection between oral and written language) point directly to the need to use whatever children say, whereas others point in different directions. If what children say, for instance, is not spoken in sentences and one preestablished goal for the material is to teach that a period signals the end of a sentence, a teacher will need to compose sentences based on the fragments.

For anyone who might frown upon support for a teacher's sentences in a discussion of language experience material, let me relate what one highly effective remedial reading teacher did with seven boys ranging in age from ten to thirteen. (The description will also show that language experience materials—as the term is used in this book—are not just for younger children.) Contrary to what has been suggested, these boys were *not* interested in having what they said written. In fact, anything even dimly related to reading or school quickly turned them off. Having tried everything she could think of to get them involved—yet failing to do so—this teacher finally hit upon the possibility of capitalizing on the boys' enthusiastic interest in cars and in eventually getting a driver's license.

To start, she procured copies of *Rules of the Road* for her state. An examination of the pictures and chapter titles constituted the boys' initial contact with the book, which, fortunately, was enough to spark interest in a more careful study of the content. That proceeded as follows.

Since the material was too difficult for the boys to read on their own, the teacher started by reading aloud the first couple of pages. This was designed to add authenticity to her own highly simplified version of the book, copies of which were distributed next. At first, key words were selected for identification and practice. Meanwhile, common words like *the, from,* and *you* were reviewed.

Figure 14.3

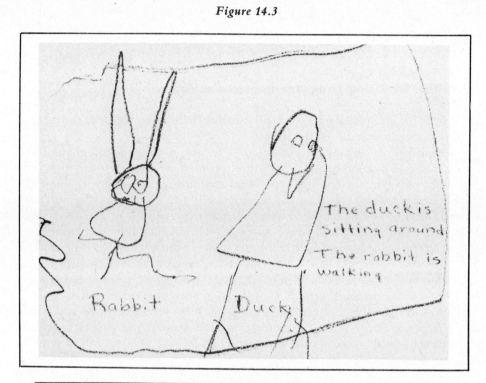

Once vocabulary was taken care of, comprehension took on importance. Generally, details were the focus of the silent reading, since they are commonly tested in drivers' examinations. As was recommended earlier, the silent reading was preceded by questions and followed by answers and discussion—and often more questions. Whenever disagreement about an answer occurred, parts of the text were read aloud as a way of verifying the correct answer.

The seven boys were tested periodically since that is a requirement for getting a driver's license. Periodically, too, the simplified material allowed for attention to structural analysis *(multilane, intersection, crosswalk)* and to phonics *(rule, road, rural, red, right)*. Often, it necessitated a study of word meanings *(pedestrian, minimum, merge)*. In fact, one product of the work was a glossary with definitions that the boys themselves provided. Preparing the glossary made it natural to review alphabetical order and how it functions in organizing or finding something.

What the practices of this excellent remedial teacher underscore for the present discussion is that, under certain circumstances, teacher-composed sentences elicit as much interest as does student-composed material.

How can a teacher ever know who is learning what? The teacher just referred to had no trouble keeping track of what she attempted to teach or of who was learning what. She met with the seven boys for forty-five minutes daily, and she knew them well enough to be fairly certain about what to select and how to proceed. Additionally, the group was sufficiently small and homogeneous in ability that she was often able to work with all seven at once. Whenever individual students needed extra help or one more explanation, she had time for that, too.

With classroom teachers, life is more complicated. Not only are there more students but there also are greater differences among them. Certain students, therefore, may be working with one basal reader whereas others are in a different one. Meanwhile, their teacher is trying her best to allow time for language experience materials to add the personal touch. It goes without saying that managing all this can be difficult; thus it is normal to hear questions about keeping track of who is learning what. To answer, a few preliminary comments are necessary.

To begin, even primary-grade teachers should not try to develop an instructional program based solely on language experience materials unless they are exceedingly knowledgeable about reading, highly skillful in teaching it, and *very well* organized. Since not everyone has all these qualifications (plus a willingness to spend a great deal of time on preparations), language experience materials typically supplement, rather than replace, one or more basal reader series. Within that framework, keeping track of who is learning what can be accomplished in connection with the basal program. This allows for less concentrated efforts to identify exactly what is being learned when language experience materials are the focus. The more relaxed (not indifferent) posture is easy to defend when the two main reasons for using these materials are kept in mind: to motivate students to want to read and to personalize what is done with reading in school. One further contribution lies in the fact that language experience materials present no comprehension problems. They may, however, provide material for comprehension instruction about such topics as words signaling opinions, cause-effect relationships, and distinctions between important and unimportant details. In addition to helping with connected text, language experience material also allows for attention to individual words in the form of word practice, or instruction in phonics and structural analysis.

Use of Language Experience Materials with Younger Children

Now that guidelines have been offered for using language experience materials, a more specific consideration can be accomplished by examining what a kindergarten and a first-grade teacher did. Correctly, what each did was affected by preestablished goals.

Goals: *To teach what is meant by* word.
           To teach the function of empty space in establishing word boundaries.

After lunch, a magician from the community put on a show for kindergarten and first-grade children. Subsequently, one of the two kindergarten teachers wisely took advantage of the special event to work on the two goals just named. Following is the conversation that took place after the children had made spontaneous comments about the show. (In this case, the interest of all in the topic allowed for whole class work.)

Teacher: To make sure you don't forget some of the things we saw the magician do, I want to write them for you here [pointing to the chalkboard]. Who wants to tell us one thing the magician did?
Kevin: He pulled a rabbit out of a hat!
Teacher: He sure did. Let me write what you said, Kevin. Say it one more time.
Kevin: He pulled a rabbit out of a hat.
Teacher: Who remembers something else that the magician did? Margie, what did you see him do?
Margie: Pick a black ace out of a deck of cards.
Teacher: Yes, he did that, too. Let's see now. Kevin said, "He pulled a rabbit out of a hat." What do you want to say?

Soon the chalkboard displayed:

He pulled a rabbit out of a hat.

He pulled an ace out of a deck of cards.

He threw up lots of balls and always caught them.

To realize the two preestablished goals, procedures similar to the following should be used. (They are listed now to underscore and demonstrate a guideline that has been mentioned many times before: *How* anything ought to be done depends on *why* it is being done.) A teacher should:

1. Say aloud each word as it is written. This allows children to watch talk become print.
2. Read the entire account in a natural speaking fashion, pointing to each word as it is identified.
3. Suggest to the children that they might like to read it. (As the children "read," the teacher reads along with them, all the while moving her hand across each line of text from left to right.)
4. Identify and point to the words that appear more than once. If the children are interested, let them "read" those words again.
5. Make a comment like, "There are so many words up here!" Then count them, pointing to each one. Show how a space separates one word from another. Next, have the children count the words. Point to each as it is counted.
6. Reread the entire account. Encourage the children to read along.

In addition to specifying what a word is and indicating the function of space to show word boundaries, the procedures just described (a) demonstrated how words are read from left to right; (b) showed that identical words look alike when they are written; (c) gave the children a chance to pretend they could read; and (d) gave them the opportunity to learn some words. If the group had been fairly small or if the help of an aide was available, the teacher might have asked each child for her or his favorite word. Named words could have been printed on small cards to be taken home to be read to parents and anyone else willing to listen. The cards could also be used to initiate individual and personal collections of word cards.

Goal: To teach the word red.

Wanting to teach *red* (*blue* and *green* are known), a first-grade teacher assembled a group of nine children near a chalkboard and began a discussion.

Teacher:	This really is a beautiful morning, isn't it? It was a good morning to look at things on the way to school. As I was driving, I saw leaves that were the most beautiful colors—green, yellow, red, orange. Did you notice anything as *you* walked to school?
Tonia:	My mother drove me.
Annamarie:	I saw some noisy motorcycles!
Teacher:	What color were they?
Annamarie:	I don't know. They were too noisy.
Teacher:	David, what did you see?

David:	I saw Tommy's new bike.
Teacher:	What color is it?
David:	I forget.
Teacher:	Let's see if we can think of some things whose colors we remember. When you think of something, I'll write what you say up here [points to chalkboard]. I'll pick one color to get started. I'll take red. That's a good, bright color for a good, bright morning. Let me first show you what the word *red* looks like [writes *red* on board]. What does this word say?
Children:	Red.
Teacher:	To help you remember it, let's spell it [points to letters].
Children:	*R, e, d.*
Teacher:	What does this word say?
Children:	Red.
Teacher:	I'll name one thing that's red. My blouse is red. Watch me write what I just said. Now I'll read it [points to each word]. My blouse is red. What does this word say [points to *red*]?
Children:	Red.
Teacher:	Let's see if you can read all the words I just wrote [points to each].
Children:	My blouse is red.
Teacher:	Can you tell me something else that's red? George?
George:	Chicken pox and measles are red.
Teacher:	Wonderful! Watch as I write what George just told us.

Soon the chalkboard showed:

A fire truck is red.

Chicken pox and measles are red.

Lipstick is red.

A red crayola is red.

Part of the flag is red.

My daddy's pants are red.

What else should be done with *red* to make sure it is remembered depends on what the children know. If their entire reading vocabulary is *blue* and *green*, a teacher can use a ditto sheet showing something like a clown whose clothes will be colored according to one-word written directions: *red, blue, green*. With slightly larger vocabularies, word practice with connected text may be possible. Now a teacher might ask individuals to read cards like:

red, white, and blue	the green top	a little red hat

To personalize experiences with the new word, the attention given it might conclude with children's pictures of something red. All could start with "Red" printed at the top of their paper, which allows for a discussion of titles and capitalization. As the children finish their drawings, the teacher could print whatever comments or descriptions they want to add.

Other child-dictated material is in Figure 14.4, with possible goals for each listed on the page facing it.

Use with Older Students

All of the reasons for using language experience materials with young children tell why they are equally suitable for older ones who are struggling to achieve a modest amount of reading ability. The remedial reading teacher described earlier effectively verified their suitability for such students when she composed and used material relevant for those who drive automobiles. So, too, does another teacher who, if she is working with older girls, takes advantage of their interest in clothes, cosmetics, and hair styles both to stimulate an interest in reading and to develop materials. In this case, magazines and store catalogs are especially helpful.

A consideration of the potential of language experience materials for middle- and upper-grade students who are average or above average in reading brings creative writing into the picture, for it is a natural outcome of earlier uses of child-composed materials. When it is not, a teacher's greatest concern is how to get students' writing started. "They don't have anything to say" is the way one teacher recently expressed it. Coincidentally, on the very day she showed the concern, I saw a television ad for a cereal that underscored what is essential to remember: *To write, students must have something to write about.* The television commercial showed a group of young children watching a huge bowl filled with milk and cereal. As they listened to the pieces pop and crackle, an adult in the background inquired, "What do you suppose they're saying?" Promptly the children responded with contributions like "Watch me swim," and "I'm drowning," "Save me," and "Get out of my way."

What some teachers have done in classrooms to get thoughts and words flowing will be described now. Illustrations start with younger children and older ones with reading problems, then shift to what has been seen in middle- and upper-grade classrooms.

Taking advantage of children's self-interest, one teacher distributed paper at the top of which was printed "My name is _____." The children were asked to think of something that they especially liked and to draw its picture. Children who could print and spell explained their picture at the bottom (for example, *I like my swing set*). The teacher did the printing for those who either could not, or chose not to, print themselves.

The same "I like" theme was executed differently in another room. Following an interesting discussion of colors, the children were asked to name something that they liked, including its color. Later, individual responses (for exam-

Figure 14.4

①
Bobby:	I cut my leg yesterday.
Mary Pat:	A fire engine woke me up last night.
Vivian:	I'm going to my cousin's house right after school.

②

Guess Who?

This is a girl in our room.

She has very long hair.

It's brown.

Sometimes she has a ribbon in her hair.

She has a new baby sister.

Who is she?

③

Look for Spring

Look for the sun in the sky.

Look for bugs in trees.

Look for green grass.

Look for a robin.

Instructional Possibilities of the Material in Figure 14.4

① Basic understandings about written language

1.   *What is said can be written.*
2.   *What is written is read from left to right and from top to bottom.*
3.   *The meaning of* word.
4.   *An empty space marks the end of one word and the beginning of the next one.*
5.   *The end of a line is not always the end of a thought.*

② Vocabulary

1.   *Teach* she *and* has.
2.   *Review* is, a, in.

Function of question mark
What constitutes "sameness" in words

Reason why She *and* she *are the same word even though they look different.*

③ Vocabulary

1.   *Teach* for.
2.   *Review* the, in, *and* look.

Distinction between words that might be confused

four *(taught previously) and* for.

ple, *"I like purple farmer jeans," "I like brown ground," "I like white shoelaces"*) became captions for pictures.

A class in another school had been discussing feet: size, shape, function, and so on. Afterward, members cut outlines of one of their own feet to serve as covers for a one-page book. Soon they were writing such observations as:

> *Feet*
> They run.
> Feet can tiptoe.
> Feet get stepped on.
> Feet hurt.

In another room, "Numbers in My Life" was the theme of a discussion, which led to drawings and single-sentence captions like:

> There are eight rooms in my house.
> I am seven years old.
> We drove 300 miles on our vacation.
> I am exactly five feet tall.
> My mother says she's thirty but she's really more.

Other samples of writing in the early grades constitute Figures 14.5 through 14.7.

What older and abler students write is more substantial and, as a result, too long to quote or show. Instead of presenting illustrations, therefore, descriptions of what middle- and upper-grade teachers have done to stimulate writing will be provided. To be kept in mind is that what one student writes is reading material for others.

Intermittently over a period of several months, one fifth-grade teacher had adult show-and-tell. In this instance, adults in the community were invited to talk about their hobbies or interests. Among the topics discussed and illustrated were braille writing, cake decorating, shadow puppet plays, shell collecting, and radio-controlled model airplanes. Adults who traveled were also invited to bring slides and special items representative of a particular country or city. (One noticeably popular visitor, a woman who had lived in Liberia for two years, displayed a boa snakeskin "about three kids long.") Students prepared for a visitor by listing questions they hoped would be answered. After a visitor left, they discussed, wrote about, and sometimes illustrated what had been especially interesting, informative, or surprising. A class book for each visitor was the final product.

In another classroom, the final product of discussions was a book of illustrated descriptions of the oldest item in each student's home. Earlier, all had been encouraged to find out what was likely to be the oldest, to discuss it with their parents, and to note all its details. Along with other information about its origin and use, what was learned about the item resulted in interesting illustrated material for all to read and discuss.

Figure 14.5

it was   a   antalope   it   lived
in a   field   it had   a baby.
The End

Amy   A D   A   Dragon
A Dragon is bry. big.
My Dragon is Sik.
My Dragon is very very,
tall?

Figure 14.6

> What is a friend?
>
> A friend is some one who is fun.
> My friend are Connie
> Paula Julie Kataleen
> Jana Angela
> Rebecca

> I saw a red spiter and
> it had perpple spots he looked
> sille. and it had babys all
> difrot colrs and thay looked
> sille too.   Kathleen

Figure 14.7

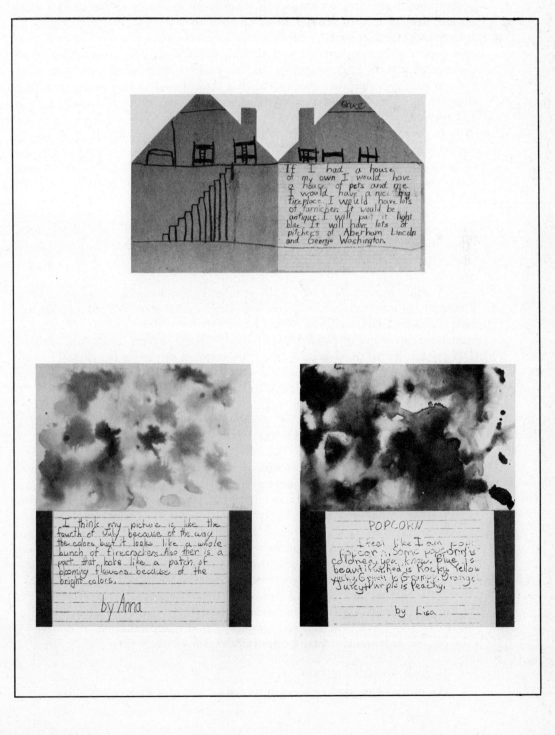

Working with some able boys who were less interested in school than she wished they were, another teacher used sports to get some reading and writing started. Resulting from her plans was a brief book per sport, each starting with a colorful magazine picture. Accompanying it was a glossary of terms that figured in the sport (including references to equipment), followed by an account of how the sport is played. In certain cases, the boys had to do research—consequently, some reading—when they discovered that they were less familiar with a sport than they at first thought they were. This was true for polo, soccer, jai alai, and rugby.

In another school, a teacher followed a similar plan except she took advantage of boys' interest in cars. In this case, the student-composed book had pictures of cars accompanied by accounts of the car's name, the company that made it, and its special features. Hunches about the kinds of people most likely to buy each kind of car were included.

In still another school, a teacher used wordless picture books to stimulate writing. In this case, students volunteered to compose text for the illustrations. When it was done, an author read his text while another child showed the pictures. (Reference 1 at the end of the chapter contains an annotated list of picture books.)

Another teacher used Pickle Week to enliven classroom activities in May. This seemingly unprovocative celebration produced slogans ("Send a pickle to a friend"), stories, and cartoons. The research that was done uncovered information about the origin of pickles, the kinds that exist, and the uses made of them. (Did *you* know that the average yearly consumption of pickles per person is eight pounds?) "What a perfectly delightful way to bring the year to a close" was the teacher's observation when the project ended.

TRADE BOOKS

Any teacher wise enough to remember that the constant assignment of ditto sheets is not the best way to motivate reading—or to characterize its true nature—sees to it that trade books are always close at hand. (As was explained in Chapter 12, a *trade book* refers to any that is written for library and bookstore markets rather than for instruction.) Paperbacks, large library loans, and temporary contributions from the teacher's and students' personal libraries do away with excuses for not having sizable, attractive collections. Garage sales and second-hand bookstores can also help bring classroom libraries into existence.

Whenever a library is being assembled, thoughts about variety should be in the foreground so that differences in students' interests and abilities can be accommodated. This is also the time to remember that independent-level material is valuable for such fundamentally important reasons as:

Promotes self-confidence.
Allows for the consolidation and realistic use of a variety of skills.

Develops good habits insofar as rate is concerned.

Moves attention away from individual words to the meaning of connected text.

Develops an interest in reading.

Reminders about the contributions of independent-level material are necessary because of the widespread, Puritan-like notion that only what is hard is good.

Realistically, it has to be recognized that the mere availability of suitable and interesting books is not always sufficient to get students to want to read them. This means that teachers sometimes have to take special steps to change their minds.* Allowing students to make their own selections (and doing away with such obligations as book reports) is one helpful step; however, if freedom of choice is to have any meaning, what is available must be known. Therefore, each time all or part of a classroom library is changed, the new possibilities must be announced—some might even be advertised—by showing a few illustrations or by reading just enough from each to spark curiosity about the rest of the book.

Other steps that teachers have taken to motivate reading are described next.

- Whenever students show special interest in a topic, our school librarian and I seek out books that pertain to it. Together, we usually succeed in finding material written at a readability level that each child can handle. Initially, I meet with the group of interested children to discuss the topic, to distribute books, and to set a date for a subsequent meeting. Often, postreading discussions are as mature as any that adults might have. One bonus feature is the opportunity that the discussions give to less able readers to make significant contributions, for very often what was in their books is just as informative as what originated in more difficult sources.

- Because my contacts with students are often impersonal, I meet as often as I can with individuals, ostensibly to discuss what they have been reading on their own. At such times I am more eager to learn how children feel about reading than to assess their abilities or deficiencies. These meetings give me a chance to recommend books or to find some that match expressed interests. I especially try to find out the questions that are important to students and then try to locate books that might offer answers.

- If children enjoyed a book, they may, if they wish, tell in writing why they enjoyed it. Recommendations are displayed on a board to assist anyone who is looking for a book. If multiple copies of a really good book are available, I feel no compunction about asking certain students to read it. We first meet as a group so that I can introduce the book and set a date for getting reactions. When we meet again, I am ready with questions, but I ask them only if something is needed to get a discussion started. If the children appear

* Ways to move from a basal reader selection to reading trade books were described in the previous chapter.

to have enjoyed a book, I am also ready to show others by the same author or similar books by different authors.

- Many of the new informational books—even those written at fairly simple levels—are more interesting than textbooks. Students like them better, too. That's why I encourage groups to do extra reading on topics that originate in social studies and science texts. With the supplementary reading, we often get contradictory information, which results in lively discussions and, very often, in further reading.

- Sometime each year I suggest the possibility of looking for interesting new words in self-selected books. To fan some interest, I couple the suggestion with a few examples I've come across in my own reading. (I always go out of my way to let students know that I am an avid reader.) At some designated date, interested students and I get together to discuss our findings.

- By the time children get to third grade, some are effective oral readers. With guidance from me or the school librarian, they select books that kindergartners and first graders would enjoy. After reading the books silently, they take turns reading them aloud to small groups of younger children.

- Whenever parents or other adults in the community have interesting hobbies, I invite them to tell my students about them. I then try to find books that relate to the hobbies. Parents who have traveled and have taken slides also speak to us. Again, I work with our librarian to find books about the places each person has been to.

- Into some of the trade books in my room I tuck cards that make a request. (Students call them the "Would you" cards.) One is: "Would you pretend that you're the author of this book as you read it? When you're finished, be ready to tell which parts of the book were the hardest to write." A card in another book might ask, "Would you get a friend to read this book when you're finished? Together, the two of you can make a mobile whose parts will show drawings of characters or scenes or happenings in the book. Later, you can use the mobile to tell others about it."

STILL MORE MATERIALS

Not to be forgotten in this discussion of materials that encourage reading are children's magazines. Like its adult counterpart, *National Geographic,* the one called *School Bulletin* is colorfully illustrated and highly popular.* Other magazines that attract young readers in large numbers are *Highlights*† and *Playcraft,*‡

* National Geographic Society, Washington, D.C.
† Highlights for Children, Inc., Columbus, Ohio.
‡ Parents' Magazine Enterprises, Inc., Bergenfield, N.J.

Figure 14.8

Melville, Herman. *Moby Dick*. West Haven, Conn.: Pendulum Press, Inc., 1973, p. 29.

both of which offer short articles, riddles, and many opportunities to make things with the assistance of written directions. Other magazines are available for older students who are below average in reading ability (4).

When the goal is to motivate reading, comic books cannot be overlooked for, like it or not, they have great appeal for some children. If "comic book" only conjures up thoughts of violence and monsters, you are invited to examine Figure 14.8, which shows a page from a collection of comic books based on classical tales like *Moby Dick, The Red Badge of Courage,* and *Kidnapped.* Anyone who questions using comic books in school is also invited to take note of the following observation in an article written by someone who is both a mother and a teacher:

> As the mother of three boys who, one after the other, were notoriously unmotivated to read and had to be urged, coaxed, cajoled, threatened, and drilled in order even to stay in the super slow group in reading, I wish to thank comic books for being a conduit, if not a contribution, to culture. [7, p. 54]

When older students have limited ability, another way to motivate reading is to make material available that is easy but has content and a format that are not oriented to younger children. One of the first set of materials to meet these criteria was the Reader's Digest *Skill Builders.** Following the format of *Reader's Digest,* these soft-covered books, which are revised periodically, contain brief and usually interesting selections written at readability levels ranging from first to ninth grade. "Audio units" (cassette tapes), which offer help with vocabulary and comprehension, are available too. The same publisher has *Science Readers* and *Social Science Readers* in recognition of the fact that some students are more interested in acquiring information than in reading stories. Should the latter be of interest, a number of easy-to-read books are available, some of which are suitable for older children (3). For teachers of all children, the yearly listing of books called "Children's Choices," which appears in the *Reading Teacher,* should be helpful for knowing both what to recommend and what to read to their students.

CONCLUDING COMMENTS

If the materials referred to in this chapter and the previous one were put alongside everything in the marketplace, they would look skimpy indeed, for what rolls off the presses these days seems unending. Like all forms of wealth, however, the endless array of materials has its own problems. "What in the world should I use?" pinpoints one. To answer, it is necessary to put materials into a perspective that recognizes the many different facets of an instructional program. Each will be discussed briefly in a way that highlights the relationship between the facets and materials.

* Reader's Digest Services, Inc., Educational Division, Pleasantville, N.Y.

Basic Skills, Abilities, and Understandings

No matter what educational philosophy guides a reading program, grade-by-grade attention to the basics is mandatory. That is, time must be used in such a way as to ensure that students (a) have a rich command of oral language, (b) have a substantial sight vocabulary, (c) are able to decode unfamiliar words quickly, (d) are proficient at comprehending connected text, and (e) read at varying rates depending on content and purpose.

A second requirement for every instructional program is coordination. This is necessitated by the large number of people involved (students, teachers, aides, administrators). Or to put it differently, the left hand has to know what the right is trying to do if repetition, gaps, and contradictions are to be avoided. This does not mean that left and right hands must work in identical ways, but it does mean that they must work cooperatively to ensure an organized, developmental plan. As was pointed out earlier, schools commonly rely on one or more basal reader series to take care of both the coordination and the basic skills. Even the best of such series, however, should never be thought of as "*the* program" but, rather, as one partial means for achieving certain preestablished goals.

Special Instructional Needs

Coping successfully with differences among students stands out as a key component in superior instructional programs. Typically, the success is rooted in a generous use of noncommercial materials and teacher-devised assignments, but it also goes along with a *thoughtful* selection of commercially prepared materials— for instance, workbooks dealing with a single topic, which are used only by children who need help in that area.

When highly able students are the concern, effective teachers never hesitate to use basal readers whose readability levels exceed the grade-level signs on their classroom doors. Nor would it be unusual to find in their rooms groups of students reading many different books as they pursue such interests as mythology, science fiction, mysteries, computer games, sports, or animals. All this is to say that teachers who offer individualized instruction are helped in no small way by materials, both commercial and homemade.

Usefulness of Reading

The usefulness of reading ability in the real world is often an untapped source of motivation, especially in classrooms where teachers spend most of their time giving and checking assignments that originate in workbooks and ditto sheets. In contrast, teachers who never lose sight of the need for students to appreciate the practical value of knowing how to read make generous use of materials like directions for playing games, the Yellow Pages in a telephone directory, store catalogs, cereal box offers for miniature toys, *TV Guide,* the sports page from the local newspaper, ads in children's magazines, and words for a popular song.

Literary Experiences

Any avid reader knows that reading ability has much more than just utilitarian value. For them, *not* to be able to read would result in a life drastically reduced in its ability to provide vicarious experiences, consolation, inspiration, relaxation, and enjoyment. Recognizing the tremendous potential, conscientious teachers do whatever they can to bring students and good books together. The same potential is the reason this chapter has singled out trade books as being an important part of classroom libraries and why it also recommended free-choice reading.

SUMMARY

Since the previous section provided a summary, let me conclude the chapter with quoted material from an article by a high school teacher. Although he makes the point somewhat dramatically, this author does succeed in underscoring the importance of selecting materials that have significance for those who will be using them:

> I have taught in high school for ten years. During that time I have given assignments to a murderer, an evangelist, a pugilist, a thief, and an imbecile. . . .
>
> The murderer awaits death in the state penitentiary; the evangelist has lain a year in the village churchyard; the pugilist lost an eye in a brawl in Hong Kong; the thief, by standing on his tip-toes, can see into my window from the county jail; the once gentle moron beats his head against a padded cell in a state asylum.
>
> All of these people once sat in my class. They sat and looked at me gravely across the worn desks. I must have been a great help to them—I taught the rhyming of the Elizabethan sonnet and how to diagram a complex sentence. [8, p. 57]

REVIEW

1. Exactly how does Chapter 14 underscore what was said earlier in the book, namely, that the most important question a teacher can ask is, "*Why* am I doing what I'm doing?"
2. Assume you are a first-grade teacher who uses language experience materials along with a basal reader series. During a parent-teacher conference, a mother says that if you would forget about "modern stuff" and spend more time with workbooks, her son would be a better reader. It turns out that

language experience materials are the "modern stuff." How would you respond to this parent's suggestion?

3. Were you surprised at the recommendation in Chapter 14 to use more independent-level material than is commonly the case in classrooms? Why (not)?

4. Starting with the instructional program, how would you explain the following diagram to someone who did not read Chapters 13 or 14? Be sure to refer to materials in your explanation.

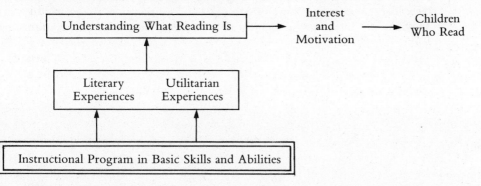

5. Explain the following: Providing an effective instructional program at all grade levels is one of the best ways to ensure that children not only *can* read but *do* read.

REFERENCES

1. Abrahamson, Richard F. "An Update on Wordless Picture Books with an Annotated Bibliography." *Reading Teacher* 34 (January 1981): 417–421.

2. Allen, Roach Van, and Allen, Claryce. *Language Experience in Reading.* Chicago: Encyclopedia Britannica Press, 1966.

3. Cunningham, Pat. "Books for Beginners." *Reading Teacher* 34 (May 1981): 952–954.

4. Graves, Michael; Boettcher, Judith; and Ryder, Randall. *Easy Reading: Book Series and Periodicals for Less Able Readers.* Newark, Dela.: International Reading Association, 1979.

5. Hacker, Charles J. "From Schema Theory to Classroom Practice." *Language Arts* 57 (November–December 1980): 866–876.

6. Hall, Mary Anne. *Teaching Reading as a Language Experience.* 3d ed. Columbus, Ohio: Charles E. Merrill Publishing Co., 1981.

7. Haugaard, Kay. "Comic Books: Conduits to Culture?" *Reading Teacher* 27 (October 1973): 54–55.

8. Lajoie, Ronald. "More Than Teaching." *Elementary English* 52 (January 1975): 55–58.

9. Lee, Dorris M., and Allen, R. V. *Learning to Read through Experience*. New York: Meredith Publishing Co., 1963.

10. Moss, Joy. "The Fable and Critical Thinking." *Language Arts* 57 (January 1980): 21–29.

11. Nessel, Denise, and Jones, Margaret. *The Language Experience Approach to Reading: A Handbook for Teachers*. New York: Teachers College Press, 1981.

12. Quandt, Ivan. "Investing in Word Banks—A Practice for Any Approach." *Reading Teacher* 27 (November 1973): 171–173.

13. Stauffer, Russell G. *The Language-Experience Approach to the Teaching of Reading*. New York: Harper and Row, 1970.

14. Troy, Anne. "Literature for Content Area Reading." *Reading Teacher* 30 (February 1977): 470–474.

PART VI

IDENTIFYING INSTRUCTIONAL NEEDS

CHAPTER 15

ORGANIZING FOR INSTRUCTION

PREVIEW

If a knowledgeable classroom teacher had no more than about ten students who were alike in such critical factors as reading ability, family background, interests, and personality, delivering successful and relevant reading instruction would be fairly easy. As it is, large numbers of students and great differences among them combine to make both teaching and classroom management very difficult.

Possible means for working with as many as twenty-five or thirty children who vary in ways that are significant for teaching reading is the subject of Chapter 15. It deals with the logistics of instruction by considering the three possible "audiences" to which a teacher can offer instruction, namely, the entire class, one student, or a small group.

Underlying all of Chapter 15 is the most important point that can be made about classroom organization: it is a means for attaining individualized instruction. Together with decisions about other features of a program, whatever is done to organize both students and available time should reflect that end.

Also underlying the chapter is the fact that no one best way exists for managing a classroom. What Chapter 15 does, therefore, is describe possibilities, not formulas. If you are teaching, you might want to use what is described as a standard against which your own organization can be evaluated. Or, if you are not teaching, compare what is said with what you remember about classrooms when you were an elementary school student. Before any comparison is made, all readers of the chapter should profit from reading the summary at the end of the chapter.

Even a few visits to classrooms are enough to underscore the need for well-organized teachers. A successful teacher, in fact, might be compared to a symphony orchestra leader who is able to synthesize into a meaningful, harmonious whole a large number of different instruments and musicians.

I know nothing about the intricacies of successful orchestration, but I do know from experience that organizing a classroom in a way that facilitates individualized instruction is no small feat. A speaker I once heard expressed my own feelings when he said, "Effective organization is the end product of trial and error." Inherent in his observation is that getting students, materials, and time organized in the most productive way possible is an evolutionary process that gradually progresses with decisions made throughout the year.

DIFFERENCES AMONG TEACHERS

One decision that is not always made consciously has great impact on all the others. I refer to teachers' priorities—that is, to the importance that they assign to such things as individualized instruction and practice, oral and silent reading, basal reader materials, free reading, and students' interests.

Why a decision about priorities (whether made consciously or unconsciously) is an encompassing one can be shown by comparing two teachers. The first views her major responsibility as having all students complete a basal reader, the workbook that goes with it, and all the ditto-sheet exercises that the publisher of the series provides. As a result, she uses the time assigned to reading in a way that differs greatly from what a second teacher does whose priorities can be identified in the following statement:

> The major goal of my instructional program is to develop each child's potential for comprehending print via silent reading. To attain it, instruction and practice must focus on whatever it is that will advance each child's abilities. To keep children involved and trying, every effort must be made to help them see the relevance of reading in their own lives. The importance of motivation for learning also makes it important to have materials that match not only their abilities but also their interests. In the end, I evaluate myself not just on the basis of how well the children read but also by the frequency with which they *do* read.

While teachers' priorities are undeniably significant for the way classrooms are run, so too are their personalities. On this point, Wallen (17) offers sound advice to teachers:

You should be frank about the fact that the best degree of structure is largely how *you* define it. Some teachers cannot tolerate much movement in the classroom. They feel distinctly uncomfortable when a child moves around the room in an apparent search for adventure. On the other hand, some teachers feel the same degree of discomfort if children are too quiet and too still. They enjoy movement and the ambiguity that characterizes it. Because you must live comfortably in the classroom, you should . . . allow for as much structure as you and the children find comfortable. [p. 475]

DIFFERENCES AMONG STUDENTS

Although differences in teachers inevitably lead to variation in how instructional programs are organized and executed, the effect of the differences that characterize their students is less predictable. In some cases—and this is the ideal—teachers match their instructional program to particular children to the greatest degree possible. Now, individualized instruction is common, not rare. In other instances, what is done at each grade level is set (generally in accordance with a basal reader series) even though the students at each level vary from year to year. You will recall that this rigidity was depicted earlier as follows:

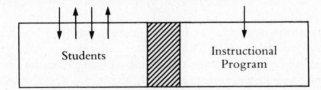

If large numbers of students are ever to realize their potential insofar as reading is concerned, certain differences among them *must* be taken into account whether teachers are making plans for a year or a day. In this chapter, differences are identified and discussed in the context of the three ways in which teachers can spend their time: working with an entire class, working with one child, and working with a small group. Although each possibility will be discussed separately, spending time in all three ways is characteristic of the most effective of teachers.

WORKING WITH AN ENTIRE CLASS

When classroom organization is viewed as a means for realizing individualized instruction, it is natural to wonder, Should teachers *ever* work with an entire class? Both the means-end framework and the need for efficiency suggest an answer: Whenever an entire class has need for the same instruction or practice, it makes very good sense to work with everyone together. Let me describe, therefore, examples of whole class needs.

If just about everyone in a third grade reads aloud in a way that lacks luster and sparkle, their teacher might have the entire class participate in choral reading, using material that everyone can read. This means that selections might be fairly easy for some; however, since the purpose is to improve oral reading, it is unnecessary—even undesirable—to give each student the most difficult material he is capable of reading. About once each month, then, time will go to choral reading as a way of fostering appropriate expression.

Another illustration of whole class work comes from a second grade in which the current topic in science is magnetism. Demonstrating that what is said in the present chapter applies to content subject instruction as well as to the reading period, this example describes another set of circumstances that makes intermittent work with an entire class defensible.

Let us assume, first of all, that certain concepts and vocabulary dealing with magnetism need to be taught. It will also be assumed that some students are able to read the science textbook without help whereas others have to struggle with every page. Such differences make one-textbook teaching inappropriate, so what should one do? As always, a variety of procedures is possible. One teacher begins by showing a film. With interesting equipment and a variety of experiments, it teaches the whole class about magnetism, emphasizing the meaning of words like *magnet, attract,* and *metal.*

What should be done after the film is shown and its content is discussed? One teacher may decide to work with the seven children who need further review of the film's content as well as help in learning to read words like *magnet, attract,* and *metal.* While this instruction takes place, the remaining children divide between those using reference materials to get more information about magnetism and those reading about the experiments they will soon be demonstrating to the class. One of these children might also be asked to prepare to read orally from a brief but interesting book about magnets.

Later, the teacher shifts to the more advanced children in order to discuss what they learned from their independent reading. Simultaneously, the student who prepared for the oral reading is instructing the less able children by reading aloud from the book about magnets.

Current research with comprehension suggests that having a teacher (or able child) read aloud to a group is a procedure that should be used more often than it is. I refer to studies that show the fundamental importance of background information for reading comprehension, whether the text is a story or a chapter in a science textbook (1, 2, 7). One such study, for example, demonstrates how understanding the nature of fables (in particular, how certain animals serve to personify certain traits) contributes substantially to the ability to comprehend this genre (7). The oral reading of fables, therefore, coupled with discussions and comparisons, is still another example of productive work that can be carried on with an entire class.

While something like a carefully chosen story read aloud (or, for example, choral reading) can get and keep every student's attention, classroom observations point out that other activities are much less successful in this regard. To illustrate, in one second grade the teacher introduced new basal reader vocabulary to the entire class. Explaining the procedure later, she said that she was a strict disciplinarian and thus was able to maintain sustained attention from everyone. Observing from the back of the room, however, revealed a sizable number of inattentive children while the words were being identified and discussed at the front.

Joined with many other observations in classrooms, what was seen in the second grade provides ample evidence that even when an entire class does stand to profit from a given piece of instruction, certain members may learn very little because of inattentiveness. This suggests that only when what is being done is likely to capture everyone's attention should whole class instruction take place.

WORKING WITH ONE STUDENT

At first glance, working with one student seems so inherently valuable that neither an explanation nor a defense of this use of a teacher's time appears necessary. Examples of such work, however, sometimes prompt a different conclusion. More specifically, a practice found to be exceedingly common when thirty-nine grade three through six classrooms were visited (10) goes as follows. The teacher distributes the same assignment sheets to the whole class, briefly describes what is to be done, and then walks around the room helping individual students who have problems completing the sheets.

By itself, the description does not explain why, in this instance, the individual help is questionable. Watching the practice repeatedly, however, made it apparent that the need to help individuals was the consequence of giving the same assignments to an entire class even though the ability of its members to do them was unequal. The moral of the story? "Private lessons" are desirable when the instruction that a particular student requires deviates substantially from what others need. Commonly, the requirement will be easier instruction.

Right now, easier instruction comes from personnel other than the classroom teacher—for instance, from a reading specialist. While, in theory, the potential of these sources of help for achieving individualized instruction is great, in practice problems may arise because of insufficient (or no) communication between the classroom teacher and the "special" teacher. One survey (9), for example, reached the following conclusion:

> A large proportion of teachers in the survey, 70%, reported that a specialist instructed students in their classes. However, less than half of these teachers reported ever receiving suggestions from the specialist. In other words, the addition of a specialist to a school staff typically means that selected children are taken out of the classroom on what is often called a "pull-out" basis. It is not typical for the specialist to give suggestions to the teacher or provide diagnostic feedback or materials. [p. 286]

Unquestionably, what any specialist does with or for a student ought to be coordinated with what that student's classroom teacher does and expects. Otherwise, the two plans may be at odds with each other, hardly helpful to a child who already has problems.

With a child whose "problem" is advanced ability, special teachers are not likely to be available. Classroom teachers, therefore, must do whatever they can to provide interesting challenge as well as the possibility for further advancement. With these students, instruction can focus on topics not customarily covered—at least not in any depth. Meriting attention, for instance, are the various literary genres and subjects like etymology and mythology. When the use of a basal series is mandatory, such students can also be challenged when materials that match their abilities (*not* the sign on the classroom door) are used.

WORKING WITH SMALL GROUPS

It probably is true to say that in effective instructional programs, teachers spend most of their time with individuals and small groups (14). To achieve individualized instruction, the small groups, hereafter referred to as *subgroups,* are organized in relation to the kinds of differences that characterize students in relation to reading. Two kinds that must be taken into account in every instructional plan are (a) differences in *general* achievement and (b) differences in *specific* abilities and deficiencies. Before discussing the two, let me comment generally about work with subgroups.

To begin, concentrated attention to subgroups is possible only after classroom routines and expectations have been established. (How quickly they *are* established depends on many factors, including students' past experiences with other teachers.) One important expectation is that children will not usually interrupt a teacher working with a subgroup. Since uninterrupted time *is* important, instruction with subgroups should take place in an area of the classroom that is away from the main flow of traffic, close to a chalkboard, and removed from distractions. (One observed teacher who neglected to think about distractions placed interesting science equipment right next to where she met with reading groups. It took but a few minutes for her to learn that children can be counted on to succumb to temptation.) Bookshelves and portable bulletin boards can separate the reading area from the rest of the room.

Two other reminders about subgroups apply equally to work with a whole class:

- Do not begin instruction until it appears that everyone is paying attention.

- When individual responses are requested, do not always call on the ones who are the first to raise their hands. That only encourages those who think that it is more important to respond in any fashion than it is to think first and then answer.

The last and most important point to make about subgroups is that they are meant to allow for differentiated instruction. To divide a class into groups and then give each either the same or closely similar instruction is to lose sight of the very reason for having small groups.

GENERAL ACHIEVEMENT SUBGROUPS

One way in which students differ is in what might be called general achievement. (Comments like "He's reading at a second-grade level" or "She's pretty much a fifth-grade reader" or "In the reading test, she scored at a third-grade level" refer to general achievement.) Differences in general achievement, therefore, are the basis for one type of subgrouping. Because texts in basal programs are organized around general achievement levels, it is common for teachers to use a basal reader with a general achievement subgroup that is written at their instructional level. This means that the basal reader lessons that have been discussed in prior chapters describe a type of work that often takes place with such groups.

Since identifying students' general achievement is easier and less time-consuming than pinpointing specific abilities and shortcomings, general achievement subgroups can function almost as soon as a school year begins.

IDENTIFYING GENERAL ACHIEVEMENT

While no teacher should be slipshod in efforts to identify general achievement levels, no teacher, either, should turn those efforts into an end in themselves. This point needs to be emphasized because if a teacher spends considerable time organizing subgroups, there is a tendency to want to keep the membership of each intact for the whole year even when what is natural occurs: shifts and changes in abilities. Placing subgroups in a correct perspective (means for accomplishing individualized instruction) leads to one conclusion: As changes occur in abilities, corresponding changes ought to take place in the membership of subgroups.

Sources for learning about students' general achievement at the beginning of the year are cumulative records, standardized tests, and oral reading tests. Each will be discussed.

Cumulative Records

When children first enroll in school, information about them begins to accumulate. The cards on which it is kept are called *cumulative records*. These records are linked to decisions about general achievement subgroups because they include information about reading. For general achievement estimates, the most helpful kind describes the materials that each student completed during each year in school. This allows a teacher to know at a glance something about the general achievement of everyone in the room. If certain children, for instance, completed but did not go beyond a certain basal reader in second grade, the third-grade teacher will have some idea not only of their general ability but also of a suitable text. Most often, cumulative records can be examined before students arrive to start a new year.

Standardized Test

In addition to keeping an account of the books that each child completes, most schools use standardized reading tests to obtain information about achievement. These tests are comprised of several subtests usually dealing with word recognition and various kinds of comprehension abilities. Rate of reading may be assessed, too. When scores from subtests are added, the total raw score can be converted to a grade-level score that is supposed to indicate a student's general achievement. Grade-level scores are helpful with decisions about general achievement subgroups only when two of their limitations are recognized.

The first relates to all test scores: they derive from a very small sample of behavior during a brief amount of time. The other limitation, which has special relevance for this discussion, is that reading test scores reported as grade-level scores usually overestimate ability. This means that a score ought to be used not as an index of a student's general achievement but only to rank that child's ability in relation to that of classmates. More specifically, when a teacher lists from the highest to the lowest all the raw scores for all the children—even when they were obtained the previous May or June—she is left with a picture of the kind and range of differences that she is going to have to cope with. She also has some idea of the number of subgroups likely to be needed, as well as the possible membership of each one. If this same teacher also knows the materials that each student completed the previous year, she is in a very good position to (a) form general achievement subgroups, (b) assign texts, and (c) get suitable instruction underway.

Oral Reading Test

As you were reading about how to identify general achievement, you might have thought, "What if neither records nor test scores are available for one or more children?" Since that is a possibility, let us next consider an oral reading test whose purpose is to identify instructional-level material and, along with that, a suitable text. With that as a goal, three terms concerned with the difficulty of material in relation to a given child need to be reviewed:

Independent level. Material easy enough that a child can read it without assistance.
Instructional level. Material that is sufficiently difficult that, with the help of a
    teacher, a child could improve his ability by reading it.

Frustration level. Material that is so difficult for a particular child that he would be frustrated in trying to read it even if assistance was available.

When teachers work with a general achievement subgroup, material at the students' instructional level is used—at least most of the time. (Independent-level material would be suitable for some purposes.) Since a basal reader is the common choice for such work, knowing which reader in a given basal series is at a child's instructional level allows for an appropriate placement.

For the oral reading test designed to identify instructional-level material, word-identification and comprehension abilities are taken into account in the following way.

Level	Unidentified or misidentified words	Unanswered or incorrectly answered questions
Independent	One (or fewer) words per 100	10 percent
Instructional	Five (or fewer) words per 100	25 percent
Frustration	Ten (or more) words per 100	50 percent

As you can see, the criteria leave some gray areas open to question. Coupled with a teacher's own judgment, however, they can provide helpful guidelines (not rules) for selecting a text written at a child's instructional level.

Passages for an oral test.   Basal reader passages of about 100 to 300 words are used. When making selections, it is important to keep in mind that understanding their content should not be dependent upon knowing what was said prior to the selected passage. (If it is, the earlier material must be reviewed or summarized before the test commences.)

To make the test suitable for more than one student, the difficulty of selected passages should range from at least two grade levels below the classroom in question to at least two grade levels above it. Because the concern of the test is diagnosis, what is chosen should be unfamiliar material.

Questions for an oral test.   Since the testing takes into account both word-identification and comprehension abilities, questions are required for each passage. While their number and kind will be determined by the passage, questions should vary whenever possible. Ideally, they would focus on content that is both stated and implied.★

Administering an oral test.   "Trying a book on for size" is an apt description of the oral test being discussed. To make sure that the first one is comfortable, a

---

★ Asking comprehension questions about orally read material is defensible when the purpose is to learn as quickly as possible about appropriate material and subgroup placement. On the other hand, as Chapter 16 will explain, when the goal is to learn about particular comprehension abilities (or the lack of them), silent reading is called for.

Figure 15.1

Level: third grade

Words: 284

Word errors: ___7___

Missed questions   ___2___

Level for child   _____instructional_____

The witch very quickly brewed a magic potion "Drink this, and you will go as quick as the wind," said the old woman.

The princess thanked her, and the two girls set out on their way. They went as fast as the wind. It seemed as if the trees and bushes were flying by. When it began to grow dark, however, the magic potion lost its power.

The princess and Kakila went more and more slowly and became more and more tired. Finally, they got themselves ready to spend the night.

When the princess had fallen asleep, Kakila got up and took the ring from the princess's finger.

"Now I will be the princess," she said to herself. "If I show this to the king, he will believe that I am the Princess Maraya, and he will take me in as his niece."

With these thoughts, she set out on the way. The princess was sleeping quietly all the while. But around her, life was stirring. All the animals came and gazed at her, for never before had they seen such a lovely girl.

Suddenly, there was a huffing and a puffing. Terrified, the animals scattered. Makulu the giant was coming.

He was very ill-tempered, for he had not yet captured a single human. But what did he see here? A little girl. "Ha!" Now he was grinning from ear to ear, and he snatched up the poor little princess in his hand. When the giant raised her up, she was terribly frightened. But when Makulu saw how beautiful the princess was, he could not find it in his heart to harm her.

So he said, "Don't be afraid. I will not hurt you."

109

From "Makulu," an African tale, in *Cities All About,* © 1979 Open Court Publishing Company.

Questions:
1.   Is this a story that could really happen? Why do you think so?
2.   Whom would you rather have for a friend, the giant or Kakila? Why?
3.   What in the story gives you a hint about how big the giant is?
4.   It said that, at first, the giant was ill tempered. What does that mean? (If necessary, explain the meaning.)
5.   Did the giant stay ill tempered? Why (not)?
6.   It said that the giant was "grinning from ear to ear." Does this mean his smile was so wide that it went from one ear across to the other? (If no, what does it mean?)

passage thought to be at a student's independent level is used initially. A request to read the passage orally, accompanied by a brief explanation for the testing and of how it will be conducted ("When you finish reading this, I'll ask you a few questions about it"), gets things started. Sometimes a student will display so much competence that completing the passage is unnecessary. A comment like, "This certainly is too easy for you, isn't it" allows for a shift to another more difficult passage. Almost from the start, a selection might also be identified as being at the child's frustration level. Again, a quick change is called for.

When a child is reading a passage that might be at his instructional level, the teacher keeps track of the number of word errors. (Inability to pronounce a difficult proper name should not be counted as an error, nor should a misidentified word that is corrected by the reader.) If the child is reading from one copy of a passage and the teacher has another, errors can be noted on the second copy. If the oral reading is recorded on tape, an evaluation can be made later. Whether recorded or not, each oral reading of a passage is followed by questions about the content. Figure 15.1 shows a sample passage, questions for it, and the results of one student's efforts to read it.

To sum up, three sources are available to learn about students' general achievement at the start of a year: data from school records, scores from standardized tests, and the results of an individual oral reading test. Since the oral test is time-consuming, it is usually given only when information from records and group tests is either unavailable or confusing.

ESTABLISHING GENERAL ACHIEVEMENT SUBGROUPS

Aware of the general achievement levels of the students (or of the material that is at their instructional level), a teacher is in a position to organize subgroups. Theoretically, the range of differences determines how many subgroups to establish; practical considerations, however, cannot be ignored. More specifically, if a teacher is unwilling or unable to spend the time required to plan for a large number, fewer subgroups than what the differences suggest should be used. This guideline would apply to a recently observed third grade in which there were five general achievement subgroups. Meeting with one of them, the teacher's first question was, "Did I assign you a story to read over the week-end?" Meeting with another group later, she started by inquiring, "What book are we reading in?" While one visit is hardly sufficient to reach reliable conclusions, it is possible that fewer subgroups would have allowed for more effective teaching in this particular room.

The obvious lesson to be learned from an incident like the one just described is that having many groups is neither good nor bad. What counts is whether subgroups allow for a close match between what students need to learn and what is taught. Within that framework, compromise may be necessary. Legitimate compromises, therefore, are illustrated on the next page.

Ms. Greyson is beginning her first year of teaching. General achievement levels of the twenty-nine third graders in her class are distributed as follows:

Grade III:
Reading Grade Levels

	I	II	III	IV
Number of Children	2	9	16	2

Ms. Greyson is convinced of the need to match instruction with student needs but is unsure of her ability to manage subgroups. As a start, therefore, she decides to have two. Eleven students will be in one group, eighteen in the other. She is aware of the compromise and plans to make adjustments as the school year progresses and her self-confidence increases.

Another teacher, Mr. Poli, makes compromises for different reasons. Unlike Ms. Greyson, he feels competent to work with groups, but he has just transferred to a school in which whole class instruction is all that is used in both fourth and fifth grades. One consequence is that his sixth graders are unaccustomed to working on their own and need experience in doing assignments while he works with others. That is why Mr. Poli begins with two subgroups, even though the following general achievement range exists:

Grade VI:
Reading Grade Levels

	I	III	IV	V	VI
Number of Children	2	0	9	12	9

Mr. Poli plans to change gradually either to three or four groups, but he correctly feels that the first job is to help his students establish work habits that will allow him to give uninterrupted attention to instruction.

In another school, Ms. Thorpe is a second-grade teacher with thirty students reading at the following general achievement levels:

Grade II:
Reading Grade Levels

	I	II	III	IV	V
Number of Children	1	13	8	5	3

Of the thirteen students who are reading at a second-grade level, four are very sure of themselves and nine are not. With that in mind, Ms. Thorpe begins the year by establishing three general achievement subgroups:

Group 1	Group 2	Group 3
10	12	8

If Ms. Thorpe finds that Group 1 is too large to get the kind of help it needs, she will divide the ten students into two groups.

Together, the three teachers exemplify how a variety of factors affect decisions about the number and membership of subgroups. While such decisions ought to be made carefully, in no sense should they be thought of as final and unchangeable. In fact, an essential feature of productive subgrouping is that it remains flexible throughout the year, allowing for the peaks, valleys, and plateaus that characterize all human learning.

SPECIAL NEEDS SUBGROUPS

As observant teachers work with general achievement subgroups, they soon learn that differences exist in what members of a group can and cannot do.★ At less advanced levels, one or more in a group might have difficulty remembering and using the short vowel sounds. Others in the same or a different group might not be able to identify important service words automatically. Still others may not really understand what it means to answer questions. At more advanced levels, individual problems might be concerned with inappropriate rates of reading, paying needless attention to trivial details, inability to use the structure of a word to learn its meaning, or the failure to treat literal and figurative uses of language differently.

Specific problems like those just described indicate that general achievement instruction alone is not enough to promote everybody's progress. Instead, students who share a deficiency need to be temporarily grouped for instruction and practice that concentrates on the problem. Once it is resolved, the group disbands.

Special Needs Lessons

In some instances, additional practice may be all that is required to remedy a problem. That would be the case, for example, if it was insufficiently quick recall of certain service words. At other times, the need will be for carefully planned lessons that include instruction, application, practice, and evaluation. To show what one such lesson might be like, let us say that a teacher adheres to a basal reader manual's suggestions for teaching the suffix -er to a general achievement subgroup. Later, while checking students' responses to two workbook pages dealing with -er, she learns that three children did poorly, suggesting confusion

★ How to learn about such differences is the subject of the next chapter, "Diagnosis for Instruction."

not only about -*er* but also about the nature of a suffix. Since the manual provides no help, the teacher offers her own lesson to the three, which proceeds as follows.

Five familiar roots are written on the chalkboard. After the three children read the words aloud, the teacher reminds them of how they learned earlier that adding *s* to words like these makes them mean more than one. The board now displays pairs of words:

bat	toy	girl	door	cap
bats	toys	girls	doors	caps

Once all of the pairs are identified and discussed, the teacher writes three other words *(was, bus, has)* in order to make a distinction between words to which *s* has been added to the root and words in which *s* is part of the root itself. To specify the latter type, the teacher demonstrates that removing *s* from these words results in letters that do not spell a word:

was	bus	has
wa	bu	ha

Keeping the goal of the lesson in mind, the teacher next writes four other known roots on the board *(work, catch, teach, paint),* which the three students read aloud. This is followed by a series of questions starting with, "What do we call somebody who works?" Eventually the board displays:

work	catch	teach	paint
worker	catcher	teacher	painter

After the children take turns offering sentences that include *worker, catcher, teacher,* and *painter,* the teacher reminds the three that *e, r* at the end of a word might be part of the word itself, *not* an ending telling who is doing whatever is named in the root. For this part of the lesson, therefore, the board shows:

winter	under	her	water
wint	und	h	wat

Once the instruction is completed, the teacher will write still more words, this time asking the children to identify which have the ending *er* telling who did something and which are words in which *er* is part of the word itself.

Following the application, the teacher plans to distribute copies of the same two workbook pages that allowed for the earlier diagnosis. The children's responses will show whether the special needs instruction succeeded in clearing up the confusion.

How Special Needs Groups Function

To show how special needs subgroups function, another reference to Ms. Thorpe will be useful. She teaches second grade and has thirty students, who are divided into three general achievement subgroups:

Group 1	Group 2	Group 3
10	12	8

Let us say that Ms. Thorpe works for about the first month of school with the three groups. During that time, she makes decisions both about some goals she will try to reach and the materials that will be instrumental in attaining them. Meanwhile, she is learning about specific needs of individuals; she is also beginning to make plans to include special needs instruction. The fifth week of the school year, therefore, shows the following use of a seventy-five-minute reading period:

Monday	Tuesday	Wednesday	Thursday	Friday
General achievement groups	Special needs groups	General achievement groups	Special needs groups	General achievement groups

Resulting from the experiences of the fifth week is a revised schedule for the sixth week:

Monday	Tuesday	Wednesday	Thursday	Friday
Special needs groups	Special needs groups	General achievement groups	Special needs groups	General achievement groups

Right now there are two special needs subgroups, with children from the three general achievement groups distributed as follows:*

Blending sounds into syllables and words	Practice in identifying service words
1 1 1 1 1	1 1 1
2 2 2 2 2 2	2 2 2 2 2 2
3	3 3 3 3 3 3 3

Later, more detailed information coupled wth different learning rates result in three special needs groups:

* In these examples, the numerals pertain to the three general achievement subgroups. For instance, "1" refers to a student from Group 1, the lowest achievers.

Blending sounds into syllables and words	*Practice with service words*	*Practice with service words*
1 1 1 1 1	1 1 1 1	3 3 3 3
2 2 2	2 2 2 2 2	3 3 3 3
	2 2 2 2	

Now, students doing the same work (practice with service words) are divided into two groups because some can identify many more words than others.

Let me use the circumstances of another previously mentioned teacher, Mr. Poli, to provide one further illustration of a classroom employing special needs groups. Mr. Poli, you will recall, found himself with thirty-two sixth graders who were unaccustomed to working independently. To allow them to develop the habit of completing assignments while other students had his attention, Mr. Poli began the school year with just two general achievement subgroups. After a few weeks, he redistributed students to form three:

Group 1	*Group 2*	*Group 3*
2	13	17

Several weeks later he was using easy materials with Group 1 (eleven-year-olds with second-grade reading ability) but dividing his time in various ways with the others. Sometimes he would stay with the two general achievement divisions (Groups 2 and 3). Frequently, however, he changed to special needs groups like the following:

Using structural analysis to figure out word meanings	*Using signal words to follow a sequence*
2 2 2 2 2 2	3 3 3 3 3 3 3 3 3 3 3
2 2 2 2 2 2	
3 3 3 3 3 3	

or

Comprehending similes	*Varying rate of reading according to purpose*
2 2 2 2 2	2 2
2 2 2 2 2	3 3 3 3 3 3 3 3 3
	3 3 3 3 3 3 3

Unquestionably, the wide range of achievement in Mr. Poli's sixth grade presents major organizational problems. Even in classrooms like his, however, there may still be occasions for whole class projects. Nonetheless, the greater the disparity in reading ability within a class, the greater is the need for subgroup instruction.

INTERCLASS ORGANIZATION

At the middle- and upper-grade levels, the amount of disparity in reading ability found in Mr. Poli's class is not uncommon. A valid generalization, in fact, is: the higher the grade level, the wider the range in students' reading abilities.

Problems encountered in trying to adjust instruction to differences prompt some schools to use an interclass organization, usually starting at grade 3 or grade 4. In such cases, students from various classrooms with similar general achievement meet together for the daily reading period, commonly the first sixty or ninety minutes in the morning. Most often, placements are based on test scores and teacher recommendations. Supposedly, the end result is groups of homogeneous children insofar as reading ability is concerned. What actually results, however, are groups in which the range of achievement is smaller than would be likely in a self-contained classroom. And in theory, that should help a teacher who is earnestly trying to put together an instructional program that matches what students need and are ready to learn.

What happens in practice varies considerably. All too often, for example, the reduced range of abilities is mistakenly interpreted as justifying whole class instruction based on one textbook (3). Even when teachers do work with subgroups on suitable goals, interclass arrangements can lead to much wasted time. In one classroom-observation study (10), for example, almost 10 percent of the time officially allotted to reading instruction went to "transitional activities," described as those occasions when the teacher waits while (a) some students leave and others arrive and (b) students settle down for instruction.

Other observations of interclass arrangements point to the need to match teachers and students with care. A teacher who has never taught at the primary-grade level, for instance, may be ill prepared to "begin at the beginning" should she be assigned to work with the lowest achievers. Someone else, on the other hand, may be intimidated by a group of bright, articulate, highly skillful readers.

Whether teachers and students are carefully matched or not, one consequence of between-class arrangements is the failure of each homeroom teacher to know in detail the reading achievements and problems of the students in her own classroom (with the exception of those who are in her reading group, too). The lack of detailed information about everyone can be a real problem when she makes plans for teaching subjects like social studies and science. The lack of information also creates difficulties for students when they try to do required assignments.

Put together, the potential shortcomings and problems of an interclass organization should be enough to make elementary school personnel think twice before they abandon self-contained classrooms. Reminded of the possible problems, one administrator recently defended using what he called "departmentalization for reading" by pointing out that changing classrooms and working with more than one teacher was good preparation for junior high. Another, more defensible position is that offering individualized instruction is the best way to prepare for the future.

STUDENTS' INDEPENDENT WORK

Except when whole class instruction takes place, some students will need to work on their own. Ideally, what they do independently should advance their ability to read. Assignments that make that contribution contrast sharply with *busy work:* assignments designed to keep children occupied and, hopefully, out of mischief.

Many ideas for productive assignments were given in Chapters 5 through 12. Now, therefore, independent work will be discussed more generally in the framework of classroom organization.

Learning to Work Independently

To be noted immediately is that working independently is something students *learn* to do. In a school in which whole class instruction is rare and independent work is characteristic, children can become highly proficient in taking care of their own business while a teacher gives time to classmates. On the other hand, when whole class instruction dominates, unsupervised work is less natural and therefore less productive. With that in mind, teachers who recognize the need for a more individualized approach must allow time for students to get acquainted with new expectations and procedures.

Features of Desirable Independent Assignments

Other factors also affect the productivity of independent work, the most important of which has to do with the nature of the assignments themselves. From a teacher's perspective, each should be concerned with what a student or a group needs to learn, practice, or use. From the child's point of view, an assignment should be something that he understands and is able to do and that is not unbearably monotonous. Because a combination of assignments minimizes monotony, illustrations of combinations in one fourth grade will be given.

We'll say the month is February, the day is Wednesday, and the week's schedule for the reading period (9–10:15 A.M.) is as follows:

Monday	Tuesday	Wednesday	Thursday	Friday
General achievement groups	Special needs groups	General achievement groups	Special needs groups	General achievement groups

The teacher's plan for Wednesday shows this distribution of time:

9:00–9:25	Group 1 (third-grade reading level)
9:25–9:50	Group 3 (fifth- and sixth-grade reading levels)
9:50–10:15	Group 2 (fourth-grade reading level)

The time is 9:25. Tom is in Group 1 and has just finished spending time with the teacher. His group worked on a story in a basal reader and was assigned three pages in the workbook, all dealing with material that extends the story. Tom and the others were asked to complete that assignment before doing anything else because the workbooks are to be collected at 10:15, corrected, and returned on Friday.

The second job for Tom is connected with his special needs group, which met the day before. Comprised of students from two different general achievement subgroups, its members are excessively slow in finding alphabetically organized material; so on Tuesday, the teacher discussed and demonstrated procedures to make such a search easier. After the discussion, she gave the following three assignments, which she described as "practice in learning to find something quickly":

1. Spend work time on Tuesday acquiring information about a given animal in an encyclopedia. (Each child had a different animal so that each would be using a different volume.) Some will be discussed.
2. At home on Tuesday, make a telephone directory for any ten children in the room. Find their numbers in the local directory.
3. Spend work time on Wednesday finding words in a dictionary. (Each child received a list of words and a dictionary.) Write one possible definition for each.

The plan for Thursday is to have the children talk about problems they encountered in finding names and words quickly or perhaps some short cuts they discovered.

Whether this special needs subgroup remains intact will depend upon the ability of its members to find words on Thursday as they work under the supervision of the teacher. It is likely that some will need further help and others will not. If that is the case, the focus of the special needs subgroup will remain the same during the following week, but its membership will be altered.

To show another way in which assignments can be combined and thus varied, let me describe a second student in the same fourth grade. Anne is a member of the most advanced general achievement subgroup (Group 3) and reads comfortably at a sixth-grade level. To show how she and other members of Group 3 are spending the week, let me repeat the schedule shown earlier.

Monday	Tuesday	Wednesday	Thursday	Friday
General achievement groups	Special needs groups	General achievement groups	Special needs groups	General achievement groups

Wednesday's Plan	9:00–9:25	Group 1 (third-grade reading level)
	9:25–9:50	Group 3 (fifth- and sixth-grade reading levels)
	9:50–10:15	Group 2 (fourth-grade reading level)

The eight members of Group 3 are studying words and their histories. (Uncertain about the group's reactions to her plans, the teacher is taking just one week at a time.) On Monday, when general achievement subgroups met, the teacher introduced Group 3 to the idea that words have histories and that studying them can be very interesting. To support her statement, she related how certain words and expressions came into our language and how their meanings took shape over time. Having already been introduced to the dictionary, these students were also told about Noah Webster, of his special interest in words, and of the work of lexicographers.

The introductory discussion on Monday set the stage for three assignments that are to be completed by Friday:

1.   The two most advanced readers (one is Anne) were told about unabridged dictionaries and the attention they give to word histories. They were asked to go to the school library, where the librarian will be waiting to show them a copy of a dictionary. Their job for Friday is to bring in and discuss an unabridged dictionary (with the approval and help of the librarian), to show its content, and to tell the history of a few particularly interesting words.
2.   The next two most advanced children in Group 3 were asked to read *Noah Webster, Boy of Words* (12). The objective is an oral report of the book, also to be ready by Friday. (The teacher would like to have assigned the biography to all eight children, but only two copies were available.)
3.   Books dealing with the history of American English were distributed to the remaining four children. Their job is to read parts of each in order to select words whose histories they will relate on Friday.

According to the teacher's plan, Tuesday was to be for special needs groups. During this week, however, the Group 3 general achievement subgroup is a special needs (or special opportunity) group; consequently, plans for these students proceeded differently. The two dictionary children worked in the library while the two who are reading about Noah Webster continued with that. The teacher was thus free to give time on Tuesday to the four children who were reading about words from a variety of books. They talked about some and began to make decisions about the words to discuss on Friday. In certain instances, word families will be referred to (for example, *act, react, action, reactionary*), so plans were made to construct charts showing word relationships.

From 9:25 until 9:50 on Wednesday, the teacher divides her time between the two children who are working with the dictionary and the two who are reading about Noah Webster. With both pairs, her aim is to identify what these students have been learning, to provide suggestions about what might have been overlooked or underplayed, and to make plans for Friday's oral presentations.

On Thursday, usually a special needs day, the eight children in general achievement Group 3 will meet with the teacher to coordinate plans for Friday. Having concluded that they will be presenting highly interesting material, the teacher plans to use the reading period on Friday as a time for the children to discuss with the rest of the class what they have done and learned. Following the presentation, she herself will show easier books that also deal with word histories. They will become part of the classroom collection and, it is hoped, part of what the students will select during free-reading periods. The attention to word histories might eventually result in a focus for a subgroup brought together because of a mutual interest in this kind of study.

Further Considerations for Independent Assignments

In addition to focusing on something that will be profitable, either because it advances students' abilities or increases their interest in reading, independent assignments need to be made within a framework that reflects such considerations as the following.

1. Why a particular assignment is being given ought to be explained. Even a brief explanation makes it more meaningful for students and helps portray the teacher as someone who is there to help them become better readers. This point is stressed because, all too often, students are simply moved from one job to another with no explanation of why they are being asked to do any of them. And, only rarely, are the jobs seen as something that will advance reading ability.
2. As was demonstrated in the illustrative material, combinations of assignments may include both short-term and long-term jobs. When this is the case, they function most effectively when a student has a written description of what is to be done. Older students can be responsible for keeping their own reminders in a notebook, or the teacher might ditto a brief description of assignments and the sequence for completing them. Or—and this is especially helpful for younger children—a teacher can print simply worded descriptions or directions on a large sheet of paper thumbtacked to an easel placed close to the students for whom the directions are intended.
3. Regardless of the form written directions take, they are useful in providing students with extra reading practice. They also are helpful in reducing interruptions that occur with queries like, "I finished my workbook. What should I do now?"

LEARNING CENTERS

In some classrooms, all or part of what students do on their own takes place in *learning centers*. A learning center (or station) is a given amount of space; it also is a collection of materials assembled to (a) accomplish a particular goal or (b) feature a given theme or topic. Among the latter, both the space and the materials might highlight something like creative writing, art, living things, the environment, nyms (synonyms, antonyms, homonyms), mythology, or communication.

Learning centers established to realize a particular goal can be highly productive for reading; consequently, most of the comments that follow focus on that kind. They will be given as answers to questions frequently raised about centers.

Should all teachers have learning centers? Like everything else in a classroom, a learning center should exist if a teacher believes it will be more successful than anything else in attaining a particular goal. Thus the first question is *not,* Should I have a learning center? Instead, the initial consideration ought to be, What are some goals that are important and as yet unattained? If one or more can be realized more effectively and efficiently with a learning center than with something else, it should be assembled.

Are learning centers more suitable for younger or older students? Since one central reason for centers is to encourage independent work and reading, they *are* more suitable for middle- and upper-grade classes since more advanced abilities are found there. Nonetheless, observations reveal that they are scarce at those levels. This is unfortunate because life in middle- and upper-grade classrooms sometimes needs rejuvenation, which learning centers have the potential to provide. In addition, the concerns of the various subject matter areas are fruitful for center themes and topics.

Whether used with younger or older students, centers should be introduced gradually. When the availability of a center is a new experience, it might even be necessary to walk small groups through one in order to identify what is available and to explain what is expected. If problems develop in the use of materials, students should be encouraged to tell about the difficulty so that it can be remedied. All this is to point up that only when students are well prepared for centers are they likely to make a significant contribution to an instructional program. Similarly, only when teachers are well organized is a significant contribution likely.

Should students be assigned to centers, or should they be free to choose or ignore them? Again, the answer depends on a center's purpose. To illustrate the dependency, let me describe a few highly commendable uses of centers.

In one third grade, a general achievement subgroup was introduced to tall tales with a basal reader selection. To extend their understanding of this genre, the teacher prepared a center comprised of materials for three tasks. (Each child could complete the three whenever he or she wished but within a week's time. What was done would be shared and discussed.) One job was to select a tall tale from a shelf of about a dozen books and to do whatever was on the assignment card tucked into it. Another assignment was to illustrate one exaggeration chosen from a list entitled "Hyperbole," which included statements like *The building was so tall that it scraped the sky* and *I'm so hungry I could eat a bear.* The third task was to write an original tall tale that could be as short as a paragraph or as long as an author wished to make it. This center, then, was not a place to which students could go when they finished their work. It was where they did it.

In contrast, another teacher had a center that students used when assignments were finished. It was an outgrowth of a basal story about a circus and a tiger and featured old issues of *National Geographic* that had articles and beautifully colored pictures of jungle animals. Side by side with the magazines was a collection of fiction and nonfiction books about animals. Students were free to use any of these materials, once assigned work was done.

To demonstrate the *value* of being able to read (which is often neglected in classrooms) and, second, to provide practice in using and consolidating acquired skills, another teacher set aside one hour per day for a period of a week for work in centers. Students could choose from any of the five that had been prepared as long as the number permitted in each one had not been reached. A student could select the same center on all five afternoons or could work in each one for an hour. While the children were thus occupied, the teacher met with individual students for whatever purpose was meaningful at the time. (Other teachers might elect to work with general achievement or special needs subgroups.) The five centers provided opportunities (with the help of written directions) to carry out simple, interesting experiments and to make (with the assistance of written directions and sketches) puppets, collages, and papier-mâché animals.

Knowing that a story's presentation on television prompts many children to go to a library to get the book version, another teacher periodically organized a center where students could listen to recordings of stories that were available in book form. Kept by the teacher, the books were loaned to any child who had heard a tape and wanted to read the book. Earphones allowed several students to use the center at the same time without disturbing each other.

Shown by all the descriptions of centers is one of the most important contributions that anything or anyone can make: fostering an interest in reading.

SUMMARY

Organizing a classroom to facilitate a maximum of individualized instruction is not an easy, quickly accomplished task. Nor is it one that will be performed in a uniform way. Factors that account for variability from one classroom to another pertain to teachers and include at the top of the list their knowledge of reading instruction, their experience and competence in teaching and in keeping track of who knows what, and their ability to plan for, and manage, different activities that are occurring simultaneously. Unquestionably, teachers' personalities and their educational philosophies also enter into and complicate the picture.

Other, equally significant variables pertain to students. Not to be taken lightly, for instance, are their number and their past experiences with school, with other teachers, and with different expectations. In addition, and central to all organizational decisions, are students' abilities in reading. In fact, it is *differences* in those abilities that are the most fundamental consideration of all when teachers are making decisions about the use of their time and that of students.

Chapter 15 discussed differences in general achievement and in specific abilities and problems. The discussion of how to identify students' general achievement at the start of the year took into account three sources of information: cumulative records, standardized tests, and oral reading tests. While how to learn about specific abilities and problems was referred to intermittently, that topic is the main concern of the next chapter.

The three possible ways for working with students (whole class, individual, subgroup) were discussed and illustrated with examples. Variety in the illustrations was meant to show that there is no such thing as one best way to organize. Nonetheless, every type must be evaluated in relation to one question: To what extent does individualized instruction exist?

The need for individualized assignments and practice was also underscored when independent work was discussed. Since what students do on their own may be just as important for advancement in reading as what they do with a teacher, readers of the chapter were urged to avoid thinking of assignments as a means for keeping students busy. To show that they can be both productive and interesting, some assignments were described; many more have been listed in prior chapters. What is important for teachers to remember about assignments is that they are justified only when, first, they concentrate on what is significant for reading ability, and, second, they deal with what one or more students still need to learn, review, or practice. Explaining to students the reason for an assignment was highly recommended.

REVIEW

1. When teachers use general achievement subgroups, they commonly end up with three. Why do you think that is so? Are three subgroups desirable or undesirable? Why?

2. With one example, the chapter showed that helping an individual child is not necessarily something that merits praise.

   (a) What was the example?
   (b) Describe other circumstances that would make individual help questionable.

3. Certain things about reading should be so familiar to teachers that they are recalled automatically at the appropriate time. Such is the case with oral reading and its two different functions. What should teachers remember when they are considering the possibility of having students read aloud?

4. Assume that you have been asked to evaluate the organizational pattern that a fourth-grade teacher uses. Keeping in mind the central purpose of organizational decisions, compose three to five questions that will provide a basis for the evaluation.

REFERENCES

1. Anderson, R. C.; Pichert, J. W.; Goetz, E. T.; Schallert, D. L.; Stevens, K. V.; and Trollip, S. R. "Instantiation of General Terms." *Journal of Verbal Learning and Verbal Behavior* 15 (December 1976): 667–679.

2. Anderson, R. C.; Reynolds, R. E.; Schallert, D. L.; and Goetz, E. T. "Frameworks for Comprehending Discourse." *American Educational Research Journal* 14 (Fall 1977): 367–381.

3. Austin, Mary C., and Morrison, Coleman. *The First R: The Harvard Report on Reading in the Elementary Schools.* New York: Macmillan, 1963.

4. Barbe, Walter B. *Educator's Guide to Personalized Reading Instruction.* Englewood Cliffs, N.J.: Prentice-Hall, 1961.

5. Borko, Hilda; Shavelson, Richard J.; and Stern, Paula. "Teachers' Decisions in the Planning of Reading Instruction." *Reading Research Quarterly* 16, no. 3 (1981): 449–466.

6. Brogan, Peggy, and Fox, L. K. *Helping Children Read.* New York: Holt-Rinehart, 1961.

7. Bruce, Bertram. "What Makes a Good Story?" *Language Arts* 15 (April 1978): 460–466.

8. Chambers, D. W., and Pyle, W. J. "Individualized Reading Questioned." *Reading Teacher* 25 (March 1972): 535–537.

9. Cohen, Elizabeth G.; Intili, Jo-Ann K.; and Robbins, Susan H. "Teachers and Reading Specialist: Cooperation or Isolation?" *Reading Teacher* 32 (December 1978): 281–287.

10. Durkin, Dolores. "What Classroom Observations Reveal about Reading Comprehension Instruction." *Reading Research Quarterly* 14, no. 4 (1978–1979): 481–533.

11. Harris, Albert J. *Effective Teaching of Reading.* New York: David McKay Company, 1962.

12. Higgins, Helen B. *Noah Webster, Boy of Words.* Indianapolis, Ind.: Bobbs-Merrill, 1961.

13. Leinhardt, Gaea; Zigmond, Naomi; and Cooley, William W. "Reading Instruction and Its Effects." *American Educational Research Journal* 18 (Fall 1981): 343–361.

14. Rouk, Ullik. "Separate Studies Show Similar Results of Teacher Effectiveness." *Educational R and D Report* 2 (Spring 1979): 6–10.

15. Veatch, Jeannette. *Individualizing Your Reading Program.* New York: Putnam, 1959.

16. Veatch, Jeannette. *Reading in the Elementary School.* New York: Ronald Press Co., 1966.

17. Wallen, Carl J. *Competency in Teaching Reading.* Chicago: Science Research Associates, 1972.

CHAPTER 16

DIAGNOSIS FOR INSTRUCTION

Intelligence and Expectations for Reading
Some General Comments about Diagnosis
Diagnosis in the Context of a Basal Reader Lesson
    Preparation for Reading: New Vocabulary
    Preparation for Reading: Use of Cues
    Preparation for Reading: Comprehension
    Postreading Activities
    Basal Reader Tests
Special Efforts to Diagnose
More Teacher-Devised Diagnosis
Guidelines for Teacher-Devised Diagnosis
Record Keeping for Teacher-Devised Diagnosis
Commercially Produced Group Tests
    Survey Tests
    Diagnostic Tests
    Criterion-Referenced Tests
Commercially Produced Individual Tests
    Diagnostic Tests
    Informal Reading Inventories
        Description
        Critique
Summary
Review

PREVIEW

As early as Chapter 1, it was said that the underlying thrust of this book is the desire to increase individualized instruction, defined as any that (a) deals with what contributes to reading ability, (b) concentrates on what has not yet been learned by the student or group receiving the instruction, and (c) proceeds at a suitable pace. The concern of the next and final topic, diagnosis, is closely linked to individualized instruction since it has to do with attempts to identify what students do or do not know about something that contributes to the ability to read. Since what does contribute has been covered in Chapters 5 through 12, it is time now to consider ways for learning what students have achieved in specific areas.

To be stressed immediately is that efforts to learn what has been achieved do not necessarily constitute special events that are scheduled ahead of time. In fact, the diagnosis that is the major concern of Chapter 16 is an integral part of everyday teaching. It thus has to do with questions like, Is this necessary? Do they know this? Can they apply it? Now that they can, what comes next?

Although what advances reading ability must be understood before a discussion of diagnosis is meaningful, placing a chapter on diagnosis at the very end of a methodology textbook has one drawback. It could unintentionally communicate the idea that classroom diagnosis also takes place "at the end"—for instance, at the end of a marking period or a school year. With the possibility of that misunderstanding occurring, let me state explicitly that Chapter 16 is not about grading, passing, or failing students. Instead, its central objective is the improvement of instruction through knowing what the particular needs of particular students are. The chapter views diagnosis, then, as a daily occurrence, not an optional addition to an instructional program.

As the previous chapter pointed out, one concern of teachers at the start of a new school year is organization, which means that some questions about students' abilities have to be answered almost immediately. How to get answers that provide guidelines for establishing general achievement subgroups and selecting instructional-level materials was discussed in that chapter. Getting answers about what to teach, review, practice, or skip is the focus now.

INTELLIGENCE AND EXPECTATIONS FOR READING

Answers about what to teach, how quickly to teach it, and what to expect are affected by a number of variables, one of which is a student's intelligence. Theoretically, then, anyone responsible for planning an instructional program would find it helpful to know about the intelligence of those to whom the instruction will be offered. In practice, however, problems are inevitable when attempts are made to assess intelligence.

To begin, the best tests for approximating it must be administered individually by a psychometrist, which makes them prohibitively expensive. While group-administered tests are affordable, their shortcomings are major. In fact, the shortcoming related to cultural bias has reduced the number of schools that use group intelligence tests almost to zero. Still another flaw led to problems and misconceptions: doing well on group-administered tests depends on reading ability. Because of the dependence, students with reading problems inevitably come out looking like mentally slow children whether or not that is the case.

Since it is better to have no data than poor data, teachers should take the stance that superior instruction can compensate for many deficiencies in students and that *their* responsibility is to deliver a maximum of individualized instruction executed in a way that shows how important and useful it is to be able to read.

SOME GENERAL COMMENTS ABOUT DIAGNOSIS

Anyone who equates testing with diagnosis is bound to conclude that the latter is common. This is so because testing has become such a major part of the educational enterprise that one is often tempted to inquire, "But whatever happened to teaching?"

That teaching is sometimes put on the back burner to allow for testing is especially obvious when *skills management systems* are used. These are commercially prepared materials in which hundreds of objectives (referred to as subskills) are defined with tests accompanying each one. What Walter Loban has said about such testing is worth quoting:

> . . . the tests typically measure what is easy to measure, not what is important. . . . Almost every commercial test . . . can be likened to the inadequate actor who runs the gamut of emotions from A to B. [15, p. 486]

Even though it is hard to see what some of the identified skills in management systems have to do with the requirements of reading, and, further, even though it is equally difficult to understand how all the bits and pieces add up to reading ability, interest in such materials persists because of their close connection with accountability and statewide competency testing. That it does persist means that in some classrooms, assigning exercises that are like test items comes close to replacing instruction. Or, as Michael Strange has observed, "Children are often expected to teach themselves through interaction with dittoed materials (21, p. 198).

The belief that direct, explicit instruction from a teacher is mandatory if every student's potential is to be realized has been underscored throughout this book. You will recall from earlier chapters the recommended sequence for that teaching: goal, instruction, application, practice. What needs to be stressed about these facets of a lesson was stated in Chapter 11 when it was said that "application and practice both yield information that helps a teacher know if more (or different) instruction should follow. They are an important part, therefore, of diagnostic teaching." This statement implies what is the most important point to make about diagnosis: *If what it uncovers does not improve instruction, it is pointless.*

DIAGNOSIS IN THE CONTEXT OF A BASAL READER LESSON

Whether instruction comes in the form of a lesson that is guided by a single goal or in the context of a basal reader lesson in which several goals are the concern, it should be executed in a way that gives teachers an opportunity to learn who knows what. Because of the common, even daily, use of basal materials, the framework of a typical basal reader lesson will be used again, this time to show how everyday activities provide diagnostic information. Later, special efforts to diagnose will be described.

Preparation for Reading: New Vocabulary

If students are expected to read a basal selection that includes new words, they must be given the chance to learn any that they cannot decode themselves. (How to select such words was explained in Chapter 9 under the heading "Teachers' Decisions about New Vocabulary.") Prereading attention to vocabulary (including what the words mean) allows members of an instructional group to respond and thus to give teachers a chance to learn which words need to be practiced before the selection is read.

Once it *has* been read, further attention should go to vocabulary (including the words that the students presumably figured out themselves) in order to see if identifications are automatic. Now, diagnostic information can be collected in a variety of ways. For instance:

- Show the new words on cards (alone or in a brief context) several times. Have individual students read them aloud.

- Refer students to the sentences in the selection in which the new words occurred. Have individual students read the sentences aloud.

- Show other sentences that include the new words. Ask questions about their content that could only be answered by those who know the new vocabulary.

If responses indicate that all or some students need more practice with certain words, it can come in the form of a written assignment. (Ideas for written practice were described in Chapter 5.)

Preparation for Reading: Use of Cues

The occurrence of new vocabulary in a basal selection may be a time (whether or not the manual suggests it) to instruct about (a) a use of contexts for help with word identifications or meanings, (b) a phonics generalization, or (c) a particular prefix or suffix. Whenever new words do enter into instruction about contextual, graphophonic, or structural cues, lessons should reflect the sequence referred to before: goal, instruction, application, practice. As was also pointed out before, both the application and practice allow for diagnostic information, now pertaining to students' ability to use a particular type of cue to decode words that are visually unfamiliar.

Preparation for Reading: Comprehension

Typically, when basal manuals do offer suggestions for teaching comprehension, they come after a selection has been read. However, as the earlier chapter on comprehension stated, it is sometimes better to use them (as they are offered or in some altered form) before the reading begins, especially if what is taught can be applied to what is about to be read. Either way, instruction should allow for diagnosis and for subsequent decisions about the need to review or to move on to something else.

As the chapter on comprehension also indicated, examination of a selection may point to the need to deal with some aspect of the text that may cause problems. In these cases, instruction can proceed in a way that is similar to the sample lessons described in Chapter 11. Like them, it should allow for diagnostic information.

Postreading Activities

What is taught about comprehension before a basal selection is read is designed to improve the *process* of comprehending. Once the selection has been read, reviewing what was taught is often desirable. After the selection has been read is also the time to check up on the *products* of comprehension. This can be initiated with the questions posed before the reading began and can proceed with whatever additional probing seems necessary. Consideration of answers should focus not just on whether they are correct but also on what they reveal about instructional needs. Meanwhile, students should be encouraged to ask about anything that is unclear.

Typically, a basal lesson includes workbook and ditto sheet assignments that are usually done after a selection is read. Any that pertain to what was selected for instruction earlier will provide additional diagnostic information. If none pertains to what received special attention, teacher-composed assignments ought to be given in order to see whether students understand and are able to use what was taught.

Basal Reader Tests

In recent years, one obvious addition to basal programs is numerous tests. (This is a response to the widespread interest in testing referred to before.) Some are *inventories,* which will be discussed later. Other tests in basal reader series assess the achievement of objectives covered by manual suggestions. Since not all deal with what contributes to reading ability, this second type of test should be used selectively.

SPECIAL EFFORTS TO DIAGNOSE

Teachers intent on offering a maximum of individualized instruction identify what students need to learn or review not only by paying close attention to their responses and questions during basal reader and other types of lessons but also by having special diagnostic sessions. What three such teachers did will be described.

As you read the descriptions, note how special needs subgroups come into existence. Watch, too, for the way a diagnostic goal affects how the diagnosis is carried out. And, finally, notice how diagnosis is concerned not only with shortcomings but also with strengths.

Ms. White. Over a period of five years, Ms. White taught both third and fourth grades. While she always believed that the basal materials prescribed for those grades give excessive, even tedious, attention to dictionary skills, it was only now that she felt sufficiently confident to omit nonessentials. To pinpoint what was unnecessary, she conducted brief, individual tests close to the start of the year—she was now teaching third grade—in which the goal was to learn who was unable to use a dictionary sufficiently quickly. Five words made up the test. Results indicated that only two children had trouble; consequently, they became a special-needs group, and it was only to them that instruction and assignments with location skills would be given. Meanwhile, the whole class worked on using a pronunciation key in dictionaries and on choosing meanings that fit particular contexts. Sentences taken from science and social studies textbooks were used.

Approximately one month later, more individual tests were scheduled. This time the purpose was, first, to see whether the students could pronounce words with the help of diacritical marks and, second, to learn whether additional help with selecting appropriate meanings was needed. Now, words were presented in sentences. One result of the testing was the establishment of a special-needs group composed of thirteen students to whom further help with choosing relevant definitions will be given. The other sixteen will get no further dictionary assignments even though the assigned basal reader workbook continues to dwell on dictionary exercises for what seems like an endless amount of time.

In reflecting upon her experiences, Ms. White said she had to laugh at how uneasy and even guilty she felt when she first skipped workbook pages and worksheets. In time, however, such feelings were replaced with self-confidence plus the assurance that she was on the way to becoming a professional person who makes the instructional decisions.

Ms. Paul. This teacher has twenty-six bright second graders, all of whom read well. Like others in her building, Ms. Paul is obligated to use basal readers and workbooks written for the grade she teaches. Once these materials are completed, anything else is permissible.

To make the best of what she believes is an indefensible policy—at least insofar as her present class is concerned—Ms. Paul started the year determined to eliminate any manual segment, workbook page, or ditto sheet that dealt with what her students knew or with what was not essential for reading. Falling into the latter category is what is sometimes done with contractions, specifically, having children write the words for which contractions substitute and having them note the letters that the apostrophe replaces. Aware that all that is required for reading is the ability to identify contractions and to understand their meanings, Ms. Paul decided to begin by eliminating nonessentials insofar as contractions are concerned.

She first listed all the contractions that were reviewed or introduced in the basal series she has to use and then composed sentences that included them all. For the diagnosis, each child read the sentences aloud, which permitted Ms. Paul to learn whether they were pronouncing the contractions correctly. Following that, they told in their own words what each sentence meant. This procedure was used because the meaning of the sentence depended upon knowing the meaning of the contraction. In the end, the test confirmed what had been suspected: time did not have to go to contractions because the children knew them as well as their teacher.

Thanks to other eliminations, Ms. Paul got through the prescribed reader and workbook in less than three months, after which she gradually moved to the use of trade books and to instruction carried on for the most part with individuals and special-needs groups.

Mr. Oliver. This teacher has a third-grade class in which eleven students are mature in their behavior and proficient in their reading. The two characteristics encouraged him (unwisely) to give them numerous written assignments at the start of the year. In fact, their reading program was composed of reading basal selections, completing workbook pages and worksheets, and doing written reports. Recognizing both the shortcomings and monotony of the combination, Mr. Oliver decided in November to collect diagnostic information so that suitable instruction could begin.

He started by meeting with each of the eleven students to learn what they do with unknown words. Because the specific goal was to learn what is done when only spellings are available to help, he compiled a list of twenty words, some of which were likely to cause problems. That was mentioned at the start of each session, as was the reason for having it: to learn whether further help with decoding is necessary.

In the initial conferences, only root words were used; for the second, derived and inflected words were listed. By asking the students to think out loud whenever they came to a word they were unable to identify immediately, Mr. Oliver ended up with a number of notations that pinpointed what still needed to be taught about phonic and structural analyses.

In the end, only one child in the group was so proficient at decoding as to require no further help. Mr. Oliver offered her the chance to read self-selected trade books while the others had advanced decoding instruction; however, she preferred to stay with the group. As it turned out, her observations about difficult words (especially derived and inflected words) made a useful contribution to the fast-paced work of these advanced students.

COMMENTS. As the descriptions of all three teachers point up, each was concerned not about covering material but about teaching particular students. All three, therefore, could readily respond to a questionnaire like the following:

TEACHING QUESTIONNAIRE
READING

1.   List below what you attempted to teach today, and to whom.

Instructional goals   *Students*

2.   Why did you select those goals for those individuals?

3.   Did the students learn what you planned for them to learn?

_____ yes   _____ no

4.   If yes, why do you think they did?

If no, why do you think they did not?

If no, what is the next step?

Teachers who find it easy to respond to a questionnaire like this one are doing what is at the core of this textbook: teaching diagnostically. Others who could only respond with references to the pages in readers and workbooks that were covered need to develop the habit of asking themselves, "*Why* am I doing what I'm doing?"

MORE TEACHER-DEVISED DIAGNOSIS

Special efforts to diagnose are not always carried out with basal materials. To demonstrate that, two more diagnostically oriented teachers will be described.

Ms. Bowler. It was the start of Ms. Bowler's third year of teaching. All three had been in fourth grade. At the end of September, she was working with general-achievement subgroups; she was also eager to supplement basal readers with other materials and to use somewhat different organizational arrangements.

A decision already made was to use newly acquired booklets designed to provide practice with two products of comprehension: main ideas or themes, and details. One positive attribute of the booklets is interesting expository material presented at various readability levels, which allows for a matching based on general achievement, as well as on particular comprehension needs.

To find out who needed which practice, Ms. Bowler scheduled individual conferences in which each student silently read three unrelated paragraphs of expository text that were somewhere between the instructional and independent levels. For each passage, questions about its main idea or theme and the details that related to it were posed prior to the reading. (While they read, students were free to request help with troublesome words.) Afterward, answers to questions determined who would get which booklet, as well as who had no need for any of them. To record (thus remember) what she learned, Ms. Bowler used a sheet similar to the one shown here:

X = No help needed	Details	Main Ideas
Art	X	X
Betsy	X	
Beverly		
Billy		X
Helen	X	X

For a while at least, the plan is to use the booklets to help remedy some comprehension deficiencies, once further instruction is offered. Meanwhile, basal reader selections will be used as a vehicle for extending reading vocabularies and adding to decoding skills.

Ms. Antley. This second-grade teacher is just starting the second month of a new year. Earlier, while listening to children read selected passages in order to organize general-achievement levels, she noticed that two boys, both spending a second year in second grade, seemed content to say anything whenever they encountered a word they were unable to identify. It was as if they did not realize that reading is a sense-making process. To learn more about them, Ms. Antley met with each separately to see what he knew about contextual cues.

With this objective in mind, she had the boys read aloud fifteen sentences with deleted words—for instance, "When you come in, _____ the door." Any word was accepted for a blank as long as it made sense. Since the diagnostic focus was on using contexts, the boys were given help whenever they were unable to identify a word.

Results of the brief conferences showed need for attention to the semantic aspects of reading, as well as to the use of contextual cues for help with word identifications. Therefore, Ms. Antley plans to concentrate at first on material that she will read to the boys (much like the kindergarten teachers referred to in Chapter 6). Later, written sentences similar to the ones that figured in the original diagnosis will be used. Still later, Ms. Antley plans to learn how the two boys use contextual cues plus minimal graphophonic cues, since they know most letter-sound relationships. In a subsequent diagnostic session, therefore, she will use sentences like: *When you come in, cl_____ the door.*

GUIDELINES FOR TEACHER-DEVISED DIAGNOSIS

Now that some preplanned diagnosis has been described, guidelines for all teacher-devised diagnosis will be considered.

As with teaching, the basic one is found in the question, "*Why* am I doing what I'm doing?" That question is of fundamental importance because the objective of each attempt to diagnose should determine what is done. To illustrate the dependence, two of the teachers whose diagnostic plans were just described will be referred to again.

Mr. Oliver wanted to learn what certain students did when they came across words they could not immediately identify; consequently, he chose difficult, unknown words for the assessment. (To reduce anxiety, he let the students know they were difficult.) Because of the objective, what was done was done aloud. This contrasted with Ms. Bowler's procedures. She wanted to learn more about comprehension abilities; for her assessments, therefore, questions about a selected passage were posed and then the material was read silently. Deliberately, the passages were not so hard that individual words would cause problems. In addition, students were free to ask for help with troublesome words. All this was done in order to distinguish between problems with vocabulary, which were not the concern, and deficiencies in comprehending main ideas and related details in expository material.

Obviously, if diagnostic procedures are to be affected by the goal of diagnosis, the latter needs to be specifically defined. Over the years, the importance of specifically defined objectives has encouraged some to support what are called *behavioral objectives* (22). A behavioral objective is stated in a way that (a) pinpoints the focus of the diagnosis by describing the expected behavior of the student and (b) indicates what the diagnostic procedure will be. The two dimensions can be seen in sample behavioral objectives such as the following:

Students will be able:

1. to state what is the cause of a behavior described in a paragraph.
2. to perceive /b/, /f/, and /t/ in spoken words in which they appear in initial or final position.
3. to use visual cues to divide unknown VCCV words into syllables.
4. to distinguish between *ing* as an inflection and *ing* as an integral part of a root in unknown words.
5. to identify roots in unknown inflected words in which the spelling of the root has been altered.
6. to cite the sequence of events that occur in a paragraph of text.

The importance of pinpointing the focus of diagnosis indirectly suggests another guideline: Do not try to learn everything at once. This advice stems from the fact that since instruction usually deals with one thing at a time, it makes sense to diagnose only one aspect of reading at a time. Even with the circumscribed focus, however, the need to write down what is learned still exists. In fact, not to record it in some form is to risk losing the value of diagnosis; for, you will recall, *diagnosis is a waste of time if the results are not used to make decisions that will increase individualized instruction.*

Key points about classroom diagnosis can now be summarized as follows:

GUIDELINES FOR DIAGNOSIS

1. Select a specific objective that, if achieved, will advance students' reading ability.
2. Use procedures that are suitable for that objective.
3. Record what is learned about each student.
4. Use what is learned to make future instructional decisions.

One final point: Do not overlook the information that students might provide about their own reading. Answers to questions like the following (posed to individuals or to a group) might be enlightening.

"What was there about this story that was so hard?"
"I wonder why you keep confusing *quarrel* and *quiver*. Do *you* know?"
"You seem to be having trouble finding the roots in these new words. What do you think the problem is?"
"You took longer to read this story than I had expected. Was there anything in it that slowed you down?"

RECORD KEEPING FOR TEACHER-DEVISED DIAGNOSIS

No matter how good a diagnostic procedure is, it will be fruitless if what is uncovered is forgotten. This makes record keeping very important. Even so, records should never be allowed to become ends in themselves, a point that can be specified with a reference to a very conscientious teacher who started a new school year with the firm resolution to keep better accounts of what diagnosis revealed. Before school began, therefore, much time was spent preparing a large, elaborately sectioned record book in which considerable space was allotted to each student. What was the outcome once school began? Record keeping became so detailed and time-consuming that it never did have much of an impact on instruction. The moral? It echoes a warning sounded many times in earlier chapters, namely, means should not become ends in themselves. This suggests that two adjectives characterize useful records: *simple* and *brief*.

Simple, brief, and effective record keeping gets started with everyday observations kept in a small notebook that should never be too far away. Written observations might include:

"Tom gets lost in details. Can't seem to see the difference between important and unimportant details."
"Mary Pat finishes everything immediately. Needs more challenge."
"Jimmy H. still loves dinosaurs. More books needed."
"Teresa gets so hurt when her answers are wrong."
"Mark still confuses short vowel sounds. Doesn't seem to hear differences among them."
"Jerry gets right answers but always is the last to finish."

Another type of record sheet that should be available shows all the students' names at the left and a nameless column at the right:

1.	
2.	
3.	
4.	
5.	

Multiple copies (dittoed) allow for both flexible and instantaneous use. To illustrate, if a teacher decides to learn about a given skill or ability, the names of the students to be involved in the diagnosis are underlined, the focus of the diagnosis is described at the top of the second column, and what is learned is recorded after each name.

A more specific record sheet was shown on page 435. Another is sketched here:

Short Vowel Sounds						
✓= Knows	Arlene	Joanne	Mark	Michael	Pat V.	Trish
ă	✓	✓	✓	✓	✓	✓
ĕ	✓		✓			
ĭ		✓	✓			✓
ŏ			✓			
ŭ			✓	✓		✓
Letter with diacritical mark presented. Asked for sound.						

The advantage of this record sheet is that it tells not only who knows what but also how responses were elicited. Still more kinds of written records will be dealt with later.

COMMERCIALLY PRODUCED GROUP TESTS

Everything that is known about teaching and reading suggests that the most valuable sources of information for instruction are those that have been discussed: (a) students' everyday responses, oral and written, and (b) teacher-devised diagnosis that focuses on a particular piece of an instructional program. Nonetheless, commercial tests are still used in great numbers even though test experts themselves do not hesitate to point out their flaws. Oscar Buros (2), for example, in an article entitled "Fifty Years in Testing: Some Reminiscences, Criticisms, and Suggestions," comments:

> Except for the tremendous advances in electronic scoring, analysis, and reporting of test results, we don't have a great deal to show for fifty years of work. Essentially, achievement tests are being constructed today in the same way they were fifty years ago—the major changes being the use of more sophisticated statistical procedures for doing what we did then, mistakes and all. [p. 10]

Buros continues:

> Today's tests are more attractively printed and are generally machine scorable, but otherwise they show little improvement. . . . In fact, some of today's tests may even be poorer, because of the restrictions imposed by machine scoring. [p. 10]

Since commercially produced tests continue to be used in great numbers, they merit some attention. Because of the special popularity of those that are administered to groups, they will be considered first.

Survey Tests

Survey tests are designed to provide information about students' overall achievement in reading. That is why these tests were referred to in the previous chapter when ways to place students in general-achievement subgroups and to select instructional-level material were described. Here, let me reinforce one comment made in the earlier chapter and then add others.

The comment meriting repetition is that scores from survey tests commonly yield an inflated picture of ability, which is why the previous chapter recommended using them only to rank students when decisions about organization are being made. When what to teach is the concern, results of survey tests have little value for two reasons. First, each of the subtests samples such a limited amount of a student's ability that it cannot supply the kind or amount of information that is required for sound instructional decisions. In addition, what is assessed may bear little relationship to the goals of a given instructional program.

Diagnostic Tests

In theory, a diagnostic test should supply more detailed information than a survey test and thus ought to be more helpful for instruction. In practice, however, that hardly is the case for reasons referred to in the discussion of survey tests. That is, to keep group-administered diagnostic tests brief (which enhances their saleability), each subtest is short, which means that what they evaluate is too limited to provide adequate information about abilities or problems. Further, since authors of diagnostic tests know no more about the details of a particular instructional program than do those who write survey tests, what is chosen to be evaluated may bear little resemblance to what a particular teacher or school is trying to accomplish. Sometimes, too, what is assessed has little significance for reading. This is shown in the test that is partially reproduced in Figure 16.1

Like other tests (and many workbooks), directions for group-administered diagnostic tests are not always clear (for example, "Make a cross in the circle beside one of the last three words in each line that has the same sound as the sound which is underlined in the first word."). Laying aside the fact that sounds can hardly be underlined, directions like the one just stated make it impossible to know exactly what a score means.

Machine scoring accounts for two other reasons to question using commercially produced tests for diagnosis:

1. The insights into a student's abilities or shortcomings that may surface when the teacher scores a test are lost.
2. What authors select to test may be affected more by the ease with which it can be put into a multiple choice format than by what is essential for reading ability.

Figure 16.1

TEST 4: Phonetic Analysis

STEPS TO FOLLOW

I. Look at each line. The sound which is underlined in the first word is like a sound in one of the other three words.

II. Choose the word that has the same sound.

III. Turn to Test 4 on your answer sheet and fill in the space that has the same number as the word you have chosen.

SAMPLES

A bi̱g   1 kitten   2 ice   3 liked
B afra̱id   4 was   5 eight   6 park

1 beyond   1 beware   2 onion   3 bicycle
2 jump   4 engine   5 gum   6 finger
3 kind   1 chin   2 income 3 bank

TEST 5: Structural Analysis

STEPS TO FOLLOW

I. Read each line. In some lines three of the four choices, when put together, will make a word. The other choice is extra.

II. Find the extra choice. Turn to Test 5 on your answer sheet and fill in the space which has the same number as your answer.

III. If you *cannot* make a word with any three choices in a line, fill in the space for N, which stands for no word.

SAMPLE

1 por   2 im   3 tant   4 lag   Ⓝ

1 1 vic   2 ry   3 to   4 ed   Ⓝ
2 5 f   6 i   7 s   8 nd   Ⓝ
3 1 am   2 at   3 gr   4 pro   Ⓝ

Reproduced from the Stanford Diagnostic Reading Test. Copyright © by Harcourt Brace Jovanovich, Inc. Reproduced by special permission of the publisher.

● *The manual accompanying this frequently used test states that it is "designed to assess the major aspects of the reading process." One aspect named is decoding, and, supposedly, the page that is partially shown here evaluates that skill. (Permission to reproduce the page in its entirety could not be obtained. The "Phonetic Analysis" subtest contains thirty items; the "Structural Analysis" subtest, twenty-four items.)*

By now you should know that the task for Test 4 is a questionable way to measure decoding ability since many, if not all, of the words in the three columns will be known to the students taking the test. Working out their pronunciations, therefore, is unnecessary. If the words are known, the test is an exercise in auditory discrimination, which is elementary for this somewhat advanced test.

Test 5, according to its name, evaluates ability to use structural analysis. The nature of the task, however, makes it difficult to know just what is being measured. Is it spelling ability? Is it the ability to blend sounds and syllables to produce words? It is impossible to know for sure. As a consequence, it is also impossible to know the educational significance of a student's performance—be it good or bad.

Criterion-Referenced Tests

One product of efforts to bring testing and teaching closer together is *criterion-referenced* tests, in which achievement is examined in relation to specifically defined objectives (4, 17). The latter are referred to as *behavioral objectives,* a few samples of which were given earlier. More follow.

Some Behavioral Objectives

Student can . . .

> name all the letters of the alphabet, both capital and lowercase.
> identify all the words introduced in _____ when they appear in sentences.
> identify ten familiar roots in unfamiliar derived and inflected words.
> learn the meaning of words not in his oral vocabulary when they are presented in written contexts offering help through similes.
> scan a page to find a particular word.
> know the unstated conclusion in a paragraph of text.

Early interest in criterion-referenced tests and behavioral objectives was closely linked to the concept of *accountability*. The association progressed as follows: If teachers and school systems are to be held accountable for what they teach, tests must be made available that assess their particular goals. When these goals are stated behaviorally (for example, student is able to decode unfamiliar consonant-vowel-consonant syllables), what has been learned can be evaluated accordingly (student is presented with a selected number of c–v–c syllables and is or is not able to pronounce them). If the testing shows that too little was learned, further instruction can be provided.

Naturally, publishers did not ignore the widespread interest in criterion-referenced tests. As a result, large numbers soon became available, some dealing with objectives that would be hard to defend as contributors to reading ability. And so was born what was referred to at the start of the chapter as skills management systems. Arbitrarily established criteria for passing the tests that were an integral part of the materials led to the notion of *mastery learning* and to the production of high piles of worksheets and ditto masters modeled after test items. Such developments explain why educators like Michael Strange have concluded, "Children are often expected to teach themselves through interaction with dittoed materials" (21, p. 180). What started out as an effort to bring teaching and testing closer together, therefore, created a very different scenario in which teachers are often dispensers of practice sheets, not of instruction.

COMMERCIALLY PRODUCED INDIVIDUAL TESTS

Unlike reading clinicians and others who work with individual children and small groups, the most conscientious of classroom teachers are hard pressed to find

Figure 16.2

CHECKLIST OF READING DIFFICULTIES

A. Sight-Word Vocabulary

_____Limited	_____Slow, fumbling
_____Adequate	_____Adequate for Instructional Level
_____Good	_____Dependent upon context

B. Word Analysis Techniques

_____Adequate

_____Dependent upon spelling

_____Substitutes for meaning

Uses phonics:

_____letter-by-letter

_____in larger units

_____slowly, laboriously

_____easily, quickly

Weak in:

_____consonant sounds

_____consonant blends

_____vowel sounds

_____common syllables

_____blending

Guesses:

_____by general shape

_____by first letters

_____indiscriminately

C. Oral Reading

General:

_____head movements

_____loses place easily

_____ill at ease, tense

_____points to words

_____indifference or dislike for reading

_____holds booklet too close or too far

_____cocks head or booklet

Excessive error in:

_____addition

_____omissions

_____repetitions

_____substitutions

_____reversals

_____self-correction

Voice:

_____pitch too high, too low

_____monotone

_____volume too loud, too soft

_____articulation difficulties

31

---

time for individually administered diagnostic tests. When time *can* be found, teacher-devised procedures similar to those described earlier are recommended because they keep diagnosis and instruction in close proximity. Nonetheless, since references *are* made in schools and elsewhere to commercially produced individual tests, some will be dealt with, but briefly.

Diagnostic Tests

Figure 16.2 shows what one individually administered test evaluates. Examining the reproduction reveals not only the detailed analyses made by individual diagnostic tests but also their unfortunate tendency to be overly concerned about oral reading viewed as a performing art. Not to be forgotten, either, is a point made earlier: Since everything cannot be taught at once, it makes little sense to try to uncover everything about a student's abilities or problems.

Informal Reading Inventories

Other commercially prepared tests for use with individuals are called *Informal Reading Inventories* (IRI). They are described as being "informal" because they are not standardized, and they are referred to as an "inventory" because, like all other inventories, they attempt to identify what is available (what a student can do) and what is not available (what he or she cannot do). Commercially produced IRIs have limitations other than the one of being time-consuming to administer; consequently, they will first be described and then critiqued.

Description.   An IRI is an individual oral reading test, one of whose objectives is to identify a student's instructional level and, at the same time, to learn about his or her general achievement. For a description of one IRI, see Figure 16.3 and the comments about it. (The comments should be examined now because the following critique assumes they have been read.)

Critique.   A number of flaws are found in commercially prepared IRIs (11, 13, 16, 19). One is their erroneous assumption about the comparability of materials. That is, they are prepared with the underlying assumption that a passage written at a given readability level is comparable in difficulty to, let us say, a basal reader described as being at the same level. More specifically, it is assumed that if an IRI assessment indicates that fourth-grade material is at a particular student's instructional level, then a fourth-grade text will also be at his instructional level. Experience shows, however, that will not always be the case. When it is not, an inappropriate choice of materials for instruction results. The likelihood of this occurring (plus the expense of purchasing IRI materials) suggests that if a teacher decides to use an oral reading test to identify instructional-level material, the materials that will figure in instruction should figure in the assessment. This means that if she plans to use a given basal series for part of her instructional program and wants to learn which reader in the series is suitable for a given student, passages from readers in the series (not from an IRI) should be used. Instructions for preparing and administering a basal reader oral test are in the previous chapter.

When commercially prepared IRIs are viewed as a means for learning not about instructional-level material but about instructional needs, other flaws surface. Some have to do with comprehension, others with word identification ability.

One flaw pertaining to comprehension was implied earlier when it was said that IRIs have children read passages aloud. As Chapter 11 pointed out, when the concern is for comprehension, a selection should be read silently. Remember:

Different Concerns → Different Procedures

Diagnosis of comprehension abilities

Silent reading of unfamiliar material that is not so difficult as to prohibit distinctions being made between word identification problems and comprehension deficiencies.

Diagnosis of word identification abilities

Oral reading of unfamiliar material done as privately as circumstances permit.

Communication

Oral reading of prepared material with an audience of one or more.

Insofar as comprehension is concerned, another shortcoming in IRIs is that questioning students about a passage only reveals how well or poorly they understood that particular text. It tells nothing about specific comprehension abilities, which ought to be the major concern both of instruction and of assessment. This might be the time, therefore, to review more content from Chapter 11:

Comprehension Assessment

Diagnostic Concern	Procedure		
What will be comprehended in this selection?	Pre-reading questions	Silent reading	Answers to questions
			↓
			Assessment opportunity
Was this goal attained (e.g., understands that as . . . as signals a comparison known as a simile)?	Instruction	Application	Practice
		↓ Assessment opportunities	↓

Figure 16.3

Common Error	Symbol	Notes
Repetition	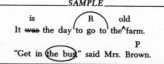 R	Mark word(s) repeated
Insertion	∧	Add additional word(s)
Substitution	—	Add substituted word
Omission	⬭	Circle word(s) omitted
Needs Assistance	P	Pronounce word when it's apparent that child does not know the word(s)

_____SAMPLE_____

    is   R   old

It ~~was~~ the day to go to the∧farm.

              P

"Get in (the bus)" said Mrs. Brown.

Observe the child's general reaction while reading. If frustrated, he is likely to manifest excessive head movement and pointing, tension, a slow-labored rate of reading, or a soft whispered voice. It is recommended that the oral reading be stopped at or before the child reaches this point.

COMPREHENSION

After each oral selection the child is asked to answer five questions about what he has just read. The questions deal with the facts, inferences and vocabulary contained in each selection. The questions for each selection are in the separate Inventory Record and labeled; F (fact), I (inference) and V (vocabulary). Answers provided for each question are merely guides or probable answers to the question. Therefore, the teacher must judge the adequacy of each response made by the child.

Partial credit (½, ¼, etc.) is allowed for responses to questions. In some cases it is helpful to record the child's responses.

SCORING

WR (Word Recognition)   COMP (Comprehension)

A scoring guide accompanies each oral selection. Each guide indicates the number of WR and COMP errors permitted within the limits of IND (independent), INST (instructional) and FRUST (frustration) levels of reading performance. Note (sample): each guide lists the number of errors permitted at each reading level. Therefore, the teacher must select the appropriate reading levels i.e., IND, INST, FRUST, based on the child's *actual errors* and the *suggested error limits* for each reading level.

_____ SAMPLE _____

Scoring Guide: Second			
WR Errors		**COMP Errors**	
IND	0	IND	0-1
INST	2-3	INST	1½-2
FRUST	5+	FRUST	2½+

xiii

Silvaroli, Nicholas J. *Classroom Reading Inventory,* 2nd ed., 1973, p. xiii. Reprinted with permission of William C. Brown Company, Publishers, Dubuque, Iowa.

●   *This shows directions for using a commercially produced IRI. (Also included is a series of passages written at a variety of readability levels, each accompanied by questions. If directions were followed, they would be posed after a student read a passage aloud.)*

Suggestions for recording word-identification errors are at the top of the page. Markings shown in the directions indicate that one student read the two sentences as follows: "It is the day to go to to go to the old farm. Get in said Mrs. Brown." (The reader needed assistance with Brown.) *According to the directions for scoring, the student made five word-identification errors.*

Guidelines for scoring are at the bottom of the page. If the oral reader made three word errors and failed to answer correctly two of the five questions, the conclusion (according to this publication) is that the passage is written at his or her instructional level. If the passage is said to have a fourth-grade readability level, the inference is that fourth-grade level material is suitable for instructional purposes.

Another major flaw in IRIs has to do with word identification and is their practice of counting word identification errors. While a total number does offer guidelines for decisions about placement in subgroups and about instructional-level material, a total number lacks significance for identifying specific instructional needs. For the latter, understanding the nature of errors is what counts, since different types of errors call for different remedies. The importance of type of error (as opposed to their number) has been effectively underscored by Pikulski (16). Discussing how two children read the sentence *The boy is sitting on a chair waiting for his mother,* he notes:

> In the first [case] . . . substitutions and insertions did very little to change the meaning of the sentence. He made four scoreable errors. The second child read in a word-by-word fashion, needed examiner help with one word and substituted *champ* for *chair* and *water* for *waits.* A very substantial amount of difficulty with word recognition is suggested and the child received very little meaning from the sentence. Yet, the first child made four scoreable errors and the second made only three. Quantitatively, the second child did better according to conventional IRI scoring systems. [p. 146]

Obtaining information about word identification ability in a way that pinpoints goals for instruction calls for oral reading and also for classifying rather than counting deviations from text. Sample classifications, therefore, follow.

EXAMPLES OF DEVIATIONS FROM TEXT

Classification	Text	What student says
Substitution	She walked toward the house.	She walked to the house.
	Climb down from there.	Get down from there.
	The signing will begin.	The singing will begin.
	His fracture is serious.	His fracture is series.
Insertion	The dog ran away.	The dog ran far away.
	Come here.	Come up here.
	The tall man can be seen.	The tall man can be seen easy.
	A red and white cab is here.	A red and white and cab is here.
Omission	The plant really grew.	The plant grew.
	They spent the whole day painting.	They spent the day painting.
	He will not do that again.	He will do that again.
	It belongs to Mike.	It to Mike.

When the essence of reading (getting meaning) is kept in mind, it can be seen in the examples that some deviations from an author's words are much more serious than others. Over the years, that fact has been highlighted by Kenneth Goodman (9, 10), who has popularized the term *miscue.* Commonly, deviations from expected responses are now divided between those that do not distort meaning (miscues) and those that do (errors).

Regardless of what deviations from text are called, analyzing rather than counting them is what makes sense when instructional needs are the concern; therefore, keeping an account of what students say when they read aloud for the purpose of diagnosing word identification ability also makes sense. One way to do that is illustrated below.

A MARKING SYSTEM

Substitution   She walked ~~toward~~ ^to^ the house.

His fracture is ~~serious~~ ^series^.

Insertion   The dog ran ^far^ away.

The tall man can be seen ^easy^ /

Omission   The plant (really) grew.

He will (not) do that again.

As was mentioned in the previous chapter, if a student's oral reading is tape recorded, an analysis of responses can be made later when he is not present.

Whether oral responses originate in individual diagnostic sessions or in everyday activities, questions like the following should be kept in mind whenever the objective is to monitor progress in word identification ability:

MONITORING WORD IDENTIFICATION ABILITY

Are high-frequency words automatically identified?

Are all available cues being used with unfamiliar words?

Do misidentifications follow any pattern? For instance, are contextual cues overused or, to the contrary, does the use of spellings dominate?

Exactly how are graphophonic cues used? For example, is the sequence of sounds commonly rearranged (*felt* read as "left")? Are sounds added (*pet* read as "pest")? Are sounds commonly omitted (*cart* read as "car")? Is equal attention given to initial, medial, and final sounds?

What is the student's strategy for working out long, seemingly complicated words? Or does a strategy even exist?

What is done with unknown inflected and derived words? Is any attempt made to sort out the root? Do altered spellings of roots cause problems? Are prefixes and suffixes recognized as such?

Are unfamiliar words worked on aggressively and persistently, or is there a tendency either to omit them or to depend on outside help?

Keeping questions like these in mind should facilitate individualized instruction, at least insofar as word identification ability is concerned.

SUMMARY

Knowing about students' achievements in reading is necessary for (a) organizing instructional groups, (b) selecting suitable material, and (c) offering appropriate instruction. The present chapter concentrated on diagnosis concerned with the latter.

Diagnosis for instruction begins with teachers who are knowledgeable about the requirements of proficient reading and proceeds with continuous efforts to learn which among the essentials has or has not been acquired by particular students. As the chapter pointed up, collecting diagnostic information so that instructional needs are clear can take many forms. Nonetheless, noncommercial kinds of diagnosis were recommended because they can be fashioned to relate not only to particular students but also to the objectives of a particular instructional program.

The various kinds of instruction that enter into a basal reader lesson allow for one type of diagnosis; so, too, does the more circumscribed lesson that concentrates on one preestablished goal. Complementing these two sources of information are specially planned diagnostic sessions in which the objective is to pinpoint what does or does not have to be taught insofar as a given skill or understanding goes.

Like instruction, the details of diagnosis should be shaped by its goal, which means that if word identification ability is being scrutinized, oral reading (and an analysis of responses) is called for. On the other hand, if the ability to comprehend a given passage is of concern, silent reading (preceded by questions) should be used. When interest lies in more specific aspects of comprehension, diagnostic opportunities are available when each is taught. This diagnosis, in fact, should be an integral part of all preplanned teaching: instruction, application, practice.

Regardless of the goal of diagnosis, or of the procedure used to attain it, what is learned should have a positive effect on future instruction. Otherwise, diagnosis is a waste of time since the *only* reason to carry it out is to improve instruction.

Chapter 16 dealt with commercially prepared diagnostic instruments, but, for a number of reasons (for example, unrelated to instructional program or to reading ability, too brief or too detailed, overly time-consuming), their use was not endorsed as a means for achieving a maximum of individualized instruction.

REVIEW

1.   Of fundamental importance to both teaching and diagnosis is the question, *Why* am I doing what I'm doing? With examples, explain the significance for both.

2. When the goal of diagnosis is to learn about a student's word identification ability, somewhat difficult material should be used. On the other hand, when a particular comprehension ability is the concern, difficult material should not be selected. Why the difference?

3. The following notations were made for the following paragraph after a child read it aloud. Based on them, what did she say when she read it?

> Every year, Susan's teacher takes her class on a trip. This year they are
> going to a ~~museum.~~ (music) The museum (they are going to) has stuffed
> animals. Some animals are ~~dinosaurs.~~ (dying) The children like dinosaurs,
> (so) they are ~~eager~~ (eagle) to go to the museum. Right now, they are reading
> about dinosaurs so (that) they will know ~~what~~ (that) they are seeing when
> they ~~arrive at~~ (get to) the museum.

Of the deviations from expected responses that show up in the notations, which are miscues and which are errors?

4. Uncovering problems is pointless unless remedies follow. What might an exercise that begins like the following help to remedy?

> I'd like to _____ them for their work.
>   price   praise
> It was _____ a beautiful day.
>   quite   quiet
> The _____ is round.
>   word   world

5. The following was heard in a fourth grade and suggests that the teacher might not be diagnostically oriented:

Teacher: Why would a good title for this story be "One Good Turn Deserves Another"?

Students: [No response]

Teacher: You're not listening. I said [this is repeated in a louder voice] why would a good title be, "One Good Turn Deserves Another"?

Students: [No response]

Since failure to listen was probably not the problem, what might the lack of response indicate? Be specific.

6. Even though what students can and cannot do is the usual concern of diagnosis, what teachers do can also be analyzed for the purpose of improving it. With that in mind, identify flaws (and suggest remedies) in what is described below.

(a) A teacher was attending to word structure to show how it offers help with meanings. The focus was on the prefix *un* meaning "not." Since *unhappy* was in a story the children would soon be reading, she used it as the first illustration. Subsequently, *untie, unlock,* and *unpack* were used as further illustrations.

(b) In another classroom, the instructional goal was to help a group understand the generalization: When there is one vowel in a syllable and it is not the last letter, it usually stands for its short sound. Correctly, the teacher used known words to illustrate the meaning of the generalization:

> and
> ask
> bad
> can

Later, in order to summarize the lesson, the teacher inquired, "Can someone tell us what we learned today?" Someone did, observing, "When a word has one vowel, it'll be an *a*."

(c) Attempting to bridge the gap between school and out-of-school reading, a teacher prepared a bulletin board for newspaper clippings brought in by students. She divided it into four parts, labeled: *Locally, Statewide, Nationally,* and *Worldly.*

REFERENCES

1. Bradley, John M., and Ames, Wilbur S. "The Influence of Intrabook Readability Variation in Oral Reading Performance." *Journal of Educational Research* 70 (November–December 1976): 101–205.

2. Buros, Oscar K. "Fifty Years in Testing: Some Reminiscences, Criticisms, and Suggestions." *Educational Researcher* 6 (July–August 1977): 9–15.

3. Calfee, Robert C.; Drum, Priscilla A.; and Arnold, Richard D. "What Research Can Tell the Reading Teacher about Assessment." In *What Research Has to Say about Reading Instruction.* Edited by S. Jay Samuels, pp. 135–164. Newark, Dela.: International Reading Association, 1978.

4. Carver, R. P. "Reading Tests in 1970 versus 1980: Psychometric versus Edumetric." *Reading Teacher* 26 (December 1972): 299–302.

5. Durkin, Dolores. "After Ten Years: Where Are We Now in Reading?" *Reading Teacher* 28 (December 1974): 262–267.

6. Durkin, Dolores. "The Importance of Goals for Reading Instruction." *Reading Teacher* 28 (January 1975): 380–383.

7. Durkin, Dolores. "Listen to Your Children." *Instructor* 81 (February 1973): 87–88.

8. Golinkoff, Roberta M. "A Comparison of Reading Comprehension Processes in Good and Poor Comprehenders." *Reading Research Quarterly* 11, no. 4 (1975–1976): 623–659.

9. Goodman, Kenneth S. "Analysis of Oral Reading Miscues: Applied Psycholinguistics." *Reading Research Quarterly* 5 (Fall 1969): 9–30.

10. Goodman, Kenneth S., ed. *Miscue Analysis: Applications to Reading Instruction.* Urbana, Ill.: National Council of Teachers of English, 1973.

11. Guszak, Frank J. "Dilemmas in Informal Reading Assessments." *Elementary English* 47 (May 1970): 666–670.

12. Johns, Jerry L. "Strategies for Oral Reading Behavior." *Language Arts* 52 (November–December 1978): 1104–1107.

13. Jongsma, Kathleen S., and Jongsma, Eugene A. "Test Reviews: Commercial Informal Reading Inventories." *Reading Teacher* 34 (March 1981): 697–705.

14. Lipton, Aaron. "Miscalling While Reading Aloud: A Point of View." *Reading Teacher* 25 (May 1972): 759–762.

15. Loban, Walter. "Commentary." *Language Arts* 56 (May 1979): 485–486.

16. Pikulski, John. "A Critical Review: Informal Reading Inventories." *Reading Teacher* 28 (November 1974): 141–151.

17. Rude, Robert T. "Objective-Based Reading Systems: An Evaluation." *Reading Teacher* 28 (November 1974): 169–175.

18. Rupley, William H. "Miscue Analysis Research: Implications for Teacher and Researcher." *Reading Teacher* 30 (February 1977): 580–583.

19. Schell, Leo M., and Hanna, Gerald S. "Can Informal Reading Inventories Reveal Strengths and Weaknesses in Comprehension Subskills?" *Reading Teacher* 35 (December 1981): 263–267.

20. Shuy, Roger W. "What the Teacher Knows Is More Important Than Text or Test." *Language Arts* 58 (November–December 1981): 919–929.

21. Strange, Michael C. "Considerations for Evaluating Reading Instruction." *Educational Leadership* 36 (December 1978): 178–181.

22. Thompson, Richard A., and Dziuban, Charles D. "Criterion Referenced Reading Tests in Perspective." *Reading Teacher* 27 (December 1973): 292–294.

INDEX